Royal Affairs

Royal Affairs

A LUSTY ROMP THROUGH THE
EXTRAMARITAL ADVENTURES
THAT ROCKED THE
British Monarchy

LESLIE CARROLL

 NEW AMERICAN LIBRARY

New American Library
Published by New American Library, a division of Penguin Group (USA) Inc., 375 Hudson Street, New York, New York 10014, USA
Penguin Group (Canada), 90 Eglinton Avenue East, Suite 700, Toronto, Ontario M4P 2Y3, Canada (a division of Pearson Penguin Canada Inc.)
Penguin Books Ltd., 80 Strand, London WC2R 0RL, England
Penguin Ireland, 25 St. Stephen's Green, Dublin 2, Ireland (a division of Penguin Books Ltd.)
Penguin Group (Australia), 250 Camberwell Road, Camberwell, Victoria 3124, Australia (a division of Pearson Australia Group Pty. Ltd.)
Penguin Books India Pvt. Ltd., 11 Community Centre, Panchsheel Park, New Delhi - 110 017, India
Penguin Group (NZ), 67 Apollo Drive, Rosedale, North Shore 0632, New Zealand (a division of Pearson New Zealand Ltd.)
Penguin Books (South Africa) (Pty.) Ltd., 24 Sturdee Avenue, Rosebank, Johannesburg 2196, South Africa

Penguin Books Ltd., Registered Offices: 80 Strand, London WC2R 0RL, England

First published by New American Library, a division of Penguin Group (USA) Inc.

First Printing, June 2008
10 9 8 7 6 5 4 3 2 1

REGISTERED TRADEMARK—MARCA REGISTRADA

LIBRARY OF CONGRESS CATALOGING-IN-PUBLICATION DATA
Carroll, Leslie.
    Royal affairs: a lusty romp through the extramarital adventures that rocked the British monarchy/Leslie Carroll.
        p. cm.
    ISBN 978-0-451-22398-2
    1. Great Britain—Kings and rulers—Paramours—Biography. 2. Great Britain—Kings and rulers—Sexual behavior. 3. Favorites, Royal—Great Britain—Biography. 4. Mistresses—Great Britain—Biography. I. Title.
DA28.8.C277 2008
941.009'9—dc22   2007051769

Set in Sabon
Designed by Jessica Shatan Heslin/Studio Shatan, Inc.

Printed in the United States of America

PUBLISHER'S NOTE
While the author has made every effort to provide accurate telephone numbers and Internet addresses at the time of publication, neither the publisher nor the author assumes any responsibility for errors, or for changes that occur after publication. Further, publisher does not have any control over and does not assume any responsibility for author or third-party Web sites or their content.

For my loving, patient, wildly supportive, and remarkably understanding husband, Scott, who endured my devoting nearly every waking hour of our first half year of marriage to a book on adultery

❧

Contents

Royal Affairs

Foreword

Sex and power have always gone hand in glove, and monarchs have been merry throughout history. Nothing can bring down a government—not even high treason—like a good sex scandal. Nowadays people yawn through newspaper accounts of civil warfare, economic downturns, even reports of appalling corporate greed. But give them a juicy sex scandal peppered with high and mighty protagonists, and it's the first story readers turn to. We can never seem to get enough of them.

Americans, in particular, enjoy a collective love affair with monarchies—probably because we don't have one, and can sanctimoniously feel superior to those benighted blighters who God and birthright have placed above the peons of their respective nations, yet who still manage to be more than human. Americans have "Hollywood royalty" instead, or myriad professional sports stars, pop icons, and politicians who behave badly. But nothing seems to be quite as alluring as a royal affair.

We're hopelessly hooked because these people with titles straight out of fairy tales or romance novels are behaving *humanly*, yet at the same time they remain larger than life. The royals have the same desires and passions as the rest of us, but the consequences of their choices are bigger—and in some cases, disastrous.

How did their spouses feel about their amorous romps? Most of the time the kings' wives were "queen consorts"—queens only by virtue of their marriage—not "regnant" queens who ruled the realm in their own right by virtue of succession, such as Elizabeth I, Anne, or Victoria. Queen consorts were expected to put up and shut up when the king strayed from the conjugal bed, and to produce the requisite heir and a spare that would guarantee the healthy succession of the kingdom.

Most marriages, especially royal ones, were primarily political and economic alliances, so it's hard to vilify these imperial adulterers for seeking sexual satisfaction outside the marital bed. And, given the state of hygiene at the time, one might imagine that an unattractive spouse was made all the more repulsive by an inattention to such delicacies. When in 1795 the future George IV was introduced to his betrothed, the odiferous, piggy-looking Caroline of Brunswick, he exclaimed to the Earl of Malmesbury, "Harris, I am not very well, pray get me a glass of brandy." The prince remained drunk for the next three days until he was dragged to the altar.

A third factor might account for all the debauchery. Any ninth-grade science student can discourse on the dangers of marrying one's first cousin, yet during the past thousand years or so, there was so much intermarriage among the royal houses that many of these inbred monarchs were mentally unbalanced to one degree or another, giving new meaning to the phrase "mad for love."

Throughout the centuries, royal affairs have engendered substantially more than salacious gossip. Often they have caused bloodshed. For example, Edward II's homosexual affairs with Piers Gaveston and Hugh Despenser the Younger infuriated his barons and alienated his wife, Queen Isabella, who decided to have an extramarital affair of her own. The vicious cycle of adultery, murder, and betrayal resulted in the overthrow of the monarchy, the king's imprisonment, and quite possibly, his assassination.

The unholy trinity of sex and politics is incomplete without religion. And a study of the extramarital affairs of Great Britain's royals also ends up chronicling the journey of the realm's religious history. Henry VIII's passion for Anne Boleyn culminated not only in their marriage but in a brand-new faith that created a lasting schism with the Church of Rome, and led to hundreds of years of strife and violence among Catholics, Protestants, and Puritans that would have a lasting impact on millions of lives.

It wasn't possible within the confines of this volume to spotlight every single monarch or to include each royal tryst, particularly when some sovereigns were such serial adulterers that one wonders how they had time to attend to affairs of *state*. Their conquests alone could fill volumes. The scuffling of silk slippers on the back stairs of Charles II's royal apartments was apparently so frequent that the king maintained a pair of discreet gatekeepers to control the flow of traffic.

And what of the mistresses? During the earlier, and more brutal, eras of British history, a woman didn't have much (if any) choice if the king exercised his droit de seigneur and decided to take her to bed. Often, girls were little more than adolescents when their ambitious parents shoved them under the monarch's nose. However, most of the mistresses in *Royal Affairs* were not innocent victims of a parent's political agenda or a monarch's rampaging lust. They were clever, accomplished, often ambitious women, not always in the first bloom of youth and not always baseborn, who cannily parlayed the only thing they had—their bodies—into extravagant wealth and notoriety, if not outright fame. In many cases, their royal bastards were ennobled by the king, making excellent marriages and living far better than their mothers could have otherwise provided.

Eventually taking their place in the House of Lords, the mistresses' illegitimate sons went on to become the decision makers who shaped an empire and spawned the richest and most powerful families in Britain.

A delicious little incident that attests to the staying power and influence of a royal mistress occurred during the reign of King George I, when the Duchess of Portsmouth (Charles II's French mistress Louise de Kéroualle), the Countess of Dorchester (a former mistress of James II), and the Countess of Orkney (William III's mistress Elizabeth Villiers Hamilton) all met at the same reception. The Countess of Orkney, known for her rapier wit, regarded her compatriots and quipped, "Who would have thought that we three whores should meet here?"

Incongruous as it may sound, England's trajectory from absolute to constitutional monarchy can be traced through the history of its sovereigns' sex scandals. Rough justice and kangaroo courts once dispatched any dissenters from the royal agenda; when an absolute monarch who ruled by divine right shouted "Off with her head!" it tended to take care of matters.

As time went on, the power of the public, from Parliament to the press, steadily eroded the sovereign's supremacy, until, by the mid-1930s, King Edward VIII, a constitutional monarch with limited input in the workings of the government, felt compelled to abdicate, believing that the tide of public opinion was against his love match. In fact, suppressed by the press, the very opposite attitude was true.

One thing is for certain: Marriage vows be damned, royals are just as randy now as they ever were. Is such behavior traceable to centuries of inbreeding or is it their sense of noblesse oblige?

From Henry II's blatant disregard of international treaties and alliances in favor of his young French mistress to Edward VIII's abdication for the woman he loved; from Henry VIII beheading his adulterous wives on Tower Green to Charles and Diana discussing their extramarital infidelities on national television, the world has in fact come a long way. Or has it? In the history of royal scandals is writ the ever-evolving story of our own society.

THE
ANGEVINS
1154–1216

HENRY II

1133–1189

RULED 1154–1189

$\mathcal{B}$ORN IN ANJOU, FRANCE, HENRY II WAS THE FIRST KING of the Angevin dynasty, a strong ruler who corralled the fractious English barons into submission and created a powerful government. Ambitious, intelligent, and rash often to the point of ruthlessness, he survived wars and rebellions, becoming one of the most successful monarchs of the Middle Ages—the greatest king England ever knew, according to the twentieth-century prime minister Winston Churchill.

Henry's mother was the Empress Matilda, daughter of Henry I, who had a claim to the English throne as the granddaughter of William the Conqueror. During Henry II's youth, the crown was in dispute. The King of England, Stephen of Blois, also a grandchild of William, claimed that his predecessor, his uncle Henry I, had willed it to him on his deathbed; and therefore, his heirs should inherit the throne. But Matilda had the backing of many of the local nobles, and men with broadswords and hundreds of knights at their disposal have a way of being very threatening. By the 1153 Treaty of Wallingford, an agreement was signed between Stephen and Matilda, granting her son, Henry II, the rights of succession.

Henry was crowned King of England on December 19, 1154, adding to his new realm Normandy (which he acquired on the death of his father in 1151), and Aquitaine, acquired through his marriage to Eleanor of Aquitaine on May 18, 1152. At the time, what we think of as France was only one of several territories in that geographical region, many of which were won and lost over the centuries by English monarchs.

Eleanor of Aquitaine was the divorced wife of the French king Louis VII. She bore Henry eight children, but their sons scrabbled like wolf cubs for primacy in their father's realm, in some cases aided and abetted by their mother to challenge Henry for the crown.

The gravel-voiced, red-haired, freckled-faced Henry was a passionate, highly political animal, capable of farseeing policies when even his most trusted advisers were blinkered. For example, it was Henry who recognized the need to guarantee the safety of the Jews in his kingdom—not because he cared a fig for their religion, but because he needed their money and their talent, particularly in matters of finance.

During his reign, jury trials were initiated, and monetary payments replaced military service as the prime duty of a vassal to his king.

Henry II was a strong king and an excellent warrior, but his temper could often get the best of him. He is probably best known for his quarrel with his former chancellor and most trusted friend, Archbishop Thomas à Becket, over the issue of clerical privilege. When Henry mused aloud that Becket had become a nuisance, exclaiming, "Will no one rid me of this turbulent priest?" four of his retainers unfortunately took him seriously. When they murdered Becket in Canterbury Cathedral on December 29, 1170, and proudly reported their deed to the king, the devastated Henry rued his words and assumed the mantle of guilt almost as if he had wielded the broadsword himself.

In June 1189, with the assistance of King Philip Augustus of France, Henry's oldest surviving son, the illustrious crusader known as Richard the Lionheart, routed Henry's army at Le Mans. On July 4, near Azay-le-Rideau, the ailing king was forced to accept a humiliating peace treaty. Two days later, he died. He was buried in the abbey church of Fontevrault. In 1204, Eleanor died at the age of eighty-two and joined him there. Their son succeeded him on the throne as Richard I.

HENRY II
and Rosamund de Clifford 1150–1176

Rosamund de Clifford, sometimes called "the Rose of the World," was the daughter of Walter de Clifford, who was one of Henry II's marchers. (The marches comprised three earldoms set up along the English-Welsh border to protect the king's lands.) Clifford was actively involved in one of the king's military campaigns when his sixteen-year-old daughter and his sire crossed paths.

Henry was a notorious ladies' man, but his affair with Rosamund turned out to be much more than a passing fancy. In fact, she was considered his Grand Passion, and their royal affair would last for a decade, until Rosamund's death in 1176. News traveled slowly in the twelfth century—or perhaps gossips got their tongues cut out—because the public did not learn of the king's long-standing liaison with Rosamund de Clifford until 1174, eight years after they fell in love. Henry's court, however, was well aware of the affair.

Gerald of Wales, a contemporary chronicler, most certainly did not approve of the royal liaison, writing, "The king, who before this had been a secret adulterer, now became a notorious one, consorting openly and shamelessly, not with the Rose of the World, as she was falsely and most frivolously styled, but, more truly, with the Rose of an impure man."

And yet Henry seemed impervious to the scratches of his detractors' quills. Ruling by divine right and possessing a sense of noblesse oblige in the extreme, he cheerfully fornicated away with little regard for the opinions of others. There were no tabloids at the time, and in any case not enough people could read for such slights to dent either his popularity or his power. And his power, not to mention his temper, could be more than somewhat violent.

Rosamund de Clifford's royal affair with Henry II successfully unhinged the most intransigent woman of the era, Henry's queen, the steely and brilliant Eleanor of Aquitaine. She bitterly referred to her rival as "the fair Rosamund."

Henry was Eleanor's second husband. In her mid-teens she had been married off to the French king, her cousin, Louis VII. But she successfully petitioned to have the marriage annulled due to consanguinity in the fourth degree—although one of the real reasons was sexual incompatibility.

In 1152, just six weeks after her annulment had been granted, the spirited Eleanor married the highly sexed Henry II, bringing England the duchy of Aquitaine in the bargain. The highly influential Eleanor bore Henry five sons and three daughters in thirteen years; introduced to England the Court of Love, with its high-flown emphasis on chivalry, poetry, and music; and was an active participant in matters of state.

But by the end of 1166, when Eleanor gave birth to her eighth child, she may have felt like an old cow. Henry's new infatuation with a sixteen-year-old Welsh blonde set her teeth on edge. Understandably, the forty-four-year-old queen resented the relationship, as most women would if their husbands had found someone younger and more nubile, someone without stretch marks and too much knowledge of his flaws.

Until he took up with Rosamund, Henry had conducted his amorous intrigues with relative discretion. But this time, it was impossible for Eleanor to turn a blind eye to his infidelities because Henry openly consorted with Rosamund. His passion for her was so overt—and evidently reciprocated—that a contemporary scribe waggishly punned on her nickame, calling her "Rosa Immundi," or "Rose of Unchastity."

The royal marriage became greatly strained, and in 1167, Eleanor had most of her possessions loaded onto ships for Argentan on the European continent. After celebrating Christmas there with Henry, she appeared to have agreed to some form of official separation, because she soon embarked with her property to her birthplace of Poitiers.

But she didn't lay low for long. Eleanor was imprisoned by Henry in 1173 for inciting their sons to rebel against him in France. The queen spent the next fifteen years of her life in captivity at various locations throughout England.

During the first three years of Eleanor's imprisonment Rosamund enjoyed the warmth of the royal bed, while the queen was left to angrily pace the chilly floors of drafty castles.

In October 1175, the king was still flaunting his affair with Rosamund, perhaps in an effort to goad the queen into demanding an annulment. But Eleanor was far too canny to take the bait, knowing that if she allowed Henry to be rid of her, he could banish her to an abbey. If she were compelled to cast off her secular being and forfeit her worldly possessions, she would lose her title as well as the continental lands that were in her name (such as Aquitaine) to the English crown.

Eleanor was not one of those queens who meekly acquiesced to her husband. She was a political animal who played to win at all costs—in war, and in love. Given her reputation, rumors abounded that she was involved in the swift dispatch of her romantic rival in 1176.

Stories that gained popularity four hundred years later, during the Elizabethan era, held that the jealous Eleanor had Rosamund poisoned, but this conjecture has never been concretely established.

True, Eleanor most certainly saw Rosamund as a threat to her power, if not to her throne. But it's doubtful for several reasons that Eleanor had a hand in her rival's demise. For one thing, Eleanor had been imprisoned since 1173, so any personal involvement in Rosamund's death would have been impossible, as Eleanor herself claimed. "In the matter of her death the Almighty knows me innocent. When I had power to send her dead, I did not; and when God wisely chose to take her from this world I was under constant watch by Henry's spies."

Nearly everything written about Rosamund is the stuff of folklore rather than of fact. Some accounts give her two sons by Henry, but their birth dates don't seem to make sense in terms of Rosamund's. Historians differ by thirteen years as to Rosamund's own date of birth. I chose the later date of 1150, which seems most logical, particularly when one considers Henry's predilection for nubile damsels. Even the extent of the footprint her royal affair left on the map of England is a matter of conjecture. One legend claims that Henry built his hunting lodge at Woodstock in her honor, and named the labyrinth there "Rosamund's Bower." Woodstock is now gone, but it stood near the current Blenheim Palace; and it certainly existed, although whether it was built specifically as a royal love nest, or as a gift for Henry's mistress, is unlikely. What everyone seems to agree on, however, is that Rosamund de Clifford was the great love of Henry's life and (with Queen Eleanor incarcerated for encouraging her sons to revolt against Henry) they lived together openly.

Though we know Rosamund died in 1176 because priory records confirm it, the reason she entered the nunnery at Godstow in the first place, like much of the rest of her life, remains a mystery. At her death, Rosamund was either all of twenty-six or she had managed to make it to the age of thirty-nine, depending on which source you read. The cause of her death remains unknown. But the legend of her life took root, and the fair Rosamund became more famous in death than she had been in life. Shortly after her demise, her tomb, which had been commissioned by Henry and placed before Godstow's high altar, began to attract pilgrims, who turned the deceased royal favorite into something of a cult figure and the tomb itself into the ultimate expression of her royal lover's undying devotion. Visitors laid their floral tributes and lit their candles about her sepulcher as though it were a monument to True Love.

But Hugh, the Bishop of Lincoln, who visited Godstow in 1191, two years after Henry's death, was not so smitten with the fairy tale. He saw Rosamund as a harlot and ordered her tomb to be moved, relegating her remains to an area beyond the church walls as a warning to other would-be fallen women. Rosamund's new resting place was a cemetery plot by the nuns' chapter house until the reign of Henry VIII, when it was destroyed during the execution of the Dissolution of Monasteries Act. The Godstow Priory itself is now only a shell of a ruin.

♛

HENRY II

and Alys (or Alais), Countess of the Vexin 1160–1220

Henry's second-most famous mistress, Alys (or Alais), was the daughter of King Louis VII of France by his second wife,

Constance of Castile, who died giving birth to her. Louis's first wife was Eleanor of Aquitaine, who was now married to the hotheaded Henry II.

Alys was the poster child for the princess–political pawn of the Middle Ages. According to a treaty arranged between France and England in 1169, when Alys was only nine years old, she was sent to Britain to become the eventual bride of Henry's son Richard (known as Richard the Lionheart). Alys pretty much grew up in Henry's court, and after Henry lost his beloved Rosamund to death in 1176, his eye alit on his pretty, sixteen-year-old French ward. With complete disregard for his 1169 treaty with Louis of France, and any feelings or opinions Richard might have had on the subject, Henry "stole" Alys, making her his own mistress.

In the long run—although it was beside the point—Alys probably wouldn't have been happy with Richard anyway. True, the prince was young and strong, well built and handsome, a magnificent horseman and an even greater warrior—but more than likely he didn't play for her team.

The match between Alys and Richard had been Eleanor's idea. Richard was her favorite son and Eleanor was always on the lookout for ways to enrich him and strengthen his political and military position in western Europe. Alys was the countess of a continental territory known as the Vexin, which was strategically important to both England and France.

But the lands that might have eventually become Henry's through Alys's dynastic marriage with Richard paled in comparison to the landscape of her body—young, firm, and evidently willing. Henry's libido recovered from Rosamund's untimely demise with relative alacrity. By 1177, only one year after her death, the royal affair with Alys was an international scandal and rumors abounded that Henry was considering divorcing Eleanor so that he could be free to marry his new paramour. Alys's reputation was roundly trashed. It was popularly bandied about that she had borne Henry a son (who died before 1190), in addition to gossip that she had always been a promiscuous girl.

King Louis was livid that his daughter, by sleeping with her fiancé's father, had become England's royal whore, instead of marrying the son to become its future queen. Then, the issue of religion was added to the scandalous cocktail of sex and politics. Pope Alexander III's emissary, Cardinal Peter of St. Chrysogonus, threatened to place England's continental possessions under an interdict (which would have effectively excommunicated all of Henry's subjects who abided there), if Henry didn't proceed with the marriage between Richard and Alys in accordance with the treaty.

Finally, when Louis demanded his daughter's return if no marriage was to take place, Henry begrudgingly agreed to permit the French princess to marry Richard, but neglected to mention a date, let alone a timetable, for this happy event.

In 1189, an ailing Henry promised Alys's brother Philip, now King of France, that he would give up his twenty-nine-year-old mistress and see that she was put under the guardianship of any one of five men (to be named by Richard), and thence married to Richard upon his return from the Holy War in Jerusalem.

But after Henry died that year, his (possibly gay) crusader son, now King Richard I, made use of the popular (and convenient) story that Alys had given birth to his father's child as an excuse to terminate their marriage treaty. Alys, who had lived in limbo for six years while Richard was a political prisoner of King Leopold of Austria, was sent home to France in 1195, shortly after Richard's return to England. Later that year her brother arranged for her marriage to William III Talvas, Count of Ponthieu, who was eighteen years her junior, hoping the union would be childless so that Philip could assume control of the strategically located Ponthieu. Alys thwarted her brother's aspirations, however, bearing the count three daughters, one of whom, Marie, inherited the county upon her father's demise in 1221.

Alys is believed to have died in 1220 at the age of sixty, still Countess of Ponthieu. The circumstances surrounding her death are unknown.

THE
PLANTAGENETS
1216–1399

EDWARD II

1284–1327
RULED 1307–1327

*E*DWARD II WAS THE YOUNGEST OF FOURTEEN (POSSIBLY sixteen) children born to the powerful, canny, and ruthless Edward I and his queen, Eleanor of Castile, but by the time he acceded to the throne in 1307, he was the only surviving son. So, perhaps the scion of the man considered the greatest Plantagenet king, even in his lifetime, was bound to be inadequate, if not a downright disaster, by comparison.

The great-grandson of Henry II, Edward I had been a conqueror, a crusader, and a lawmaker. He was also a huge bully who asserted the rights of the crown over private powers, such as those wielded by his nobles, whenever possible, but always within the confines of the law. He might not have been liked, but he was most certainly feared and respected with the deference due to one's monarch. His son, Edward II, was *just* a huge bully, the Plantagenet with the worst reputation as a ruler, and deservedly so. He allowed the decisions taken by the head inside his tights to prevail over the one between his shoulders, and the result was bloody and disastrous for England.

On the surface of it, Edward looked every inch a king—tall and handsome, with a head of golden curls and a full mustache and beard. But from his youth, his behavior was decidedly un-royal, eschewing the usual manly martial pursuits, including jousting, for the fascination of gardening and farming, and learning the skills of manual laborers and the crafts of the arti-sans.

In 1308, the twenty-three-year-old king wed the barely ado-lescent Isabella of France in a match that was entirely political; it was clear from the outset that Edward was not remotely will-ing to abandon his passionate attachment to his boyhood pal, the Gascon-born popinjay Piers Gaveston.

But the monarch managed to do his conjugal duty with yeo-manlike obligation, producing two more children than the req-uisite heir and spare. Isabella's life at court careened precipitously from trusted consort to pariah, depending on which of her hus-band's male favorites was pulling his strings or was blissfully making havoc elsewhere.

At length, Edward's involvement with the powerful Despenser family proved his undoing. Their rapaciousness sent the king-dom into revolt, culminating in Isabella and her lover Roger Mortimer raising an army against her own husband and his paramour, Hugh Despenser the Younger. Isabella's forces handily defeated them in 1326.

Consequently, Edward was brought before Parliament and tried for his crimes against the realm. On January 24, 1327, given the chance to abdicate in favor of his son, the crown prince, he accepted it, a broken man—the first King of England to be formally deposed. The following day, the fourteen-year-old prince began his rule as Edward III. He was crowned at Westminster Abbey on February 1.

In April, the forty-three-year-old Edward II was transferred from Kenilworth to Berkeley Castle in Gloucestershire, where he remained imprisoned at least until September 1327. Two attempts to rescue him proved unsuccessful. What happened to him after that has been in dispute for centuries.

The circumstances surrounding the death of Edward II are murky. Although there are no contemporary accounts of his demise, sometime during the latter half of 1327, he was believed to have been snuffed out—literally. Stories surfaced later (which were fancifully embellished over the next few centuries) that he was suffocated as he lay prone upon a table, while a hot poker was shoved up his rear in what his murderers (who may have been directly hired by Roger Mortimer) deemed a fitting end to an acknowledged sodomite.

Or not. There's an odd twist to the story, which will be discussed in the following entry.

Edward III finally grabbed the reins of power from his mother and her despotic lover in October 1330, shortly before his eighteenth birthday. Free of their manipulative influence he became a strong and respected monarch.

✺

EDWARD II
and Piers Gaveston 1284–1312
and Hugh Despenser the Younger 1286–1326

ISABELLA OF FRANCE (QUEEN TO EDWARD II)
1295–1358
and Roger Mortimer 1287–1330

The lives of these five figures are so intertwined that their royal affairs must form a single entry. This is a cautionary tale of passion and politics that began because of preferences in the

royal bed and led to civil unrest, international tensions, gruesome executions, and, for the first time in English history, the
abdication of a king.

In his youth, Edward had developed a mutually reciprocated passion for Piers Gaveston. The Gascon-born Gaveston
had grown up in the service of the court. His father was one of
Edward I's retainers, and though he was a commoner, the
young Piers, who was the same age as the future Edward II,
displayed excellent manners and breeding. In 1300, when both
boys were sixteen, the king made Piers a companion of the
prince.

It ended up being a deadly move. A contemporary historian
wrote of Gaveston that "as soon as the king's son saw him, he
fell so much in love that he entered upon an enduring compact
with him." Clearly there was nothing secret about the nature
of their relationship. And it's remarkable that they got away
with it, because homosexuality was regarded as a heinous crime
and a sin against nature. In the fourteenth century, punishment for sodomy ranged from excommunication (which was
taken very seriously) to a rather gruesome execution.

Young Edward became determined to share *all* of his possessions with Piers. For a prince to cede such power to a commoner was unthinkable; and the king (correctly) feared that his
son would inevitably share the entire English government with
his favorite, if allowed to do so.

After Prince Edward dispatched the Royal Treasurer to inform the king that he intended to grant the county of Ponthieu
to Gaveston, Edward I became so enraged by his son's prepos-
terous idea that he summoned his heir. When the prince appeared, the king grabbed him by the hair, threw him to the
floor, and literally kicked the crap out of him.

Edward's present-day biographer, Ian Mortimer, credits the
king with the following outburst: "You baseborn whoreson!
Would you give away lands, you, who never gained any? As the

Lord lives, were it not for fear of breaking up the kingdom, you shall never enjoy your inheritance!"

The sovereign made his son promise never to see his lover again, and then, before the assembled lords of Parliament, declared Gaveston banished.

But as soon as Edward I died in July 1307, the new king's first Royal Act was to recall his lover to court. Gaveston was made Duke of Cornwall—a title that Edward I had intended for his second son, and one that was traditionally conferred on a nobleman. Edward II then married off his lover to Margaret de Clare, a niece who was one of the heiresses to the vast and lucrative Gloucester estates. This, too, was another preference reserved for a high-ranking noble, because the wife in question was so near a relation to the king. The plethora of favors and titles Edward II bestowed upon his paramour angered the British barons; and the fact that Gaveston was a foreigner, and baseborn to boot, made matters even uglier.

Confident of the king's love, the arrogant Gaveston made matters worse by flaunting his newly acquired wealth and position. Understandably, the barons couldn't wait for an opportunity to get rid of him.

This was the dynamic discovered by the young Queen Isabella on the day she arrived in England.

Future historians would call her "the she-wolf of France," but Isabella the Fair, a daughter of King Philip IV, was all of twelve years old when on January 25, 1308, she was married to the twenty-three-year-old King Edward II of England. The union was designed to resolve the countries' dispute over the English possession of Gascony and England's claims to other continental duchies (Anjou, Aquitaine, and Normandy—which are also now part of present-day France), in the hope of averting any potential war between the two countries.

The preteen Isabella had probably been shielded from any

murmurs at the French court regarding her betrothed's "unnatural" relationship with Piers Gaveston, but it could not have been a secret to her father. For the sake of a political alliance Philip condemned young Isabella to a miserable marriage, sacrificing her to a known sodomite—one of the crimes for which he was expelling the Knights Templar from France.

The wedding between Isabella and Edward took place in France. The child-bride was described by Geoffrey of Paris, a contemporary chronicler, as "the beauty of all beauties . . . in the kingdom if not in all Europe," which likely meant, given the preferences of the era, that she was blond and slightly plump.

Unfortunately, she learned all too quickly that she was not to be the primary beneficiary of her tall, blond, and handsome husband's masculine magnificence; for no sooner did Edward's ship reach English shores than His Majesty bounded down the gangplank into the waiting arms of his lover, Piers Gaveston, "giving him kisses and repeated embraces." Gaveston had been named Keeper of the Realm in the king's absence, an act that infuriated the English barons, who had hoped that Edward's understudy would be (a) a nobleman, and (b) experienced in matters of governance.

With the king engaged in a very public display of quayside affection with Gaveston, the humiliated and embarrassed girl was compelled to pick her own way along the planks of the gangway. Isabella's mortification intensified when to her dismay Edward gave her wedding gifts, including her jewelry, to Gaveston!

Matters worsened at the coronation. Instead of dressing in the traditional earls' cloth of gold, Gaveston appeared in a pearl-encrusted royal purple ensemble, a color that was the purview of the monarchy. During the procession, he carried the crown of Edward the Confessor, England's most sacred relic, an honor that was customarily reserved for the highest-ranking nobleman in the land. At the coronation, Gaveston's arms, and not Isabella's, were displayed next to the king's. Most offensively to the assembled dinner guests, it was very clear who Edward considered the real queen. He spent the entire meal making out with Gaveston.

It had also been Gaveston's job to plan the event, including the coronation feast, and any bride who has had a less-than-perfect wedding reception can relate to the disasters that ensued. People were crushed into the cathedral, the food wasn't ready when it was time for supper, and when it finally arrived, it was inedible—badly cooked and unprofessionally served.

Only nine months after Edward became king, and less than two months after his marriage to Isabella, the enraged barons banded together to demand Gaveston's exile. Piers was banished twice in as many years, but the proverbial bad penny kept returning. And when Gaveston reappeared for the third time alongside the king during the Christmas celebrations of 1311, the barons were not in a holiday mood. Faced with rebellion, the lovers ran for the border—the Scottish border—where Edward pleaded with Robert the Bruce, King of the Scots, to offer Gaveston a safe haven.

"If the King of England will not keep faith with his own people, how then will he keep faith with me?" Bruce replied, refusing sanctuary.

The barons caught up with the lovers, and Gaveston was taken in honorable captivity until he could present his case to Parliament. But the Earl of Warwick had his own agenda. After forcing Gaveston to run a gauntlet through a mob of angry peasants, he tossed him into the dungeon at Warwick Castle to await the arrival of the Earl of Lancaster, the rebellious barons' ringleader.

"While he lives there will be no safe place in the realm of England," Lancaster insisted, setting the wheels in motion for Gaveston's execution. At three a.m. on June 19, 1312, the prisoner was taken to Blacklow Hill on Lancaster's estate, where two Welsh executioners ran him through with a sword and then beheaded him.

Dominican friars eventually brought Gaveston's body to their priory, stitched his head back on, and dressed the corpse in cloth of gold, before realizing that because Gaveston died an excommunicate he could not receive a Christian burial. The friars held on to the corpse until they could figure out what to do with it.

Edward's surprisingly unsentimental reaction to the news of his beloved's death was "By God's soul, he acted like a fool!" But from that moment, the king swore vengeance against Gaveston's murderers.

Despite his extramarital passion for Piers, Edward had successfully executed his royal duty in the conjugal bed. The pregnant queen welcomed her grieving husband home. Isabella was probably relieved in the extreme that Gaveston was forever out of their lives, and for a resumption of her husband's attention in the boudoir. Five months later, on November 13, 1312, she gave birth to their first son, the future Edward III.

Through Edward's diplomatic mediation, the new Pope, John XXII, overturned Gaveston's excommunication in 1315 and the king finally buried his late lamented lover with all due pomp. He also paid for masses to be said all over England for Gaveston's soul, to be repeated twice every year—on Gaveston's birthday and on the anniversary of his death—until the king's own demise.

For the next nine years Isabella counted herself surprisingly happy. She blossomed as a woman, setting new fashions with daring low-cut gowns. And she felt secure in her husband's affections, even while other pretty courtiers came and went from his bed. Isabella did enjoy the king's favors often enough to give birth to three more children between 1316 and 1321 (with at least one miscarriage during those years). Edward trusted her with affairs of state, leaving her to govern England when he was engaged in military campaigns on the Scottish border. She had grown from an innocent girl into a stunning queen, proud, strong-willed, and ambitious.

Around 1318, however, Edward's attention became focused on a new favorite, who would wreak more havoc on the kingdom than Piers Gaveston had ever done. Hugh Despenser the Elder was one of Edward's closest and most influential advisers. His son, Hugh Despenser the Younger, supplanted all the fey young men who vied for the king's favor to become not only Edward's paramour but one of the most powerful men in England. The grasping, corrupt, and ambitious Despensers soon controlled the malleable monarch, convincing Edward to decrease Isabella's hard-won influence and authority and to shift the balance of power to them.

Edward appointed his new lover Royal Chamberlain, which gave Despenser complete control of who gained access to the king. By 1320, young Despenser's greed had run amok. He extorted vast sums of money and estates and arbitrarily seized lands belonging to others, adding them to his own list of properties by bullying, manipulating, kidnapping, and torturing anyone, including women, who gave him the slightest resistance. Edward countenanced his new lover's rampant brutality, and in concert they terrorized the kingdom into submission. The younger Hugh Despenser's tyranny was unprecedented. Noblewomen and children were dispossessed and incarcerated for their lords' alleged crimes; Despenser seized and appropriated their lands for himself.

Pregnant with their fourth child, Isabella begged Edward to get rid of her rival. But it was England's barons who forced the king to banish the Despensers in 1321, only to see them return to court the following year.

In 1322, during one of the Scottish skirmishes, Despenser the Younger had persuaded the king to take flight rather than look to the queen's welfare. Consequently, Isabella nearly fell into the hands of his worst enemy, Robert the Bruce, who was plotting to kidnap her. The brave and gutsy queen somehow managed to elude her would-be captors (though two of her ladies-in-waiting perished during the attempt) in a boat bound for England. The captain of the vessel risked his life in bringing Isabella home, braving the coastal water routes, which were controlled by allies of the Scots.

By this time, Isabella had understandably suffered enough of her husband's abuse. As the Despensers gained more and more control of the kingdom, her own star sank lower and lower. In September 1324, fearing that she would ally herself with one of his former generals, Sir Roger Mortimer, the king confiscated all of Isabella's property. The queen's servants were arrested and replaced with spies handpicked by Edward to keep an eye on her. Her children were taken from her and given into the custody of Eleanor de Clare, the wife of Hugh Despenser the Younger, whose job it was to "chaperone" the queen everywhere she went.

It was then that Isabella began to consider active rebellion against Edward. She was given the opportunity to gain allies in a circuitous way. Her brother Charles, now King of France, had seized possession of Edward's lands there. Isabella departed for Paris in March 1325, to negotiate a peace treaty.

The next time she set foot on English soil would be at the side of Roger Mortimer, the man who had become her lover—and who happened to be commanding her invading army.

Because Mortimer's father, the 2nd Baron Wigmore, had died in battle when his son was still in his minority, Roger grew up at Edward I's court, ironically under the guardianship of Piers Gaveston. Married in 1301, Mortimer was knighted by Edward I in 1306, at which time he was also made the 3rd Baron Wigmore. He did yeoman service to the crown, successfully invading Ireland, where Edward II made him his viceroy, appointing him Lord Lieutenant on November 23, 1316.

But two years later, Mortimer threw his support to the growing rebel faction seeking to oust the influential and greedy Despensers. Unfortunately, the king's army outnumbered the rebels, and in 1322 Mortimer surrendered at Shrewsbury and was imprisoned in the Tower of London, his lands forfeit to the crown. Mortimer's wife, Joan de Genville, was imprisoned elsewhere, as punishment for her husband's perceived treachery.

The following year, on August 1, 1323, Mortimer effected a daring escape from the Tower, fleeing in a waiting vessel to the Continent. Isabella encountered him in France in 1325 and soon took him as her lover. Her own fate, as well as England's, was set in motion. Hell hath no fury like a woman scorned in bed, and Isabella was determined to have her revenge. Their relationship blossomed from friendship to fervor with all due speed. Motive and opportunity, as well as intense sexual frustration on Isabella's part, fueled their mutual passion. The queen was doubtless overjoyed to have a man make love to her who knew his way around a woman's anatomy.

Having heard the rumors that his wife and Mortimer were raising an army against him, Edward summoned Isabella home, but the queen stood her ground and refused to return to England. Rather than name the king as the cause of her misery, Isabella targeted the myriad abuses of Despenser, stating publicly before the French court, "I feel that marriage is a joining together of man and woman, maintaining the undivided habit of life, and that someone has come between my husband and myself to break this bond; I protest that I will not return until this intruder is removed, but discarding my marriage garment, shall assume the robes of widowhood and mourning until I am avenged of this Pharisee."

Aside from the fact that the third party referred to by the queen happened to be a guy, Isabella's statement sounds an awful lot like a fourteenth-century version of Princess Diana's famous line, "There were three of us in this marriage, so it was a bit crowded."

Charles IV stuck by his sister's resolve to remain in France, telling Edward, "The queen has come of her own will and may freely return if she wishes. But if she prefers to remain here, she is my sister and I refuse to expel her."

Isabella had already convinced her husband to send their eldest son to her, on the promise that if their heir paid homage to Charles, he would return Edward's French lands to him. With the future King of England safely by her side, Isabella's strategy began to take shape.

By March 1326, the affair between Isabella and Mortimer was common knowledge in both France and England, and their plans were well afoot to invade Britain and depose Edward. But Isabella must have had second thoughts about their decision, leading to an embarrassing public argument with Mortimer. When she considered returning to her husband after all, Mortimer grew violently angry, replying that he would sooner kill her than see her go back to Edward.

That summer, the Pope spoke out against Isabella. Her brother abandoned her, perhaps in fear of his own excommunication, or in an attempt to avoid war with England. So the queen and her paramour visited Holland, to request military aid from William of Hainault, who was married to Isabella's cousin. William gave Isabella and Mortimer eight warships in exchange for a marriage contract between his daughter Philippa and Isabella's son Edward, the crown prince.

On September 24, 1326, the queen, her son, and her lover landed in Suffolk with an army of mercenaries ready to fight King Edward for his crown.

Edward endeavored to rally his supporters, but one by one they withdrew their backing or threw their muscle behind the queen. She gained additional support and sympathy when from his pulpit one of England's most powerful bishops spread the word "that the king had carried a knife in his hose to kill Queen Isabella, and he had said that if he had no other weapon, he could crush her with his own teeth." Isabella herself declared that if the barons were to repel her forces, it was tantamount to fighting her son, their future ruler. Presented that way, the barons' choice was a no-brainer.

Hugh the Younger grabbed as much as he could liberate from the Royal Treasury and fled London with his father and the king, but Isabella's men caught up with them in Bristol. Hugh the Elder was executed there, and on November 16, 1326, Hugh the Younger and the king were captured in the open country near Neath. Edward was separated from his favorite and taken to Kenilworth Castle.

Unsure whether to brand Edward's lover as a thief or a traitor, a sodomite or a heretic, the rebels adjudged Hugh the Younger as all of the above, and he received the death sentence accorded to each of those offenses. On November 24, Hugh, whose flesh had first been crudely tattooed with scripture verses, was dragged by two teams of horses to the place of public execution and hanged like a thief on a gallows fifty feet high, while a bonfire was torched beneath him. But before the flames could asphyxiate him, Hugh was removed from the gallows and tied to a ladder, whereupon his genitals were sliced off and burned before his eyes. Hugh was then disemboweled and his entrails and vital organs consigned to the flames as well. Finally, his limbs were hacked off, followed by his head, which was spitted upon a pike atop the gates of London.

Apart from this orgy of retribution and a half dozen more minor executions of traitors, Isabella had successfully staged a bloodless coup.

It fell to Parliament to decide Edward's fate. A number of options were available, which met with varying degrees of concern from the royal family. Isabella didn't want the lords to depose him because it trampled on the notion of the divine right of kings. The crown prince most certainly objected to the execution of his father. Even Mortimer, whose life had been spared by the sovereign several years earlier, appeared uncomfortable with a parliamentary decision to kill a king.

So the lords Parliamentary decided to imprison Edward II for life, and on January 20, 1327, they read him their verdict: the king had been found guilty of (among a lengthy list of charges) gross incompetence, not listening to good advice, having lost Scotland as well as lands in Ireland and in Gascony due to poor decisions and worse governance, fleeing in the company of an enemy of the realm, losing the faith and trust of his subjects, and conduct unbecoming a monarch.

The king wept as he heard the charges, and then chose the lesser of two evils offered to him—he could relinquish the throne to an experienced governor of common blood, or abdicate in favor of his son. Sensing that the first option referred to his wife's lover, Roger Mortimer, Edward II decided to abdicate as of January 24, 1327, the tragic price and ultimate consequence of his own carnality.

The following day, his eldest son began his rule as Edward III. Just fourteen years old, he was crowned at Westminster Abbey on February 1.

That spring, the disgraced former monarch was transferred from Kenilworth to Berkeley Castle in Gloucestershire, where he remained at least until September, despite two failed rescue attempts. The true fate of Edward II may never be known.

There is no fourteenth-century account of his death. Stories surfaced much later that, according to one medieval chronicler, Edward II had been "slain with a hot spit put through the secret place posterial." Even the eminent Sir Thomas More, writing his historical biographies in the sixteenth century, gave credit to a "plumber's iron, heated intensely hot . . . introduced through a tube into his secret parts so that it burned the inner portions beyond the intestines."

Or not.

Credence has been given to a contemporary letter from a papal notary that alleges that the king escaped Berkeley Castle and fled to the Continent, hiding in an Italian castle, and surviving at least as late as 1330. Under close scrutiny of the letter's text, the case collapses for this denouement. But it was enough to make Edward III consider the possibility that his father might be somewhere out there after all, and that the body buried with pomp at Gloucester Cathedral was that of an impostor, a consideration that contemporary historians have not entirely dismissed out of hand. In any case, Edward III chose not to pursue the matter. If he had issued a new statement declaring that Edward II still lived, it would have jeopardized his own reign, and might have sparked a civil war between supporters of each of the two Edwards.

Isabella admitted her great distress at the news of her husband's death, but it was politically expedient for him to remain deceased, regardless of the truth. After all, Isabella had never enjoyed so much power. The queen and her lover coruled England as regents until Edward III attained his majority in 1330. In fact, Roger Mortimer holds a unique position in English history: he essentially ruled the country for three years with absolutely no legal right to do so. He was not a legitimate regent. He was neither the father nor the guardian of Edward III, nor was he married to the queen.

During the de facto regency, Mortimer lived large and lavishly, illegally appropriating at least as many estates as Hugh Despenser had done. He also gave himself as many titles as Edward had bestowed upon his paramours. And in March of 1330, he ordered the execution of Edward II's half brother Edmund, Earl of Kent, for plotting to return Edward II to the throne—although it was supposedly common knowledge that Edward had been gruesomely murdered three years earlier.

Edward III now feared, and not without reason, that he might be next on Mortimer's hit list. It was time to act. In the words of Edward's trusted knight Sir William de Montagu, "Eat the dog lest the dog eat us."

In October 1330, the month before Edward III's eighteenth birthday, a special session of Parliament was convened in Nottingham. Edward and a few of his trusted friends staged a mini-coup and seized his mother and her lover, imprisoning them.

"Fair son, have pity on the kind Mortimer," Isabella pleaded. But as she was probably the only person Mortimer had ever been kind to, Edward III was deaf to her entreaties and had Mortimer conveyed to the Tower of London to await execution.

On November 29, 1330, Roger Mortimer was condemned without trial for assuming royal power and other treasonous offenses. He was hanged at Tyburn and his estates became forfeit to the crown. Mortimer's hapless widow, Joan, received a royal pardon in 1336 and lived for another twenty years.

Isabella's life was spared by her son, and she repentantly reinvented herself as a loving grandmother and keeper of her late husband's flame—as well as his heart. In her last few months of life, Isabella took the habit of the Order of the Poor Clares, but was evidently too proud to be buried in sackcloth when she died on August 22, 1358.

Leave it to Isabella to have the ironic last laugh—or perhaps she was desperate to have in death what during her life her husband had so humiliatingly bestowed upon Piers Gaveston and Hugh Despenser to the detriment of his kingdom. Wrapped in her red wedding mantle, Isabella was buried holding a silver casket containing her late husband's heart, which had been delivered to her as a memento mori prior to Edward's entombment on December 20, 1327.

JOHN OF GAUNT, DUKE OF LANCASTER
1340–1399
and Katherine Swynford 1350–1403

Like so many other medieval women, Katherine Swynford might have been relegated to the musty pages of history as a minor character, but instead she became a cult fiction icon six hundred years after her birth. Her story captured the imagination of readers worldwide in 1954, when Anya Seton published *Katherine*, a popular romance novel featuring a fictionalized version of Swynford's affair with John of Gaunt, the John D. Rockefeller of his day.

The real Katherine was born Katherine de Roët, the daughter of a Flemish herald, an ambassadorial officer who traveled to England in the service of Philippa, queen consort of King Edward III. Nothing is known of her mother. Katherine's date of birth remains a subject of controversy; her two most recent biographers disagree by about five years, and I opted for the later date of 1350. No physical description of her exists, other than the occasional mention that she was very beautiful.

Katherine and her siblings were raised in the English court, where her two brothers distinguished themselves. Katherine's sister Philippa eventually married Geoffrey Chaucer, who was a distinguished civil servant and poet, and the author of *The Canterbury Tales*.

At the age of nine, Katherine was given a court position of her own. She joined the household of the handsome, strawberry blond–bearded John of Gaunt, the fourth son of King Edward III (and grandson of the ill-fated Edward II), most likely around the time of his marriage in 1359 to the beautiful, flaxen-haired Blanche, a daughter of the Duke of Lancaster, in what was as much a love match as it was a dynastic arrangement. Katherine was probably engaged as a cradle rocker or "rokestare," a position commonly held by young daughters of court favorites.

Gaunt (his name was an anglicized pronunciation of "Ghent," where he was born in 1340) stood too far down the line of succession to hope to ascend the throne. But when his father-in-law died, he inherited something far less troublesome—the Lancaster title and all the appurtenant property. In this way, Gaunt became the founder of the Lancastrian branch of the Plantagenet dynasty. Although he was never a king himself, through his Y chromosomes he quite literally became a king-maker.

John of Gaunt was tall and very slender, and quite the ladies' man, evidently; but contemporary chroniclers also referred to him as wise and reasonable, prudent, generous, imaginative, intelligent, cultivated, and accomplished. In addition to this laundry list of virtues, he had studied "science, art and letters" in his youth, according to Chaucer, who used to discuss astronomy with him. Gaunt became Chaucer's patron, commissioning a poetic elegy on his wife Blanche's beauty titled *The Boke of the Duchesse*. In the debit column, according to the chroniclers, Gaunt's contemporaries found him lofty, "jealous of honor, sudden and quick in quarrel."

By 1366, Katherine was a sort of subgoverness for the ducal children. In a match common to maids serving in medieval royal households, she was married to Hugh Swynford, an English knight in the retinue of John of Gaunt. Katherine bore Hugh a son, Thomas, in 1367, and two daughters, Blanche and Margaret. There may also have been another daughter named Dorothy. The duke himself stood as godfather to little Blanche.

Gaunt wielded considerable power in the governance of

the country. On the death of Edward III in 1367, Gaunt, a career diplomat, became the most important adult male in England. In essence, he was the real ruler of the realm for several years as the de facto seneschal for his ten-year-old nephew, King Richard II. Gaunt himself never desired the crown; in fact, he did everything he could to prop up his weak nephew's reign.

On September 12, 1368, at the age of twenty-six, Blanche of Lancaster died, a month after giving birth to her seventh child in nine years of marriage. Only three of her children survived infancy. Losing Blanche utterly devastated Gaunt, but practical concerns dictated that he remarry as soon as possible.

He wed Constance of Castile, the eldest daughter of the deposed and murdered King Pedro I, in September 1371. It was a diplomatic match; Gaunt chivalrously (and not at all altruistically) was set on placing Constance rightfully on her father's throne, and the conquest of Castile became his primary focus for the next several years. As Constance's husband, Gaunt was authorized to use the Castilian royal titles. He did proclaim himself king, minted coins, and issued state documents.

After joining Gaunt on his campaign to Spain, Hugh Swynford died in Aquitaine on November 13, 1371, leaving Katherine the lands they held in jointure, including Kettlethorpe, the Swynford estate. Being well settled allowed Katherine a rare degree of independence, and she chose to remain in Gaunt's household.

In 1372—or perhaps as early as November 1371, on Gaunt's return from Spain—Katherine began her affair with him. She was to bear Gaunt four children between 1373 and 1379. During Katherine's years with Gaunt, he became the wealthiest man in Europe without a crown on his head. By the 1370s, his family owned lands comprising one-third of England and controlled what would today amount to more

than $5 billion in annual rents. He was one of the first con-
scious capitalists, an empire builder who throughout his life
added to his vast estates. In the medieval real estate market
Gaunt was literally a "brand name"—a fourteenth-century
Trump.

Katherine's name appears regularly in Gaunt's records of
the 1370s, often referred to as *"nostre tres chere et bien
amee"* (our very dear and good friend). At first their royal affair was conducted with the utmost secrecy. Discretion was vital; Katherine was newly widowed, compelled for a full year
by societal dictates to wear the nunlike black and white mourning garments that advertised her very unattainability. Gaunt
was newly wed. If people knew he had a mistress, it would
greatly damage his chances of permanently claiming the Castilian throne.

Although a politically biased account of the era known as
the *Anonimalle Chronicle* refers to Katherine as *"une deblesce
et enchantresce"* (a she-devil and enchantress) responsible for
Gaunt's forsaking his wife, other sources report that their affair was a true love match that grew by choice out of carnal
desire as well as proximity. Katherine was tender and accommodating, and great with his kids. Outside of the nursery, she
was vivacious and shrewd, and got along famously with the
late Edward III's remaining power brokers, which made for
harmony all around, as Gaunt was the policy maker for young
Richard II.

Naming her his children's *magistra*, or governess, was
Gaunt's way of keeping Katherine close without causing tongues
to wag or eyebrows to rise. He showered her with gifts of
expensive jewelry, bolts of opulent cloth, barrels of Bor-
deaux, and cords of firewood. He deeded Lancastrian ma-
norial properties to her, so that she would have a steady
income, even though Hugh Swynford had left her well provided for.

Constance and Gaunt never bothered to learn each other's native tongue, and she evinced little interest in assimilating into English society, preferring to live apart from her husband, in the Spanish way, surrounded by an entourage of Castilians. In the spring of 1372, Gaunt gave her a generous settlement to provide for her household. Contrary to some accounts of their relationship, he did not wall her up or shunt her off to some distant Lancastrian castle after his relationship with Katherine began. The spouses mutually chose to maintain separate lives.

By 1375, Katherine's affair with the duke was common knowledge. And it clearly appalled certain segments of the population. Thomas Walsingham, a contemporary monk chronicling the age, condemned Gaunt

> . . . because he himself put aside respect for God's dread, deserted his military duties, rode around the country with the abominable temptress, seen as Katherine once called Swynford, holding her bridle in front of his own people, not only in the presence of his wife, but even with all his retainers looking on, in the most honored towns of the kingdom.

This criticism needs to be set in context. For one thing, the contemporaries who spoke ill of Katherine were really gunning for Gaunt; her reputation simply became collateral damage. For another, during the Middle Ages, among the nobility as well as the gentry, dynastic marriages were the rule. Mistresses were commonly accepted, although it was always better if they were discreet. Katherine seemed to have had that quality in spades. But many medieval chroniclers were monks, expressing the Church's attitude toward all women as Eve—the original sinner, seducer, and betrayer of mankind. Yet as far as royal mistresses go, Katherine Swynford was not poured from the mold of a gold digger. Her religious devotion is well documented and seems genuine—though how pious could she have been if she carried on an adulterous affair with her employer?

Katherine—and her royal lover—would soon be compelled to confront their guilt.

In 1381, John of Gaunt was the most powerful man in England, as well as the most despised—for the kingdom's myriad domestic problems, and for waging an unpopular war in Spain, which was seen as purely self-aggrandizing. Additionally, an oppressive poll tax on every subject was bleeding the poorer men dry. And in June 1381, the fomenting cauldron bubbled over, culminating in the Peasants' Revolt, led by Wat Tyler. Gaunt, the architect of Richard II's policies, was their convenient scapegoat. Thirty thousand strong, the mob swarmed into London. Joined by legions of apprentices, they opened the prisons, set fire to homes and brothels, and stormed the Savoy, Gaunt's magnificent white palace on the Strand, willfully destroying his priceless treasures and burning it to the ground.

Shaken by these violent events, Gaunt was convinced that God was punishing him, so he publicly confessed to the sin of lechery with Katherine Swynford.

According to the *Anonimalle Chronicle*, after renouncing Katherine in 1381, Gaunt reconciled with Constance and begged her pardon for his misdeeds. After fainting upon seeing him, "she forgave him willingly . . . and there was great joy and celebrations between them. . . ."

Although Gaunt had dumped Katherine in a most ostentatious way, he didn't fall out of love with her. In fact, he showed her how much he still cared the following Valentine's Day. On February 14, 1382, in a formal legal document known as a quitclaim, Gaunt released all claims on the properties he'd given to Katherine, meaning that all the lands, residences, and other buildings, along with the income derived from them, were hers for the rest of her life.

Katherine and Gaunt remained in touch because of their four children, and over the years he continued to send them all (including Katherine) generous and costly gifts. Gaunt had given his children by Katherine the surname of Beaufort, after one of his many territorial titles. Since Castle Beaufort was located in Anjou, which had fallen to the French in 1369, this wisely chosen name posed no threat to the duke's legitimate heirs—his son and two daughters with Blanche and his daughter Catalina (Katherine) with Constance.

In 1387, perhaps in an effort to gradually bring her closer to him again, Gaunt arranged for Katherine to have a position in the household of his daughter-in-law, Mary de Bohun.

That same year, having learned the hard way that military victory in Iberia was an impossibility, Gaunt concluded a peace treaty with Juan I of Spain, arranging the marriage of Katherine (or Catalina), his fifteen-year-old daughter by Constance, to Juan's son Enrique. With Gaunt's claim to Castile now mooted and their daughter its future queen, he and Constance no longer needed each other dynastically. Constance took up residence at Tutbury, disassociating herself from the Lancastrian household. She spent her last few years in Leicester Castle— while Gaunt once again lived openly with Katherine—dying on March 25, 1394.

Although Katherine and Gaunt were reunited while Constance still lived, there is no clear date for the recommencement of their romance, nor what the circumstances were. But once Constance died, there were no more impediments to their bliss. Gaunt loved Katherine and wanted to legalize their liaison and legitimize their four children. When he was in a position to do the right thing, he did it.

So twenty-four years after she became his lover, on January 14, 1396, Katherine wed John of Gaunt in Lincoln Cathedral.

She was forty-six years old (if born in 1350) and her husband was fifty-five. A papal dispensation was required to remove "the impediment of . . . compaternity" because Gaunt's standing as Blanche Swynford's godfather made him Katherine's "brother" under canon law. It would certainly have turned the affair into an even greater scandal if their adultery was compounded by what the Church would have deemed a form of incest. Not only did the Pope ratify their marriage, but in an unprecedented step, the four bastard children sired during Katherine and Gaunt's lengthy royal affair were legitimized by His Holiness and recognized by the king as such.

The Beauforts became mantle-children, a distinction usually given to offspring born out of wedlock to a couple that later marries, not to the children of an adulterous liaison. And Richard II's patent of legitimation of the Beauforts is unique in British history because it entitled them to all rank and titles, as well as to the right to inherit property, a privilege that was (absent a king's decree) legally denied to bastards. Richard's proclamation also clearly indicated that the Beauforts had a place in the line of royal succession.

Nevertheless, the union shocked the aristocracy, which saw no reason for the richest lord in the land to *marry* his commoner mistress. At least that was the view that was handed down through history, during an age when even the chroniclers reflected someone's political agenda.

A mid-fifteenth-century prior, John Capgrave, wrote in *The Chronicle of England* that Gaunt had wed Katherine "ageyn the opinion of many men." And the author of an early *sixteenth-*century chronicle of Plantagenet, Lancastrian, and Yorkist kings also refers to the astonished reaction their marriage received:

> . . . *the duke wedded the seyde Kateryne, the wheche wedding caused mony a monnus wondering, for, as hit was seyde, he haad holde here longe before.*

No matter what people thought, Katherine was now Duchess of Lancaster, and until the widowed king remarried she was the highest lady in the land. Her new status scandalized the aristocratic ladies, who refused to admit a baseborn woman, duchess or not, into their midst.

After waiting to wed him for nearly a quarter century, Katherine enjoyed only three years of marital happiness with John of Gaunt. He died on February 3, 1399, possibly from venereal disease.

Inscribed on Gaunt's tomb in St. Paul's Cathedral is a glowing tribute to Katherine Swynford, translated from the Latin as

HIS THIRD WIFE WAS KATHERINE,

OF A KNIGHTLY FAMILY,

AND AN EXCEPTIONALLY BEAUTIFUL WOMAN;

THEY HAD NUMEROUS OFFSPRING,

AND FROM THESE CAME THE MATERNAL FAMILY OF

HENRY VII, MOST PRUDENT ENGLISH KING

And yet he was buried beside Blanche, his first love, the woman whose connections and family fortune had brought him nearly limitless wealth and power. However, desiring that he and Katherine remain spiritually linked, Gaunt left a bequest for masses to be said jointly in their names.

On the morning of Gaunt's death he drew up a detailed will, leaving his "most dear wife Katherine" a vast amount of real estate and personal property.

Unfortunately, on his demise Gaunt's lands became forfeit to the crown because Richard II had exiled his son by Blanche, Henry, Earl of Derby, as a threat to his rule. And indeed he was. Better known as Bolingbroke, Henry eventually returned with his army and deposed Richard II, crowning himself Henry IV, the first king of the Lancastrian dynasty.

As a testament to Katherine's character, or perhaps to her savvy diplomatic acumen honed during a lifetime of association with the royal court, she was able to form close connections with *both* kings. Richard II eventually acknowledged his uncle's will and restored Katherine's entitlements from the duke's estates. And one of Katherine's sons by Gaunt—Henry Beaufort—became the chancellor for his usurping half brother, Henry IV.

Katherine retired to Lincolnshire after Gaunt's death, becoming a tenant of the Dean of Lincoln Cathedral. She died in 1403, probably at the age of fifty-two, and was buried in the cathedral. In 1644, her tomb was defaced by the Cromwellian Roundheads during the English Civil War.

The legacy of Katherine Swynford and John of Gaunt is staggering. With Blanche, John of Gaunt was the immediate ancestor of three Lancastrian kings—Henry IV, Henry V, and Henry VI.

His affair with Katherine led directly to the creation of the Tudor dynasty and to monarchs from the houses of York and Stuart. Through their eldest son, John Beaufort, Katherine and Gaunt were the great-great-grandparents of the Earl of Richmond, who defeated the Yorkist king Richard III (the grandson of Katherine and Gaunt's daughter Joan) on Bosworth Field in 1485.

Richmond, who became Henry VII, took the name Henry Tudor. His subsequent marriage to Elizabeth of York united the warring houses of York and Lancaster—each of which descended from King Edward III, Gaunt's father, and each of which believed they had a more legitimate right of succession. It was Henry Tudor who finally ended their protracted and bloody feud known as the Wars of the Roses.

The Stuarts were added to Katherine and Gaunt's family tree when John Beaufort's granddaughter (another Joan) wed a Stuart king, James I of Scotland.

In fact, every English monarch from 1461 on, including Elizabeth II, is descended from Katherine Swynford. Katherine's descendants also include Winston Churchill; Diana, Princess of Wales; and five U.S. presidents—Washington, Jefferson, John Quincy Adams, FDR, and George W. Bush.

LANCASTER

1399—1471

AND YORK

1461—85

EDWARD IV

1442–1483
RULED 1461–1470 AND 1471–1483

IN 1461, DURING THE WARS OF THE ROSES BETWEEN Edward III's descendants, Edward, Duke of York, took the throne by force from the fanatically religious and half-mad Lancastrian king, Henry VI, defeating him in a skirmish at Mortimer's Cross, near Ludlow, and proclaiming himself Edward IV. Edward's reign was divided into two periods, because he lost the crown to Henry VI in 1470 and fled to the Continent. During this period of exile, known as the "Readeption," Edward amassed an army and invaded England from Zeeland, recapturing his crown in 1471 and imprisoning Henry VI, who was quietly murdered in the Tower of London.

The spectacularly tall and regally handsome sovereign was praised for his conduct on the battlefield, his willingness to listen to the voices of domestic opposition, and his concern with the solvency of the crown. But even his staunchest supporters believed that his ignoble and rampant womanizing marred his ability to rule effectively. Although—in an ill-advised love match—Edward had secretly married Elizabeth

Woodville, a widowed commoner with two children from her previous marriage, he had always been a rover and a play-boy.

According to Sir Thomas More, writing during the first quarter of the sixteenth century,

> *The king's greedy appetite was insatiable, and every-where all over the realm intolerable. For no woman was there anywhere, young or old, rich or poor, whom he set his eye upon, in whom he anything liked, either person or appearance, speech, pace, or countenance, but without any fear of God or respect of his honor, murmur or grudge of the world, he would importunely pursue his appetite and have her, to the great destruction of many a good woman and a great dolor to her husband and their other friends.*

Edward was a great patron of artistic and cultural pursuits, including the newly invented printing press. But his appetite for cruelty (as well as for women) often overshadowed his more positive achievements. Politically he could be merciless, impris-oning and subsequently murdering one of his own brothers, the ambitious Duke of Clarence. And yet, for most medieval monarchs, this exercise of absolute power was more or less business as usual. "Use it or lose it" might as well have been the watchwords during these dark and bloody days of rebellion and counter rebellion.

On April 9, 1483, the forty-year-old Edward IV died of a fever in his bed at Westminster. His ruthless younger brother, Richard, Duke of Gloucester, once Edward's ally and seneschal in the north, imprisoned the late king's two sons in the Tower and had them declared illegitimate. It is still popularly believed that he had them murdered. He then usurped the throne, and was crowned Richard III.

👑

EDWARD IV
and Jane Shore 1450(?)–1527

Mistress Shore, as she is known throughout English literature, did not become *Jane* until after her death, when in 1599 the Elizabethan dramatist Thomas Heywood so christened her, unaware of her actual biography. The name stuck.

The real "Jane Shore" was born Elizabeth Lambert in London, the daughter of John Lambert, a prominent and prosperous City mercer and alderman. When she was still quite young, she was wed in an arranged marriage to another up-and-coming textile merchant, William Shore.

From the start, however, there was trouble in marital paradise. In March of 1476, Pope Sixtus IV commissioned a panel of three bishops to decide the case of Elizabeth Lambert alias Shore, wife of William Shore, who was petitioning for an annulment of her marriage on the grounds that her husband was "frigidus et impotens" and that she desired to have children. The annulment was apparently uncontested by William.

But by 1474, during Edward's Second Reign—and two years before her annulment took place—Mistress Shore was already the monarch's favorite paramour, though there is no credible account of how, when, and where they met. The closest we get to pinpointing a date that links Jane Shore with her tall, dark, and handsome sovereign is an entry on the Patent Rolls for December 4, 1476, that bestows the king's protection on "William Shore, citizen of London, and his servants, with all his lands, goods, and possessions in England and elsewhere."

So it's certainly possible that William Shore was not at all impotent, but reached an agreement with his wife to exchange her availability for royal favor, although he and Jane remained married for several unhappy years before she sought her ecclesiastical divorce.

Edward IV's lustful appetite was a legend in his lifetime; yet there was something about Jane Shore, above all others, that retained the king's fancy and affection until his death, more than nine years after their affair began. Thomas More—who never met Jane—was fascinated by her. In his history of Richard III's reign, written toward the end of Jane's life, he was convinced that Edward IV had genuinely adored her. "For many he had, but her he loved," wrote More.

The king often said he had three concubines: one the merriest, one the wiliest, and the third, the holiest harlot in his realm. The "merriest" of these paramours was Jane Shore, "in whom the king took special pleasure," wrote More.

It was not so much Jane's blond hair, round face, and fair complexion that captivated the king. Nor was it her exceptionally diminutive stature, for as Thomas More concluded, "there was nothing in her body that you would have changed, but if you would have wished her somewhat higher." Jane must have looked like a tiny doll next to the king, for when Edward's bones were disinterred in 1789, it was discovered that he stood six feet three and a half. In his prime, Edward IV was probably quite a handsome sight, a snappy dresser with soft dark hair, hazel eyes, and a straight nose.

Evidently, Jane had ensnared the king with her effervescent personality! More wrote that Jane "delighted not men so much in her beauty as in her pleasant behavior." At court she was an asset, witty and vivacious, and not at all grasping or avaricious in the manner of so many royal mistresses. Though she did use her influence in subtle ways, according to More, she "never abused it to any man's hurt, but to many a man's comfort and relief," achieving only the smallest recompense for her pains. "In many weighty suits she stood many men in great stead, either for none or very small rewards, and those rather gay than rich." She could also read and write very well, unsurprising for a respectable and successful merchant's daughter who probably learned to take orders and keep accounts at her father's knee.

However, Jane's ubiquitous presence at court vastly irritated the queen. The king's attachment to his favorite mistress extended far beyond the merely carnal. Elizabeth Woodville had married her husband for love, and understood that passion all too well. But even the queen had to begrudgingly admit Jane's finer qualities. At least Mistress Shore was entertaining, knew her place, and didn't have her hands in the Treasury.

During the last years of his reign, Edward IV had grown monstrously obese and was a slave to every kind of gluttony and excess, or "fleshy wantonness," as his contemporaries graphically put it. Surprisingly, given Edward's outsized libido, Jane Shore is not believed to have given her royal lover any offspring, although he sired children with other mistresses, and gave his queen ten of them, seven of whom survived him. But as Jane believed her ex-husband to be impotent, perhaps the problem really lay in her own biology; perhaps she was barren.

Although their royal affair endured for several years, Edward made no arrangements for Jane's welfare in the event of his death. So when the Duke of Gloucester usurped the throne upon her lover's demise, crowning himself Richard III, Jane's star dipped precipitously.

Ricardian societies have attempted over the centuries to rehabilitate his reputation, but Richard's reign has traditionally been characterized as one of lawlessness and terror. And he got plenty of political mileage by humiliating Mistress Shore. Richard denounced Jane for sexual immorality; and in an event that unwittingly made her a folk heroine, he had the Bishop of London command her to parade through the streets in the manner of a penitent—clad only in her white shift and kirtle, carrying a candle and reciting psalms with a conical "dunce" cap perched on her head. This Jane did with as much dignity as she could possibly muster, much to Richard's dismay. The king then imprisoned her at Ludgate on charges of sorcery and witchcraft that had contrived to aid and abet her royal lover—allegations that of course could not be proved. He even accused her of practicing the magic that had withered his arm!

Richard also accused Jane of carrying on illicit and passionate affairs with two of Edward IV's kinsmen and supporters—Lords Dorset and Hastings. In a proclamation dated October 23, 1483, Richard denounced Dorset for harboring "the unshameful and mischievous woman called Shore's wife in adultery." However, Hastings, who some historians believe became Jane's next protector, was not even in England during the time he was allegedly bedding her. In any event, Richard had Hastings beheaded in June 1483. The charges of harlotry with Dorset and Hastings were likely a smear campaign, one that bears the fingerprints of Richard's cabal. The accusations are now considered baseless, but at the time, Jane's countrymen and -women gave them credit and she was roundly denounced as a whore.

Well, the royal whore was about to land on her feet. In an undated letter, possibly written in 1484, Richard told his chancellor, the Bishop of Lincoln, that he had heard that his "solicitor Thomas Lynom, is marvelously abused and blinded with the late wife of William Shore and intends to marry her." If Lynom was indeed set on the marriage, Richard would issue his permission for Jane to be released into the custody of the bishop or someone His Grace would appoint, but the marriage itself was to be deferred until His Majesty came to London.

King Richard was too canny not to have realized that he had no legitimate case against Jane, whether for witchcraft, lechery, or any other charge beyond being his brother's lover. Nevertheless, to save face, Richard manufactured the propaganda that Jane Shore expired on a dung heap—fitting proof of her filthy lechery—and the lie soon became legend.

The *truth* seems to be that Jane was released from Ludgate prison and soon after married Thomas Lynom. The solicitor managed to extricate himself from the service of Richard III and moved to the Welsh marches, where he sat on commissions and eventually became clerk controller to Henry VII's son Arthur, Prince of Wales, in Ludlow Castle.

So the manure story was just that. As Thomas's wife, Jane more than likely lived in middle-class comfort for the remainder of her days. Thomas Lynom had died by the end of July 1518.

Jane lived to a ripe old age, even for our own era; "lean, withered, and dried up," according to More (but who doesn't look like that at the age of seventy-seven?). Most historians agree that Jane died in 1527. Her effigy is at Hixworth Church in Hertfordshire, though she may in fact be buried at Eton.

THE
TUDORS
1485–1603

MARY TUDOR

1496–1533
Queen of France 1514–1515
and Charles Brandon 1484–1545

*I*T TAKES A BRAVE WOMAN TO DEFY A KING, EVEN IF THE king happens to be your big brother and you're his favorite sister. But that's precisely what Mary Tudor did.

Mary Rose Tudor, tall, graceful, and fine-boned, with the same red-gold hair as her brother, was considered one of Europe's most beautiful princesses. She was also one of its greatest pawns. In 1507, Mary was betrothed to Archduke Charles of Austria, heir to both the throne of Spain (occupied at the time by Ferdinand of Aragon, the father of Henry's queen, Catherine) and to the title of Holy Roman Emperor, held then by Maximilian of Austria. But the sands of political alliance were always shifting, and the wedding plans were scotched when Ferdinand and Maximilian went behind Henry's back and signed a truce with France.

On Henry's behalf, his new Archbishop of York, Wolsey, negotiated their own arrangement with France. As part of their treaty, on August 13, 1514, Henry's younger sister, Mary, "a nymph from heaven," was married by proxy to Louis XII, the fifty-two-year-old French monarch.

The Brandon family had an illustrious relationship with the Tudors. Charles's father, Sir William Brandon, had been Henry VII's valiant standard-bearer. He had paid the ultimate price for his service to the crown when he was killed during the Battle of Bosworth by Richard III himself.

Charles Brandon, who was said to resemble Henry so much that some people thought he was the king's "bastard brother," was one of Henry's favorite courtiers. In 1513, Henry made him a Knight of the Garter and Master of the Horse, and that same year created him Viscount Lisle. That summer, Lisle distinguished himself in battle during Henry's campaigns in France.

In 1514, Brandon was made Duke of Suffolk, and his rise through the ranks of the peerage had many nobles from older and more established families bristling. But Brandon had his fans as well. "A liberal and magnificent lord," wrote a Venetian visitor to the court. "No one ever bore so vast a rise with so easy a dignity."

Brandon took part in the jousts that Henry had organized to celebrate the marriage of Mary to the King of France. It is not known for certain, though it is surmised, that although he was a dozen years her senior, Suffolk caught young Mary's eye during the tournaments.

Henry rejoiced in the match with the French monarch, but the bride was miserable at the prospect of being wedded to an aging, ailing man for whom she had no love. Henry was quite aware, as was Wolsey, of Mary's unhappiness, but her feelings were of no importance when compared with matters of international politics. Yet she may have been canny enough to see a way out of her dilemma. Letters were exchanged among the parties wherein Mary had proposed a bargain, conveying to her brother that she had "consented to his request and for the peace of Christendom, to marry Louis of France, though he was very aged and sickly, on condition that if she survived him, she should marry whom she liked."

The wedding festivities in England proceeded as though the groom himself had been there. The young bride was placed in the huge bed of estate with a stand-in, the duc de Longueville. He "consummated" the marriage on his sovereign's behalf by removing his red hose and touching one of Mary's bare legs with his own.

Then the great preparations began to send Mary across the Channel to France with her trousseau and her retinue—which included Thomas Boleyn's two daughters, Mary and Anne. On October 2, about to sail from Dover, Mary Tudor reminded her brother of their agreement. Henry did not acknowledge her remarks, instead telling her quite formally, "I betoken you to God and the fortunes of the sea and the government of the King your husband."

And on October 9, in Abbeville, France, Mary Rose Tudor and Louis were married in person. She was crowned Queen of France at St. Denis on November 5. After that, Mary and Suffolk may have crossed paths at her own court, where Henry had entrusted him with diplomatic missions to Louis XII.

Under Salic law, the French crown could only pass to a male heir, and although Louis was nicknamed *Le Père du Peuple*—the father of his people—he was unable to father any sons with his first two wives. Hope, however, sprang eternal in the king's soul. In fact, after his wedding night to Mary, he announced that "he had performed marvels."

But on New Year's Day 1515, less than three months later, Louis XII passed away, quite possibly during, or at least due to, his amatory efforts to beget an heir. Mary had never been happy in the marriage, and now she was free, only eighteen years old, and, she believed, with the rest of her life ahead of her to do as she pleased.

Wrong.

Mary's rank as the English king's sister as well as her youth and (assumed) fecundity made her a key player in international relations. Henry VIII was legally in control of her future, and it was important for him to see her settled in a second advantageous match.

In late January 1515, after promising Henry that he would not propose to his sister, Suffolk was dispatched to escort Mary—now the dowager Queen of France—back home, and to offer England's official congratulations to the new king, François I. But rather than hurry swiftly home, Mary and Brandon remained in France, where they secretly married on March 3. Theirs was no mere elopement; it was an act of treason. A princess of the blood had wed without the consent of the sovereign.

Suffolk had already been wed twice before. He had obtained an annulment of his marriage to his first wife, Margaret Mortimer; and his second wife, Anne Browne, had left him a widower in 1512. At the time he eloped with Mary, he was around thirty-one years old, a handsome, sophisticated man in the prime of life. He had risked his sovereign's displeasure—and possibly his head—to marry Mary.

Writing to Wolsey, the new bridegroom confessed, "The Queen would never let me rest till I had granted her to be married. And so, to be plain with you, I have married her heartily, and have lain with her insomuch I fear me lest she be with child."

Naturally, the cardinal went straight to the king. Henry was livid—not only with Mary but with Suffolk, who had given his oath to avoid this very situation. The king's Privy Council (on which sat many peers who were jealous of Suffolk's ascendance to wealth and power) urged Henry to make an example of the wayward couple and have them executed, or at the very least imprisoned. Henry was only six years into his reign, a mere youth himself at twenty-three. And perhaps *because* he was young and lusty himself he understood Mary's passion, at least on an emotional level. He adored his sister, and would have suffered almost equally to see her immured within the Tower—or worse.

So Henry finally forgave Mary and Suffolk—or claimed to—and welcomed them back to England. On May 13, 1515, they were officially married on English soil. Although the ceremonies were modest, it was a triumph of True Love.

But sentimental attachment, and even sympathy, didn't pay the kingdom's bills. Henry had taken a huge hit in the purse by their disobedience. And he demanded restitution. So he forced Suffolk to reimburse him for the vast sum spent on Mary's wedding to the French king as well as for the luxury items, such as jewels and plate, that Louis had promised to bestow on Mary. Then there was the matter of Mary's dowry. That, too, had been forfeited to France.

The pecuniary penalty for the Duke and Duchess of Suffolk was enormous. The dowry alone amounted to £200,000, worth nearly eight hundred fifty times that sum in today's dollars. Compensation for the plate and jewels was an additional line item. And to repay Henry for the remaining expenses, Suffolk was to tender another thousand pounds per annum for the next twenty-four years.

It was Cardinal Wolsey who had brokered this financial arrangement. When Suffolk and Mary eventually returned to court, Suffolk, nearly bankrupted by it, became the cardinal's severest critic.

Mary bore Suffolk three children: a son, Henry Brandon, and two daughters, Lady Frances and Lady Eleanor. But the family did not become permanent fixtures at Henry's court, preferring the relative sanity and solitude of the duke's estates. Now that he was the king's brother-in-law, the duke's power and influence remained as strong as ever.

Suffolk was one of the diplomats present at the Field of Cloth of Gold summit between Henry and François I in 1520, where he might have first caught a glimpse of Anne Boleyn, in the train of Queen Claude. He could not have known at the time that the young lady-in-waiting with the dark eyes and sallow complexion would cause a rift with his own wife and a strained relationship between Mary and her brother.

Mary had known Anne well enough during her brief reign as Queen of France; and she didn't like her, though Mary's reasons for her early antipathy have not been preserved. After Anne became Henry's mistress, Mary came to court as infrequently as possible, and she sympathized with Katherine of Aragon during the protracted Great Matter. Because of her rank, Mary could get away with her strong opinions against Anne, although Henry didn't have to like them. It broke his heart that his favorite sister detested his mistress, because he was bound by love to prefer Anne in such circumstances.

In 1532, Mary was heard using "opprobrious language" about Anne that literally sparked violence between her husband's men and those of Anne's uncle, the Duke of Norfolk. Two of Norfolk's men, the Southwell brothers, murdered Suffolk's retainer, Sir William Pennington, as the knight sought sanctuary in Westminster Abbey. Suffolk then "remove[d] the assailants by force" from holy ground.

The court went into an uproar over the incident. Suffolk and Mary retreated to their country estate, Westhorpe Hall, but the mood at Whitehall remained so tense that Henry had to intervene by riding out to speak with Suffolk directly, and fining one of the Southwells the whopping sum of £1,000 (nearly $730,000 nowadays).

Suffolk, too, had at first not thought much of Anne. As late as May 1530, Eustache Chapuys, the ambassador from the court of Charles V, the Holy Roman Emperor, reported that the duke had been banished from court for warning Henry of Anne's unsuitability to be queen, owing to her "criminal" relations with a certain courtier "whom she loves very much and whom the king had formerly chased from court for jealousy." The married poet Thomas Wyatt was likely the man in question, and Anne was terribly upset by the gossip, though she always denied that she and Wyatt had ever enjoyed each other carnally.

Yet, when all was said and done, Suffolk was a loyal courtier, supporting the king in all he sought, and therefore became enough of a proponent of Anne's to remain in Henry's good graces. After all, a simple Act of Attainder could wipe away with one stroke of Henry's pen all the honors and titles and accumulated wealth and property that the king had bestowed upon him. So Brandon had to clench his fists and suck it up when, upon Anne's coronation, Henry replaced him in the office of Earl Marshal with Anne's uncle, his archrival Norfolk.

The Duchess of Suffolk lodged her own protest; when Anne finally became queen in 1533, Mary quite pointedly refused to come to court at all.

She fell dangerously ill that June, and in her dying wishes sought reconciliation with her brother. In her last letter to Henry, she wrote that "the sight of Your Grace is the greatest comfort to me that may be possible."

But her illness was a mere footnote amid the weeks of festivity surrounding Anne's coronation. Suffolk hurried to her sickbed with Henry's written reply to her sad little letter, offering his forgiveness and reconciling Mary to the royal bosom.

Mary died at Westhorpe Hall on June 25. First interred at the abbey at Bury St. Edmunds, her corpse was moved to St. Mary's Church after the abbey was destroyed during the dissolution of the monasteries. You would think that Henry might have tried a little harder to protect his precious sister's resting place.

Suffolk wasted little time in remarrying. On September 7, 1533, the same day as the birth of Princess Elizabeth, the forty-eight-year-old duke took a fourth wife—the barely-fourteen-year-old Katherine Willoughby, daughter of Katherine of

Aragon's trusted friend and lady-in-waiting Maria de Salinas. Suffolk had desired the girl when she was betrothed to his son. Now that he was single again, the duke broke off his own son's contract to marry Katherine himself. The scandal it created was not over the age difference between the groom and his new bride, but over the sordidness of the family dynamic. Suffolk's son, Henry, Earl of Lincoln, who passed away on March 8, 1534, was said to have died of a broken heart over his father's betrayal. Although the youth had been ill for some time, it didn't stop certain tongues from wagging, particularly Anne Boleyn's, who remarked, "My Lord of Suffolk kills one son to beget another."

Suffolk remained an influential and powerful courtier and a trusted military commander. In 1544, at the age of sixty, he was once more sent to the Continent to command the forces that besieged Boulogne.

While the court was in Guilford, Suffolk died unexpectedly on August 24, 1545, at the age of sixty-one. The cause of death is unknown, but since it came quite quickly, it was possibly a heart attack or stroke, rather than an illness. However, the legacy of his love match with Mary Tudor would enter the history books for more than its aspects of passion, intrigue, and the flagrant defying of a king.

On February 12, 1554, their granddaughter, Lady Jane Grey, known as "the Nine Days' Queen," would lose her head in the struggle for succession engendered by the death of Henry VIII's teenage son, Edward VI, who left no heirs. The hapless Jane Grey would be succeeded on the English throne by Henry's daughter Mary.

HENRY VIII

1491–1547
RULED 1509–1547

O<small>N</small> A<small>PRIL</small> 22, 1509, <small>JUST TWO MONTHS SHY OF HIS EIGH</small>-teenth birthday, Henry VIII ascended the throne on the death of his miserly father, Henry VII, from tuberculosis. The new king was flame-haired, fair-complected, over six feet two inches tall, and well proportioned with a thirty-two-inch waist, handsome and beardless, with, according to his chroniclers, a "fine calf to his leg" of which he was "exceeding proud and vain." His court became a shining citadel of art, culture, theology, and philosophy—in short, the embodiment of the Renaissance itself.

Just six weeks after Henry's accession, on June 11, 1509, he wed Katherine of Aragon, his late brother's wife. But when Katherine failed to give him a son, and Henry fell in love with one of her ladies-in-waiting, Anne Boleyn, he sought an unprecedented divorce.

Henry ignored the opinions of the Pope at the peril of his own excommunication, proclaimed himself head of the Church in England, and a reformed religion was born, which would eventually morph into the Church of England. During the thirty-eight years of Henry's reign, the monasteries were dissolved and their property absorbed by the Royal Exchequer. Dissidents, including Henry's Lord Chancellor and most trusted legal adviser, the venerated Thomas More (who so comprehensively chronicled the reigns of Edward IV and Richard III), were executed for speaking against the validity of Henry's marriage to Anne Boleyn.

But when Anne also failed to give him a son, Henry sought a way to rid himself of her as well. On May 19, 1536, she was executed on trumped-up charges of adultery and treason.

Henry married Jane Seymour just a few days after Anne's execution, and after Jane died in October 1537, just twelve days after delivering a son (the future Edward VI), Henry waited three years before remarrying. His fourth wife was the unhygienic German princess Anne of Cleves, who physically repulsed him so much that their marriage was never consummated and was swiftly annulled.

Wife number five was one of her ladies-in-waiting, Kathryn Howard, the teenage niece of the Duke of Norfolk. After Kathryn Howard's execution for treason and adultery (which were perhaps *not* trumped-up charges) in 1542, Henry dipped his gouty toes in the marital waters for a sixth time, marrying the wealthy thirty-three-year-old widow Catherine Parr on July 12, 1543, at the age of fifty-two.

Throughout his life, Henry was desperate to have a legitimate son, and there was a valid reason for his succession obsession. Although a female could by law inherit the throne of England, Henry was the product of an age when the crown had been won by arms, and not through legal succession. The Wars of the Roses provide context for this conviction, and Henry's own father, Henry VII, had been one such usurper. It was popularly believed that only a strong male could hold the throne, and lead his army, if necessary, against all challengers—

something a female (considered weak, paltry, and a second-rate gender) could not do. Queens were for begetting sons, not for ruling countries.

The chronological catalogue of Henry's six wives also mirrors the tenor of his time, and the shifting sands of religious upheaval and the swinging pendulum of his court's political factions. *Catholic, Reformer, Catholic, Lutheran, Catholic, Reformer.*

Toward the end of his days, Henry's bulk was so immense that he had to be carried from place to place in purpose-built chairs. By the time he was fifty-five, his various ailments and illnesses caught up with him; he died at Whitehall on January 28, 1547. His death was kept secret for two days so that matters regarding a smooth succession could be put in order. Henry VIII was buried at Windsor beside his beloved third wife, Jane Seymour. Their nine-year-old son succeeded him, to become Edward VI.

In 1813 the royal tomb at Windsor was opened on the directive of the Prince Regent (himself quite the ladies' man). Henry's rather large coffin was opened, confirming his height of six feet two. Russet hairs still clung to his skull.

HENRY VIII
and Elizabeth "Bessie" Blount c. 1500–1539/41 (?)

At the age of thirteen, the uncommonly pretty and talented Elizabeth Blount—one of Katherine of Aragon's ladies-in-waiting—costarred with the handsome and virile Henry in a romantic court masque, a popular courtly entertainment that combined elements of allegory, song, dance, and theatre with opulent costumes and elaborate stagecraft. The very pregnant Queen Katherine was so impressed with the performance that she asked them to repeat it by torchlight in her bedchamber.

That may have been the last time Katherine was pleased to see her husband cavorting with Bessie, that "fair damosel, who in singing, dancing, and all goodly pastimes exceeded no other," according to a chronicler of the times. Though Katherine had been taught by her parents to anticipate marital infidelity from a king, it didn't mean she was happy about it. Katherine loved Henry in every way, and wanted to be a good wife to him. And the more he cheated on her, the deeper she retreated into her religious devotions, finding solace in her Catholicism.

Katherine's reproving glances pushed Henry even further from her bed. His affair with Bessie wasn't his first extramarital liaison, but it was certainly a seminal one, because it was Bessie who gave him the son he so passionately desired.

Bessie's father, Sir John Blount of Shropshire, had fought in France alongside Henry in 1513, the same year as the court masque. Five years later, in 1518, with the queen pregnant again, the vivacious Bessie distinguished herself from her ten siblings by becoming the king's mistress, apparently offering scant resistance to the sovereign's seductive powers. In this role, Bessie was evidently the nonpareil, "thought for her rare ornaments of nature and education to be the beauty and mistress-piece of her time," according to her contemporaries.

Henry felt no guilt in availing himself of Bessie's charms because it was the custom for a king to refrain from visiting his wife's bedroom during the better part of her pregnancy, lest their amorous coupling endanger the unborn fetus. This convention provided a great excuse for monarchs to look elsewhere for sexual satisfaction during these months of imposed "restraint."

And in the summer of 1519, after Henry had been married to Katherine of Aragon for a decade with only a daughter to show for it, Bessie confirmed his virility by giving him a son—the greatest gift the king could have. Actually, it was the second greatest gift, because the son she bore was illegitimate, and therefore ineligible to inherit his throne. She named the royal bastard Henry Fitzroy, the surname being Norman-French for "son of the king," and was henceforth known as "the mother of the king's son."

Under Henry's directives, Cardinal Wolsey, who acted very much as his consigliere during the early years of his reign, arranged for the new mum to be married off. The king also named Wolsey as the baby's godfather. Bessie was wed to a commoner of "gentle" birth, Sir Gilbert Tailboys (often spelled Talboys), and little Henry was raised by Gilbert as his own son at Rokeby Manor in Warwickshire, a gift from the king as his paramour's dowry. But the king wanted to ensure that his son would have the finest possible education, so when little Henry was just a tyke, he was sent off to Kings College, Cambridge, to be tutored by Richard Croke.

Given his keen interest in his son's schooling, and the boy's lavish household with 245 liveried attendants, Henry clearly entertained the notion of legitimizing Henry Fitzroy and naming him as his successor. The king certainly contemplated arranging a marriage between his son and his legitimate daughter, the youth's half sister, Mary. In 1525, when the boy was only six years old, Henry created him Earl of Nottingham and Duke of Richmond and Somerset. At the same time, Henry also made his son a Knight of the Garter and appointed him Lord Admiral and Warden-General of the Marches against Scotland.

Although he held court from a throne as richly appointed as a prince's and was addressed as though he were legitimate royalty, Henry Fitzroy didn't get the chance to enjoy his many honors for very long. On July 22, 1536, at the age of seventeen, he died of consumption.

After Tailboys died, Bessie remarried very well, wedding Lord Clinton, who would later be made Earl of Lincoln. Her nuptial good fortune on both counts raised some eyebrows and set some tongues wagging, accusing Cardinal Wolsey of encouraging nubile young ladies of the lower and middle ranks to indulge in fornication in order to find a wellborn spouse.

Sometime between January 1539 and June 1541, at around the age of thirty-nine, Bessie was carried off by consumption herself. By that time, her former royal lover was in the process of changing the world as they knew it to marry his current inamorata, Anne Boleyn.

HENRY VIII
and Mary Boleyn 1499–1543

The French monarch François I called her his "hackney," explaining that he loved to ride her. An Italian visitor to François's court thought her *"una grandissima ribald et infame sopre tutte"* (a great prostitute and more infamous than all of them). She is probably best remembered as the older sister of Anne Boleyn. What seems clear is that this daughter of Sir Thomas Boleyn and Lady Elizabeth Howard knew how to have fun in bed.

Mary Boleyn possessed the blond, blue-eyed, curvy beauty that was the era's *belle idéale*. In 1514, she was a member of the French court in the household of the queen, Henry VIII's younger sister Mary Tudor. But after Mary's husband, King Louis XII, died on New Year's Day in 1515, Mary Boleyn remained at the French court, where she became a lady-in-waiting to the new queen, Claude, the wife of Louis's son François.

Evidently, Mary Boleyn also became the paramour of the new king, François I. But after François tired of Mary, she consoled herself in the arms of enough of his courtiers to create a scandal. In 1519, at the age of twenty, Mary was ignominiously dismissed from Queen Claude's service and packed back to England, much to the embarrassment and disgrace of her family.

But the Boleyns were a powerful family, so Mary quickly secured a place as a lady-in-waiting to Queen Katherine, the unofficial but de facto usual incubator for a royal mistress. Sure enough, soon after Bessie Blount delivered Henry's son in 1519, the regal eye began to rove, alighting before long on the new flavor in his wife's retinue.

His affair with Mary Boleyn was reputedly short but intense. And in a situation similar to Bessie Blount's, Henry saw to it that Mary made a financially brilliant marriage. So, on February 4, 1520, at the Chapel Royal in Greenwich, Mary Boleyn wed William Carey, one of Henry's favorite Gentlemen of the Bedchamber. His Majesty himself attended the wedding, bestowing an offering of six shillings, eightpence in the chapel. However, some believe that Mary was still Henry's mistress at the time she was wed to William Carey.

In any case, Henry was so immensely grateful for the gift of Mary's favors, he enriched her father as well as her new husband. Sir Thomas Boleyn was made Viscount Rochford, and William Carey's coffers were vastly enlarged.

In 1525, Mary gave birth to a son, who she named Henry. The king never claimed paternity, and Mary never pressed the point, so the boy was likely her husband's. But Mary's motherhood had the effect of dampening Henry's lust, just as it had more or less killed his ardor for Bessie Blount soon after she gave birth.

Yet there was another reason Mary was supplanted: Henry had fallen madly in lust with her younger sister, Anne.

Mary wasn't too upset about it. She devoted herself to her husband and their two children. But in 1528, after the thirty-two-year-old William Carey died during the outbreak of the sweating sickness, Mary found herself buried under a mound of debts. Petitions to her family were fruitless. Requests to Henry fell on deaf ears as well. Only Anne, who at the time of William's death was the king's inamorata, managed to procure something for her sister—an annual pension of £100 (nearly $72,000 today), and an elaborately wrought golden cup.

In 1534, Mary secretly married William Stafford, a commoner without rank of any kind. She bore him two children. For wedding a man so far beneath her station, the Boleyns disowned her for good, but Mary emphatically averred, "For well I might a' had a greater man of birth, but I assure you I could never a' had one that loved me so well. I had rather beg my bread with him than be the greatest queen in Christendom," a rather pointed swipe at her sister, as well as a triumphant declaration of True Love. But the jibe struck too close to Anne's bones, and Anne, now queen, declared that Mary and her husband would never again be received at court.

Her ostracism was probably a blessing; Mary was well rid of the vipers' nest of the Tudor court. She rusticated with her small family at Rochford in Essex while Anne and their brother George tasted the full measure of Henry's rough justice. Mary did not visit her siblings as they waited in the Tower for the executioner's blade to end their lives. Perhaps she was cannier than she'd been credited; she deliberately remained as far from the madness as possible, the better to avoid getting swept into the bloody dustbin of her family's history.

Mary died at home on July 19, 1543.

Her son, Henry Carey, was eventually made a Knight of the Garter by Elizabeth I. Mary's daughter Catherine became a maid of honor to both Anne of Cleves and Kathryn Howard. One of Catherine Carey's daughters, Lettice Knollys, was Queen

Elizabeth's bosom companion, lady-in-waiting—and later, her rival and enemy, after she married Robert Dudley, the great love of Elizabeth's life.

Mary Boleyn's twentieth-century descendants include Winston Churchill; Mary Bowes-Lyon (the mother of Elizabeth II); Diana, Princess of Wales; and Sarah Ferguson.

HENRY VIII
and Anne Boleyn ("The Most Happy")
1500(?)–1536
Queen of England 1533–1536

Anne Boleyn, the younger daughter of Sir Thomas Boleyn and Elizabeth Howard, was from the outset a political animal. She spent her teenage years in France in the train of Queen Mary Tudor, the younger sister of Henry VIII. Sir Thomas had sent both his daughters there in the hope that they would gain the polish and sophistication that would make them irresistible to a king. Sir Thomas would never exactly be father of the year, but the scheming and ambitious courtier did achieve his aim.

At François I's notoriously licentious court, Anne developed her taste for all things French—the language, the fashions, the music. She perfected the art of flirtation, her black eyes expertly conveying an entire gamut of emotions.

Anne was not a conventional beauty like her sister, Mary. She was of middling stature, and her features were angular and fine, though her mouth was considered wide. Her complexion was sallow, her bosom "was not much raised" (according to the Venetian ambassador, who evidently got close enough to evaluate it), and her hair was a brownish auburn that cascaded past her slim hips. Anne's detractors delighted in depicting her as deformed, with warts or moles all over her body, a huge wen on her throat (she was described as having a large Adam's apple, but the wen, an abnormal and unsightly growth or cyst, was a gross exaggeration that seemed to grow with the telling of the tale), and a sixth finger on her left hand. Rather than truly endowed with an eleventh digit, Anne probably had a vestigial extra nail on her left pinky, but if she had been even a tenth as malformed as her enemies painted her, the persnickety Henry, with his discerning eye for beauty, would never have looked twice at her, let alone moved heaven and earth to wed her. Still, it was believed at the time that any physical deformity was an outward manifestation of inner corruption, a superstition that would come back to haunt the dusky beauty.

Anne was in other ways very different from her giddy sister. She was smarter and brighter, quicker to pick up on nuances. Anne understood the role for which she was being groomed by her family, and assiduously applied herself to perfecting it.

In 1521, Anne was recalled to England, possibly because her father wished to arrange her marriage to a wealthy distant cousin. In the meantime, she was placed in Queen Katherine's household. Anne's cosmopolitan sophistication, her facility with languages, and her rapier wit and skilled repartee made her one of the most popular young women at court, and she soon had several admirers, including the very-married poet Thomas Wyatt, who resided near Anne's parents' Kentish home, Hever Castle.

In 1522, her hopes for a marriage to the handsome courtier Henry Percy, the son and heir of the Duke of Northumberland, were destroyed by her father and Cardinal Wolsey, acting on behalf of the duke. Anne saw the cardinal as the architect of her misfortune, her broken heart, and worst of all, her chance to marry not just for love but for wealth, status, and power. And Anne had always been ambitious.

By the middle of 1525, Anne had utterly captivated the king. She was now in her mid-twenties and Henry was then thirty-five years old, in the seventeenth year of his reign, still vigorous, handsome, and athletically built with just the slightest trace of pudginess. But it was not until the Shrovetide merriment in 1526 that people began to discern the infatuation that Henry had secretly harbored for nearly a year, scarcely daring to confess it to the object herself.

During the joust on Shrove Tuesday, 1526, Henry hinted at his feelings by wearing a tabard embroidered with the motto *"Declare je nos"* (I dare not declare), a hint to the lady who had captured his fancy.

It was not long before Henry asked Anne to be his lover, but her reply took him by surprise. "I would rather lose my life than my honesty," she told the king. "Your wife I cannot be . . . your mistress I will not be."

Where Mary Boleyn had played for love, Anne played for power. She had seen too well that once the king achieved what he desired, it soon lost all luster for him. And Anne Boleyn had no interest in becoming one of Henry's castoffs. She wanted to be his queen.

Just before Christmas 1526, after nearly eighteen months of pursuit, Henry wrote to tell Anne that

> *. . . if it pleases you to do the duty of a true, loyal mistress and friend, and to give yourself body and heart to me, who has been and will be your very loyal servant. I promise that not only the name will be due to you, but also to take you as my sole mistress, casting off all others than yourself out of mind and affection and to serve you and you alone.*

Replying in writing on New Year's Day in 1527, Anne told Henry she would accept him as her betrothed only after the king promised to make her his wife and queen—clarifying her interpretation of his plea to make her the sole mistress, or possessor, of his heart, body, and soul. She sent him a present as well—a "handsome diamond" and a brooch shaped like a ship in which a lonely damsel appears tempest-tossed. Accompanying the gift was a note that resounded with passion, but also slyly encouraged Henry to continue to press for an annulment from Katherine if he wanted to enjoy her.

From that point, Anne must have permitted Henry certain liberties with her body, because in one of his letters dating from 1527, Henry wrote, "I would you were in my arms or I in yours for I think it is a long time since we kissed." Like an infatuated schoolboy, he designed an emblem with their initials, AB and HR, entwined, and the motto *"aultre ne cherse"* (I seek no other).

And although Henry's *lust* was directed toward Anne, throughout his life his *greatest passion* was the begetting of a male heir.

Henry's desire for Anne had convinced him that God was punishing him for marrying his deceased brother Arthur's wife by denying them sons. Getting rid of Katherine was the only way to break the curse. Just before May 1527, the king conceived the idea of divorcing Katherine of Aragon—or rather, seeking to have their marriage annulled because they had violated the word of God. Brandishing a Bible, he invoked the verses of Leviticus that made it a sin for a man to lie with his dead brother's wife.

But Katherine was the daughter of Ferdinand and Isabella and her nephew was Charles V, the Spanish king and Holy Roman Emperor; as such, he wielded tremendous power over most of Europe and the papacy as well. Charles would never stand idly by while the English king dared to cast off his aunt.

And Katherine had been well coached. Knowing Henry's reliance upon Leviticus, she countered the argument with the insistence that she had never consummated her marriage with Arthur. Negotiations to legally divest himself of Katherine and take Anne as his second wife and queen dragged on from 1527 to 1533, and all the while, Anne kept Henry panting after her.

Anne and Henry were initially secretive about their affair, but each was too excited about their conquest to remain discreet for long. They appeared together as a couple at a reception hosted at Greenwich Palace to honor the French ambassador on May 15, 1527. Two days later Cardinal Wolsey opened the secret trial in what came to be known as the King's Great Matter, which was the case to prove his right to annul his marriage to Katherine. Indeed, the trial was such a secret that Queen Katherine was not even informed of the proceedings!

Anne and Henry, however, were waist-deep in the Matter. They communicated daily by letter when they were not in proximity to each other. As a team they discussed and dissected the divorce, its political, religious, and social ramifications and consequences. Anne found scholars and theologians to support their theories, pushing Henry harder to think out of the box. She had developed her humanist leanings in France, and endeavored to convert the king to her views.

To "divorce" Katherine, Henry sought a papal dispensation from Clement VII that would effectively overturn, or cancel, a previous dispensation to marry his late brother's wife that he had secured from Pope Julius II, back when he thought it was a good idea. Now, nearly a quarter century later, the king was demanding that Clement's dispensation uphold the nullity of his marriage to Katherine for that very reason—*because* she had been his late brother's wife.

But Henry required two separate things from Rome: permission to divorce Katherine and permission to marry Anne. For the second half of the equation, because Henry had slept with Anne's sister, he would need a papal dispensation to ignore the subject of the first degree of affinity.

At the outset of the Great Matter, both Anne and Henry seemed to believe that the issue would be swiftly resolved. Though they anticipated resistance from Charles V, neither of them had pegged Katherine correctly. Her retreat into religious devotions had made her stronger, rather than more malleable. She was not going to go quietly. Furthermore, she loved Henry, as a queen, as a wife, and as a woman.

In February 1528, two English envoys set out for Rome with the king's petition, bearing a letter from Cardinal Wolsey (which it must have choked him to write) extolling Anne's many virtues of character.

The events of that year reflect Anne's emergence as a Reformer, a well-informed, intelligent proponent of the burgeoning Protestant religion. For all her impatient, arrogant, shrewish qualities, the truth is that there would have been no Anglican religion without Anne's scholarly reading of such banned treatises as the works of Martin Luther and her persistent encouragement of Henry to embrace many of Luther's views, break with the Church of Rome, and become the Head of the Church *in* England—which eventually led to all the British monarchs being the Head of the Church *of* England.

But that summer, Henry nearly lost the real reason for sending his envoys to Rome. Anne fell ill from the sweating sickness, a virulent strain of the flu that periodically swept through England. Always cautious about infections, the king removed himself from her company, although he wrote to her from the safety of Hundson House, passionately avowing, "wherever I am, I am yours," and assuring Anne that he "would willingly bear half" of her illness that she might suffer that much less. In another letter to his favorite convalescent, Henry wrote that he was "Wishing myself (specially an evening) in my sweetheart's

arms, whose pretty dukkys I trust shortly to kiss." ("Dukkys"
was "dugs," which is still a slang word for breasts.)

That September, Anne languished at Hever, in semi-exile
from the court. Even after she recuperated from her illness, it
was not seemly that she be omnipresent while Henry shed crocodile tears over the prospect of nullifying his marriage of more
than two decades.

Believing Anne too imperious, too arrogant, too French, the
people detested her. No matter how Henry tried to present it,
in their view he was looking for a way to cast aside a loyal and
faithful wife who had become stout, old, and barren, in favor
of his pert young mistress who was nothing but a hussy. His
subjects' attitude angered Henry at the beginning of his affair
with Anne, but by the time he wished to rid himself of Anne as
well, the king relied upon their spite and distaste to stir up public sentiment and destroy her reputation.

As the years wore on and the Great Matter remained unresolved, Anne began to lose patience with the process and with
her sovereign. At first it was probably fun and exciting to de-
vise new ways of simultaneously keeping him at bay and yet
utterly in her thrall. Anne's very unobtainability had made
her all the more alluring to Henry. But she had grown disgusted with the sympathy Katherine was engendering, not
merely from the public but at times from the king himself,
which gave her reason to fear that Henry, tired of the fight and
anxious about the enemies it was making, might from frustration or exhaustion abandon the Great Matter and return to
Katherine after all.

Anne made it very clear to Henry that she might have already
sacrificed the best years of her life, reminding the king that
children—heirs—were the real reward that lay at the end of the
fight. "I have been waiting long and might in the meanwhile
have contracted some advantageous marriage out of which I
might have had issue, which is the greatest consideration in the

world, but alas! Farewell to my time and youth spent to no purpose at all."

As temperamental as they were passionate, Henry and Anne
quarreled rather often, but she made sure to switch her seductive powers into high gear when they made up so that her royal
lover would never forget what it was he wanted from her. Anne
was a demonstrative and uninhibited spitfire, and the king
found the cocktail highly erotic. He could deny her nothing.

On December 8, 1529, Anne's father, Thomas Boleyn, was
made Earl of Wiltshire. The imperial ambassador, Eustache
Chapuys, reported to King Charles V on the festivities. Anne
sat by the king's side, taking precedence over the other ladies,
"occupying the very place allotted to a crowned queen. After
dinner, there was dancing and carousing so that it seemed as if
nothing were wanting but the priest to give away the nuptial
ring and pronounce the blessing."

In those days, Anne's presence was conspicuous, and from
late 1529 onward, she spent Henry's money lavishly. The Privy
Purse was opened wide to pay for everything from sumptuous
fabrics and furs to "playing money" for her to gamble with.
Her influence on the king was exceptional, and no one got
Henry's ear or his trust without her say-so. It was becoming
common knowledge that Anne Boleyn was the power behind
the throne. And those who for years had enjoyed Henry's
favor—such as Wolsey, Norfolk, and Henry's brother-in-law,
the Duke of Suffolk, Charles Brandon—feared they might be
cut out of the picture entirely once Anne became queen.

During the spring of 1530, Henry embarked on a Royal
Progress, accompanied by the ubiquitous Anne. The imperial
ambassador Chapuys remarked, "the king shows greater favor
to the lady every day . . . very recently, coming from Windsor,
he made her ride behind him on a pillion, a most unusual proceeding, and one that has greatly called forth people's attention
here." In his report to his sovereign, Charles V, Chapuys added

that Henry had two men imprisoned for gossiping about the incident.

Anne might not have had the people's hearts, but she had Henry's. And, no matter how long it took, she would be his queen—and theirs, like it or not. At Christmastime in 1530, Anne commissioned new livery for her attendants embroidered with the French phrase *"Ainsi sera, groigne qui groigne"* (that's how it's going to be, no matter who grumbles). She thought it was a terrific tongue-in-cheek way to get her message across. But as soon as Henry saw the uniforms, he angrily ordered Anne to dispose of them. Evidently, she had no idea that the motto had first been used as a rally cry for one of England's continental enemies, the Burgundians.

That same month, Pope Clement demanded that Henry dismiss his mistress from court while the matter of the dispensation remained under judicial review, because any children born of their union under such circumstances would be bastards. That directive spurred Henry to press Parliament even harder to agree to the swift resolution of an act that had been under discussion since November 3, 1529, granting the king supreme leadership of the Church in England. Finally, on February 11, 1531, following a secret meeting between Thomas Cromwell and the Archbishop of Canterbury, the humanist William Warham, Henry was acknowledged "Supreme Head of the Church, in so far as the Law of Christ allows." (The disclaimer at the end of the sentence would soon be struck out, leaving Henry the entirely unrestricted Head of the Church.)

Anne was ecstatic, "as if she had actually gained Paradise," a contemporary reported.

But as far as Rome and Katherine were concerned, the Great Matter remained unresolved. The pro-Katherine faction intended to reveal the real reason for Henry's petition. If it were known that he wanted an annulment just so he could marry someone else, Henry would never get his way. In 1529, seventeen of Henry's love letters to Anne were stolen by an agent of Cardinal Campeggio, one of the papal legates charged with determining the Great Matter. The letters were brought to the Pope, and to this day they remain in the Vatican's archives. Though the correspondence was not officially cited by Rome as a reason for refusing Henry's request, they got the message.

In July of 1531, Henry saw Katherine of Aragon for the last time. The king had demoted her to the rank of Princess Dowager, though for the rest of her life she refused to be addressed as such, declaring that she was still Henry's wife and England's true queen. Referring to Anne as "the scandal of Christendom," Katherine lived out her days in various royal demesnes, each one draftier than the last, struggling to maintain the modest household Henry permitted her. Even so, she was almost always in arrears.

That same month, after a contretemps between arrogant mistress and disgraced queen, Anne was seen wearing the royal jewels. It was a signal to the people of England that she wasn't going anywhere but up, and it was only a matter of time before they would have to kneel to her.

Anne's behavior had gotten out of control. Chapuys reported in one of his dispatches to Charles V, "She is becoming more arrogant every day, using words in authority towards the king of which he has several times complained to the Duke of Norfolk, saying she was not like the Queen, who never in her life used ill words to him."

In 1532, plans were under way for a continental summit meeting between Henry and François I, but for Anne to be able to accompany Henry as his consort at the celebrations surrounding the diplomatic mission, she would have to be a person of rank. So on September 1, Henry bestowed a title on his mistress, creating Anne Marquess of Pembroke, using the male form of address for the title, a common custom in Tudor times.

The honor also included five manor houses throughout the realm, to add to the pair of manors in Middlesex that Henry had given Anne earlier that year, and an additional patent settling lands worth £1,000 a year on her (close to $730,000 in today's currency).

But even with her new title, because they were not married Lady Pembroke would have to meet up with the king in Calais after the official diplomatic mission had been concluded. Still, Anne made the best of it, and at François's court she was treated like the prodigal daughter. François himself gave her an enormous diamond as an official gift. And she had a retinue of English noblewomen at her beck and call that included her sister, Mary—and a mild-mannered blonde named Jane Seymour.

Anne danced the first dance with the French king, a message to everyone in the ballroom that regardless of her official status, she was the First Woman of rank from the English court. Henry was so proud of her that he ran about the room pulling all the masks off the ladies' faces, so that everyone could see his lover partnered by the king of France.

Following the festivities, while most of their attendants returned to England, Anne and Henry spent a fortnight in Calais enjoying a romantic idyll that resembled a honeymoon. Rumors abounded that the couple exchanged vows. And finally—finally—Anne surrendered her body to Henry and they made love for the first time since the king's infatuation with her had sparked nearly seven years earlier. We can only hope that it wasn't a letdown for either lover.

Regardless of whether their coupling was enjoyable, it was certainly fruitful, for by the end of the first week of December 1532, when she was about thirty-two, Anne was pregnant.

She and Henry were secretly wed on St. Paul's day, January 25, 1533. The king lied outright to Dr. Rowland Lee, who officiated at their wedding, claiming that he had a document from the Pope giving him permission to marry again—though he refused to produce it. Actually, Henry was not yet legally divorced according to the Church of Rome, but in his mind he had *never* been legally married to Katherine, and therefore, he was a bachelor and free to wed whomsoever he chose.

By mid-February, the queen-to-be felt the urge to flaunt her condition, announcing in company that she had "a fearsome and unquenchable longing to eat apples." Henry remarked that it was a sure sign Anne was pregnant, to which Anne responded she "was sure [she] was not." A silvery peal of laughter issued from her lips and she returned to her room without another word. Eyewitnesses were shocked by her lack of discretion.

On April 12, Easter Sunday, Anne appeared for the first time as Queen of England. "All the world is astonished at it, and even those who take her part do not know whether to laugh or to cry," wrote Chapuys.

On May 28, from a gallery in Lambeth Palace, Archbishop Cranmer—having reached his formal decision on the Great Matter, with the assent of the learned divines of the court, that Henry's marriage to Katherine of Aragon was "null and absolutely void," and "contrary to divine law"—publicly declared Henry's marriage to Anne "good and valid." Anne was now Henry's legal bride and the child she carried in her womb would be legitimate. But Katherine's daughter, Princess Mary, was declared a bastard, and would henceforth be referred to as the Lady Mary.

Cranmer was about to crown the king's pregnant new wife, but he wasn't altogether comfortable about it, despite the fact that he and Anne were England's keenest supporters of Reform. As archbishop, he was technically the Pope's legate and not the king's servant; therefore, Cranmer felt obligated to threaten Henry with excommunication if the monarch didn't "put away" Katherine—who still considered herself Henry's wife and queen. There could not be two wives and queens; that much was clear.

So Henry shoved a history-making law through Parliament called the Act of Restraint of Appeals, which proclaimed England "an empire governed by one supreme head and king," who answered to no one but God for his actions. It was also made an act of treason to write or speak against his marriage to Anne, and all adult males were compelled to uphold it.

Anne's household now numbered two hundred retainers and attendants, liveried in her chosen colors of purple and blue embroidered with the motto *"La plus heureuse"* (the most happy).

Preparations then began in earnest for the four-day coronation celebration. At last, Anne Boleyn would receive what had been more than six years in the making. On May 29, 1533, she sailed in state up the Thames from Greenwich in a richly appointed barge, accompanied by a flotilla of fifty other vessels. Cloth of gold adorned her burgeoning figure. At the Tower of London, Henry greeted her with great pomp and the royal couple spent the next two nights celebrating under its battlements.

Unfortunately for Anne, during her progress through the City, the pageantry was marred by the official banners that lined the streets, emblazoning the entwined initials of the monarch and his new queen consort. "HA HA," they read, and the public loved the unintentional joke on Anne. But she made a beautiful picture, her chestnut hair cascading down her back in the manner of medieval queens and virgin brides. Her crimson brocaded gown was encrusted with precious stones, the pearls she wore about her neck "larger than chick peas."

On June 1, Whitsuntide, the six-months-pregnant Anne was crowned queen at Westminster Abbey, the folds of her gown cleverly concealing her condition. According to tradition, the king did not attend the coronation. Greeting Anne afterward at Westminster, Henry asked her, "How liked you the City, sweetheart?"

The new queen replied, "Sir, the City itself was well enow, but I saw so many caps on heads and heard few tongues."

This jibes with Chapuys's assessment of the mood in the streets, as he noted that it was so far from being jubilant that it was funereal.

After that, it was all downhill.

On July 11, Pope Clement issued a Bull declaring void Archbishop Cranmer's verdict on Henry's first marriage. His Holiness demanded that Henry put Anne away, adding that any child of theirs would be deemed illegitimate. The Pope also excommunicated Henry, but by then the king was past caring. A Pope's will had no validity to the newly appointed Head of the Church in England.

Yet after Anne had endured so much and waited so long to realize her ambition, the royal honeymoon was short-lived. Henry was already experiencing buyer's remorse. And his little blue eyes had begun to stray.

The heavily pregnant new queen, with her sharp tongue and shrewish temper, was not a pleasant companion; and of course Henry had to find outlets for gratifying his lust without endangering the health of the son he hoped she was carrying. Anne found herself unable to control or contain her jealousy over Henry's little infatuations and dalliances with her ladies-in-waiting; she may well have feared that one of Henry's flings might displace (or worse, replace) her. "Coldness and grumbling" characterized their arguments. When Anne complained about his infidelities, using "certain words" that Henry disliked, he advised her to shut her eyes and endure as those who were her betters had done, reminding his new wife that he could "lower her as much as he had raised her."

Henry had confided to François I that he had to have a son "for the quiet repose and tranquility of our realm." However, at three p.m. on September 7, 1533, Anne gave birth to a flame-haired daughter, who the monarchs named Elizabeth after both of their mothers. Henry could not conceal his displeasure at the birth of a girl. Nor, at the outset, could Anne. After all those years of struggle and sacrifice, the risks Henry had taken to reform the religion, the lives that had been ruined so that Anne could become his queen, the best she could do was bear a girl.

They both knew that she had "failed," though Anne would in short order become so devoted to Elizabeth that she breast-fed the baby herself, scandalizing the court. But Henry canceled the joust and the other grand celebrations that had been set to take place upon the birth of his son. He had been so sure Anne would give him a boy that the formal documents had been drawn up with the word "Prince" on them. All that was lacking was the insertion of the heir's name and date of birth. Henry seethed as "ss" was added to every announcement.

In March 1534, Pope Clement finally concluded that Henry's marriage to Katherine had indeed been *valid*—no surprise to anyone by then. He died that September, by which time Anne was several months pregnant again, her "goodly belly" a subject of discussion since April 27.

Henry was now forty-three years old, and Anne was in her mid-thirties. To their mutual consternation, she miscarried. Anne was pregnant again by October 1535, though her condition did not deter Henry from paying a visit early in the month to the Seymour family at their home of Wulfhall. There, Sir John Seymour made certain that his demure and modest daughter, Jane, fell under the royal gaze as much as possible. It was not long before Henry gave Jane a miniature portrait of himself, which she ostentatiously wore about her throat at court. Anne was so infuriated by Jane's impudence that she ripped the chain from her neck.

At the end of December, Henry received the news that Katherine lay dangerously ill, but he refused to see her. In her final days, she wrote one last letter to the king averring her everlasting passion for him, poignantly ending with the words, "Lastly, I make this vow, that mine eyes desire you above all things."

The letter was signed "Katherine the Queen."

On January 7, 1536, just days after her fiftieth birthday, the cancerous tumor on Katherine's heart claimed her life. On learning of the former queen's demise, Anne and Henry donned yellow garments, a color of rejoicing in England, but the traditional color of mourning in Spain. Katherine of Aragon was buried with modest pomp at Peterborough. Not until the twentieth century did her resting place receive the honors it deserved, when Mary of Teck, the queen consort of George V, ordered the symbols of queenship to be displayed over Katherine's tomb. The two banners bearing the royal arms of England and Spain hang there still.

Anne miscarried a male fetus said to be fifteen weeks old on the day of Katherine's funeral, blaming it on two incidents that had caused her great anxiety—catching her husband with Jane Seymour (who evidently wasn't particularly modest) on his lap, and the jousting accident he suffered on the day of her miscarriage. Henry had lain unconscious for two hours, and naturally Anne feared for his life and for her own future, should the king die of his injuries.

But Henry wasn't buying either reason. Utterly insensitive to Anne's grief at losing another baby, he lamented, "I see God will not give me male children," leaving his fragile wife devastated and terrified of losing his love.

Anne had good reason to despair. For Henry was already beginning to map out a more fertile pasture. In April, the king was very indiscreetly boasting to his ambassador in France that God might yet see fit to "send us heirs male," averring, "You do not know all my secrets."

If Anne ever gave birth to a boy, her enemies knew her power over Henry would be nearly invincible. Timing was everything. She had to go—and sooner rather than later. After Anne's miscarriage in 1536, the anti-Boleyn and pro-Seymour factions at court coalesced, convening to determine the best way of getting rid of Anne to make way for Jane. Thomas Cromwell, once Cardinal Wolsey's trusted secretary and now Henry's Chief Minister, made the point that there were international matters just as pressing as Henry's need for a son. France and Spain were now at war, and England stood to gain much from an alliance with Spain. But for obvious reasons, Henry's marriage to Anne was a stumbling block to any negotiations. Why would Spain's king, Charles V, aid the man who had dumped his sainted aunt for the French-bred hussy?

It had therefore become not just biologically but politically expedient for Henry to eliminate Anne.

As the Seymours were moved into apartments at Greenwich, and a pro-Seymour courtier was made a Knight of the Garter in preference to Anne's brother, George (now Viscount Rochford, after the death of their father), Anne felt it all slipping away, everything she had clawed and scratched and waited for with her last fiber of patience. Her only "crime" was that she had failed to give Henry a son.

On April 24, 1536, at Cromwell's prompting, the king signed a document appointing a committee to investigate Anne's possibly treasonous activities. It was not difficult to find people cheerfully willing to testify to Anne's innate lasciviousness. In fact, Anne's own uncle, the Duke of Norfolk, even as he reaped the benefits of her favor, called her *"la grande putain"* (the great whore).

On April 30, a court musician and dancer named Mark Smeaton was arrested on the grounds that he had committed adultery with the queen. After being put to the rack the hapless Smeaton confessed to the blatant lie.

The following day three men of Henry's Privy Chamber

were arrested, also charged with having bedded Anne. It was a travesty of justice, for Henry knew these knights, Sir Francis Weston, Sir Henry Norris, and Sir William Brereton, too well to ever suspect them of treachery. The witch hunt was well under way.

Hoping something would stick, Henry saw to it that Anne was charged with so many treasonous acts that it would have been impossible for the council not to have convicted her of at least one of them. Anne was even accused of sleeping with her own brother, a charge made by George's jealous wife, Lady Rochford, a lady of Anne's bedchamber. She thought her husband spent far too much time in his sister's company, and therefore accused the Boleyn siblings of "undue familiarity."

Cromwell had been a tremendous supporter of Anne's during the Great Matter, but had jumped to a safer barge when he saw that hers was sinking. He became one of the prime architects of Anne's downfall, and her bitterest enemy during her final days. Cromwell hoped that the charge of incest would suitably shock and appall the council, with its titillating allegations of Anne's "alluring [George] with her tongue in [his] mouth and his tongue in hers."

The anti-Boleyn machine banked on the assumption that people who swallowed that story would believe anything. This was the grotesque version of Anne Boleyn they wished to perpetrate and disseminate—the "goggle-eyed whore" with the gross cyst on her neck, moles all over her body, six fingers on one hand, and three breasts.

And if people didn't believe that Anne and George were lovers, they might credit some of the other allegations—that she had conspired to kill the king, Queen Katherine, the Lady Mary, and Henry's illegitimate son by Bessie Blount, Henry Fitzroy. Many times Anne *had* in fact angrily urged Henry to execute his first wife and their daughter for treason, but he had never entertained her suggestion.

The indictment against Anne stated that "she, following daily her frail and carnal lust, did falsely and traitorously procure by base conversations and kisses, touchings, gifts, and other infamous incitations, divers of the king's daily and familiar servants to be her adulterers and concubines."

Anne was arrested on May 2, 1536, on the charges of adultery, incest, and conspiracy to kill the king.

During her imprisonment in the Tower, Anne's every word and movement were jotted down by the wardresses who had been entrusted with watching her, in the hope that the queen might say something to implicate herself and give Henry legitimate proof of her infidelity or other treasonous act. Throughout her confinement, she suffered violent mood swings, veering wildly from laughter to remorse to boastfulness to tears.

And because Henry refused to see her, on May 6, 1536, Anne wrote him a letter, in which she begged him not to dishonor their daughter, Elizabeth, and asserted her loyalty and innocence:

> . . . let me receive an open trial, for my truth shall fear no open shames; then shall you see either mine innocence cleared, your suspicions and conscience satisfied, the ignominy and slander of the world stopped, or my guilt openly declared. So that . . . Your Grace may be at liberty, both before God and man, not only to execute worthy punishment on me, as an unfaithful wife, but to follow your affection already settled on that party Mistress Seymour. . . . But if you have already determined . . . that not only my death, but an infamous slander, must bring you to the joying of your desired happiness, then I desire of God that He will pardon your great sin herein. . . .

Anne's trial began on May 15 in the Great Hall of the Tower of London. Her brother was to be judged by the same council of peers. Two thousand spectators watched the circus from purpose-built stands. The Duke of Norfolk presided over the proceedings as High Steward, while Anne's former sweetheart, Henry Percy, now the Earl of Northumberland, was impelled by his rank to sit on the peer council. But Percy was dying and the exigencies of his illness did not permit him to remain for the verdict. Possibly, he was unable to witness the sham trial of the woman he had once adored.

According to the herald, Charles Wriothesley, Anne gave "wise and discreet answers" to her examiners, concealing her terror beneath a calm and regal demeanor. How much hope did she hold out for an acquittal? A princess of Spain had been powerless to fight Henry's vast machine; dared the descendant of a lowly mercer—however much her family had risen over the past half century—expect to triumph where those of royal blood had failed?

No one believed the charge of incest, and George Boleyn spoke so persuasively that an acquittal looked imminent. However, a note penned in French was read in open court, its contents attributed to George. According to the note, based upon a conversation with Anne, "the king was incapable of copulating with his wife, and he had neither skill nor virility [potency]." Even though Anne—who had remained sexually faithful to Henry—had become pregnant four times in three years, by maligning the king's mojo in open court George had sealed his death warrant.

All four men accused of adultery with the queen were found guilty and sentenced to a traitor's death—beheading, followed by castration, disembowelment, and quartering. However, in a fit of generosity, Henry commuted the sentence to a simple beheading, probably because he knew that the men were innocent—sacrificial lambs in the campaign to get rid of Anne.

At the trials of the two peers, Anne and George, their uncle

Norfolk read the sentence: the queen and her brother were to be burned at the stake, or executed, according to the king's pleasure.

Two days after the verdict, George Boleyn, Mark Smeaton, and the men of the Privy Chamber were beheaded on Tower Hill. But Henry allowed the corpses their dignity; the heads were not displayed on Tower Bridge, which was the customary punishment for dead traitors. Anne grew hourly more fearful that her turn would come at any moment.

But before she was executed, Anne suffered another ignominy. She was stripped of her title as queen, and her marriage—after all the struggles to achieve it—was declared invalid. The Decree of Nullity was dated May 17, though it was not signed until June 10, and it would be another two weeks before both houses of Parliament subscribed to it. Henry had gotten his marriage to Anne annulled on the grounds that his affair with her sister, Mary, had placed them within the first degree of affinity, even though, in 1528—*at Henry's urging*—the Pope had issued a special dispensation that set aside the subject of Henry's affinity to Anne based on his romantic history with Mary Boleyn.

But Henry had cleverly inserted into the 1534 Act of Supremacy that any existing papal dispensations would no longer be considered valid if they were contrary to Holy Scripture and the law of God. This phraseology was relied upon to justify the invalidity of Henry's marriage to Anne as incestuous. Their daughter, Elizabeth, not yet three years old, was made a bastard by it.

On May 18, Anne made a full confession to Cranmer, though she went to the block maintaining her love for Henry and her innocence of the crimes for which she had been convicted.

As a final gesture of kindness to the woman he once called his "fresh young damsel," Henry had spent £24 (roughly the equivalent of $14,400 in today's currency) to hire the executioner from St Omer in Calais. This agent of death wielded a sword rather than an axe, ensuring a swifter and less painful demise.

In a letter to Thomas Cromwell on May 19, 1536, the day of Anne's execution, Sir William Kingston, Constable of the Tower, recorded his conversation with Anne when she heard the news.

> This morning she sent for me . . . and at my coming she said, "Mr. Kingston, I hear I shall not die afore noon, and I am very sorry therefore, for I thought to be dead by this time and past my pain." I told her it should be no pain, it was so little. And then she said, "I heard say the executioner was very good, and I have a little neck," and then put her hands about it, laughing heartily. I have seen many men and also women executed, and that they have been in great sorrow, and to my knowledge this lady has much joy in death.

The time of the execution had been kept a secret so there wouldn't be a tremendous crowd to witness her demise. The customary hour was dawn, but as noon approached, Anne grew increasingly anxious, eager to finally be put out of her misery. She had no idea that the delay was caused by the headsman's being detained on the Dover Road. Because her executioner was stuck in traffic, Anne's death had been postponed for a few hours, pending his arrival.

Though she was to die as the Marquess of Pembroke, Anne looked every inch a queen as she walked to the block on Tower Hill wearing a red petticoat under a loose, dark gray gown of damask trimmed in fur. A mantle of ermine enveloped her slender shoulders. Her long chestnut hair was bound up under a simple white linen coif over which she wore a gabled head-dress in the English style, rather than one of the French half-moon caps she had introduced to Henry's court fifteen years earlier.

Witnesses described Anne's steps as light, almost blithe. Perhaps she was relieved to be released from her mental torment, knowing there was nothing left for her in the temporal world.

With all the buildup to Anne's denouement, no one bothered to be sure that there was a coffin to receive her remains. Anne's body and head were placed into an arrow chest that was close at hand and buried in an unmarked grave in the Chapel of St. Peter ad Vincula, adjoining the Tower Green. Her skeleton was one of those identified in renovations of the chapel during the reign of Queen Victoria, so Anne's final resting place is now marked in the marble floor.

After the most famously protracted courtship in the world, Anne Boleyn had been queen for only a thousand days.

She was not an easy person to like. Many times Anne seemed like the pushy power behind the throne when Henry was reluctant to pursue a thing to its conclusion. Yet Anne was as capable of being generous and compassionate as she was angry, vicious, and spiteful. She annually gave away £1,500 to the poor—over $1 million in today's economy. But the average Renaissance Briton, perhaps even the recipients of her charitable largesse, remembered her instead as the trophy wife from hell who had seduced their sovereign and made him cast aside their beloved queen.

As a result of her royal affair, Anne Boleyn's legacy is enormous. By encouraging Henry to break with Rome and adopt some of the teachings of Luther and of Renaissance humanist theologians, she was arguably one of the most influential persons on the development of the Christian religion in western Europe.

Anne was innocent of the charges for which she forfeited her head. But neither her bloodline nor her spirit perished on Tower Hill, for she left behind a daughter. Henry restored Elizabeth's legitimate birthright three years before his death in the Succession Act of 1544. The redheaded princess would become England's most venerated queen, and perhaps the greatest female monarch the world has ever known: Queen Elizabeth I.

HENRY VIII
and Jane Seymour ("Bound to Obey and Serve")
1509–1537
Queen of England 1536–1537

After the dragon, Henry wanted a doormat—but was Jane Seymour really that bland? Her conduct, first as a royal lady-in-waiting and later as a queen, indicates that she was more of a steel magnolia—a fragrant, seemingly fragile, ultrafeminine exterior concealing a tensile core.

The Seymours were a respected family within the Tudor court, but their connections were nowhere near as powerful, nor their lineage as illustrious, as the Boleyns or the Howards. Sir John Seymour, Jane's father, had served with Henry in France in 1513. Her mother, Margery Wentworth, was descended from Edward III. And Jane, the fifth child of ten, had been one of Anne Boleyn's ladies-in-waiting, just as Anne was for Katherine of Aragon.

Jane's brother had been in service to the Spanish king and Holy Roman Emperor Charles V, and Jane herself had also been a lady-in-waiting to Katherine of Aragon, so it stands to reason that Eustache Chapuys, the imperial ambassador to Henry's court, would have something nice to say about her. But the best the diplomat could manage was to describe Jane as being "of middling height and nobody thinks she has much beauty. Her complexion is so whitish that she may be called rather pale."

So, after two fiery and temperamental auburn-haired forces of nature, what did Henry see in this whey-faced woman with the washed-out blond locks and pointy little chin? The answer is obvious, actually. The king wanted peace and tranquility. He craved harmony, not just in his marriage but throughout his realm. And the modest and docile twenty-five-year-old Jane was the perfect antidote to his first two wives. So, okay, she was a drip and a pill, but that was the medicine the self-diagnosing Henry required. She was also likely as anyone else to produce sons. Her mother had given birth to ten children, so her fecundity pedigree was high.

Yet this young woman knew how to play the hands that were dealt her. A speck on the palaces' walnut-paneled walls until 1536, Jane had spent a lifetime observing and absorbing what to do and, more to the point, how not to behave around the king. She was clever enough to remain chaste in a court renowned for its flirtatious, if not outright licentious, behavior.

Even Chapuys wasn't certain Jane was as innocent as she appeared, remarking of her that "you may imagine whether being an Englishwoman and having been long at court, she would not hold it a sin to be a maid."

Although Jane was likely coached on how to massage the king-sized ego once his infatuation with her had begun, she was more than likely smarter than the average dishrag, and she was not without a certain degree of ambition for herself. She simply kept it better concealed than her black-eyed predecessor. Jane told the king what he wanted to hear and appeared to be everything he now sought in a consort. And Henry believed what he wanted to.

Jane did have two patrons who were eager to advance their own agendas and saw in her the best means to achieve them. Gertrude, Marchioness of Exeter, and Sir Nicholas Carew, Master of the Horse, who had bested Anne Boleyn's brother for the Garter, staunchly supported the claims of Henry's daughter Mary. Carew and the marchioness were convinced that Jane, who had always been passively sympathetic to the disinherited Mary's plight, would repair the relationship between Henry and Mary. The result would be that the Catholic Mary would reacquire her rights of succession and perhaps even Henry's Reformation would come to a grinding halt.

It's unfair to cite Henry's passion and priapic urges as the only reason he so rapidly went from Anne to Jane. Once Anne was clearly destined for the history books, the king's Privy Council began pressuring him to find another bride, and beget a male heir ASAP for the sake of the smooth succession of the realm.

Jane was their choice as well. But Jane was proving not such an easy mark. Though she openly flirted with Henry, even to the point of sitting on his lap and accepting his presents of jewelry, she'd learned how to play hard-to-get from the best of them.

Taking a leaf from Anne Boleyn's courtship playbook, Jane made it clear to the king that if she was not to become his wife, she would have nothing to do with him. Pretty brave for the girl who was supposed to be the doormat. When Henry sent Jane a bag of gold sovereigns and what was presumably a passionate love letter, Jane's reaction was swift and decisive. Acting as appalled as if Henry had left the money on the nightstand, in front of the king's messenger she kissed the love letter, but pointedly left it unopened, returning it, along with the purse, begging the courier to remind the king that she was "a gentlewoman of fair and honorable lineage without reproach," and modestly insisting that she had "nothing in the world but my honor, which for a thousand deaths I would not wound."

According to Chapuys, Jane asked the courier to convey to Henry that "if the king deigned to make her a present of money, she prayed it would be when God might send her a husband."

Henry got the point. And he relied upon his ever-faithful Archbishop of Canterbury, Thomas Cranmer, to secure him a dispensation to marry Jane, because they were within the forbidden degree of affinity, as Jane's grandmother was a cousin of Henry's great-grandmother. Cranmer signed the dispensation on the same day as Anne Boleyn's execution.

Although Anne had been universally detested, Jane was not particularly admired by the average Briton. A love letter to her from Henry describes not only his feelings for her but those of lesser mortals:

My dear friend and mistress,
The bearer of these few lines from thy entirely devoted
servant will deliver into thy fair hands a token of my true
affection for thee, hoping you will keep it for ever in your
sincere love for me. There is a ballad made lately of great
derision against us; I pray you pay no manner of regard to
it. I am not at present informed who is the setter forth of
this malignant writing, but if he is found out, he shall
straitly be punished for it. Hoping shortly to receive you
into these arms, I end for the present
Your own living servant and sovereign
H.R.

Although she wisely removed herself from public scrutiny while Anne's trial was under way, as soon as the queen had been declared guilty, Jane permitted herself to be seen once again in the king's presence. And on the afternoon of Anne's execution,

the two enjoyed a sumptuous meal amid much unrestricted canoodling. They were secretly betrothed the following day.

On May 30, 1536, just eleven days after Anne's death, Jane
married Henry in the same manner as did his two previous
spouses—in as private a ceremony as possible. They were wed
quickly and quietly at Whitehall in the Queen's Closet—
though, ironically, there was no actual queen at the time.

Henry was going through wives with such velocity that at the
myriad royal demesnes, England's laborers and artisans had not
even finished replacing Katherine's pomegranates of Granada
with Anne's Tudor roses and heraldic leopards. Now—instead
of starting from scratch with newly made devices—a clever artisan might skillfully transform Anne's leopards into Jane's emblem of the panther. Jane's other emblem was a castle, from
which a flaming phoenix rose, code for the rebirth of Henry's
love life and his household as well as his realm—and of course
for the son he desperately coveted after so much wifely failure.
Not for nothing did the court call Jane Seymour "the Peacemaker," a role she was ambitious to embrace and maintain, going to her grave with that legacy.

The Seymour family did well for itself once Jane was anointed
Henry's chosen one. The celebrated court artist Hans Holbein
designed jewelry and a golden cup for the new queen. Jane's
dowry (from the king to Jane, not from her father to the king)
included 104 manors, 5 castles, and a number of forests, chases,
and woodlands. And a week after the royal wedding, Jane's
brother Sir Edward Seymour was created Viscount Beauchamp.
More blatantly ambitious than his sister, the new viscount harbored dreams of one day becoming regent if Jane should bear
the increasingly ailing Henry a son.

On June 4, Jane was proclaimed queen; three days later, the
royal couple entered London by barge from Greenwich to
Whitehall. The new queen was pasty-faced and lusterless, but
her new bridegroom was a piggy-eyed, forty-five-year-old with

a head "as bald as Caesar's," according to one contemporary report. Henry disguised his follicle issue by wearing hats. A beard hid his nonexistent chin. Actually, Henry had reached the life expectancy for Tudor times, and though he was balding, he was still relatively fit for a man of any age and era, though his waist was thirty-seven inches and his chest measurement a burly forty-five.

As the months wore on, the plans for Jane's grand coronation were postponed. The Exchequer insisted that the Treasury could ill afford it at the time. Henry claimed it was because the plague had returned to England that September, but the real reason may have been because he was waiting for her to be pregnant. Regardless of the lack of a formal coronation, Jane was still Henry's queen consort.

And Jane set to work making the role her own.

The conservative new queen had some definite ideas about how the court ladies should dress, as well. The sexy "French-style" garments cut from opulent cloth that were so favored by her predecessor Anne Boleyn were not only discarded, they were banned. The delicate caps that showed more of a woman's hair were to be replaced by the dowdy gabled headdresses that offered total coverage and transformed even the prettiest maiden into a homely matron. And speaking of coverage—no more plunging square necklines à la Anne. As an antidote to the dreaded décolletage, Jane ordered her women to wear "chests"—dickie-like inserts—that served as modesty panels. The bright colors that had made Anne's ladies resemble exotic birds of plumage were replaced by a somber palette of drab hues. Black was the new crimson, gold, and purple.

In the political arena, Jane usually kept her mouth shut, but for a religious woman who did not embrace the new reform, Henry's dissolution and destruction of the monasteries was too much. On bended knee, she pleaded with the king to restore the abbeys, but Henry growled at her to get up. The French ambassador reported, "He had often told her not to meddle with his affairs." The issue was particularly sensitive for Henry because he had just crushed a rebellion that had begun in the north, demanding the restoration of Christ's Church.

A shiver probably went through Jane as Henry unleashed his temper full bore on his usually timid wife. Immediately chastened, if not entirely cowed, she never again interfered in matters of policy or state—except in one instance, but it was one where she knew she would eventually have more success. Jane was very aware that—issues of politics and religion aside—Henry really did love his children. She was also a devout Catholic (as was Henry's firstborn, Mary) and had received no small degree of urging from Chapuys, the imperial ambassador, to see that Mary was restored to her father's good graces.

So Jane pressured Henry to reconcile with Mary, and even with little Elizabeth, but the new Act of Succession continued to shut out both of Henry's daughters in favor of any sons Jane might bear.

Mary was no happy camper. As if the depression, headaches, and menstrual problems the twenty-year-old princess endured (unsurprising given the ill-treatment she'd suffered since Katherine of Aragon's fall from favor) had not been punishment enough, she was forced to sign documents averring that Henry was the true Head of the Church in England, and repudiating the Pope, disrespectfully referred to in the documents as "the Bishop of Rome." And if she did not sign a paper acknowledging the invalidity of her mother's marriage to the king and her own illegitimacy, she would be imprisoned in the Tower. To save her own skin, poor Mary was compelled to swallow her last shred of dignity and conscience in relinquishing her own birthright and declaring her bastardy.

Mary's capitulation did reconcile her with her father. Even if nothing changed legally, at least she was once more treated like a member of the royal family, officially named the second-ranking woman in England after the queen.

In early January 1537, during the climax of the Twelfth Night pageantry, Jane evidently became pregnant. When courtiers began to whisper about her burgeoning condition, it had also not escaped their notice that the queen had not become enceinte during the six months since her wedding—which says more about the lusty forty-six-year-old king's possible potency issues than of Jane's fecundity. In fact, on August 12, 1536, less than three months after the royal wedding, Henry had confided to Chapuys that he was feeling old and doubted he should sire any children with the queen.

But in October 1537, as Jane gazed upon the panthers and phoenixes that detailed the cornices of her apartments in Hampton Court—the rooms where only eighteen months earlier leopards roamed and Tudor roses bloomed—she went into labor.

Jane gave birth to Henry's miracle child—the much desired son, who he nicknamed "God's imp"—on October 12, in the wee hours of the morning at Hampton Court. After twenty-eight years of rule, the monarch finally had his heir. He was named Edward after his great-great-grandfather and because he was born on the eve of the saint's feast day. Henry's infant son was placed in his arms, and witnesses reported that the king wept to see him.

Bishop Latimer teetered on the verge of heresy when he said, "We all hungered after a prince so long that there was as much rejoicing as at the birth of John the Baptist."

Three days later, wrapped in velvet and fur, Jane forced herself to be up and about at her son's lavish christening. According to custom, she made the official announcement of the prince's birth. Henry's daughter Mary was the infant's godmother. And Elizabeth, though only a toddler, was given the honor of holding her stepbrother's christening garment.

A game but hopelessly fatigued Jane stood on her feet

for nearly the entire day to receive the compliments of the hundreds of guests who were permitted to witness the ceremony and take part in the celebrations afterward. She carried out her consort duties in Hampton Court Chapel, and the festivities went on into the wee hours of the next morning. Jane's family was granted additional honors the following week.

But the exertion of childbirth and the exigencies of playing hostess when her body was utterly exhausted contributed to Jane's swift demise. She fell ill within a day or two after giving birth, possibly due to a tear in her perineum, which became infected, owing to the general ignorance of and inattention to hygiene, particularly in medical situations. Jane developed puerperal (or childbed) fever, which turned into septicemia and eventually led to delirium. The king was wont to place the blame "through the fault of those that were about her, who suffered her to take great cold and to eat things that her fantasy in sickness called for." Twelve days after giving birth, on October 24 at eight a.m., Jane's confessor was summoned. After receiving extreme unction, she died shortly before midnight, at all of twenty-eight years old.

Was Henry present as Jane slipped into the next world? It is not likely. This king of passive-aggressive behavior had a history of running away when it came time to dispose of, or otherwise lose, a wife. The man renowned for ordering executions was unable to deal with death.

The inconsolable king ordered the churches to be draped in black. On November 12, 1537, Jane's body was taken in great pomp and solemnity to Windsor, the only one of Henry's six queens to be buried in St. George's Chapel there. A decade later the dying Henry requested that he be interred beside her.

Jane Seymour's epitaph, inscribed in Latin, translates roughly to:

HERE LIES JANE, A PHOENIX
WHO DIED IN GIVING ANOTHER PHOENIX BIRTH.
LET HER BE MOURNED, FOR BIRDS LIKE THESE
ARE RARE INDEED.

Henry wore full black mourning for three months, but despite his grief, he agreed with surprising alacrity to the notion of taking a fourth wife. After all, he had but one heir, and for "insurance" purposes, someone had to give birth to the requisite spare.

Edward, Prince of Wales, acceded to the throne on his father's death in 1547, to become Edward VI. He died in 1553, at the age of fifteen, of a pulmonary disease, possibly consumption, his constitution already weakened by a previous case of the measles.

HENRY VIII
and Kathryn Howard ("No Other Will Than His")
1521–1542
Queen of England 1540–1542

KATHRYN HOWARD
and Francis Dereham ?–1541
and Thomas Culpeper 1514–1541

After Jane Seymour died, the king waited three years before nuptializing number four, Anne of Cleves, on Twelfth Night, January 6, 1540. The match was the brainchild of Henry's Chief Minister, Thomas Cromwell, who believed that Henry would strengthen his ties to Protestantism by espousing a German princess. But Henry was famously repulsed by Anne's physical appearance and lack of hygiene. So by April, tongues were wagging about his new infatuation with the girl the French ambassador had marked for her exceptional grace.

The previous December, Kathryn Howard, yet another auburn-haired niece of the powerful Duke of Norfolk, had come to court to serve the new queen as a lady-in-waiting. Kathryn was still a teenager, as much as thirty years Henry's junior, but the king was utterly thunderstruck, behaving like an adolescent boy in love, positively giddy with desire over the dark-eyed, curvaceous redhead. Evidently, Kathryn was exceptionally diminutive, described by one contemporary as *"parvissima puella"* (a really tiny girl). Next to Henry, who had grown so massive that three large men could fit inside one of his doublets (in 1540, his waist measured fifty-four inches and his chest a whopping fifty-seven), she must have resembled half of a Tudor *Mutt and Jeff* cartoon.

Kathryn's father and Anne Boleyn's mother were siblings, making the young women first cousins, but Kathryn lacked Anne's intelligence, canniness, and political acumen. Her father, Lord Edmund Howard, was the third son of the 2nd Duke of Norfolk. Being so far down the line of inheritance, he had little hope of advancement. The best that he and Kathryn's mother, Jocasta Culpeper, could do was to place some of their brood with more affluent relatives who could afford to give them a better upbringing.

Many things about Kathryn Howard's early life remain a mystery because they are not well documented. The spelling of her name has been variously Catherine, Katherine, and Kathryn— the last of which, though a contemporary spelling, comes closest to the way she spelled it herself (Katheryn) in a love letter to her paramour.

Her date of birth has been variously given as anywhere from 1520 to 1525. If she was born at the latter end of the spectrum, she would have been only fifteen years old in 1540 when she married Henry. I chose to fall closer to the earliest date, given the level of sexual experience Kathryn had by the time she came to court.

Kathryn's mother had already passed away when her father sent her to live with her step-grandmother, Agnes Howard, the dowager Duchess of Norfolk. Kathryn was supposedly twelve years old at the time, one of a number of poorer female Howard relations who served the duchess as ladies-in-waiting of a sort and were schooled and boarded in her homes.

Kathryn was housed, dormitory-style, with the other girls in the Maidens' Chamber. More or less orphaned when she needed the guidance of her parents most of all, desperate for love, attention, and approbation, the pubescent Kathryn devoted herself to the pursuit of hedonism.

The music tutor, Henry Manox, who taught the virginal Kathryn the virginals, also provided her training wheels in carnality. But even as she flirted with the lowly musician, Kathryn haughtily reminded him, "I will never be naught with you, and able to marry me ye be not."

When the duchess caught them canoodling, she "gave Kathryn two or three blows and gave straight charge both to her and to Manox that they should never be alone together."

But soon Kathryn moved on, commencing a torrid affair with one of her step-grandmother's clerks, Francis Dereham. Although the duchess locked the Maidens' Chamber every night and pocketed the key, Kathryn contrived to bribe Agnes's maid, Mary Lascelles, into stealing it. Dereham became Kathryn's regular nocturnal visitor. He called Kathryn his "wife," and she called him "husband," and they may have entered into some form of a precontract of marriage. The adolescent girl saw nothing wrong with their carnal knowledge of each other, since she considered herself Dereham's wife.

The two of them enjoyed fruits and wine and foreplay in

Kathryn's bed and exchanged love tokens. But the jealous Manox arranged to have an anonymous letter delivered to the duchess, disclosing her niece's affair with Dereham.

The duchess sent Dereham back to Ireland and found a position at court for the spirited Kathryn. Luckily for the dowager, absence from Dereham made Kathryn's heart grow colder. In late 1539, when she was about to join the train of Anne of Cleves, Kathryn made it clear to him that she was moving on. "All that knew me and kept my company, know how glad and desirous I was to come to the court," she told Dereham.

She had not been at court for too many months when she noticed one of Henry's higher-ranking courtiers, Thomas Culpeper, a distant relation on her mother's side, and a gentleman of the king's Privy Chamber.

Culpeper was in his mid-twenties at the time. He and Kathryn were the male and female equivalent of each other—gorgeous, ambitious, charming, and oversexed. There were rumors of marriage plans between them, but Kathryn hotly contradicted the gossip: "If you heard such a report, you heard more than I do know."

In fact, Kathryn had caught the eye of the biggest fish of all: His Majesty.

Kathryn was courted by Henry in a big way. On April 24, 1540, the king bestowed upon her a gift of lands that had been confiscated from a felon. A month later, she received several bolts of silk. The French ambassador reported that Henry could not "treat her well enough." She was showered with jewels, depicted in them by the king's Master Painter, Hans Holbein, and given such authority and power as she had never known—all heady stuff to a teenage orphan who had been raised in genteel poverty.

Around that time, Kathryn consented to come to the king's bed. Little did Henry know that his new mistress was a skilled seductress and quite experienced in the boudoir. He was a guy; she was great in bed. Who needed to ask questions?

The king had his marriage to Anne of Cleves annulled as swiftly as possible. On June 24, the queen was utterly blindsided when she received a document declaring her marriage to Henry invalid. It had never been consummated because the German princess's homeliness repulsed Henry to the point where he could not even get an erection. It's entirely possible that the king wasn't impotent at all at this stage in his life; he was simply disgusted by the thought of making love to Anne.

Anne's wedding ring had been inscribed with the words "God send me well to keep." But Henry had unceremoniously discarded her instead. Queen of England for less than seven months, Anne was demoted to the role of the king's "good sister." At first, she was hysterical, crying for days in her chamber. But she came away from the deal with palaces and property, and most important, her head. The only thing she'd lost to Henry's insensitivity was her heart. Although she had arrived in her adopted country in December 1539 without a word of English, she had fallen in love with the stout sovereign, and genuinely wanted to make a go of it as his devoted wife. She was terrified that if Henry sent her back to her brother, the Duke of Cleves would kill her with his own hands for mucking up the marriage and embarrassing their royal house.

So Henry arranged for Anne to remain in England for the rest of her days, and she gamely put up with the king's new wife. Things could have become awkward between them, particularly since Anne had been beloved by all at court but Henry. But when the roles were reversed and the former queen had to pay homage to her recent lady-in-waiting, Anne was all humility and Kathryn all graciousness. Anne addressed her replacement on her knees, whereupon, according to Eustache Chapuys, the ambassador from the Holy Roman Emperor, Kathryn begged Anne to rise and "received her most kindly, showing her favor and courtesy."

On July 28, during the middle of a particularly hot and dry summer, in a secret ceremony conducted by Bishop Bonner, Kathryn and Henry were wed. That same day, Henry's former Chief Minister Thomas Cromwell was executed on Tower Green for, among other things, having been the architect of the king's disastrous marriage to Anne of Cleves.

Henry's ambassadors to foreign lands were informed in a statement issued on August 8, 1540, that "upon a notable appearance of honor, cleanness and maidenly behavior . . . His Highness was finally contented to honor that lady with his marriage, thinking in his old days—after sundry troubles of mind which had happened to him by marriage—to have obtained such a perfect jewel of womanhood and very perfect love towards him as should have been not only to his quietness but also to have brought forth the desired fruits of marriage."

For her motto, Kathryn chose the submissive phrase *"non aultre volonté que le sienne"* (no other will than his). On the royal properties, the stone and stained glass were embellished with *H*s entwined with *K*s. Because Kathryn was Henry's "blushing rose without a thorn," she selected a crowned rose as her emblem.

Constantly caressing her in public, "the king's affection was so marvelously set upon that gentlewoman, as it was never known that he had the like to any woman," wrote Ralph Morice, secretary to Archbishop Cranmer. He spent more on Kathryn's gowns, jewels, and household expenses than he had for any of his other wives. It cost Henry £46,000 a year— nearly $36 million in today's economy—to maintain Kathryn's personal establishment.

Although Kathryn was indeed something of a good-time girl, she was warm and loving, a good-natured soul who just wanted everybody to be happy. And unlike each of Henry's previous wives, she had no political agenda of her own.

Kathryn found places in her household for most of the young ladies from her Maidens' Chamber days. And at Agnes Howard's insistence, she made her former lover Francis Dereham one of her clerks, a move that was ill-advised at best, but the dowager duchess had pressed her for the favor. During her brief tenure as queen, Kathryn's detractors accused her of favoritism in making these appointments, but this was an accepted practice at the time—protocol observed by each of Henry's queens, as well as by the king himself.

But Dereham abused his position, behaving like one of his betters. When he was caught lingering over his dinner, a perquisite reserved for members of the Queen's Council, he retorted somewhat cryptically, "I was of the Queen's Council before [his accuser] knew her, and shall be when she hath forgotten him."

In October 1540, the Queen Consort Act was passed by Parliament, giving Kathryn the right to "act as a woman sole, without the consent of the King's Highness." Unfortunately, the teen queen would end up taking her privileges too literally.

The following July, the court embarked on a Royal Progress, and it was during this journey that a change in Kathryn's behavior began to be noted.

At their stop in Lincoln, Henry retired to his apartments early, but the queen's rooms were lit until the wee hours of the morning. The night watchman observed that the door to her back stairs was ajar, so he locked it; but not too much later, he saw two figures approach the door. They fumbled with the lock and somehow got it open, slipping wordlessly into the queen's rooms.

A few days later, on a hunting break at Hartfield Chase, Kathryn's ladies spied her glancing out the window of her bedchamber at Thomas Culpeper, fixing him with a look of purest lust. It was a gaze her minions would long remember.

The next destination on the Royal Progress was Pontefract

Castle. A page, sent by the king to Kathryn's bedchamber (presumably to summon her to the royal fourposter), found the door bolted shut. Apparently, he did not dare report this to His Majesty. Did he tell Henry instead that he found Kathryn fast asleep, snoring loud enough to shake the battlements?

Kathryn later claimed that she and Culpeper had a platonic relationship and were simply conversing all night, but a locked door never looks good.

On November 1, with the Progress over and the court back in London, Henry declared his happiness in a solemn thanksgiving, ironically (or perhaps pointedly) giving thanks for the virtuousness of his wife. Immediately after his pronouncement of perfect bliss, everything turned ugly. A Hollywood screenwriter couldn't have done better with the timing.

Sliding into the pew beside him, Thomas Cranmer, the Archbishop of Canterbury, approached Henry with news that would destroy the king's fantasies and bring down the fragile house of cards that was his fifth marriage. Cranmer had received a letter from John Lascelles advising him of Kathryn's infidelity. John was the brother of Mary Lascelles, the maidservant at step-gran Agnes Howard's house who used to procure the keys to the Maidens' Chamber so that Francis Dereham could sneak in to have orgiastic sex with Kathryn. And Kathryn had made a cardinal goof by finding a place in her royal household for each of her former acquaintances—except Mary Lascelles.

But there was more to the picture. The Lascelles family were staunch Reformers (as was Cranmer—who in happier days had been the sidekick of the über-Reformer Anne Boleyn). The Reformers wanted to bring down the powerful (and Catholic) Howards before they gained so much influence at court that Henry would become dissuaded from reforming the religion. Cranmer didn't really have anything against Kathryn per se, but he weighed the consequences and concluded that it would be all right with his conscience to sacrifice the queen if it meant saving his infant Church.

When Henry read the accusations against Kathryn, his first reaction was disbelief. He insisted that the investigation into these allegations be conducted in secret. Meanwhile, his beloved queen was kept at Hampton Court, and Henry developed excuses for not visiting her. In fact, true to form when the going got tough on the domestic front, Henry absented himself. He would never see his wife again.

The investigative hearings began on November 5, 1541. Kathryn stood accused of fornicating before marriage with both Henry Manox and Francis Dereham. The transcripts of the hearings include testimony so graphic that a twenty-first-century tabloid couldn't print it without running afoul of the pornography laws.

Mary Lascelles, the first to testify, claimed that she had reproved Manox for his presumption in thinking that Kathryn would ever be his. She added that on hearing this, Manox had laughed in Mary's face and boastfully replied, "I know her well enough, for I have had her by the cunt, and I know it among a hundred . . . And she loves me and I love her, and she had said to me that I shall have her maidenhead, though it be painful to her, and not doubting but I will be good to her hereafter."

According to Manox, Kathryn had withheld her virginity from him but had promised that he should not go entirely unsatisfied.

"Yet let me feel your secret place," the music teacher had insisted. Kathryn assented, "and I felt more than was convenient," he admitted. However, Manox swore "upon [his] damnation and the most extreme punishment of [his] body" that he never did more with Kathryn than that act of groping, and had never known her carnally. And throughout the hearings, he would not be budged from this testimony. It would ultimately free him, as there was nothing for which he could be convicted. Manox would be the only one implicated in the scandal to walk away with his head on his shoulders.

But Dereham was another story. Under oath, he confessed "carnal knowledge with the Queen . . . lying in bed by her in [his] doublet and hosen divers times and six or seven times naked in bed with her."

Mary Lascelles titillated the investigators with descriptions of Kathryn and Dereham's marathon lovemaking sessions in the Maidens' Chamber, "for they would kiss and hang by their bills together as if they were two sparrows."

"There was such puffing and blowing between them that [she] was weary of the same," testified Alice Restwood, Kathryn's former bedfellow in the Maidens' Chamber.

Henry was moved to tears by all this testimony. His virtuous wife had turned out to be nothing but a harlot.

Even as the council heard witness after witness shred Kathryn's virtue, the queen herself, holed up at Hampton Court, remained unaware of the investigation. But on November 7, two days after the first day of hearings, when the king's men came to place her under house arrest and found her making merry with her maids, they informed the queen that it was "no more the time to dance."

The evidence against her had been so well rehearsed that a refutation of the charges was impossible. She could only counter them with resignation and abject humility.

The authorities gave Kathryn every chance to admit a precontract with Dereham, which would have saved her life, as the precontract was itself tantamount to a marriage. If she had been contracted to Dereham, her marriage to Henry would have been null and void, and—if she was not Henry's wife—he could not possibly charge her with adultery.

But Kathryn, too hysterical and unable to parse the nuances

of the situation, insisted that Dereham had forced himself upon her, averring that she had never welcomed his advances. However, no one believed her because of the duration of the relationship and the numerous love tokens exchanged.

She was arrested on November 12, 1541. When the king refused to see her, Kathryn wrote him a desperate plea for clemency. She pleaded with Henry for forgiveness, confessing that

> *First, at the flattering and fair persuasions of Manox, being but a young girl, I suffered him at sundry times to handle and touch the secret parts of my body which neither become me with honesty to permit nor him to require.*
>
> *Also, Francis Dereham, by many persuasions procured me to his vicious purpose and obtained first to lie upon my bed with his doublet and hose and after within the bed and finally he lay with me naked, and used me in such sort as a man doth his wife many and sundry times, but how often I know not.*
>
> *Our company ended almost a year before the King's Majesty was married to my Lady Anne of Cleves and continued not past one quarter of a year or a little above.*

Henry wasn't entirely sure she had committed any offense with Dereham since it had all taken place long before she had become queen. Why not be merciful? Kathryn was guilty of being young and lusty, something Henry understood firsthand. For that, he could consign her to a convent, but at least her life would be spared. In fact, on November 14, Henry did tell Kathryn, "to a nunnery, go!" packing her off to Syon, a former convent, while the whole sordid business could be sorted out.

But Henry's council, realizing how much his passion for Kathryn might soften his resolve, couldn't allow him to be lenient. They convinced him that to forgive Kathryn's transgressions was a sign of regal weakness.

Conveniently for the council, Kathryn's Lady of the Bedchamber, Jane Rochford (the sister-in-law of the late Anne Boleyn), decided to unburden her conscience. The scheming yet craven Lady Rochford had acted as go-between and gatekeeper on numerous occasions when Kathryn was wont to admit Thomas Culpeper to her bedchamber.

Now Kathryn's ordeal took on a different tone, and the stakes could not have been higher. If Kathryn had slept with Culpeper during the Royal Progress, she had indeed committed adultery—high treason because she had cuckolded a king. And the penalty was death.

A rapid-fire round of finger-pointing began. Francis Dereham told the council that the reason Kathryn had terminated their relationship was because the queen had fallen for Thomas Culpeper.

Kathryn blamed Lady Rochford, insisting that her lady-in-waiting had *encouraged* her to consort with Culpeper, convincing her that she could get away with it. Kathryn admitted that she had indeed given Culpeper some relatively insignificant gifts, but that it had not been her idea; Culpeper had asked for them.

On November 12, 1541, Culpeper was arrested and taken to the Tower. His rank prohibited him from being subjected to torture or undue duress, but he did have more to say on the matter. Though he insisted that Kathryn had initiated their relationship, he did admit his feelings for her. Since some historians have painted Culpeper as an ambitious schemer and Kathryn the dupe of her own hormones, it's almost refreshing to note that—since everyone was to die for it—at least Culpeper did care for her.

At the Tower, Culpeper delineated in chapter and verse the

extent of his affair with the queen, stating that on Maundy Thursday (April 14, 1541), he was summoned by one of Kathryn's servants to the queen's presence, where Kathryn gave him "by her own hand a fair cap of velvet garnished with a brooch, along with three dozen pairs of aglets [decorative pins] and a chain. 'Put this under your cloak [and let] nobody see it,'" Kathryn had allegedly told Culpeper. To which he claimed to have replied, "Alas, madam, why did you not do this when you were a maid?"

This was not what Kathryn wanted to hear, according to Culpeper, because at their next encounter, she had grumpily asked him, "Is this all the thanks ye give me for the cap? If I had known ye would have [said] these words, you never should have had it."

They'd been playing a flirtatious high-stakes game of cat and mouse; the more one of them withheld their favors or interest, the more it sparked the other's flame. And yet in a rare moment of self-awareness, Kathryn had told Culpeper that their love was impossible—which he had interpreted as a directive to satisfy his urges elsewhere.

"I marvel that ye could so much dissemble as to say ye loved me so earnestly and yet would and did lie so soon with another," she'd complained.

Culpeper replied that Kathryn "was married [to the king] afore [he] loved the other," adding that he had "found so little favor at her hands at that time, that [he] was rather moved to set by other."

Although she was not ready to give herself to him, Kathryn did fear that Culpeper would forget her, so she sent him a pair of bracelets "to keep his arms warm."

As early as April 1541, when Culpeper had become ill at Greenwich, Kathryn had taken a keen interest in his welfare and dispatched her pages to bring him meat and fish for dinner, a gesture that could be construed as coming from the kind heart of a sovereign—but what would consign Kathryn to the block was the letter she subsequently wrote to her paramour:

> *Master Culpeper,*
> *. . . It was showed me that you was sick, the which thing troubled me very much till such time that I hear from you, praying you to send me word how that you do. For I never longed so much for a thing as I do to see you and to speak with you, the which I trust shall be shortly now.*
> *. . . it makes my heart to die to think what fortune I have that I cannot be always in your company.*
> *My trust is always in you that you will be as you have promised me, and in that hope I trust still, praying you then that you will come when my Lady Rochford is here, for then I shall be best at leisure to be at your commandment. . . .*
> *I would you were with me now, that you might see what pain I take in writing you.*
>
> > *Yours as long as life endures,*
> > *Katheryn*

Though this letter provides no proof of *sexual* passion, let alone intercourse, to write it and send it was spectacularly ill-advised. No court is without its intrigue and surely the note was bound to come to light.

Culpeper confessed that their affair had heated up during the summer's Royal Progress. It had been Thomas and his servant who had picked the lock to Kathryn's bedchamber door in Lincoln after the watchman had shut it. Culpeper admitted that when he entered the queen's rooms he found only Kathryn and Lady Rochford there, and they stayed up throughout the night reminiscing about old times and old loves. He acknowledged that Kathryn had been very anxious about the watch, fearing they'd be discovered.

Culpeper's volubility at the Tower continued to condemn himself as well as the queen, admitting that at Pontefract, during the Progress, Kathryn had sent him a note: *"As ye find the door, so to come."*

And though she was probably jesting, during a lovers' spat Kathryn had boasted to Culpeper when the Progress stopped at York that "she 'had store of other lovers at other doors as well as he,'" to which Culpeper claims to have replied, "It is like enough."

Although there is no evidence of any other paramours, with all the dangers of being overheard, it was not a bright thing for Kathryn to say.

But there is more to Kathryn than the heedless hedonist, and it doesn't do her justice to paint her in broad strokes as an empty-headed, oversexed ninny. She is not a fictional character intended to represent an archetype. During these all-night tête-à-têtes with Culpeper, Kathryn's vulnerability emerged. Admitting that Kathryn did have "communication with him how well she loved him," Culpeper testified that the queen had poured out her heart to him, confiding that "when she was a maiden how many times her grief was such that she could not but weep in the presence of her fellows."

Acknowledging that she and Culpeper were playing with fire, Kathryn admitted that she feared Henry, urging Culpeper not to mention anything about their relationship when he went to confession, or ask to be shriven for it, because "surely the king, being Supreme Head of the Church, should have knowledge of it."

"No, madam, I warrant you," Culpeper had assured her.

It was an open-book test—the painful lesson of Anne Boleyn's fall from grace staring at her from the pages of recent history—and still, Kathryn managed to fail it.

Perhaps they were not having sex all those nights they spent together during the Progress. Perhaps it *was* just a friendship, but, as Culpeper admitted, it was flirting with intent. He "meant to do ill with the Queen, and that likewise the Queen so minded with him."

And it would be enough to convict them both.

It was tough on the royal ego to face the possibility that this time his wife had thrown *him* over, rather than the other way around. The Howards had sold Henry a damaged bill of goods and he had been cuckolded in the bargain. The entire court knew it. And so would the rest of the world, once the foreign ambassadors sent their dispatches.

It's hard not to feel somewhat sorry for Henry, so self-deluded was he about his virility. Or was he? To condemn Kathryn was to air his own fragile insecurities about his age, his health, and his sexual prowess. More than anything else, he wanted a son, and the older he got, the more he realized that Holy Grail of paternity was slipping from his grasp. Though he would not acknowledge it publicly, Henry could see just as well as anyone else did that he was hugely obese, and that for nearly fifteen years he'd endured an oozing, ulcerous wound on his leg that often gave him a fever, made him limp, and stank to high heaven when it was time to change the dressing. His mortality mocked him, and with each passing day it became more impor-tant to insure the succession of his crown and the propagation of the Tudor dynasty. Yet court insiders claimed that Henry seemed to age overnight when he learned that his beloved rose without a thorn might have played him for a fool.

The imperial ambassador, Chapuys, reported that he had never seen the king "so sad, pensive and sighing," and ". . . He has certainly shown greater sorrow and regret at her loss, than at the faults, loss or divorce of his preceding wives."

Henry openly "regretted his ill luck in meeting with such horribly ill-conditioned wives." He called for his sword that he might kill her "that he loved so much." All the pleasure "that wicked woman" had derived from her "incontinency" should not equal the pain she should receive from torture. Her suffering should be of a far *greater* magnitude.

Kathryn had been demoted from queen on November 22, 1541, to be called simply Kathryn Howard from then on. That day she was indicted for having led "an abominable, base, carnal, voluptuous, and vicious life before her royal marriage," behaving "like a common harlot with divers persons, maintaining however the outward appearance of chastity and honesty." She was accused of leading the king "by word and gesture to love her," and "arrogantly coupled herself with him in marriage," concealing her precontract with Francis Dereham "to the peril of the king and his children to be begotten by her." She was also accused of seducing Culpeper and telling him that she preferred him to the king.

A passel of Kathryn's relatives were conveyed to the Tower, including the elderly dowager Duchess of Norfolk, all charged with misprision of treason, in knowing that Kathryn had either committed treason or planned to do so. The only relation who emerged unscathed was Kathryn's uncle, the Duke of Norfolk, who had distanced himself from Kathryn as vociferously as he had once promoted her.

On December 1, 1541, although both men refused to confess carnal knowledge with Kathryn after she had become queen, Culpeper and Dereham were tried for treason and found guilty.

They were executed on December 10. Dereham was dragged on a hurdle from the Tower to Tyburn, where he was hanged. Then, while he was still alive, he was castrated and disemboweled. Finally, he was beheaded, and quartered—and all that for sleeping with a lusty teenage girl who had not yet *met* Henry VIII.

Because of his rank and his position as a member of the King's Bedchamber, Culpeper received a more lenient sentence. He was simply beheaded.

In mid-January 1542, a Bill of Attainder in the form of a petition was drawn up, permitting Henry to execute Kathryn and her lady-in-waiting Lady Rochford for high treason, the penalty for which was "death and the confiscation of goods." Although Kathryn had never confessed to adultery with Culpeper, Henry decided to put her to death under the "violent assumption" that she had been unfaithful to him.

Additional clauses of the act were ridiculously retroactive, stating that it was treason if any nonvirgin should marry the king "without plain declaration before of her unchaste life unto his majesty." Adultery by or with the queen or the wife of the Prince of Wales was likewise a treasonable offense. It was also considered misprision of treason for anyone to conceal knowledge of such an offense—and that's what convicted Lady Rochford.

There was some hesitation about using an Act of Attainder against the queen without her being afforded the opportunity to speak for herself, so a delegation was dispatched to Syon House to hear her side of the story.

But Kathryn refused to defend herself, openly acknowledging her guilt instead. She did request that Henry spare her relations from being punished, that he "would not impute [her] crime to [her] whole kindred and family." She also asked that Henry give some of her fine attire to her household, "since she had nothing now to recompense them as they deserved."

On February 10, Kathryn, clad in black velvet, was taken by barge from Syon to the Tower, amid a bout of perfectly understandable last-minute hysterics. At least her boat was fully canopied, sparing her the sight of two recently decapitated heads—Dereham's and Culpeper's—rotting atop pikes on London Bridge. In the Queen's Apartments at the Tower, according to the Calendar of State papers, Kathryn spent her final days enjoying the same honors and ceremonies that had been accorded to her when she was Queen of England, despite the fact that she had been stripped of her title.

The following day, the Act of Attainder received Henry's assent in absentia. Although the words *"le roi le veut"* (the king wills it) had been printed at the top of the document, *Henry never actually signed it*—and both women would meet their gruesome ends without the king's formal imprimatur.

Kathryn was brought before Cranmer to make her confession. It was a pitiful sight. Cranmer said, "I found her in such lamentation and heaviness as I never saw no creature, so that it would have pitied any man's heart in the world to have looked upon her."

Endeavoring to calm her troubled soul, the archbishop gave her some (false) hope for the king's mercy. Her agitation somewhat soothed, the queen now believed that Henry would simply denounce her and she would be punished, but afterward, she would be received back into his good graces, even if they were never to dwell together again. "What a gracious and loving prince I had," she wept. "Alas, my lord that I am still alive; the fear of death grieved me not so much before, as doth now the remembrance of the king's goodness."

But there was to be no clemency.

On Sunday, February 12, Kathryn was told that she would die the next day. Utterly terrified, she asked for the block to be brought to her, so she could "make trial of it, that she might know how to place herself." She may not have lived every day of her life with dignity, but she was determined to spend her last one dying with it. She tearfully confessed to Cranmer that she deserved a thousand deaths for so offending a king who had treated her so graciously.

Kathryn Howard was executed on the same block where

Anne Boleyn had met her end six years earlier. She was probably only twenty years old at the time of her death, and had been queen for just over eighteen months.

The legend that has traveled through the centuries that Kathryn's last words were "I die a queen, but I had rather die the wife of Thomas Culpeper," is the stuff of fiction, a line that wouldn't be out of place coming from the Underwood typewriter of a Hollywood hack. First of all, Kathryn wasn't queen anymore. Second, a girl so terrified of her execution that she insisted on rehearsing with the block would scarcely be so arrogant in her final moments.

According to Ottwell Johnson, an eyewitness at Kathryn's execution, the queen mounted the platform and stood before the block, then "uttered [her] lively faith in the blood of Christ only." She "desired all Christian people to take regard unto [her] worthy and just punishment," adding that she had offended "God heinously from her youth upward, in breaking all His commandments." She had transgressed "against the King's Royal Majesty very dangerously," and was "justly condemned by the laws of the realm and Parliament to die."

Just as she had practiced, Kathryn laid her head upon the block. She merited no expensive French executioner wielding an extra-sharp sword. Her red head was struck off with an axe. The weeping ladies-in-waiting wrapped her bleeding body parts in blankets and Kathryn's remains were placed in a coffin that was buried alongside Anne Boleyn's in the little Tower church of St. Peter ad Vincula.

Swooning with fear, Lady Rochford was dragged to the blood-soaked scaffold. In her final words, she maintained her innocence as to being Kathryn's procuress, but admitted that she had "falsely accused" her late husband "of loving in an incestuous manner, his sister, Queen Anne Boleyn. For this I deserve to die."

She was beheaded on the block still red with Kathryn's blood.

Following the executions, Kathryn's relations were released from the Tower.

Though Henry enjoyed a court banquet and feasted his eye upon numerous attractive young ladies just two weeks later, it would be eighteen months before he had recovered from the blows to his heart and his ego engendered by the queen's infidelity.

He would take one more wife—the much-married Catherine Parr. The author of at least one devotional work, Catherine's intellectual accomplishments were rare for her day; she was one of only seven early-Tudor-era females to be a published author. Her first book, printed in November 1545, went through nineteen editions during the sixteenth century.

The Act of Attainder against Kathryn and Lady Rochford stood until 1553, when Henry's daughter, Mary I—the monarch whose moniker was "Bloody" because of her execution of hundreds of religious dissenters—reversed the act because it lacked the sovereign's signature. It was far too late to do her late stepmother any good, but it was a noble gesture nonetheless.

ELIZABETH I

1533–1603
RULED 1558–1603

*E*LIZABETH I, THE DAUGHTER OF HENRY VIII AND ANNE Boleyn, was twenty-five years old when she became queen upon the death of her half sister, Mary I, on November 17, 1558. She reigned for nearly forty-five years, creating the cult of the Virgin Queen by staunchly refusing to marry, claiming she was wed instead to England and her subjects were her children.

Mary I had only ruled for five years, but she'd left the realm in a sorry state. She'd lost Calais, the last English territory on the Continent, to the French. Religious tensions abounded between Catholics, Protestants, and the new evangelical Puritans. The Treasury was bankrupt from financing the foreign wars fought by her husband, King Philip of Spain. The cities were crowded, squalid, and dangerous.

One of Elizabeth's key political concerns during her lengthy reign was the subject of her marriage (or not) to ensure the smooth succession of her crown. Over the years, several suitors, foreign and English, vied for her hand, but she had a valid political reason for rejecting each of them.

Her personal aversion to the institution aside, marriage presented a minefield of obstacles. Most foreign princes were Catholic, and Elizabeth staunchly refused to renounce her own religion. Additionally, if she married a foreign prince, England would end up a vassal to his crown. And if she chose an English husband, it would create factions among her nobles, which might result in civil strife. There was also the issue of the man's birthright and nobility. Every man in England was beneath her.

Elizabeth put her realm on the road to becoming a great empire. She decimated the Spanish navy with the defeat of its legendary Armada, and risked her popularity and her reputation by executing a foreign queen—her cousin, Mary, Queen of Scots—for plotting against her.

Elizabeth was the first English monarch to lend her name to an entire age, shaped by the force of her policy and personality. During her reign, poetry and theatre blossomed and flourished. It was an era of adventure and piracy on the high seas and exploration in the New World, embodied by the dashing Francis Drake and Sir Walter Raleigh.

In the late winter of 1603, Elizabeth began to slow down. Although she had lost the power of speech in her final days, she pantomimed a crown above her head with her hands, which was interpreted as a sign for King James VI, the son of Mary, Queen of Scots, to succeed her. At her behest, her Secretary of State, Robert Cecil, had been working behind the scenes since 1601 to ensure James's smooth accession to the English throne, so there was little question that James was Elizabeth's legitimate choice to succeed her.

In the wee hours of March 24, 1603, the sixty-nine-year-old Elizabeth died in her sleep. A sapphire ring was prized from her finger by her trusted lady-in-waiting, Lady Scrope, and sent to Scotland in a horseback ride that made history for speed; it was the official signal for James to take his place on the English throne.

👑

ELIZABETH I

and Robert Dudley, 1st Earl of Leicester 1533–1588

One of the greatest love stories in British royal history became a scandal even though the parties *weren't* having sex.

Elizabeth and Robert Dudley, the son of the Duke of Northumberland, were childhood playfellows. Ironically, Dudley was the first to learn of Elizabeth's intention never to marry; and yet, if she had been free of political constraints and considerations, he was the one man she would have chosen for a husband. Speaking to Elizabeth's ministers, Dudley once affirmed the intimate nature of their long-standing friendship, insisting, "I have known her better than any man alive since she was eight years old." That was their age in 1542, when Elizabeth's third stepmother, Kathryn Howard, received the full measure of her husband's wrath and met her grisly end. "I will never marry," the little red-haired princess had said resolutely. And she meant it.

Robert Dudley's father lost his head for backing a plot to place Mary Tudor's granddaughter, Lady Jane Grey, on the throne as Edward VI's successor. In the fallout, Robert was imprisoned in the Tower for a while on suspicion of treason. Some have posited that Robert renewed his friendship with Elizabeth when she was remanded to the Tower for three months in 1554, for her suspected participation in Thomas Wyatt's plot against her half sister Queen Mary's marriage to Philip of Spain. This scenario is not likely, as Elizabeth was heavily monitored and housed in another area of the Tower from young Dudley. He was also married, and his wife was permitted visits at any hour. Additionally, if Elizabeth were to be seen conversing (or more) with Dudley, the son and grandson of convicted traitors, her guilt by association would have quickly led her to the block.

Dudley had wed an heiress, Amy Robsart, in 1550. As the years wore on, their childless marriage, begun for love, became lackluster.

It was really Elizabeth who was the great love of his life.

As soon as Dudley heard the news that Queen Mary had died, he rode hell for leather to Hatfield on a white charger and offered Elizabeth his services. Faced with such a wildly romantic gesture, how could she possibly refuse him? On November 18, 1558, the day after she learned she was queen, she appointed Dudley Master of the Horse. It was an appropriate fit; Robert was an expert equestrian and a superb jouster. As a military man he had acquitted himself well, fighting with valor at the Battle of St. Quentin in 1557.

As Master of the Horse, Dudley was entitled to a suite of rooms at court and his own retinue of servants, who would be permitted to wear the green and white livery of the Tudor court. His job was to purchase, train, breed, and maintain the horses for the queen and her court, at a salary of £1,500 a year—nearly $700,000 in today's economy.

The appointment had another perquisite: Elizabeth adored riding and Dudley's position put the two of them into daily contact. Often they would ride out together for hours, as alone as they could possibly be.

They made an attractive couple, both tall, slim, and good-looking. A contemporary described Elizabeth by saying, "Her face is comely rather than handsome, but she is well formed and has fine eyes." Elizabeth was fine-boned, with long, tapered fingers, high cheekbones, piercingly intelligent eyes, a long, slightly hooked nose, a small bosom, and a tiny waist. She had inherited her father's curly Tudor-red hair, and her mother's sallow complexion, which she always endeavored to lighten with a facial scrub mixed from eggshells and egg whites, alum and borax, and poppy seeds.

The six-foot-tall Dudley's complexion was so swarthy that he had earned the nickname of "Gypsy." But to Elizabeth he would always be her "bonny sweet Robin." Dudley was thought to be "a very goodly person and singular well-featured, and all his youth well-favored, but high-foreheaded." His mustache and beard were lighter and redder than his hair, his nose was high-bridged, and his heavy-lidded eyes lent him a sardonically sexy appearance. He was a true Renaissance man—athletic, artistic, musical, literary, well-read and informed in science and philosophy, and a consummate linguist.

It was soon abundantly apparent to the entire court, including the foreign envoys, that Dudley was the queen's favorite, and their relationship several cuts above the ordinary preferment. She leapt into his arms as he partnered her in lively galliards, and they were openly affectionate, leading to the charge that Dudley was overly familiar with the person of the queen. The court hummed with gossip.

On April 18, 1559, just five months after Elizabeth's accession, Count de Feria, ambassador to Philip of Spain, wrote to his sovereign:

Lord Robert has come so much into favor that he does whatever he likes with affairs. It is even said that Her Majesty visits him in his chamber day and night. People talk of this so freely that they go so far to say that his wife has a malady in one of her breasts, and that the Queen is only waiting for her to die to marry Lord Robert. I can assure Your Majesty that matters have reached such a pass that I have been brought to consider whether it would be well

to approach Lord Robert on Your Majesty's behalf, prom-
ising your help and favor and coming to terms with him.

The Venetian ambassador arrived at the same conclusion: if
Lady Dudley "were perchance to die, the Queen might easily
take him for her husband."

It would never have been "easy." Nevertheless, the issue
eventually came to haunt both "lovers."

Baron Breuner, a suitor for her hand, correctly summed up
the temperature of the times: "If she took my Lord Robert, she
will incur so much enmity that she may one evening lay herself
down as the Queen of England, and rise the next morning as
plain Mistress Elizabeth."

On April 23, 1559, Elizabeth made Dudley a Knight of the
Garter, angering some of his fellow courtiers, who felt that a
descendant of traitors should never receive such an honor. There
were men among them who had served England long and valiantly. Why were they overlooked for a man whose only qualifi-
cations were his good looks and his equestrian prowess?

But to Elizabeth, Dudley was everything a man should be.
She admired his robust taste for adventure, his bravery and
nerve. She made it clear that his presence raised her spirits, and
for that reason she must see him every day. She granted Dudley
money, state offices, and property. In the Privy Council he enjoyed a place of preference, and Elizabeth entertained nothing
that had not been reviewed and vetted by him. Naturally, factions formed against him, and before long he was the most despised man in England, even though his detractors could ill
afford to publicly malign him, since the queen might one day
be mercurial enough to marry him.

Dudley's personality made it too easy for his enemies to
align against him. He was haughty and ambitious and had an
unpleasant tendency to speak ill of his "friends" behind their
backs. And he very much wanted the crown matrimonial. But

he wanted Elizabeth just as much. *Any* crown was not an acceptable consolation prize if he could not have her hand.

People were talking and gossip was getting ugly. Elizabeth's oldest friends and closest confidantes, such as her former schoolmistress Kat Ashley, urged her to marry Dudley or stop flirting with him and caressing him before the entire court. Her lovestruck behavior was ruining her reputation, something she could ill afford.

Elizabeth gave Kat her stock answer about weighing the pros and cons of any union and marrying for the good of the country or not at all. In that case, Kat replied, put some distance between Dudley and yourself.

But Elizabeth would have sooner lost her sight. And yet she knew she could never marry him.

In 1560, Elizabeth embarked on one of her famous progresses throughout the kingdom; Dudley was her constant companion. They spent entire days cozily closeted together, giving the impression that they were lovers in every way. One envious courtier exclaimed, "Not a man in England but cries out at the top of his voice, this fellow is ruining the country with his vanity."

Meanwhile, Amy, Lady Dudley, was in the country, living a peripatetic existence between the homes of friends and family, where she would stay for weeks or months at a time. The queen had given Dudley a house in Kew so he could reside near the court, but Her Majesty had a habit of dropping in unannounced and Amy was too mortified to ever risk being there at the same time. In 1560, she had been married to Dudley for a decade, and yet they rarely saw each other, because Elizabeth insisted that he remain at court and spend each day with her.

Elizabeth made it very difficult and expensive for courtiers to house their wives at court, and greatly discouraged the practice. With Amy in particular, Elizabeth made it abundantly clear that even a reference to her name was displeasing to her ears. Rumors must have reached Amy of her husband's flirtatious dalliances with Her Majesty, but what was the poor woman to do about it? If she complained, who knows what might befall her? So she kept her thoughts to herself, as illness and melancholy replaced Dudley as her daily companions. Her material needs were always provided for; Amy lacked for nothing but her husband's love and attention.

By early September of 1560, it was widely known that Amy was very depressed. The doctors told her that she was suffering from a terminal illness in the breast, and no doubt she was in considerable physical pain. She was then residing at Cumnor Place, a house leased by Dudley's former steward. Along with the home's usual residents, she was accompanied by a female chaperone and attended by a small staff of servants. On September 8, Amy urged her servants to attend a local fair, almost anxious to get them out of the house. The only one to remain behind was her traveling companion, who refused to rub shoulders with a bunch of peasants. When the servants returned to Cumnor Place that evening, they found Amy dead, at the foot of a shallow flight of stone steps leading from her bedroom to the hallway. Her neck was broken.

On September 9, when she heard the news of Amy's death, the queen was shocked speechless. Dudley appeared bewildered. He ordered a full inquiry, and two days later Elizabeth declared that the entire matter should be made public so that it would not appear as though the crown had willfully concealed anything. Despite the suspicious circumstances, the coroner's inquest deemed her death the result of an accidental slip and fall.

Amy got her revenge from the grave, for now Elizabeth and Dudley could never marry. Apart from the fact that Dudley's rank and general unpopularity made him an unsuitable candidate for king consort, he had become tainted with suspicion, even though no complicity in Amy's death was ever proved.

Amy's body lay in state on September 22 and was buried the

next day. Dudley did not attend the funeral, as it was the custom at the time for mourners to be of the same sex as the deceased.

Tongues continued to cluck when Elizabeth welcomed Dudley back to court. How could a sovereign admit to her favor a courtier who might have killed his wife?

But she shocked them further on September 28, 1564, when she elevated Dudley to the peerage, creating him Baron Denbigh and Earl of Leicester. Sir James Melville, a Scottish envoy, noticed that when the queen smilingly bestowed the collar of his earldom on her dear Robin, she affectionately tickled his neck.

After the ceremony, Elizabeth coyly asked Melville, "How like you my new creation?" Elizabeth had recently conceived the notion that her bonny sweet Robin should marry Mary, Queen of Scots. Perhaps she'd chosen this moment to make Dudley Earl of Leicester so that he might be a stronger candidate for her cousin's hand. That way he would get his kingdom, and Elizabeth would be assured that her northern neighbor was being governed just the way she would rule it herself.

But the idea met an early demise. None of the parties truly wanted it, not even Elizabeth. And Dudley (Leicester) didn't want to be just *any* redheaded queen's king consort—he wanted Elizabeth.

After the notion to marry Leicester to Mary was tabled, Elizabeth and her paramour were as close as ever. People saw them kiss when Leicester visited her chamber in the morning, the queen still in her night-shift or spilling out of her dressing gown.

So close, and yet so far. Leicester's willpower could not be expected to last forever.

In 1565, he commenced a flirtation with "one of the best looking ladies of the court," Elizabeth's married cousin and former waiting woman, the beautiful, red-haired Lettice Knollys. Lettice, a granddaughter of Mary Boleyn who had been married at twenty to Walter Devereux, the 1st Earl of Essex, was a near look-alike for Elizabeth.

Elizabeth retaliated by flirting with other courtiers, which had the intended effect of inflaming Leicester's jealousy. The two quarreled furiously, accusing each other of casting them aside for another. Elizabeth's nerves grew raw; where Leicester was concerned, she could not muster her famous ability to conceal her feelings. When Elizabeth learned that he had been arrogant to one of her servants, she exploded in front of the entire court, venting the full measure of her thwarted sexual and emotional frustration.

"God's death, my lord, I have wished you well, but my favor is not so locked up for you that others shall not participate thereof. And if you think to rule here, I will take a course to see you forthcoming. I will have but one mistress and no master."

Their relationship had turned a corner. Leicester didn't love her any less, but he could no longer hold out hope of being her lover in every sense of the word. He would never bed her. He was tired of being blamed for Elizabeth's not marrying a foreign prince, and thereby making a politically advantageous match for England. He was tired of her humiliating flirting with other men in front of everyone. He was even tired of her flirting with *him,* stringing him along for so many years, and never making a commitment.

But he made one more try. At Christmas 1565, Leicester again asked the queen to marry him. Elizabeth equivocated, telling him she couldn't give him a reply until early February, at Candlemas, a date that seems rather arbitrary. Buoyed by hope, Leicester began to act as though his marriage and kingship were in the bag, alienating yet more nobles.

But Elizabeth did not say yes. And the years dragged on.

In May 1573, Leicester was the object of affection of the twenty-five-year-old widow of Lord Sheffield, a woman with

the unfortunate first name of Douglas. Douglas became Leicester's mistress, but soon demanded marriage from him, since he
had compromised her reputation. Leicester—perhaps hoping
against hope that Elizabeth would finally come around—
caddishly offered Douglas an alternative: she could remain his
mistress or he would help her find a suitable husband.

The lady rejected his offer and instead got her way. That
May, Leicester secretly married Douglas. But by the end of
1575, he had tired of her, and the thirty-five-year-old Lettice
Knollys, still beautiful, came back into the romantic picture.
By now, she had given her husband, the 1st Earl of Essex, five
children, although the marriage was not a happy one. When
Essex died of dysentery in 1576, his nine-year-old son, Robert,
inherited the title. Lettice was now marriageable, although she
was deeply in debt.

Leicester was no longer the dashing figure he had been in his
youth. By 1577, he was forty-four years old and past his prime.
He'd grown portly, "high colored and red faced," and had not
waged a military campaign in twenty years.

Despite the wildfire spread of gossip at court, Lettice may not
have known about Leicester's clandestine marriage to Douglas
Sheffield. In any event, both Lettice and Leicester behaved as
if he were available. Then Lettice discovered she was pregnant and insisted that her lover legitimize the child. Leicester
capitulated. In the spring of 1578, he wed Lettice in secret at
his estate of Kenilworth, in Wanstead, Essex—a home he
had purchased so that he could sneak away from court to be
with her.

An anonymously written note was left at Elizabeth's garden
doorstep, which one can safely assume spilled the beans on
Leicester's marriage to Lettice.

True, the queen had strung him along for decades, but it
stung to learn that he had well and truly moved on. Elizabeth
banished him from court for marrying without her permission—

which she likely never would have granted. In May, Leicester traveled north to Buxton for the spa waters, and remained away from court for two months.

And yet, Elizabeth missed him dreadfully. When Leicester returned to court, he still behaved toward her as he had always done, and Lettice's name—like Amy Robsart's—was never mentioned. Elizabeth detested Lettice with a vengeance. And now that the woman had taken her bonny sweet Robin from her, Elizabeth did her level best to pretend the new Lady Leicester didn't exist.

In her famous speech to the final Parliament of her reign in 1601, known as "the Golden Speech," Elizabeth remarked, "to be a king and wear a crown is more glorious to them that see it than it is a pleasure to them that bear it." It was a sentiment that she carried with her daily. Discovering that Leicester had married another—and a near relation who had always been a rival for beauty—must have been the single occasion when Elizabeth most wished herself a mere mortal, a "normal" noblewoman free to choose love with one of her own. The weight of the crown must have felt very heavy during those long days. Leicester's marriage had put her in a perpetually foul mood. He might be welcomed at court, at her pleasure, but Lettice was pointedly persona non grata.

Lettice showed up once, so opulently dressed that her appearance rivaled the monarch's, and Elizabeth utterly lost her temper. In the presence of several courtiers and ladies, she strode up to Lettice and boxed her ears. "As but one sun lights the East, so I shall have but one queen in England!" Elizabeth shouted. The new Countess of Leicester dared not show her face again for years.

Technically, Leicester was a bigamist; his marriage to Douglas Sheffield, though performed in secret, had been perfectly legal. And although their ardor had mutually cooled, Douglas was devastated when Leicester told her it was over and tried to buy her off with an annuity of £700 per annum (almost $270,000 today) on the proviso that she pretend their marriage never took place. Leicester also demanded custody of their son.

Douglas ultimately agreed to all of Leicester's proposals, fearful of some sort of retribution if she did not comply.

On September 21, 1578, Leicester and Lettice had a more public wedding ceremony. The bride was pregnant, but the baby was stillborn at the end of the year.

Still smarting from what she viewed as Leicester's betrayal, in 1579, Elizabeth headed full tilt toward marriage. The youthful duc d'Anjou had sent his envoy, Jean de Simier, to woo Elizabeth in Anjou's name. Elizabeth behaved like a giddy schoolgirl in his presence—so much so that her councilors got very nervous as to just what sort of proxy wooing de Simier was engaging in.

Leicester was insanely jealous. Envy gnawed at him even further when the duc d'Anjou himself arrived in England, and proved to be an extremely pleasant surprise to Elizabeth. Rumors of his pockmarked condition had been greatly exaggerated. Anjou was handsome, debonair, charming, suave—and, okay, so he was only twenty-three years old to her forty-five— and she was nuts about him from the start. Despite the vast difference in their ages, their sexual chemistry was powerful. And indeed, despite her years, she still hoped to beget an heir.

But the queen dithered and delayed and second-guessed herself, politically, diplomatically, and emotionally. Finally, the French determined that the match was a bad idea after all. Her own Parliament was discouraging the marriage as well. On October 7, Elizabeth burst into tears in front of them, realizing that Anjou represented her last, best hope for some semblance of a normal marriage.

During the summer of 1580, Douglas Sheffield married Sir

Edward Stafford. Elizabeth remained jealous over Douglas's relationship with Leicester, and she sought to make trouble for Lettice by revealing that Leicester had legally married Douglas, had never divorced her, and therefore, Lettice's marriage to Leicester was invalid. But when no one could attest to a wedding between Douglas and Leicester, Elizabeth's attempt to create a rift fizzled.

That December, Lettice gave birth to another child, Robert, Baron Denbigh, whom she and Leicester lovingly called their "noble imp."

In 1584, the duc d'Anjou died of a fever. When the news reached England, Elizabeth erupted in a flood of tears and cried in public for three full weeks. She wore black for six months and referred to herself as "a widow woman who has lost her husband."

Leicester lost his noble imp during the summer of 1585 and the grief aged him considerably. He considered retiring to private life in the country, but Elizabeth had need of his martial skills. She dispatched him to the Netherlands in command of an expedition, leading an army of six thousand men and one thousand horses. His young stepson, the Earl of Essex, accompanied him as Master of the Horse. The Dutch treated Leicester like the prince he'd always aspired to be, urging him "to declare himself chief head and Governor General."

Perceiving this as an attempt at self-aggrandizement, Elizabeth was so incensed that she withheld the soldiers' pay and removed Leicester from his commission. But on June 25, 1587, she sent him back to the Netherlands with three thousand troops. However, Anglo-Dutch relations were becoming increasingly tense and Elizabeth recalled him on November 10, displeased with his failure to forge a union with the Netherlands and put the Spanish alliance in check. Back on English soil, he relinquished his post as Master of the Horse, persuading Elizabeth to bestow it on his stepson, Essex.

In August of 1588, after enjoying the triumphant victory celebrations over the Spanish Armada, the fifty-five-year-old Leicester asked Elizabeth to give him permission to leave London for the healing waters of Buxton. He took the journey by stages, an exhausted and ailing campaigner who had fought his last good fight commanding Elizabeth's army against the threat of the Spanish invasion.

On August 29, suffering from ague and fever, he wrote to Elizabeth from Rycote in Oxfordshire:

> *I most humbly beseech your Majesty to pardon your old servant to be thus bold in sending to know how my gracious lady doth, and what ease of her late pain she finds, being the chiefest thing in the world I do pray for, for her to have good health and long life. For my own poor case, I continue still your medicine, and it amends much better than any other thing that hath been given me . . .*

At four a.m. on September 4, Leicester died at his hunting lodge in Cornbury Park, near Woodstock. He was buried beside his son in the Chapel of St. Mary the Virgin at Warwick.

Elizabeth had lost her "brother and best friend," and was too heartbroken to attend to affairs of state. She shut herself in her bedchamber, refusing to speak to or see anyone, until her treasurer broke down the door, needing to discuss a matter of urgency.

On the missive from Rycote Elizabeth scrawled "his last letter" and tucked it into a little box that she kept beside her bed. After that came the process of sorting out. She took back Leicester's estates without a care for Lettice's welfare. However, as he had acquired it through marriage and not by the crown, Leicester's town house on the Strand passed to his eldest stepson, Robert, the dashing Earl of Essex, who renamed it Essex House.

Lettice landed on her feet, though. Within the year she married Sir Christopher Blount, a young friend of her son's.

As for Elizabeth . . . after her brilliant defeat of the Spanish Armada, the queen was at the zenith of her powers—"Eliza Triumphant." If only Leicester had lived to see it.

👑

ELIZABETH I
and Robert Devereux, 2nd Earl of Essex 1566–1601

It was a May–December romance between two strong-willed egomaniacs that would end up destroying them both. Elizabeth lost all dignity. And Essex lost his head.

Robert Devereux, 2nd Earl of Essex, was Elizabeth's first cousin twice removed, the son of Lettice Knollys, her former lady-in-waiting. His stepfather was Robert Dudley, 1st Earl of Leicester, Elizabeth's precious favorite and platonic paramour.

A precocious youth, Essex entered Trinity College, Cambridge, at the age of ten, and at fourteen graduated as a Master of Arts. He first came to court in 1584, an eighteen-year-old stripling in the company of his stepfather. Because of his special relationship to Elizabeth's favorite courtier, Essex secured her preferment as well.

He accompanied Leicester in 1585 on a successful campaign in the Netherlands—where, for his valor, Leicester knighted him on the field. By May of 1587, Essex was one of the brightest lights at a court renowned for its brain trust. He was a handsome twenty-one-year-old, tall and dashing, with soft auburn hair that grazed his broad shoulders, graceful hands, a lively wit, and an infectious energy.

Although thirty-three years separated them, Elizabeth could not bear to be a moment without Essex. By day they enjoyed sparkling conversation, long walks, and rides through the royal parks. In the evenings, there was music and dancing, and after everyone had departed for bed, the queen and her young protégé would remain together into the wee hours of the morning, playing cards.

Ever the clever courtier, Essex knew what his queen desired most. His letters to her contained fervent protestations of love, and the L word was always on his lips. Elizabeth and Essex were "lovers" in the old-fashioned, high-flown style of courtly love. What physical intimacy passed between them—and Elizabeth, though ostensibly a virgin, always had an amorous and flirtatious disposition—was only of the most innocuous variety. No matter how head over heels she seemed, Elizabeth was a canny politician. It seems unlikely she would ever allow any man, especially a callow youth, a power over her by dominating her sexually.

After England's spectacular defeat of the Spanish Armada, Essex became hungry to distinguish himself on the field of battle, although it was not where his strengths lay. An older, wiser courtier and philosopher, the twenty-seven-year-old Sir Francis Bacon, took Essex under his wing. Bacon coached Essex on how to behave in the queen's presence, cautioning him against his customary displays of petulance and bad temper when he didn't get his way.

"A man must read formality in your countenance," Bacon told his friend. There were better ways to accomplish his purpose: "Your Lordship should never be without some particulars afoot, which you should seem to pursue with earnestness and affection, and then let them fall, upon taking knowledge of Her Majesty's opposition and dislike."

Bacon also tried to instill a sense of realism into the idealistic upstart. He urged Essex to aim for an appointment to the

Privy Council, astutely suggesting that the witty cavalier fared better in the rarefied atmosphere of the court than amid the deprivations and din of a battlefield.

But Essex wasn't listening. He begged Elizabeth to let him join Sir Francis Drake's Counter Armada, leading the English fleet to raid Corunna and detach Portugal from Philip of Spain's rule. Elizabeth refused him leave; but Essex flagrantly disobeyed her order. The queen dispatched an angry and frantic letter to Drake:

> ... We will and command you that you sequester him from all charge and service and cause him to be safely kept. . . . If [Essex] be now come into the company of the fleet, we straightly charge you that you do forthwith cause him to be sent hither in safe manner. Which, if you do not, you shall look to answer for the same to your smart. For these be no childish actions. Therefore consider well of your doings herein.

But Essex remained with the English fleet. And on his return, Elizabeth forgave him, a pattern that characterized their relationship. Aware that the queen's fondness for him allowed him to get away with just about anything, Essex played the court-favorite card at every possible opportunity. He continually behaved as though he were Elizabeth's equal, bragging to fellow courtiers that he was capable of mastering her. He treated her with such abominable disrespect that any other man who spoke so rudely to the queen would have been beheaded within the day.

Elizabeth even bailed him out financially. When Essex's extravagant spending put him £20,000 (about $7 million today) in the hole, she advanced him £3,000. But then she called in the debt right away. Essex didn't have the funds. So Elizabeth demanded one of his estates as repayment. Essex forfeited his precious manor at Keyston in Huntingdonshire, but Elizabeth then turned around and gave him a perquisite—the right to farm the customs duties on the imports of sweet wine for a period of years, thereby enabling him to have a steady source of income.

Elizabeth notoriously bridled with thinly veiled rage when a courtier married, and her reaction was no different when she learned in 1589 that the twenty-three-year-old Essex had wed Frances Sidney, the widowed daughter of Francis Walsingham, the queen's spymaster. Elizabeth's objections were voiced loud and clear, but before long she recognized the prudence of the match. The age-appropriate Frances was a virtuous girl from a good family. Nevertheless, Elizabeth pretended that, as his wife, Frances didn't exist, and continued her flirtations—which, at age fifty-six, were getting a bit gruesome. Elizabeth consoled herself with the notion that the love that she and Essex enjoyed was on a higher plane. Frances could have her cozy domesticity.

In 1591, after the French king, Henri IV, appealed to Elizabeth for aid to help the Protestant Huguenots fight the Spaniards and the Catholic League, she agreed to send four thousand men.

Three times Essex begged his sovereign lady to put him in command of this special force, and each time, Elizabeth refused. Finally, he knelt before her for two hours and refused to budge until she relented.

But the reality didn't match the fantasy and Essex made a cock-up of things. He lost his favorite brother in a skirmish, deserted the main body of his troops to go hawking, and rashly challenged the governor of Rouen to a duel. Finally, he left his men to meet Henri, which almost resulted in his being cut off and isolated by the opposing army.

Hearing about Essex's raft of blunders, an infuriated Elizabeth considered pulling the plug on the entire campaign. But the immature earl could not handle her scolding. "Unkindness and sorrow have broken my heart and my wits. I wish to be out of my prison which I account my life," he lamented.

The pair of them routinely engaged in a twisted tango. Whenever Essex would leave court in one of his sulks, Elizabeth would mirror it, descending into a black and foul mood and becoming even testier than usual. She and Essex quarreled often, but the eruptions, though ugly, were brief. And reconciliation was delicious when her favorite assured her how beloved she was in his eyes.

In Essex's company, Elizabeth felt lit from within, girly and coy, but the earl was exhausted by the game. He looked at the vain, wrinkled woman in her inappropriately revealing necklines, her red fright wigs and layers of cosmetics that turned her once-lovely face into a caricature, and he saw an obstinate sixty-something virgin who changed her mind as often as she changed her gowns. She was grasping at her long-lost youth, trying to re-create in him another Dudley. He would collapse from the strain, his body shivering with ague, lying in the dark for days, incapable of action.

And yet, Essex was insanely jealous of any other courtier on whom Elizabeth bestowed her smiles and favor—particularly Sir Walter Raleigh, his greatest rival in the dash and élan department.

Early in 1593, Elizabeth appointed Essex to the Privy Council. His new prestige gained him some enemies at court, most notably Robert Cecil, Elizabeth's new secretary, who was assuming his aging father's duties. But Essex took his new responsibilities very seriously, arriving at the House of Lords at seven in the morning every day, emerging as a burgeoning statesman.

On December 28, 1597, on Cecil's genuinely considered recommendation despite his personal dislike for the youth, Elizabeth made Essex Earl Marshal of England, charged with arranging state events, such as the opening of Parliament. But without a military campaign, Essex was bored. In 1598, he began philandering with a number of ladies of the court, fathering a bastard child by Mistress Elizabeth Southwell, even as he slept with other women. His wife was dismayed, and his queen was despondent, lapsing into fits of melancholy. Elizabeth's temper grew shorter and sharper, and her ladies bore the brunt of it.

Essex saw his opportunity to distinguish himself in September 1598. That's when an army of Irish rebels led by Hugh O'Neill, 2nd Earl of Tyrone, ambushed the English forces there, leaving twelve hundred men dead or wounded, and the north of Ireland all the way down to Dublin unprotected.

Elizabeth was bent on sending Essex's uncle, Sir William Knollys, to quash the uprising. Essex proposed a counter-candidate and he and the queen nearly came to blows over it. In the middle of their argument, Essex made the cardinal mistake of contemptuously turning his back on the queen.

Elizabeth literally boxed his ears, shouting, "Go to the Devil!"

Her arrogant young adversary then did the unthinkable. Swearing loudly, he grasped the hilt of his sword. Getting right up in Elizabeth's face, he screamed, "This is an outrage that I will not put up with! I would not have borne it from your father's hands!"

The room went frighteningly silent. The Earl of Nottingham grabbed hold of Essex before he did something even more rash. Elizabeth remained absolutely still. Either utterly mortified or still in high dudgeon, Essex fled the room.

What happened next was even more remarkable, given Elizabeth's penchant for mercilessly castigating those who crossed her.

She did nothing.

Not another word was said about the incident.

Utterly unchastened, Essex reopened the wound by writing to her from Wanstead. In a display of colossal gall, he had the temerity to scold his sovereign for her cruel treatment of him.

Elizabeth finally grew disgusted. "He hath played long enough upon me. And now I mean to play awhile upon him," she vowed, "and stand as much upon my greatness as he hath upon stomach." She instructed her messenger to "tell the Earl that I value *myself* at as great a price as *he* values *himself*."

Essex's disrespectful written reply was "I do confess that, as a man, I have been more subject to your natural beauty than as a subject to the power of a king."

Elizabeth had sent Sir Richard Bingham to crush Tyrone's rebels, but in October, Bingham died. Essex begged Elizabeth to send him to Ireland as Bingham's replacement—arguing that only he could put down the rebellion and pacify Ireland. Finally, he got his wish. Essex was given the command of the largest army Elizabeth had ever amassed—sixteen thousand infantrymen and thirteen thousand cavalrymen.

The English settlers welcomed Essex with open arms. But from there, it was all downhill. Filled with bravado, Essex loved the *idea* of a military campaign, the glory and honors that would come to him for a job well done. But as a tactician and strategist, and as a commander, he was a disaster. He dithered, squandering time and resources, and far worse—lives. In addition to casualties, desertion and disease claimed his men. He dispatched them to distant outposts, thereby reducing the numbers he needed to fight Tyrone. When one of his detachments displayed cowardice in the field, he had every tenth man in the rank and file summarily executed, and cashiered his lieutenants, executing one of them as well. He did not request Elizabeth's permission to alter his marching orders or inform her of his troop movements. He knighted dozens of men, though Elizabeth had expressly forbidden him to do so. One wag grumpily quipped that Essex unsheathed his sword only to make knights.

Elizabeth anxiously waited for a dispatch from the front. "I give the Lord Deputy a thousand pounds a day to go on progress," she lamented bitterly, and ordered Essex to march forthwith into Ulster.

Essex replied that her command was impossible to fulfill, because the army was vastly depleted. Only four thousand infantrymen remained. At great expense, the queen sent two thousand reinforcements, ordering Essex to attack Tyrone and not to leave Ireland until he had succeeded. Instead of engaging Tyrone in battle, Essex did the most humiliating thing a general could do: meeting Tyrone one-on-one in the middle of a river, Essex negotiated a truce.

And then, without permission to depart, Essex left for England. To avoid any unpleasant news of his conduct reaching the queen's ears before he had a chance to explain his actions, Essex headed straight for London. With his riding boots muddy and his clothes dirty and dusty from his long journey, he strode uninvited and unannounced into Elizabeth's bedroom as she was making her toilette.

A wizened, bare-faced woman with straggly gray hair glanced up, startled, at the intruder. With queenly aplomb, Elizabeth recovered her composure, and even her vanity, and burst out laughing, once she realized he meant her no harm. She told Essex she would speak with him when they were both properly dressed.

But it wasn't long before she ascertained what had happened in Ireland. Elizabeth remanded Essex to the custody of the Lord Keeper at York House until she determined the appropriate course of action.

On November 29, the Star Chamber met, and Essex's litany of transgressions was read aloud. He had mismanaged the Irish campaign, had brokered a humiliating treaty, and had deserted his commission without permission, returning to England in direct contravention of the queen's orders.

And yet no punishment was meted out. Essex languished under house arrest at York House until the spring, when Elizabeth ordered him back to his own estate. By then she was determined that a tribunal of her own should hear the case.

On June 5, 1600, after an eleven-hour hearing before Elizabeth's special commission, Essex was declared guilty and stripped of his offices. Elizabeth granted his wish to return to his own home.

Aware that the patent for the duties on the sweet wines was coming due, Essex wrote her honeyed letters in the hope that the queen would renew it. But the rose-colored scales had finally fallen from the royal eyes. Elizabeth told Francis Bacon, "My Lord of Essex has written me some very dutiful letters, and I have been moved by them; but what I took for the abundance of the heart I find to be only a suit for the farm of sweet wines."

And yet, the earl still had the power to move her, writing:

Haste, paper, to that happy presence, whence only unhappy I am banished; kiss that fair correcting hand which lays new plasters to my lighter hurts, but to my greatest wound applieth nothing. Say thou comest from pining, languishing, despairing ESSEX.

Nevertheless, she did not renew his warrant. Henceforward the profits from the sweet wines would be reserved for the crown.

At this, Essex became apoplectic. A friend, Sir John Harington, wrote:

He shifteth from sorrow and repentance to rage and rebellion so suddenly as well proveth him devoid of good reason or right mind ... The Queen well knoweth how to

humble the haughty spirit, the haughty spirit knoweth not
how to yield, and the man's soul seemed tossed to and fro,
like the waves of a troubled sea.

During a conversation about Elizabeth's conditions of his
return to court, Essex lost command of his temper to such a
degree that it finally cost him her love. In his view, she had
banished him; and by refusing to renew his license on the
sweet wine imports, had reduced him to poverty. "Her conditions!" he exclaimed. "Her conditions are as crooked as her
carcase!"

The remark was repeated to the queen. And finally, after giving Essex enough rope to hang himself ever since she met him,
Elizabeth refused to forgive him. Essex had mortally wounded
the powerful queen's most vulnerable spot: her vanity.

The earl then embarked on the most foolhardy project of his
life. He decided that Elizabeth must be deposed. In the early
weeks of 1601, he wrote to James VI of Scotland, who sent
back a letter of encouragement. Essex wore the letter about his
neck in a small black leather purse.

On February 7, the earl was summoned to present himself
before the Privy Council, but he pled illness, assuming that he
would be arrested as soon as he arrived. The following day, Essex gathered three hundred supporters and, by telling them
that Cecil and Raleigh planned to assassinate him, tricked
them into marching behind him through the streets of London,
shouting, "For the Queen! For the Queen! The crown of England is sold to the Spaniards! A plot is laid for my life!"

But the good people of London kept their doors and windows shut. The golden boy's credit with them had turned to
dross. Essex managed to get down to the riverside, where he
found a small boat and rowed up the Thames to Essex House,
where he sought refuge, but his respite was short-lived. The
queen's guards caught up with him. He surrendered himself

into their custody and was immediately brought to the Tower.

Essex was tried for treason on February 19, 1601. In such proceedings, a guilty verdict was a foregone conclusion.

Elizabeth was heartbroken, not only because her favorite was about to die but because he had betrayed her trust in his ability, and by extension her love for him. Yet she could not, would not, alter the verdict. After years of vacillating where Essex was concerned, Elizabeth showed no regret at ordering his death.

On the frosty morning of February 25, the thirty-four-year-old Essex walked to the place of execution on Tower Green. In addition to the usual paeans to God and queen, in his final speech on the scaffold Essex confessed that "my sins are more in number than the hairs on my head. I have bestowed my youth in wantonness, lust, and uncleanness; I have been puffed up with pride and vanity, and love of this wicked world's pleasures."

It took the executioner three strikes of the axe to get the job done.

After her husband's death, the long-suffering Frances, Lady Essex, remarried twice more. Essex's ambitious mother, Lettice Knollys, widowed once again by the execution of Christopher Blount, one of her son's coconspirators, lived to the astonishing age of ninety-four.

THE
STUARTS
1603–1714

MARY, QUEEN OF SCOTS

1542–1587
MONARCH OF SCOTLAND 1542–1567
QUEEN CONSORT OF FRANCE 1559–1560

MARY, QUEEN OF SCOTS, THE DAUGHTER OF KING James V and Marie of Guise, his powerfully connected French-born wife, was only a week old when her father died and she became queen. It was a time of civil unrest. By 1548, when Mary was just five years old, her mother sent her to France for her own safety, while she remained in Scotland as Mary's regent. Mary was raised in the court of Henri II. Slender and pale, she was nicknamed *"la reine blanche"* (the white queen). In 1558, she married François, the frail and sickly dauphin. A year later, Henri II died, and Mary and her young husband—now François II—became the king and queen of France.

In June 1560, Marie of Guise died of dropsy. But just as Mary was beginning to cope with her mother's death, on December 5, her fifteen-year-old husband died of an ear infection. The widowed, eighteen-year-old Mary returned to Scotland in 1561 to claim her crown. The country was in turmoil, governed by a body of regents that included the evangelical Protestant John Knox and Mary's bastard half brother, James Stewart.

Mary's efforts to strip the nobles of their power and instead consolidate it within the purview of the crown angered many of the lairds (the Scottish lords) whose support she needed most—misogynists who were already malcontented at being ruled by a lassie.

In addition to the crippling poverty facing her wild and rugged nation, Mary had a lot of institutionalized hostility to handle. She was a female, a foreigner (having been raised in France), and she was a devout Catholic in a Protestant country that had embraced the Reformation with a vengeance.

Mary's domestic policy was always the pursuit of peace. She had a horror of violence, saying of herself that she would "rather pray with Esther than take the sword of Judith."

In a love match, Mary wed her ambitious cousin, Henry Stuart, Lord Darnley. Shortly after Darnley was murdered by a conspiracy of lairds in February 1567, Mary married the alleged ringleader of the plot, James Hepburn, Earl of Bothwell. Then, the nobles who had so vociferously supported Bothwell turned traitor, raising their swords against Bothwell and arresting Mary.

On June 24, 1567, imprisoned at Lochleven Castle, Mary was forced to abdicate her throne in favor of her infant son, James, who was crowned at Stirling that day.

Aided by some of her sympathetic captors, Mary managed to escape on May 2, 1568, and fled to England, hoping that Elizabeth would grant her asylum as a fugitive queen. Mary's plan was to regroup an army and return to Scotland to reclaim her crown.

However, for the next nineteen years, Mary remained in Elizabeth's "honorable custody," detained as a potential threat to Elizabeth's person and her crown because she might stir up

Catholic sympathy and challenge the Protestant Elizabeth's sovereignty. Civil war was unthinkable. In the summer of 1586, Mary indeed implicated herself in a plot to depose Elizabeth, fomented by Anthony Babington, a Catholic zealot.

Mary was arrested and taken to Fotheringhay Castle. Her trial itself was utterly illegal: she was a foreign queen and therefore was not bound by their laws. And she could not be properly judged by a panel of peers, because a sovereign—who ruled by divine right—by definition *had* no peers. Nonetheless, Mary was convicted of high treason, and on February 1, 1587, Elizabeth signed her death warrant.

On the morning of February 8, 1587, the forty-four-year-old Mary Stuart, dowager Queen of Scotland and France, was executed in the Great Hall at Fotheringhay Castle. After three inept chops, the executioner finally raised the severed appendage, and Mary's red wig came off in his hand. Her head, with its scraggly gray locks, ignominiously thudded to the floor. And then, Mary's little Westie, who had been hiding within her skirts the entire time, crawled out from beneath her petticoats and nestled himself between Mary's head and shoulders. The terrier was thoroughly scrubbed of Mary's blood and every shred of the queen's clothes was burned so that they could not become relics of a Catholic martyr, a role in which many of her fellow Papists had cast her since her incarceration in England began.

Mary's corpse was encased in a lead coffin that remained at Fotheringhay for nearly half a year until her son, King James VI, arranged a proper funeral at Peterborough Cathedral. It was a Protestant service.

On the death of Elizabeth I in 1603, James VI of Scotland became James I of England, jointly ruling both realms. He erected a white marble monument for his mother in Westminster Abbey, where her body now reposes—*la reine blanche* forever.

MARY, QUEEN OF SCOTS

and Henry Stuart, Lord Darnley 1545–1567
and James Hepburn, 4th Earl of Bothwell c. 1534–1578

Though she had once glimpsed him years earlier when he was no more than a gangly boy, Mary, Queen of Scots, met her first cousin, the golden-haired Henry Stuart, Lord Darnley, when his pushy mother, Margaret Lennox, sent him to France to express his condolences on the death of Mary's husband, King François II. Lady Lennox viewed her son as the next candidate for Mary's hand because Mary and Darnley were both grandchildren of Margaret Tudor, the elder sister of Henry VIII. Like Mary, Darnley's veins ran thick with both Stuart and Tudor (Scottish and English) royal blood. And, like Mary, he was Catholic.

At the time, Darnley did not make much of an impression on the grieving eighteen-year-old queen. It was not until five years later, in 1565, that Mary saw him in an entirely new light and fell madly in love with him.

By then, her English cousin, Queen Elizabeth I, was trying to fob off her own paramour, Robert Dudley, Earl of Leicester, onto Mary. Mary's advisers thought it was a joke, since Leicester was damaged goods. His father, Northumberland, had been executed for treason and the title attainted (meaning that it, and the appurtenant lands, reverted to the crown); and Leicester's wife, Amy Robsart, had died under suspicious circumstances, some thought a victim of Leicester himself.

Mary would only have agreed to marry Leicester if Elizabeth named her the heir to the English throne; and though Elizabeth's envoys first dangled that carrot, the promise was withdrawn. The hope of a union with Don Carlos, the heir to King Philip of Spain, had dimmed as well. So Mary focused her attentions on Darnley, a curly-haired, nineteen-year-old, six-feet-one-inch-tall playboy, "the properest and best proportioned long man she had ever seen."

But Sir James Melville, one of her envoys to the English court, didn't understand the attraction, sneering, "No woman would make choice of such a man that was liker a woman than a man, for he is very lusty, beardless, and lady-faced."

John Knox, the formidable clergyman and leader of the Protestant Reformation, believed that Mary should secure *his* approval before choosing a husband—and the *last* thing this puritanical evangelical wanted was a Catholic consort for the queen.

An enraged Mary, all of twenty-one years old at the time, summoned the fifty-year-old Knox to Holyrood Palace. Choked with tears, she demanded, "What have you to do with my marriage? What are you within this commonwealth?"

"A subject born within the same," Knox replied tersely.

In April 1565, when Darnley fell ill and was confined to Stirling Castle for his recuperation, Mary's ardor blossomed. She was at Darnley's bedside every day, and at each visit they exchanged love tokens, proximity working its magic on her feelings.

Elizabeth was enraged to learn that Mary intended to marry Darnley without asking for her permission to wed an English subject. Mary angrily informed Elizabeth that "Her Majesty desires her good sister to meddle no further." She would marry Darnley, no matter what.

The two tall figures made an elegant couple, and together they enjoyed the pastimes of hawking, hunting, and billiards. Exceedingly feminine, Mary possessed a striking, though fragile, beauty—slender and unusually tall for the era at nearly six feet, with high cheekbones, hazel eyes, and the Tudor red-gold hair. Her speaking voice was praised as *"très douce et très bonne"* (very sweet and very pretty).

On July 22, 1565, Mary made Darnley Duke of Albany. One week later, the heralds proclaimed that the man so recently introduced to the Scots as "Prince Henry" would henceforth be known as "King of this our kingdom" with Mary's full blessing.

The sun was not yet up on the morning of July 29, 1565, when Mary was led down the aisle of the Chapel Royal at Holyrood by Darnley's father, Lord Lennox, and the Earl of Argyll. Though her smile was radiant, the bride wore black, emblematic of her status as a widow, and by extension, the dowager queen of France.

Darnley entered the chapel and the bridal couple exchanged vows. Since they were first cousins, a papal dispensation was necessary in order for them to marry. It had not arrived in Edinburgh by July 29, but Mary blithely assumed the document was en route and married Darnley without it. Although the dispensation finally made it to Scotland, the July 29 marriage was technically not legal because the bride and groom still remained within a proscribed degree of affinity.

As soon as the ceremony was over, Mary cast aside her mourning garments and days of festivities began.

Darnley was a handsome popinjay who stirred Mary's lust and evidently gave her what she craved after a celibate marriage to the French dauphin—fabulous sex. The English ambassador to Scotland, Thomas Randolph, was disgusted that the "poor Queen, whom ever before I esteemed so worthy, so wise, so honorable in all her doings" was behaving like a giddy schoolgirl, mooning over a man who was so vastly her inferior.

But Darnley's lower birthright was nothing compared to the

fact that he turned out to be an adulterous, syphilitic alcoholic who abused the "poor queen" almost as soon as he bedded her. Having learned that her beloved husband was no stranger to the brothels of Edinburgh, how must she have felt to realize that her body alone could not satisfy him?

Darnley had become King Henry, so self-aggrandizing that he would go hunting or hawking on a day when important government business was being transacted so that he had to be fetched in order to affix his signature—which he deliberately wrote larger than Mary's own. But he wanted more—and not just from the whores along the Canongate. Darnley wanted the *crown matrimonial*, which would have made him a coruler rather than a mere consort, giving him the full powers of kingship on Mary's death. To that end, he began to make deals with some of the Scottish lairds; but he was too dim to realize that they were using him as a pawn.

Darnley's ego was considerably larger than his brain and he swallowed the lords' bait, entering a conspiracy to dethrone his wife. Meanwhile, Mary, six months pregnant, was platonically taking comfort in the company of her correspondence secretary, an Italian from Savoy named David Riccio, perhaps the only man at court to have the queen's ear and her full trust. The xenophobic nobles distrusted Riccio because he was a Catholic and a foreigner. The thirty-five-year-old Riccio, short and ugly, also became the lairds' convenient scapegoat for all baseborn men who the queen had elevated to positions of influence at court.

"Woe is me for you when Davy's son shall be a king of England," was the pestilence poured into the gullible, egotistical Darnley's ear. The lords persuaded Darnley that the first step in effecting a coup was to destroy Mary's confidant. And Mary and her unborn child had to be put out of the picture for Darnley to step into his own.

Curiously, the English knew of the plot, while Mary was

utterly unaware of it. On February 13, 1566, Elizabeth's ambassador, Thomas Randolph, wrote to the Earl of Leicester:

> *I know for certain that this Queen repenteth her marriage, that she hateth Darnley and all his kin. I know there are practices in hand contrived between father and son to come by the crown against her will. I know that if that take effect which is intended, David, with the consent of the king, shall have his throat cut within these ten days. Many things grievouser and worse than these are brought to my ears, yea, of things intended against her own person.*

At Holyrood Palace on the night of March 9, 1566, Riccio and Mary were in her supper-room enjoying a game of cards amid servants, guards, and other companions, when a group of men, led by Patrick Lord Ruthven, sneaked up the privy stairs from Darnley's apartment below and began to batter at the door.

"Let it please Your Majesty that yonder man David come forth of your Privy Chamber where he hath been overlong," they demanded.

Mary refused to open the door, insisting that Riccio was there by her invitation. This proved no deterrent to Ruthven, who then barged into the room. He denounced the secretary for offending the queen's honor.

Mary turned to her husband and asked Darnley if he had anything to do with the unwanted intrusion. He muttered an incoherent and sheepish demurral. Ruthven railed against Mary for banishing the Protestant lairds. Her servants were so cowed that they could not stir, and yet Ruthven shouted, "Lay not hands on me, for I will not be handled." It was the cue for the coconspirators to enter the room.

As Ker of Fawdonside leveled his pistol at Mary's swollen

belly, Riccio, dandyishly dressed in his nightgown of furred damask and a satin doublet and hose of russet velvet, was dragged into the next room kicking and screaming in Italian and French, "*Justizia! Justizia! Sauvez ma vie, madame! Sauvez ma vie!*" He was stabbed more than fifty times, and his bloody, battered body was tossed down a staircase.

Darnley's coconspirators made the queen a prisoner in her own palace. Although she feared for her life and privately grieved (and seethed with rage) over Riccio's assassination, Mary concealed her emotions behind a mask of pure charm. Lucky for her that her husband was too stupid to spot a trap once it had been laid. By the following evening she had convinced Darnley that his life was as endangered as hers. By midnight, he had become her ally.

Only fifty-two hours after Riccio's murder, Mary and Darnley tiptoed down the privy stairs that led from her apartment to his, through the servants' quarters, and out of the palace. All through the night, they rode to Dunbar Castle and safety, managing a twenty-five-mile journey in five hours. Mary, riding pillion (on a cushion behind him), urged Darnley to have more care for her condition, to which he angrily replied that if she lost the baby, they could just as easily make another.

Mary's courage rallied her subjects. By March 18, she had amassed eight thousand men behind her, and rode victoriously back into Edinburgh.

On June 19, 1566, after a painful and difficult labor, Mary gave birth to a son, the future James VI. Now that the heir was born and healthy, Mary raged at Darnley, "I have forgiven, but will never forget!" She saw him now for a craven, scheming traitor. "What if Fawdonside's pistol had shot, what would become of him and me both? Or what estate would you have been in? God only knows, but we may suspect."

David Riccio's murder had engendered in Mary an abiding,

seething hatred of her husband. She had been in ill health ever since her son's birth, collapsing in October 1566 with vomiting and convulsions, losing consciousness for two days. Darnley did not even visit her sickbed. "He misuses himself so far towards her that it is an heartbreak for her to think that he should be her husband," lamented William Maitland, one of Mary's most trusted advisers.

Mary now toyed with the idea of divorcing Darnley, but the nobles would only consent to it if the queen would pardon the conspirators, who had scattered to the four winds after Riccio's murder. Mary agreed—as long as it was formally stipulated that her son, James, was legitimate, without the slightest taint of bastardy. She had never been intimate with Riccio, and wanted the idle tongues silenced.

At Stirling Castle on December 17, 1566, Mary's son was christened. In absentia, Elizabeth I was his godmother. Darnley was conspicuously missing from the festivities. At the end of the month he departed for Glasgow, a center of Lennox Stewart power, where his family would welcome him. Around the New Year, he was diagnosed with syphilis.

Mary convinced Darnley to return to Edinburgh to recuperate. Rather than take up residence in Holyrood, on February 1, 1567, he moved to a modest house just inside the city wall, known colloquially as Kirk o' Field. Mary was all cordiality toward her husband, even staying at the house with him, though in a bedroom upstairs from his. Darnley congenially unburdened himself, informing Mary of certain plots against her, adding that even *he* had been approached by malfeasors who had suggested that he murder Mary himself! You can just hear the nervous laughter.

On the night of February 9, Mary attended the wedding masque for one of her favorite valets. While she was out, the house at Kirk o' Field was filled with gunpowder. At two a.m. on February 10, the house was blown sky-high.

Hours later, one of Darnley's servants, who had somehow

survived the blast, stood atop the town wall, crying for assistance. Darnley's body, naked beneath his nightgown, was found in the little garden outside the house. He had been strangled to death. Evidently, he had peered out the window and saw the conspirators outside, including some of his kinsmen from Clan Douglas. Fearing that they were about to set the house afire with him inside, Darnley had tried to escape. Only twenty-one years old, the king died at their hands.

At Holyrood, where she had gone after remaining at the wedding masque past midnight, Mary was awakened with the news of Darnley's death. She vowed to punish those who "have taken this wicked enterprise in hand," since "we assure ourself it was dressed always for us as for the king; for we lay the most part all of the last week in that same lodging."

Mary usually became distraught at scenes of bloodshed and violence and had been physically ill over the deaths of her mother and François, but she shed no tears when she was shown Darnley's corpse. Perhaps she was as much relieved that he was gone as that she had survived an attempted coup. Or perhaps she was just in shock.

Mary observed the traditional forty days of mourning, during which she was said to be melancholy and pensive. Maybe she wondered who her friends were. Was there anyone left who she could trust? Ill health and depression brought on by stress and grief increased her dependence on the Earl of Bothwell, "a glorious, rash, and hazardous young man" whose power seemed to grow daily.

On March 19, Bothwell began to act as Mary's policy director. He was already Lord High Admiral, as well as one of Mary's key advisers on matters relating to the border territories. Bothwell was ambitious to be king of Scotland himself now that Mary was once again marriageable.

A somewhat simian-looking serial adulterer, the five-feet-six-inch-tall Bothwell was dwarfed in stature by the queen. John Leslie, Bishop of Ross, thought the earl "of great bodily strength and beauty, although vicious and dissolute in his habits." He was also brutal and striving, though perhaps no more so than many of his era, particularly in a time and place where money and family ambition were the Scottish nobles' two driving forces. And he was up to his elbows in conspiracies.

On her way back to Edinburgh after visiting her infant son at Stirling Castle, Mary's party was accosted by Bothwell and eight hundred of his men. He told Mary that her safety was in jeopardy, urging her to place her trust in him and permit him to escort her to Dunbar Castle. In order to avoid bloodshed, Mary assented. The incident was so odd and Mary's conciliation so easily won that many people believed (and still do) that she had been complicit in the "abduction." It is possible, given that she was utterly exhausted, physically and emotionally, and thought there might be worse fates than joining forces with Bothwell. But what happened next was most certainly not what she expected.

At Dunbar, Bothwell raped her. The violation placed her in an untenable position. According to Sir James Melville, "the Queen could not but marry him, seeing he had ravished her and lain with her against her will."

But Mary was vulnerable and resigned herself to marrying Bothwell for three reasons: he had convinced her that he was the skilled and masterful consort she needed to rule Scotland; he showed her a bond signed by several powerful nobles pledging their support to him as their overlord; and the rape had "consummated" their union, so that Mary could not go back on her word to marry him once they reached Edinburgh.

She had angered the nobles by wedding Darnley, against their advice. If they supported Bothwell, and her marriage to him, perhaps the civil strife would cease.

On Thursday, May 15, 1567, in a Protestant ceremony, Mary and Bothwell were married in the Great Hall at Holyrood Palace. The queen had lost so much control over her destiny that she had allowed herself to be wed according to a religion she did not espouse.

According to one of Mary's advisers, "not one day passed" that the new bride was not in tears. Bothwell prohibited Mary from enjoying the leisurely pursuits she had so enjoyed—hawking, hunting, and music. He accused her in the crudest language of frivolity and wantonness. Only twenty-four years old, she seemed to age overnight.

It was not long before the rebels turned on their leader. Bothwell had served their purpose; now it was time to get rid of him. Mary was urged to abandon her new husband to save herself, but she refused—for two reasons. She did not trust the conspirators to see her safely restored to her throne (she was right; they were already hastily forging documents to implicate her in Darnley's murder); and by now she realized she was pregnant.

On June 15, 1567, at Carberry Hill, Bothwell was deserted by his supporters, leaving him to face the rebels alone. He had enjoyed the perquisites of power for only five weeks. After a final, very public embrace with Mary, Bothwell galloped north toward Dunbar Castle to amass more troops. Mary never saw him again. The rebels took her prisoner as soon as the rear end of Bothwell's horse had faded from view.

"Burn her, burn the whore, she is not worthy to live!" The soldiers' taunts rang in the queen's tender ears as they conveyed her to Edinburgh. Her clothes were streaked with grime; her cheeks were hot with tears.

In Edinburgh, Mary was conveyed to a modest home owned by a brother-in-law of one of the conspirators. The following day, her unwashed hair streaming about her shoulders, her bodice so ripped that her breasts were nearly exposed, Mary stuck her head out of the window and begged her subjects to aid her. In the four weeks since she had been married to

Bothwell, she had endured humiliations she never could have imagined possible.

Mary was then taken to Lochleven Castle, a Douglas clan stronghold on an island so small there was little else on it but the castle keep. At Lochleven, Mary lived in less than genteel incarceration, although several members of the Douglas family were enchanted by her, eventually aiding her escape in 1568.

On June 16, 1567, the warrant for Mary's imprisonment was signed by a number of the rebels. The initial charges included the murder of Darnley (for which the conspirators themselves were guilty), and for governing her realm under Bothwell's undue influence. But it was hard to make the latter allegation stick with Bothwell out of the picture. Her captors pressured Mary to divorce Bothwell. Although she never loved the man, she feared the child she was carrying would be denounced as a bastard if she agreed to a divorce.

Confined indoors, Mary's health, already fragile, began to deteriorate even further. She miscarried on July 24, with some accounts referring to twin fetuses. She had been pregnant for approximately eight weeks. The only positive to be extracted from her sorrow was that there was no longer a reason to remain married to Bothwell.

On the day of Mary's miscarriage, Lord Lindsay brought her a sheaf of documents that would change history. "Sign them, or else the rebels will be compelled to slit your throat," Lord Lindsay threatened. Having lost a great deal of blood, under extreme duress, and in tremendous pain, Mary affixed her signature and resigned her crown, abdicating in favor of her infant son, James.

James VI, barely a year old, was crowned King of Scotland on July 29, 1567. Mary's bastard half brother, James Stewart, the Earl of Moray, was named regent.

Bothwell traveled north to Scandinavia in the hopes of raising another army. In Norway, a former paramour, Anna

Throndsen, accused him of never returning her dowry. Both-well was about to face imprisonment when the Danish king, Frederick, learned that he was wanted for Darnley's murder. Frederick brought Bothwell back to Denmark and threw him into the dank and remote fortress of Dragsholm Castle, where he remained for a decade, dying of madness in April 1578. As of the mid-1990s, his mummified body was still preserved under glass at Fårevejle Church, near Dragsholm.

James I of England
and Ireland (also
James VI of Scotland)

᯾

1566–1625
RULED SCOTLAND 1567–1625
RULED AS JAMES I OF ENGLAND AND IRELAND
1603–1625

*J*AMES STUART WAS THE ONLY CHILD OF MARY, QUEEN of Scots, and her useless wastrel of a husband Robert Darnley. He was crowned King of Scotland on July 29, 1567, when he was just thirteen months old, after a faction of rebel Protestant nobles forced his mother to abdicate in his favor. So James grew up parentless, raised as a strict Calvinist by a gaggle of regents with competing interests that sometimes escalated into violence. Though the young king preferred the sexual society of men, when he wed the fourteen-year-old Anne of Denmark in 1589, by all accounts James thought her very beautiful and was actually in love with her.

After his mother's death in 1587, James corresponded secretly with Queen Elizabeth and her ministers in the expectation that he would succeed the Virgin Queen. He was proclaimed King of England upon Elizabeth's death on March 24, 1603, and was crowned on July 11.

An avid peacemaker, James finally ended the fifteen-year war with Spain. He also tackled the perennial issue of religious tolerance (or lack thereof), brokering a sit-down between the Catholic bishops and the evangelical Puritans. His greatest legacy is the English-language translation of the Bible to which he lent his name. The Papists weren't too happy about it. A cabal of Roman Catholics conspired to blow up the Houses of Parliament. But their plan (referred to then as the Powder Treason, but now known as the Gunpowder Plot) was thwarted on the eve of destruction, when at midnight on November 4, 1605, one of the conspirators, Guy Fawkes, was discovered in the cellars of Parliament surrounded by barrels of gunpowder. The plotters were ultimately caught, tried, and executed.

The king was a talented scholar and a notable patron of the arts. During what would be known as the Jacobean Age, English drama and literature flourished.

Still, no matter how good a king he might be, to the English, James was a "double-other"—being both a Scot and a homosexual. James and his voluptuous blond queen had a rather unusual arrangement whereby Anne would vet James's favorites. Perhaps she sought to ensure that they were not dangerously grasping—or diseased. After all, James was still sleeping with her as well. She bore the king five children, three of whom survived, and by all accounts they had a relatively accommodating relationship, as far as royal marriages go.

So, does that make James *bi*sexual? Yes—and no. In the sixteenth century, gender identity was not viewed in today's black-and-white terms. Men of noble birth learned from the cradle that it was their dynastic responsibility to beget heirs.

Without someone to inherit their estates and the wealth they yielded, their line would become extinct and the lands and titles reapportioned to another family. For *kings*, ensuring the succession was an imperative, in order to prevent a civil war over the fate of the crown.

So *of course* James did his duty and fathered at least the requisite heir and a spare. But when it came to his preference of a lover for an extramarital affair, his choice was always a man.

James died of dysentery on March 27, 1625, at the age of fifty-eight. He was succeeded by his bellicose and divisive son, Charles I.

JAMES I OF ENGLAND AND IRELAND
(ALSO JAMES VI OF SCOTLAND)
and George Villiers, Duke of Buckingham 1592–1628

I desire only to live in this world for your sake . . . I had rather live banished in any part of the Earth with you than live a sorrowful widow's life without you . . . God bless you, my sweet child and wife, and grant that ye may ever be a comfort to your dear dad and husband.

These words were written to George Villiers, 1st Duke of Buckingham, by his devoted lover, King James—the same King James who lent his name to an English-language translation of the Bible.

Courtiers and clerics rhapsodized about Villiers's flawless good looks, his childlike face, and his long slender legs that put one in mind of a thoroughbred colt. Simon d'Ewes described

Villiers as "full of delicacy and handsome features; yea his hands and face seemed to me especially effeminate and curious." And Bishop Godfrey Goodman praised Buckingham's "very lovely complexion," adding that the king's favorite "was the handsomest bodied man of England; his limbs so well compacted, and his conversation so pleasing, and of so sweet a disposition."

George Villiers was the second son of a second marriage made by a Leicestershire knight whose family had come over with William the Conqueror. George's widowed mother stage-managed his court career, steering him directly into the lap of King James I. In his formal portraits, the russet-haired, red-bearded James appears tall and dashing. But by the time young George captured the king's fancy, James was an aging queen of forty-seven, obese, fidgety, and prematurely senile. His skinny legs couldn't support his massive bulk. His tongue was too big for his mouth and lolled when he spoke.

Long before he was married to Anne of Denmark, James's favorites were men. When he was thirteen years old he fell madly in love with the 6th Seigneur d'Aubigny, his cousin Esmé Stuart, a dashing, worldly older man, whom he openly (and frequently) kissed. He also appointed him to the highest positions of honor and prestige, creating him Duke of Lennox and First Gentleman of the Bedchamber—the position given to each of James's subsequent favorites. The First Gentleman slept in the same room as the king, and more important, controlled all access to the monarch. However, the duke's greatest claim to fame may be that he taught his young cousin how to drink—a pastime at which the king would excel for the remainder of his life, to the immense consternation and embarrassment of his queen.

"The King drinks so much, and conducts himself so ill in every respect that I expect an early and evil result," she lamented. In 1604, one year after he became King of England, she predicted that he only had a few good years left before his drinking would either kill him or turn him into an imbecile.

Lennox, James's imbibing instructor, ended up getting himself kidnapped by a cabal of envious nobles. He escaped and fled to France, where he died a year later, leaving instructions for his heart to be embalmed and sent to his seventeen-year-old royal lover.

He was replaced in James's favor by a handsome young courtier named Robert Carr, who drew the king's attention when he was injured in a tournament. The king sent his personal physician to heal the wounded combatant, and soothed his pains by making him Earl of Somerset and Lord Chamberlain, succeeding Lennox in that office.

A contemporary wrote of both Carr's and Villiers's effect on their sovereign lover: "Now, as no other reason appeared in favor of their choice but handsomeness, so the love the King shewed was as amorously conveyed as if he had mistaken their sex, and thought them ladies, which I have seene Sommerset and Buckingham labor to resemble in effeminateness of their dressings; though in W[horeson] lookes and wanton gestures, they exceeded any part of woman kind my conversation did ever cope withal."

In 1614, when he was first introduced to the king, the twenty-two-year-old George Villiers was devilishly handsome, with chestnut-colored locks cascading past his shoulders, a rakish Vandyke beard, and a mustache that curled insouciantly upward. Villiers seems to have been chosen for his role as the king's favorite by opponents of his former favorite, the Earl of Somerset, Robert Carr.

James fell in love with Villiers, loading him with honors, the first of which was appointing him cup bearer, a position previously held by Somerset. Then the king promoted Villiers through three ranks of the peerage in as many years, making him a viscount and Lord High Admiral in 1616, an earl in 1617, and a marquis in 1619. In 1623, on St. George's Day, April 23, James made his lover Duke of Buckingham and a Knight of the Garter.

Gobsmacked by his generosity, the newly made Buckingham told the king, "You have filled a consuming purse, given me fair houses, more land than I am worthy of . . . filled my coffers so full with patents of honor, that my shoulders cannot bear more."

To his courtiers, James's passion for Buckingham was obvious. Simon d'Ewes wrote in his diary that James was often wont to exclaim, "Becote [by God] George, I love thee dearly," and "Begott, man, never one loved another moore than I doe thee."

This affection was corroborated by George Gerrard, who wrote in 1617 that "the king was never more careful, or did more tenderly love any that he hath raised than this Lord of Buckingham."

The contemporary writer Théophile de Viau, who also happened to be gay, immortalized the relationship in his poem *"Au marquis de Boukinquan"*:

> Apollo *with his songs*
> *debauched young Hyacinthus,*
> *And it is well known that the king of England*
> *fucks the Duke of Buckingham.*

The love affair became a topic of international gossip. The Venetian ambassador wrote that James was a man "who has given him all his heart, who will not eat, sup, or remain an hour without him, and considers him his whole joy."

Monsieur Tillières, the French ambassador, claimed that James chose his favorites "not on the basis of any skill or talent in governance or statecraft, but instead, the king simply allowed himself to be carried away by his passion."

And in 1617, the Spanish ambassador reported to his sovereign that James had summoned his Privy Council and reiterated before them his preference for Buckingham above all others. This was not a "defect," James insisted, because, "just as 'Christ had his John; so have I my George.'"

The king's remark was *not* biblical heresy; it was gay code. James, and other cultured men of the day, would have been familiar with the plays of the popular (and probably gay) Elizabethan-era dramatist Christopher Marlowe (1564–1593), who had said that not only were Christ and John "bedfellows," but more specifically, that "he used him as the sinners of Sodoma."

Even if James's ministers didn't get the reference, James himself was having his own sly joke on them. His meaning was crystal clear, however, in 1619 when he christened a new ship *Buckingham's Entrance*. Apparently, the attendant giggles, snickers, and blushes were too much to withstand, and the vessel was renamed the *Happy Entrance*.

Interestingly, James's queen, Anne of Denmark, accepted her husband's passion for Villiers. In letters to the latter, she would ask George to promise to remain "always true" to her husband. When Queen Anne died on March 2, 1619, James did not remarry.

But in 1620, Buckingham did—a duty that was completely expected from a man of his rank and position, regardless of his sexual preferences outside of wedlock. Initially, the king had hoped that his lover's marriage would produce "sweet bedchamber boys to play me with," as he confided to George, but Lady Buckingham gave birth to a daughter, sparing everyone the skin-pebbling results of such a royal inclination. James ultimately (and chastely) delighted in his lover's wife and subsequent children, playing the role of benevolent uncle.

Over the years, Buckingham became a force to be reckoned with, and in the waning years of James's life, the duke solidified his power with the Prince of Wales, the future Charles I. In 1623, the two young men embarked on a diplomatic mission to Spain. James sent his lover passionate letters, lamenting,

Alas, I now repent me sore that ever I suffered you to go away. I care for match nor nothing, so I may once have you in my arms again. God grant it! God grant it! Amen, amen, amen.

The duke flirtatiously replied,

. . . my thoughts are only bent on having my dear Dad and Master's legs soon in my arms.

He also expressed the passionate desire to get "hold of your bed-post again." Of the myriad images conjured by this phrase, none are chaste.

When Buckingham and the Prince of Wales returned to English soil, they jointly encouraged King James to declare war on Spain. The king's ministers viewed his overweening pacifism as a defect, because it was considered effeminate—and effeminacy was but a hop, skip, and a jump from homosexuality. As it was, James's contemporaries were alarmed that his court was controlled by a gay mafia, and the licentiousness of the court undermined the subjects' respect for their sovereign.

Still, James refused to be dragged into the Thirty Years War, a conflict that had erupted in 1618 as a German civil war with factions either supporting or attacking the Hapsburg rulers. It was also a religious war among Catholics, Lutherans, and Calvinists.

Over the next couple of years, James grew increasingly ill and unable to attend to affairs of state. In 1625, he was plagued by attacks of arthritis, gout, and frequently recurring ague, and the business of running the kingdom was left to Charles and the Duke of Buckingham, who assiduously pressured James to enter the war. His health failing and his spirit flagging, James finally relented. After decades of effeminism and peace, war was looked on as "the most manly and English way." Buckingham, in his capacity as Lord Admiral, assumed the chief responsibility for England's disastrous entry into the conflict.

In early March, James was felled by an apoplectic fit; and in his weakened condition, an attack of dysentery claimed his life on March 27, 1625. He died in his bed at Theobald House with his beloved Buckingham at his side.

Buckingham then became a tremendous influence on the policies and strategies of the twenty-four-year-old Charles I. But a year after James's death, Parliament attempted to impeach the duke. The new king protected him, but in 1628 Parliament tried once more to oust him.

Later that year, while preparing to lead another naval expedition to the Continent, Buckingham was stabbed to death by John Felton, a disgruntled sailor. The killer claimed he had been encouraged to assassinate the duke by the collective anger over the disastrous condition of the economy and the unpopular Thirty Years War.

The ugly legacy left by James and his George includes England's lengthy involvement in a costly foreign war, engendering such widespread disillusion and unrest that it led to the overthrow of the monarchy by Oliver Cromwell.

CHARLES II

1630–1685
RULED 1660–1685

CHARLES WAS THE ELDEST SURVIVING SON OF CHARLES I
and Henrietta Maria of France. In the climactic event of the
English Civil War between the Parliamentarians (the "Roundheads") and the Cavaliers loyal to the crown (the "Royalists"),
his father was beheaded on January 30, 1649. Oliver Cromwell, the MP for Cambridge who had distinguished himself as
a leader of the Parliamentary forces, proclaimed himself Lord
Protector of the Realm. The period that followed, between the
execution of Charles I and the Restoration of Charles II, was
known as the Interregnum.

Charles II was crowned King of Scots at Scone on January 1,
1651, and attempted to regain his English title. But after his
defeat at the Battle of Worcester on September 3, he fled to the
Continent, spending the next nine years in France and in the
United Provinces of the Netherlands. There, he held court as
the exiled King of England, and his supporters continually
sought ways to restore him to his father's throne.

The Protectorate collapsed in 1659, and on May 23, 1660,

Charles sailed for England to reclaim his crown, triumphantly entering London on May 29, his thirtieth birthday.

In 1662, Charles married the Portuguese princess Catherine of Braganza, a tiny brunette who had the misfortune to fall in love with her handsome, philandering husband.

Charles's reign was marred by the Plague of 1665, which decimated the English population, and the Great Fire of London, which began on September 2, 1666, destroying more than thirteen thousand homes and eighty-seven churches in the city.

Politically, his rule was marked by a tug-of-war between Popish supporters and Anglicans. Plots and counterplots were hatched to assassinate Charles and crown his Catholic brother James, or to exclude James, and all Roman Catholics, from ever sitting on the English throne. Charles equivocated, unwilling to cut his own brother out of his rights of succession.

Charles died on February 6, 1685, and James did indeed succeed him without incident.

The Plague, the Great Fire, and the religious dissent notwithstanding, the most discussed subject of Charles II's Restoration is his prolific sex life. George Villiers, the witty, rakish 2nd Duke of Buckingham (and son of James I's favorite), once remarked, "A king is supposed to be the father of his people and Charles certainly was father to a good many of them."

He acknowledged and ennobled a total of seventeen children. Of the twenty-six dukes in England today, five of them are direct descendants of Charles II and his mistresses.

However, none of Charles's children were legitimate, and therefore the succession of his kingdom became the salient political issue of the day. It eventually led to the Glorious Revolution—in which Charles's brother, King James II, duked it out with his son-in-law William of Orange, *and lost*—and to the 1701 Act of Settlement, which prohibited a Catholic from sitting on the throne of England (or taking a Catholic as his or her consort).

That act is still in effect today.

♔

CHARLES II
and Lucy Walter 1630–1658

In the decade after his father, "the Royal Martyr" Charles I, was summarily beheaded at Whitehall, his son, the future Charles II, actively fought to claim his kingdom. But from the lengthy list of mistresses he accumulated during that time, the young prince appeared equally consumed with having sex as often as possible. According to one biographer, Charles was first seduced by the woman who had been his wet nurse. Between that liaison and his accession to the English throne in 1660, he had enjoyed the favors of no fewer than seventeen mistresses, starting with his first real love, the Welsh-born Lucy Walter, a noblewoman's daughter–turned-courtesan.

The chestnut-haired Lucy, whom the contemporary writer John Evelyn described as a "brown, beautiful, bold but insipid creature," was not bound by any political loyalties when it came to spreading her charms—the mistress of both Roundheads and Royalists. Regardless of civil strife, a girl's got to earn a living, after all.

Already a professional temptress, Lucy met Charles while he was in The Hague. The fruit of their passionate affair was the nineteen-year-old Charles's first child, James Crofts, whom he created Duke of Monmouth in 1653, when the boy was only four years old.

Because he would have been the legitimate Prince of Wales

had Lucy ever married Charles, the teenage Monmouth encouraged the rumor that there had been a secret wedding between his mother and the king, the marriage contract locked away in a black box. But during their affair, and even after his son's birth, Charles had apparently told Lucy he would never marry her and harbored no intentions of changing his mind.

Their royal affair lasted until 1651, the same year that Charles was crowned King of Scotland. Lucy, sometimes referring to herself as Mrs. Barlow, raised their son on her own until Charles's courtiers came to claim him from her in 1658.

Lucy died of syphilis that year, long discarded by Charles and likely forgotten by all except her son, whose entire adult existence was predicated on the precarious line he walked between pride and embarrassment at his lineage.

♔

CHARLES II
and Barbara Villiers, Lady Castlemaine, Duchess of Cleveland
1641–1709

If Charles and his younger brother James, the Duke of York, and their cabal of witty courtiers—Buckingham, Sedley, and Rochester—were the Restoration Rat Pack, then Barbara Villiers was their Ava Gardner, a tempestuous temptress, moody, alluring, and demanding. Her hair-trigger temper was as legendary as her sexual magnetism.

The auburn-haired beauty came from noble stock. Her father, Viscount Grandison, died in the service of King Charles I when Barbara was just a baby. Her first cousin George Villiers, the 2nd Duke of Buckingham, was a close confidant of Charles II.

Sexually precocious, Barbara began her courtesan's career at the age of fifteen as one of several lovers of the widowed Earl of Chesterfield, a man nearly twice her age. Their affair continued even after she wed Roger Palmer on April 14, 1659. The affluent, twenty-four-year-old Palmer belonged to a group of Royalist conspirators. In early 1660, the plotters needed an emissary to journey to the Netherlands, where Charles's itinerant court was living in exile. Required for more pressing business in England, Palmer could not be spared for the enterprise, and clever Barbara, all of eighteen years old, was chosen to go to Breda in her husband's stead.

It didn't take long for her to ensnare the twenty-nine-year-old Charles. The king became utterly smitten by her dazzling good looks and her outstanding amatory skills. By the time he returned to England to claim his throne, Barbara was well established as his mistress.

On Restoration Day, May 29, 1660, Barbara watched the all-male procession, more than twenty thousand strong, triumphantly make its way through London. Charles II spent his first night back at Whitehall in her arms. That evening, or quite soon after, Barbara became pregnant; their first child, Anne, was born on February 25, 1661.

Later that year, Roger Palmer was made Earl of Castlemaine, "the reason whereof everyone knows," wrote the contemporary diarist Samuel Pepys. Soon, Lady Castlemaine was pregnant again. Palmer was conveniently dispatched on diplomatic missions, but was just as routinely brought back to London each time his wife was about to give birth, an annual occurrence between 1661 and 1665.

Even during her advanced stages of pregnancy, Barbara shared her bed with Charles, whether from lust or the fear of losing her position to another mistress if she denied the king her charms for too many nights at a stretch. Barbara bore three sons and two daughters that were acknowledged and ennobled by the king, and during their eight-year affair, she amassed an enormous fortune, acquired any way she could get her hands on it.

With a bachelor king on the throne, Barbara was the uncontested prima donna at Whitehall. But Charles's ministers were pressing him to make a good marriage, to strengthen England's base of power against her usual enemies, France and Spain. Recognizing the importance of an alliance between Britain and Portugal, Charles settled on Catherine of Braganza.

Barbara was obviously none too thrilled. The last thing she wanted was for Charles to marry a beautiful princess who would give him a passel of legitimate children, thereby leaving her and her bastard brood to fend for themselves.

As it turned out, Barbara needn't have worried about the queen's beauty or her fertility. "She has nothing viable about her capable to make the king forget his inclinations to the Countess of Castlemaine, the finest woman of her age," wrote Sir John Reresby, who officially welcomed the new queen to English shores.

Catherine of Braganza arrived in Portsmouth from Portugal in 1662. She resembled a fragile sparrow, more childlike than womanly in appearance. Though her eyes sparkled with intelligence, buck teeth marred her smile and made her upper lip protrude. Her thick dark hair was dressed in the height of fashion—for Portugal—in tight clusters of curls that sprang like squarish wings from either side of her head, mirroring the image made by the old-fashioned farthingales on her hips.

"I thought they had brought me a bat instead of a woman," a shocked Charles wrote to his chancellor, the Earl of Clarendon. Yet the king was determined to be loyal to his odd little wife, whom he actually fancied—sort of—remarking to Clarendon, "I am confident never two humours were better fitted together than ours are . . . I must be the worst man living (which I hope I am not) if I be not a good husband."

The thought was not father to the deed, however. Charles could never deny himself Barbara's charms for very long, no matter how much she drove him crazy and how often he tried to dump her. The king admitted that he was "no atheist but [he] could not think God would make a man miserable for taking a little pleasure out of the way."

And Barbara certainly knew how to provide it. It was said that she was expertly versed in all the erotic tricks illustrated in Pietro Aretino's banned book of sixteen sonnets, an Italian Renaissance *Kama Sutra* of sorts. She was an utterly confirmed voluptuary, the rare female rake.

So enamored of Barbara was Charles that he had spent the entire first week of Catherine's arrival at Barbara's King Street residence while his bride-to-be cooled her heels amongst a bunch of courtiers in Portsmouth. Across the land, church bells pealed and bonfires were lit in celebration, but there was no fire outside Barbara's London home, even though the king was inside it.

Barbara's brazenness knew no bounds. On the day of the royal wedding, she hung up her lingerie to dry on palace grounds for all the world to see, a gesture that titillated Pepys, who wrote on May 21, 1662, ". . . in the Privy-garden saw the finest smocks and linnen petticoats of my Lady Castlemayne's laced with rich lace at the bottom, that ever I saw, and it did me good to look upon them."

Barbara was heavily pregnant with her second child by Charles. She insisted on the privilege of giving birth at Hampton Court, a deliberate power grab intended to upstage the new queen's arrival and redirect the court's focus to the royal mistress's favor and fecundity. Barbara badgered, threatened, hectored, and cajoled until the reluctant Charles relented.

Now twenty-one, Barbara had been Charles's mistress for nearly two years. Aware that she would inevitably lose some ground now that Charles had married Catherine, she extracted his promise to appoint her as one of the Ladies of the Queen's Bedchamber, the highest honor a lady of the court could achieve. However, the twenty-three-year-old Catherine had been warned by her mother not to tolerate Lady Castlemaine's presence at court—and, in fact, to insist that all of the king's mistresses be dismissed from Whitehall.

As Charles presented a number of ladies to their new queen, he slipped Barbara in among them. Catherine extended her tiny hand and a warm smile to the stunning woman curtsying before her. But as Charles uttered the words, "My Lady Castlemaine," Catherine, registering the connection, made a strangled gasp for air, and fell back into a dead faint, blood gushing from her nose.

Charles did not even follow the pair of servants who bore the stricken queen to her chamber. Poor Catherine's reaction had made him cross. A struggle then ensued over Barbara's appointment as a Lady of the Queen's Bedchamber. According to custom, Charles presented Catherine with a list of possible candidates for her approval. The queen promptly struck Barbara's name from it. The king presented the list again, and once more, Catherine vigorously crossed off his mistress's name.

Charles issued a lengthy statement, insisting that "my wife shall never have cause to complain that I broke my vows to her if she will live towards me as a good wife ought to do, in rendering herself grateful and acceptable to me, which it is in her power to do. But if she continues uneasy to me I cannot answer for myself that I shall not endeavor to seek other company."

Catherine's temperament would not suffer such indignities. "The king's insistence upon that particular can proceed from no other ground but his hatred of my person. He wishes to expose me to the contempt of the world. And the world will think me deserving of such an affront if I submit to it." She then threatened to board the next boat for Lisbon.

In retaliation, Charles dismissed Catherine's train of somber

Portuguese ladies and musty-robed monks, leaving her with a handful of servants chosen at his pleasure, none of whom spoke her language.

Barbara had scored another triumph.

In the early 1660s, Barbara reveled in the knowledge that Charles was still in the first flush of his infatuation for her. "The lewdest, as well as the fairest of his concubines," anything she requested, no matter how great or petty, was hers. If a minister dared refuse her demands, Charles made it clear that an enemy of Barbara's was an enemy of the crown.

One man who dared to test the king's policy was his chancellor, Edward Hyde, Earl of Clarendon. Clarendon refused to recognize Barbara's elevated position as *maîtresse en titre* and would not seal any document that bore her name. All royal patents and warrants passed through Clarendon's hands, and as long as he was chancellor, Barbara would not be granted a single English title—which was why Roger Palmer was created Earl of Castlemaine, an Irish peerage.

Having had enough of public cuckoldry, Palmer managed to secure a legal deed of separation, indemnifying himself for up to £10,000 (currently more than $1.8 million) against her debts. Husband and wife met publicly for the last time in August 1662, at Whitehall, where they watched the king and queen make their state entry into London via river from Hampton Court.

As time went on, Barbara's promiscuity and her infidelity to her royal lover became well known at court. The Bishop of Salisbury remarked that Barbara was "most vicious and ravenous, foolish but imperious, very uneasy with the king, and always carrying on intrigues with other men."

She was once accosted by two masked courtiers in St. James's Park, who called her a "vile whore," adding that she was likely to suffer the same fate as Jane Shore, the mistress of Edward IV—who, legend had it, died on a dung heap. And when a group of disgruntled apprentices razed a number of London brothels, the cry went up to pull down the biggest stew of them all—Whitehall Palace.

Charles finally refused to acknowledge Barbara's sixth child, a daughter, whose father might have been Henry Jermyn, the dwarfish Earl of St. Albans—or John Churchill, a handsome youth who would go on to a distinguished military career, earning him the title Duke of Marlborough. However, Barbara was not one to let a dodgy paternity stand in the way of her rage for honors and titles—for her children as well as for herself. Well aware that her emotional blackmail always worked on Charles, late in her pregnancy Barbara threatened the king with everything from public humiliation to infanticide. "God damn me, but you shall own it!" she shrieked. "I will have it christened in the Chapel at Whitehall and owned as yours . . . or I will bring it into Whitehall gallery and dash its brains out before your face."

Charles stood his ground, convinced the child was not his, but Barbara's sexual power was like a drug, and he was hopelessly addicted. Two weeks later, the lovers were hot and heavy again. Barbara made the *king* kneel before *her* and promise never more to offend her in the same way.

In 1666, the same year that the Great Fire destroyed a third of London, the Royal Navy was given worthless chits instead of pay, but £30,000 (approximately $6.4 million today) of Barbara's debts for purchases of jewelry and gold and silver plate were cleared by the king. Barbara then greedily helped herself to the treasures of the Jewel House at the Tower of London, signing documents that promised their safe return. But as always, she managed to turn the loan into a royal gift.

Two years later, in an effort to silence her clamoring for more wealth, Charles gave Barbara Berkshire House, which also effectively removed her presence from Whitehall. Barbara named the residence Cleveland House in 1670 when Charles ennobled her further, creating her Baroness Nonsuch, Countess of Southampton, and Duchess of Cleveland. These honors were bestowed "in consideration of her noble descent, her father's death in the service of the Crown, and by reason of her personal virtues." There was another reason not stated in the warrant: Charles was about to install a new mistress, the orange-girl-turned-actress Nell Gwyn, in a posh town house in Pall Mall, and the insanely jealous Barbara required further proof of Charles's devotion.

Of course Barbara required the funds to sustain her new titles, so she demolished the spectacular Palace of Nonsuch, which had been built by Henry VIII. The exotic pinnacles and turrets and the lavish plasterwork and intricate carvings were dismantled and sold for scrap.

Dipping her grasping hand into every possible pot, she amassed annual revenues totaling as much as £43,200 ($10.6 million today) from various excises and taxes, along with a raft of leases and real estate. And during the 1660s and 1670s, she made at least an additional £15,000 (nearly $3.7 million) a year through influence peddling and selling offices.

Barbara entertained her own cabal of courtiers to pursue her personal agendas, though the political advice she often gave the king proved wildly unpopular because it was always self-aggrandizing. And she routinely pushed through the appointments of men who would be in a position to steer more wealth and influence her way.

John Wilmot, the Earl of Rochester, who skewered his contemporaries with his wicked wit, continually lambasted Barbara's avarice and rapacity:

> Castlemaine is much to be admir'd
> Although she ne'er was satisfied or tired.
> Full forty men a day provided for this whore,
> Yet like a bitch she wags her tail for more.

Whenever Charles took up with another mistress, Barbara would avenge herself with other men, flaunting their liaison in public. After the king pensioned her off, Barbara took as her paramour Charles Hart, an actor from the King's Theatre who had been Nell Gwyn's lover on *her* way *up* the social ladder. Barbara's other subsequent bedfellows included a studly footman with whom she shared a bath; Jacob Hall, a rope dancer with the flexibility of a contortionist, whom she seduced in his booth at Bartholomew Fair; and the celebrated playwright William Wycherly. Yet from time to time over the years Barbara and Charles would reignite their passion. More than any of his other mistresses, she understood the nature of his character, his need for variety and excitement sexually; in that respect they were very much alike.

Occasionally, Barbara was caught in the act. Once, when the king surprised her with a visit, she had to send the gnomelike Henry Jermyn crawling under her bed. And one morning, after Barbara had just spent the night with John Churchill, Charles made another startling appearance in her boudoir. As Churchill endeavored to sneak out the window, Charles phlegmatically quipped, "I forgive you, for you do it for your bread."

Though Barbara regularly raped the Royal Treasury, she was perpetually short of funds. She was a compulsive gambler, and also footed the bill for her string of low-rent lovers. But after Lord Treasurer Danby clamped down on Treasury funds going to royal mistresses, Barbara received only £6,000 (now nearly $1.5 million) a year for life, plus £3,000 apiece for each of her royal bastards.

After 1670, when the baby-faced Bretonne Louise de Kéroualle became the king's new *maîtresse en titre*, their passion began to cool. In 1676, Barbara went to live in Paris, consoling herself with a bouquet of posh French lovers. She briefly returned to London in 1679 for the wedding of one of her sons. She took the opportunity to launch a final raid on the Treasury, filching £25,000 (over $6.2 million today) after a fight with the acting Lord Treasurer, the Earl of Essex, who told Charles he would rather be dismissed from his position than pay Barbara the funds she demanded. Charles took him at his word, and a new Lord Treasurer was installed who had no qualms about releasing vast sums of money to the king's former paramour.

By March of 1684, Barbara had returned to London for good, and had once more taken up residence in Cleveland House opposite St. James's Palace. Her live-in lover was the handsome and devilishly sexy Cardonell "Scum" Goodman, an actor at the King's Theatre and sometime highwayman.

On his deathbed in February 1685, Charles seemed to have forgiven Barbara for all her bad behavior, whispering to the Duke of York, "Be kind to the Duchess of Cleveland. . . ."

Soon after the king's demise, Barbara plummeted into debt, descending below the ranks of the demimonde into the shadow world of thieves and sharpers. Ever the nymphomaniac, her judgment was often impaired by her hormones.

In 1705, her husband, Roger Palmer, died at his mother's estate in Wales, and that November 25, the sixty-four-year-old Barbara wed Robert "Beau" Feilding, who was several years her junior. He also turned out to be a bigamist.

Beau was tried and convicted the following year, but was ultimately pardoned by Queen Anne. He returned to Barbara and began selling off her valuables and household effects. When she protested, he beat her, locked her in a room, and starved her until she acquiesced to his plunder of her property. Abused physically, mentally, and emotionally, during one such thrashing Barbara literally cried "Murder!" and finally got the attention of the neighbors. Her grandson, the Duke of Grafton, intervened and Beau was carted off to Newgate. On his release, he took up with the wife he had married not two weeks before he wed Barbara.

In 1709, Barbara contracted dropsy. The accumulation of

fluid beneath her skin swelled her body to the size of a beached whale. She died on October 9 at the age of sixty-eight, the disease having obliterated what remained of her once-spectacular beauty.

CHARLES II

and Frances Teresa Stuart 1647–1702

Frances Stuart created a scandal by just saying no, becoming the embodiment of an empire without ever yielding her body.

Her father, a distant relative of the Stuart monarchs, had been a physician in the court of Charles I. He managed to get his family safely to France after the beheading of his sovereign; and from her infancy, Frances was raised across the Channel in the court of Louis XIV.

Charles II's sister "Minette," who was married to Louis's brother the duc d'Orleans, sent the fourteen-year-old Frances back to England to serve as a maid of honor at Charles's wedding to Catherine of Braganza on May 21, 1662. After the ceremonies, Frances was asked to remain in England as a lady-in-waiting to the new queen.

Her remarkable beauty, in a court known for its plethora of pretty faces, earned Frances an extraordinary measure of adoration. The popular poet-playwright John Dryden praised her looks in verse. And Samuel Pepys, the ultimate seventeenth-century eyewitness, rhapsodized about her in his diary:

> . . . *into the Queen's presence, where all the ladies walked, talking and fiddling with their hats and feathers, and*

*changing and trying one another's by one another's heads,
and laughing. . . . But, above all, Mrs. Stewart [sic] in this
dress, with her hat cocked and a red plume, with her sweet
eye, little Roman nose, and excellent taille, is now the
greatest beauty I ever saw, I think, in my life; and, if ever
woman can, do exceed my Lady Castlemaine, at least in
this dress nor do I wonder if the King changes, which I
verily believe is the reason of his coldness to my Lady
Castlemaine.*

In the same entry, Pepys fantasized about making love with
her!

*So home to supper and to bed, before I sleep fancying my-
self to sport with Mrs. Stuart with great pleasure.*

Before long, Frances had earned the nickname *"La Belle
Stuart,"* and the king was curly head over cavalier boots infatuated with her. Charles installed her at Whitehall in the rooms
just below his own. How convenient for His Majesty—who
had Barbara Castlemaine in the apartment just above his! In
fact, the only time Charles did not cave in to Barbara's she-
nanigans was when she banished the beautiful Frances from
her rooms, where the king would visit nightly for lively conversation. Charles darkly warned Barbara that if Frances wasn't
there the next time he came upstairs, he would have nothing
more to do with her.

Though La Belle Stuart gave some of her contemporaries the
impression that she was a bit of a bubblehead, she was probably just a wildly romantic young girl in a nest of cynics. And, in
fact, she kept her head about her when all around her seemed
to be indiscriminately opening their legs.

Already a popular girl with the courtiers and the queen,
Frances gently told her sovereign that she was saving herself

for marriage, which had the effect of rousing his lust even more. Having spent her girlhood in the French court, she knew how to flirt and tease, but that was as far as things would go. With the pick of the handsomest cavaliers in England at her feet, she intended to wed for love. And why jeopardize her position in the queen's train by incurring Catherine's anger unnecessarily? Frances had observed enough of the lusty court to know how to play the game; in fact, she was a cannier player than most, despite the fact that she seemed to spend the bulk of her time at Whitehall building houses of playing cards.

Barbara Castlemaine often pimped for her royal lover when she realized that the king was tiring of her demanding antics; yet she needed to be certain that any new conquest would be pliant enough to let her continue to pull the strings. Soon after Frances came to England, Barbara had sought to get the girl into his bed by staging a mock marriage between the two ladies, where Charles leapt into the breach at the moment of "consummation." According to Pepys's diary,

> . . . my Lady Castlemaine, a few days since, had Mrs. Stuart to an entertainment, and at night began a frolique that they two must be married, and married they were, with ring and all other ceremonies of church service, and ribbands and a sack posset in bed, and flinging the stocking [much like our custom of tossing the bouquet]; but in the close, it is said that my Lady Castlemaine, who was the bridegroom, rose, and the King came and took her place with pretty Mrs. Stuart.

A year after Frances came to court, her mistress was taken gravely ill, and many feared the queen would die. Pepys, with his finger on the court's pulse, wrote on November 9, 1663:

... The king is now become besotted upon Mrs. Stuart, that he gets into corners and will be with her half an hour together kissing her to the observation of all the world; and she now stays by herself and expects it, as my Lady Castlemaine used to do. ... But yet it is thought that this new wench is so subtle, that she lets him not do anything than is safe to her, but yet his doting is so great that, Pierce [the royal surgeon] tells me, it is verily thought if the Queene had died, he would have married her.

But the queen survived the fever and Charles continued to woo Frances, bestowing upon her an honor that no other royal mistress had ever gained. In 1664, to celebrate English naval victories over the Dutch fleet, Charles had commemorative medals struck, featuring the face of Frances Stuart as the personification of the realm. Samuel Pepys observed,

At my goldsmith's did observe the King's new medal ... there is Mrs. Stewart's face as well done as ever I saw anything in my whole life, I think: and a pretty thing it is, that he should choose her face to represent Britannia by.

For the next couple of years, Frances seemed content to do no more than flirt and tease (despite Pepys's diary entry of April 15, 1666, where he wrote—having gleaned the gossip from Pierce, the royal surgeon—"for certain Mrs. Stuart do do everything with the king that a mistress should do"). The more La Belle Stuart was adamant about keeping her maidenhead to herself, the more ardent grew the monarch. But it was also clear that despite the queen's inability to bear children, Charles had no intention of divorcing her. So Frances was faced with two choices: succumb and become another royal mistress (with the certainty that the king would tire of her eventually, especially when age and beauty began to fade), or find a husband with whom she could live happily ever after.

In March 1667, the twenty-year-old Frances snagged herself another Charles Stuart—the 3rd Duke of Richmond and 6th Duke of Lennox. When the king got wind of their wedding plans, like a jilted lover he sought a way to thwart the match. Frances and her swain outwitted Charles by eloping.

He took his revenge by dispatching Frances's new husband to the Continent on numerous far-flung diplomatic missions. Although Charles swore he would have nothing whatever to do with Frances from then on, when she was infected with smallpox in 1669, he knelt at the new duchess's bedside and forgave her for marrying without his consent. Frances survived the disease and Charles elevated her status to Lady of the Queen's Bedchamber. For retaining her dignity as well as her virginity in the face of such a skilled assault upon it, Frances may be the only one of Charles II's mistresses to have earned the full measure of respect from his queen and court.

In 1672, when Frances's husband died without issue at the age of thirty-four, his estates reverted to the crown; but Charles pensioned off Frances with £1,000 (roughly $258,000 today) per annum for life. She invested her earnings wisely, eventually purchasing an estate in Scotland, which in her late husband's honor she renamed Lennoxlove. She died in 1702.

In many ways, the lovely Scots lass proved more immortal than the monarch. When coinage was introduced as a form of currency, Frances's image from the victory medals was chosen to represent the realm; she remained the face of Britannia for three centuries, her profile gracing every English penny until 1971.

CHARLES II
and Nell Gwyn 1650–1687

The brave and witty know no fear or sorrow.
Let us enjoy today, we'll die tomorrow.

—APHRA BEHN, 1660s

That couplet was written by a popular playwright and a dear friend of the actress-turned-royal-mistress Nell Gwyn. It sums up Nell's vivacious spirit as well as the merry licentiousness of the Restoration. When Charles II was crowned in 1660, the kingdom joyously cast off the repressive shroud of Puritanism and the pendulum swung wildly in the opposite direction. It was time to party—and no woman better embodied the ethos of the era than "pretty, witty Nell Gwyn," as the king's friend and noted diarist Samuel Pepys had dubbed her.

To say that Nell was lowborn is to sugarcoat her childhood. Although her birthplace is disputable, with three locations (London, Oxford, and Hereford) each claiming paternity, she grew up in Coal Yard Alley amid the London slums. Her father, who had been jailed in Oxford for being a Royalist, died in prison, most likely a debtor as well. Nell's mother, a beauty reduced by hard luck and hard times to an obese, brandy-swilling soak, sold ale at Mrs. Ross's in Drury Lane. Nell used to tell people that she was "brought up in a bawdy house to bring strong waters to the gentlemen."

With her flame-colored curls streaked with gold, her oft-praised dainty feet, her flawless peaches-and-cream complexion, perfect teeth hidden by a full and sensuous mouth that poets swooned over, and hazel-green eyes framed by soft brown brows, Nell was a petite, yet voluptuous, spitfire. She had an infectious laugh, an earthy sense of humor, swore like a sailor; and, though illiterate and uneducated, had a lightning-quick wit. Her secret girlhood crush was the new king, twenty years her senior, six feet two, and swarthy with blazingly intelligent black eyes, a dashing mustache gracing the upper lip of a sexily sardonic mouth. He also disdained wigs, because he didn't need them with his head of inky black curls that tumbled past his shoulders.

Upon his accession, Charles immediately set about reopening the theatres that the Lord Protector, Oliver Cromwell, had shut down. Charles had tapped Thomas Killigrew to form a company in the king's name and it was at the new King's House in Drury Lane that the twelve-year-old Nell and her older sister Rose got jobs hawking oranges to the gallants in the pit, honing their skills at flirtation and witty repartee. Rose followed the predictable trajectory for such a pursuit and ended up a prostitute.

But Nell's destiny would be somewhat different. After eighteen months, the theatre manager, impressed with Nell's pluck, asked her if she'd ever considered taking acting lessons.

In March 1665, the fifteen-year-old Nell, having been coached by Shakespeare's great-nephew Charles Hart, made her stage debut in Dryden's *The Indian Emperor*. Her performance was an instant success, leading to Nell's prompt receipt of an invitation to join the company.

Nell not only possessed a strong, clear voice that could be heard above the rowdiest crowd, but had an effortless gift for mimicry and improvisation and matchless comic timing. Her vitality was contagious. By the end of 1666, "Sweet Nell of Old Drury," as she was affectionately called, was the indisputable queen of the London stage.

One early evening in April 1668, after watching a performance of *She Wou'd If She Cou'd*, Nell and her date repaired to a nearby tavern. Dining there was the king himself and his brother James, the dour Duke of York (who Nell called "Dismal Jimmy"). The royals invited Nell and her friend to join them. When the bill came, neither the monarch nor the duke had the means to pay it. Nell suddenly found herself stuck with the tab.

Making as much light as possible of her predicament by employing the king's favorite expression, Nell cried, "Od's fish, this is the poorest company I ever was in!"

The king, utterly charmed, laughed uproariously. Nell had made a conquest for life. Her life, anyway.

The illiterate actress and the erudite, worldly sovereign found common ground in myriad ways, drawn to each other by a mutual passion for the theatre, a shared ribald sense of humor, and a love of sport and the outdoors. Charles had great respect for honesty, and in a world of perfumed artifice, Nell's was a bracing tonic. Above all, their royal affair was born of an ever-deepening friendship, which can't be said about any of Charles's other mistresses.

Aphra Behn told Nell, "You glad the hearts of all that have the happy fortune to see you, as if you were made on purpose to put the whole world into good humor." No wonder Nell captured the heart of a king.

The only one of his harem to genuinely love the countryside, Nell had Charles all to herself each summer when the court went to Newmarket for the races, and for hunting, fishing, and hawking. There, the lovers could almost pretend they were man and wife in a pastoral Arcadia. Charles, who had learned as a youth to conceal his true emotions, allowed himself to feel vulnerable around Nell. And she made him laugh, a gift that can never be underestimated.

With Charles, Nell felt appreciated and adored. He was her best friend and there was nothing she wouldn't do to please him, even if it meant sharing his affection with other mistresses. Still, Nell acknowledged that her position was precarious, and necessitated some sort of insurance policy. To that end, she didn't quit the stage for the first three years of her royal affair. She even returned to the theatre soon after giving birth on May 8, 1670, to their first child, Charles. It sent a clear message to her adoring public that the monarch was not providing them with enough to live on. In February 1671, the king, publicly shamed, ensconced Nell and their baby in a fashionable town house at 79 Pall Mall, which he paid for and furnished.

She was soon pregnant again, and on Christmas Day 1671, she gave birth to their second child, James, the king's eighth son by five different mothers. That year, at age twenty-one, Nell finally retired from the stage.

Soon, it was common knowledge that a person had to visit "Mrs. Neslie" if they wanted the ear of the king. Charles trusted Nell implicitly, fully aware that she was looking out for his interests in preference to her own. Foreign ambassadors adored her. Because Nell herself was of the people, she kept her lover connected with the needs of his subjects. And yet it was her low birth that precluded her from becoming his *maîtresse en titre*.

However, noblewomen who felt compelled to accept Charles's other mistresses, such as Barbara Castlemaine and the French Louise de Kéroualle, because they were wellborn ladies, refused to be in the same room with Nell. Nell would on occasion lament her outcast state to her lover, who tried to ameliorate matters by letting the hypocritical biddies know that "those he lay with were fit company for the greatest woman in the land."

To the lower classes she became a cult heroine. Nell was the goddess of the guttersnipes, as close to a queen as one of their own could ever aspire. The tradesmen adored her because she was the only one of the king's mistresses who always paid her bills promptly. And there were others who countenanced Nell's presence in their king's bed more easily than that of his Papist mistress Louise de Kéroualle. At least Nell was a Protestant. In 1681, during a time of open anti-Catholic sentiment, Nell's coach was stopped in an Oxford street by a mob who believed the passenger to be the detested Louise. The shade was lifted and out of the window popped Nell's pretty face amid a profusion of red curls. "Pray good people, be civil. I am the *Protestant* whore!" she cheerily announced, turning the jeers of the angry swarm into a rousing chorus of cheers.

Though Nell wasn't above competition, she always had a sense of fun about it—the sexy jester of the Restoration court, popping people's pretensions like balloons. She was particularly adept at affecting Louise de Kéroualle's lisping French accent, deliberately mangling her surname into the decidedly prosaic "Cartwheel." Nell's imitation of her continental rival (who she nicknamed "Squintabella" because of the slight cast to one of Louise's eyes) even had bishops in stitches. Louise also had the annoying habit of turning on the crocodile tears at the drop of a hat, earning her another nickname from Nell—"the Weeping Willow."

When Louise de Kéroualle had a portrait of herself painted in a revealing white shift, with her son (by Charles), portrayed as Cupid, hovering in the background, Nell commissioned a portrait of herself in the same pose and garment— flanked by her *two* cherubic royal bastards.

The Frenchwoman's penchant for donning mourning whenever a noble personage (of any nationality) passed away was another affectation mocked by Nell when she threw on widow's weeds and announced to the court that she was mourning the death of a wildly obscure potentate, the Cham of Tartary.

One afternoon Barbara Castlemaine (who by that time was sleeping with the playwright William Wycherly) flaunted her royal bounty by ostentatiously parading in front of Nell's house in her lavish coach pulled by three teams of horses. The following day, Nell (though she envied Barbara's expensive equipage) put the powerful mistress in her rightful place. She drove back and forth in front of Castlemaine's home in a rickety oxcart drawn by three teams of cattle, calling out at orangeseller volume, "Whores to market, ho!"

Charles's other mistresses didn't appreciate being mocked, but the king loved her sense of mischief. Surprisingly, he even found it refreshing when *he* was the butt of her pranks. One sultry evening, Nell suggested a fishing party. Though her idea appeared spontaneous, in fact, she'd had it all planned out, complete with silken fishing nets and gold hooks. But as the merriment progressed, the king became visibly peeved that he had not caught anything. When he wasn't looking, Nell dived into their picnic hamper and pulled out a string of fried smelts, which she managed to attach to his rod, then sweetly suggested to her lover that he check his line. The astonished monarch laughed uproariously when he realized what Nell had done. Baronne d'Aulnoy, an eyewitness to the event, wrote that Nell told the king, "It was only right that a great king should have unusual privileges. A poor fisherman could only take fish alive, but His Majesty caught them ready to eat!"

Nell was furious that Charles had bestowed a title on his French mistress. Louise, the new Duchess of Portsmouth, knew it and lorded it over her rival. Though Charles had, from time to time, hinted that he would ennoble Nell, his treasurer, Lord Danby, insisted that to elevate an orange-girl would upend the entire class system, challenging the entire notion of an aristocracy. Much as the king might desire to compensate Nell with a title, the Establishment would never countenance it.

Despite her disappointment, Nell petitioned Charles for something approaching equal compensation. Charles pleaded poverty. After all, the war with France was costly. All the more reason not to have given an English title to a French whore, thought Nell. "I shall tell you how you shall never want," she fumed. "Send the French into France again, set me on the stage again, and lock up your own codpiece!"

Unfortunately, the king did not take her advice.

After ennobling Louise de Kéroualle's three-year-old royal bastard as the Duke of Richmond, to appease the unhappy, slighted Nell (whose own royal bastards had received no titles), Charles made her a Lady of the Queen's Bedchamber—a prestigious honor, though it might have been the queen's idea and not Charles's, to throw the baseborn Nell a bone. Nell was the only one of Charles's mistresses whom the tiny, fragile Catherine actually liked. Having already resigned herself to her husband's numerous affairs, perhaps Her Majesty acknowledged that she and Nell were the only women at court who really did have the king's interests at heart.

Another thing that set Nell apart from Charles's other mistresses was that she never meddled in state affairs. Nell happily admitted her ignorance on such subjects, perfectly aware that the role she played in the king's life was that of a sexy pleasure giver, not a political adviser, "the sleeping partner on the ship of state." No doubt the "Merry Monarch's" ministers were very grateful for her self-awareness and wished that more of Charles's mistresses had felt the same way. In the words of a popular ditty from the 1670s:

> Hard by Pall Mall lives a wench call'd Nell
> King Charles the Second he kept her.
> She hath got a trick to handle his prick
> But never lays hands on his scepter.

The only time Nell took such matters into her own clever hands was when she thought Charles should be sensitive to the mood of his people and pay more attention to running the country. After the king had been neglecting to attend Council meetings, which was costing him both support and respect, Nell, who always had her lover's interests at heart before her own, bet the Duke of Lauderdale £100 (almost $25,000 today) that she would have better luck than His Grace in lighting a fire under the king.

She then summoned her former employer and mentor Tom Killigrew and coached him in his role. A day or two later, the old actor-manager burst into the King's Closet in full traveling costume.

The startled Charles exclaimed, "What, Killigrew, where are you going in such a violent hurry?"

"To hell," Killigrew replied, panting, "to fetch up Oliver Cromwell to look after the affairs of England, for his successor never will."

Nell's scheme worked.

Though Barbara Castlemaine's numerous royal bastards were given titles (which their mother fought and scratched to obtain), Nell's two sons by the king were, in her own words, "princes by their father for their elevation, but they had a whore to their mother for their humiliation." In fact, the boys had never even enjoyed a surname!

Nell wasn't happy about it.

One day when Charles paid her a visit, Nell hammered home her point. Her way of informing their six-year-old son that his father had arrived was to shout into the next room, "Come hither, you little bastard!" Charles was appalled. But Nell's remark achieved the desired result. On December 27, 1676, her paramour signed a royal patent, granting little Charles the titles of Baron Heddington, Earl of Burford—and in 1684, the boy was made Duke of St. Albans. He ended up living better than his mother did, with apartments in Whitehall and an allowance of £1,500 (today more than $367,000) a year. Among all seventeen of Charles's royal bastards, Nell's Charles was always a favorite of the king.

In January 1677, little James was given the title Lord James Beauclerk, the surname King Charles chose for both boys.

It was perhaps the best the king could do—but it wasn't parity. Still, Nell retained her sense of humor and consoled herself by cheerfully reminding her aristocratic rivals that when all was said and done, they were providing the same service to the king.

Yet Nell did ultimately convince Charles to give her the free-hold of 79 Pall Mall, where she was a popular hostess, and where Charles so often met his ministers and foreign emissaries to conduct affairs of state. After all, Nell teased, she deserved the freehold because she "had always offered [her] services for free under the crown!" Though her £4,000 (nearly $1 million) pension was a fraction of her rivals' allowances, Charles did give (and built for) Nell a number of houses, as well as a passel of Irish properties, from which Nell derived an income during her lifetime.

And because she was the mother of an earl, she was accorded the status (though not the title) of a lady and entitled to receive a coat of arms. Nell immediately had it applied to her vast services of silver plate.

The year 1679 was a particularly devastating one for Nell. Her mother died after falling into a ditch in a drunken stupor; and typical of Nell's loving heart, she honored the fat old bag with a lavish funeral. Later that year, Nell's younger son, James, who had been sent off to France to be educated, died, purport-edly "of a bad leg." Nell thought the cause of death preposter-ous and was certain that Louise de Kéroualle had somehow contrived to have the boy poisoned.

Endeavoring to cheer and console her, Charles built his little Nelly a house just inside the grounds of Windsor Castle, where rumor had it that a secret tunnel connected Burford House with the king's own apartments. Together the lovers poured their energies into improvements to Windsor, adding tennis courts, an orangery, and a bowling alley. Because Nell loved hawking, Charles made their surviving son Master of the Hawks and Grand Falconer, a sinecure the future Dukes of St. Albans would enjoy for centuries. And on June 11, 1679, a royal warrant reaffirmed Nell's pension.

On February 1, 1685, Charles spent the evening in the company of Nell and his other mistresses, past and present. The following morning, Nell's thirty-fifth birthday, while he was waiting to be shaved, the king's eyes suddenly rolled back into his head, he began foaming at the mouth, and he slipped off the chair, hitting the floor with a heavy thud.

When Nell heard the news, she came running to Whitehall, but the Establishment had already surrounded the monarch and, in case he was about to die, refused to allow a fallen woman to sully his royal presence. For the next four days, as the king swung from violent convulsions to periods of lucid tranquility, his team of physicians tried every medical method in the book to revive his health. But all the bleeding, cupping, purges, purgatives, and quack remedies did not avail. Nell was desperate for news of her lover's condition. As a duke, their son was permitted to be present (along with the king's other ennobled illegitimate children), and he reported back to his frantic mother on the monarch's progress.

During the king's final hours, he bestowed on their son the ring that the boy's paternal grandfather, Charles I, wore on the scaffold the day he was executed—the ring the king had passed to Bishop Juxon for safekeeping, and which the bishop had ultimately given to the future Charles II. In fact, Charles had worn the ring during his triumphant Restoration Day procession through London on his thirtieth birthday, May 29, 1660. If ever there was an indication of Charles's preference for Nell above all other mistresses, it was his gift of this most personal, and most treasured, possession to their only surviving son.

On Charles's deathbed he was said to have told his brother James, "Let not poor Nelly starve." Romantic last words perhaps, but those who adore Nell Gwyn's unique spark and her insatiable vitality might argue that Charles could have ensured that she would never hunger for anything while he lived. He had plenty of opportunities to do so. A king's mistress was expected to live large and entertain lavishly, as a society and court hostess, and to maintain herself in style after his demise. Nell's £4,000 pension was actually considered exceptionally modest for one in her circumstances.

Nell was in desperate financial straits following Charles's death in 1685. She began selling off her possessions, and feared that her lover's last words would go unheeded by the new king.

But three months later, James did send Nell some money to live on, paid the lion's share of her creditors' bills, and in January 1686, granted her an annual pension of £1,500 (a shade over $382,000 today). Nell was the only one of Charles's mistresses ever to receive her funds directly from the Treasury, as only she could be depended upon to spend the money on what it was intended for.

Still faithful to the memory of her lover, Nell repulsed the advances of several suitors after the king died, sorrowfully telling one expectant gent that she would "not lay a dog where the deer had lain."

She spent the brief remainder of her life as she had always lived it, gaily and in the company of good friends. It was rumored she was ailing, possibly suffering from the clap, the only unwelcome gift from her royal lover of twenty years. In March of 1687, Nell suffered a stroke, then was felled by a second one in May that left her paralyzed. For months, from her sumptuous silver bed, attended by Charles's former physicians, she waited for death to reunite her with the king. Nell Gwyn died on November 14, 1687. She was only thirty-seven years old. Nell would never live to see her royal son become a war hero, nor dandle any of her thirteen grandchildren.

As a measure of her fondness for Nell's memory, the dowager

Queen Catherine awarded Nell's oldest royal bastard a pension of his own, granting the young Duke of St. Albans £2,000 a year (over half a million dollars today), adding to the annuity of £4,000 that the late king had already given the boy.

On November 17, the day of Nell's funeral, the streets were mobbed with mourners from all strata of society. Her eulogy was delivered without irony by the vicar of St. Martin-in-the-Fields. Contained in her will were numerous charitable bequests to Protestant and Papist alike, consistent with Nell's lifelong generosity and her refusal to become mired in state or religious politics.

The Earl of Rochester's advice, ". . . with hand, body, head, heart, and all the faculties you have, contribute to his pleasure all you can . . . ," had been Nell's credo. Of all Charles's mistresses, she was the only one who never accepted a bribe to influence him on another party's behalf. Although she was jealous of the material gains of her rivals, Nell seems to have genuinely loved the king, and was utterly devoted to him and his welfare. Beyond her obviously stunning looks, wicked wit, and tremendous sense of playfulness and fun, it was Nell Gwyn's *character* that made her so special to Charles II.

CHARLES II

and Louise Renée de Penancoët de Kéroualle,
Duchess of Portsmouth 1649–1734

In 1670, when Charles's beloved sister, Henrietta Anne, Duchesse d'Orleans, came over from Versailles to negotiate the Secret Treaty of Dover between England and France, she brought with her a number of unexpected gifts. First were some presents for the bastard child that the royal mistress Nell Gwyn was about to bear; second was the young woman who would become Nell's chief rival for the king's affections—"Minette's" young and pretty lady-in-waiting Louise Renée de Penancoët de Kéroualle.

Louise's skin was pale, her baby face framed by a puffy halo of soft dark curls. Her almond-shaped, heavy lidded eyes conveyed dreaminess to some, dullness to others. Her placid, even icy, expression never seemed to change. Gorgeous but vacuous is probably how she was viewed by most of Charles's courtiers.

On the eve of Minette's departure from Dover, her brother requested a keepsake, one of the jewels he had previously given Minette. Louise opened the jewel casket as Minette asked Charles which treasure he might like.

The flirtatious king took Louise's hand, saying that she was the only jewel he desired. This response didn't sit too well with Minette, who had promised Louise's parents, impoverished though noble-born Bretons, that she would shield their daughter from the licentiousness of the English court.

The ladies returned to Paris, but three weeks later, Charles's beloved Minette was dead from a sudden illness, probably caused initially by a perforated ulcer. The inconsolable monarch petitioned King Louis XIV to permit Louise to return to England, promising that the twenty-year-old Bretonne would be made a lady-in-waiting to Queen Catherine.

It wasn't a tough sell. Louis had the opportunity to place a spy for France in the English court, and in their sovereign's bed. Buckingham had already reminded Charles that if a Frenchwoman had his ear (as well as other body parts), England stood to gain a tacit alliance with Louis. The move was also a sop to the English Papists. Charles had made vague promises about converting; with a Catholic mistress he could indefinitely postpone the actual event, yet retain his pledge of good faith to become a Catholic.

Louise, who was no naïf, but in fact had been thoroughly coached in her role, was adept at playing the innocent. Her parents had schooled her in the arts of courtesanry with the hope that she would conquer their own king. However, Louis XIV already had a Louise in the position—the gorgeous, golden-haired Louise de la Vallière, and he wasn't in the market for a replacement.

Charles was so smitten by Louise's soft, gentle voice and her fragile modesty act that he offered her anything she desired—lands, titles for herself and any future royal bastards, and a generous allowance—if she would sleep with him. The king called Louise "my dear life," telling her, "I love you better than all the world besides." But she cannily realized that he was in love with love, and fired up more by the chase than the conquest.

The ambitious Louise immediately had herself installed in the finest apartments in Whitehall, fitted up as exact replicas of her opulent rooms at Louis's palace. Louise's inner sanctum was supremely plusher than the queen's.

However, after several months of coy delays, Louise was in danger of holding out *too* long. She was a natural prude rather than a sexual siren, and both the French and English envoys were becoming increasingly frustrated with her delays. But when the Duke of Buckingham mentioned that the queen, who remained incapable of bearing children, might be replaced one day, Louise's pink little ears (as well as her avarice) pricked up. Daydreaming of the crown set upon her corona of dark curls, she agreed to surrender her body to the king.

In 1671, as Charles prepared for his annual trip to Newmarket for the races, Lord Arlington made Euston, his Suffolk estate, available for the royal tryst.

The contemporary diarist John Evelyn was a houseguest of

the Arlingtons at the time. About the conquest of Louise de Kéroualle he wrote:

During my stay here with Lord Arlington neere a fort-night, his Majesty came almost every second day . . . the king often lay here . . . It was universally reported that the faire lady [Louise de Kéroualle] was bedded one of these nights and the stocking flung after the manner of a married bride; I acknowledge she was for the most part in her undresse all day, and that there was fondnesse and toying with that young wanton . . .

The surrender of Louise's much-vaunted virginity yielded valuable fruit. Nine months later, on July 29, 1672, she gave birth to a son, the fifth of Charles's royal bastards to be given his forename. And from the moment of his birth, Louise considered him his father's heir presumptive. For love's labors won, in July of 1673 she was ennobled by the king as Baroness Petersfield, Countess of Farnham, and Duchess of Portsmouth.

Although Charles worshipped her, for the most part Louise was widely detested in England. Nobles were appalled (as they routinely were) that Charles had elevated a whore. Patriotic commoners were disgusted that a Frenchwoman was cleaning out the Treasury.

Louise was even disdained by thieves. When her coach was detained on the Portsmouth Road by Old Mobb, a notorious highwayman, Louise tried to talk her way out of a holdup by asking the brigand if he knew who she was, warning that he would pay dearly for robbing her. Old Mobb replied, "I know you to be the greatest whore in the kingdom and that you are maintained at the public charge." (Actually, her bills were secretly being footed by the French.) The Restoration-era Robin Hood then informed Louise that he had a whore of his own to maintain at the public expense, "same as the king," and took Louise's jewels.

Louise proved as grasping as the best of them, going toe to toe with Barbara Castlemaine over their respective sons' royal patents. Louise was ecstatic to learn that Charles was going to ennoble her two-year-old son to a dukedom, but her delight was dampened by the news that one of Castlemaine's royal bastards would be elevated at the same time. However, the Lord Treasurer Danby's signature was first required for the patent to be valid, and Louise was extremely close (if not intimate) with Danby. The two mothers, Cleveland and Portsmouth, schemed to get to Danby first. It was Louise who discovered that Danby's holiday plans had changed at the last minute, and she sent her agent to meet the Lord Treasurer's coach the night before Barbara's agent was scheduled to perform the same service. Danby therefore signed Louise's son's patent first, and to this date the Duke of Richmond takes precedence over the Duke of Grafton!

The gentle, feminine, well-read Louise, with her interest in politics and her head for strategy, set up her own salon, where with taste and decorum she entertained visiting foreign dignitaries, hostessing them lavishly as though she were herself a queen. This hubris did not sit well with a number of Charles's courtiers, including some of his closest friends. It was widely believed that the devilish Earl of Rochester penned the following couplet, which one day Louise found pinned to her boudoir door:

> *Within this place a bed's appointed*
> *For a French bitch and God's anointed.*

Another of Louise's displays of ego included having her own medal struck. Borrowing the motto of Diane de Poitiers, *maîtresse en titre* to Henri III, it bore the Latin inscription *"omnium victorem vici"* (I conquered him who conquered all).

The English were (correctly) convinced that Louise was a spy for France. And though it had been rumored that on her arrival at Whitehall she was no stranger to the secrets of the boudoir, Louise was in some ways a finer actress than Nell. She managed to snooker Charles with her performances in a variety of stock roles—beginning with the Damsel in Distress over the unexpected death of her mistress Minette, moving on to the Affronted Virgin, and finally, when her infidelities to the king were unmasked, trotting out her version of the Scorned Woman.

In 1674, Louise came down with a case of the clap, courtesy of her royal paramour—who'd likely gotten it from one of his backstairs trulls. Charles privately believed that Louise had gotten the pox from one of her own extraregal intrigues. However, since he had no proof, by accusing her he had nothing to gain and everything to lose in terms of his relations with France. Instead, while Louise posted about from Tunbridge Wells to Bath to Epsom in search of a cure, Charles sought to assuage her itch with the gift of two necklaces—one of diamonds and the other of pearls. Louise did eventually recover (or was thought to in her day), but in the course of her recuperation she had become quite stout.

Charles loved her none the less for her increasing girth, affectionately referring to her as "My darling Fubbs," "fubbs" being slang for a short, chubby person. However, by the time one of the king's old flames, the vibrant Hortense Mancini, Duchesse Mazarin, arrived on the scene in 1675, Louise realized that she couldn't compete with this new rival. She'd grown zaftig and her personality was a downer. Her frequent crying jags, which had annoyed everyone at court ever since her arrival, were finally beginning to depress the king, and Louise's handlers advised her to cut it out unless she wanted to lose his favor altogether.

Her stock dropped to its lowest point between 1678 and

1680, during the Popish Plot. This was a much-believed conspiracy said to have been instigated by the Catholics to assassinate Charles and place his brother James on the throne—when in fact it was a nearly diabolical ruse to discredit Catholics, formally *exclude* James from ever inheriting the throne, and instead install a puppet, possibly Charles's first royal bastard, the Duke of Monmouth. Louise downplayed her Catholicism by hiring Protestant servants and aligning herself with the Earl of Shaftsbury, who led the fight for exclusion. Somehow, Louise had taken it into her head that her son by Charles, the young Duke of Richmond, would be the one placed on the English throne.

Louise's disloyalty disgusted the king, but he ultimately forgave her. Because her continued presence at court was important for political, diplomatic, and financial relations with France, she was too important a chess piece to remove from the board altogether.

By the early 1680s, Louise was trusted enough by her royal lover to handle affairs of state in his absence. Yet her behavior could swing like a pendulum from entire indifference to carnality to complete depravity.

She seduced Named Achmet, the Moroccan ambassador who arrived from Tangiers on a diplomatic mission in January 1682; and there was another lover in the picture as well. Toward the end of 1681, the twenty-eight-year-old Philippe de Vendôme, Grand Prior of France, had come to England to visit his aunt, Hortense Mancini. The thirty-five-year-old Louise commenced a torrid affair with this boozing womanizer that became the talk of the court and nearly cost her her courtesan's career. After Charles discovered a sheaf of compromising love letters that Louise had penned to her young swain, he sought to expel the Frenchman from England. To avoid a diplomatic incident, Louis XIV stepped in and strongly advised Vendôme to forget he ever knew anyone named Louise de Kéroualle.

Louis XIV was enraged that his spy had been heedless enough to jeopardize her position at Whitehall, but in March of 1682, Louise traveled to France for four months and was feted everywhere she went. News of her social successes reached English ears, and when she returned to London in July, her star at court shone as brightly as ever.

According to Bishop Burnet, an eyewitness to court events, "After this the king kissed her often before all the world, which he was never observed to do before this time." So Charles must have forgiven his Fubbs her infidelities.

In February 1685, when Charles lay dying, although wellborn, Louise was not permitted to enter his chamber to pay her last respects because she had been his mistress. However, she had one more triumph to secure.

Louise told the French ambassador Paul Barillon that Charles had wanted to be received into the bosom of the Catholic faith. The story seems a bit pat to be true, but allegedly in the king's final days, while strolling through the corridors of Whitehall, Barillon happened to encounter Father Huddlestone, the same Catholic priest who had offered comfort to Charles after the Battle of Worcester. James, Duke of York, who desired nothing better than that his brother should die a Catholic, escorted the father up the back stairs to Charles's bedroom, where communion and last rites were administered. Retaining his sense of humor to the last, Charles purportedly whispered to the priest, "You who saved my life are come now to save my soul." Among the king's final words were "Be kind to the Duchess of Cleveland, and especially Portsmouth. I have always loved her and I die loving her."

After Charles shuffled off his mortal coil, Louise sought sanctuary in the French ambassador's London town house, but King James summoned her back to the palace to settle her debts before leaving the country. Acknowledging her service to the crown and her continuing political importance, the new king agreed to maintain her annual pension to the tune of £19,000 (nearly $4.9 million today).

Louise had done very well for herself as a royal mistress. Under Charles, so to speak, she had pocketed an annual pension (which had started at £18,600 in her early days), plus an annuity from taxes paid by the clergy, and £25,000 (almost $6 million) annually from Irish revenues. Over time, her pension increased to £40,000, and in some years she amassed nearly tenfold that amount. In 1681, it was reported that Louise de Kéroualle had received £136,000 (almost $33.5 million in today's economy)—a figure that probably didn't include the money she made selling pardons to wealthy criminals, or the value of her vast collection of jewels, including a pair of diamond earrings worth £18,000 that Louis XIV had given her in 1675 for services rendered to the French crown.

Louise returned to France and eventually retired to the countryside, where she lived extremely modestly, her passion for gambling having wiped out much of her fortune. She died on November 14, 1734, forty-seven years to the day after Nell Gwyn breathed her last.

CHARLES II
and Hortense Mancini, Duchesse Mazarin 1646–1699

Hortense Mancini was the favorite niece—and heiress—of the extremely powerful French cardinal Jules Mazarin. Mazarin, who succeeded Richelieu as cardinal, had been the lover of Anne of Austria, the mother of the young Louis XIV. On the death of Louis XIII, the cardinal and Anne ruled France as coregents until her son attained his majority.

The future Charles II twice petitioned the cardinal for Hortense's hand in marriage when he was a teenage exile in France, but at the time Mazarin didn't think the impoverished and itinerant youth's prospects were adequate enough, so he quashed Charles's hopes of marriage to his vibrant niece. After the Restoration, however, Mazarin was quite willing to swallow his pride and change his mind, offering to dower Hortense quite handsomely; but Charles's advisers cautioned him against choosing a French queen, and the cardinal's offer was rejected.

Hortense was quite the catch. Her black hair tumbled to her waist; her sparkling eyes changed color with the light. She was tall and slender, an accomplished sportswoman, musician, and linguist. And of course her pedigree was impeccable. In short, other than being French, she would have made the perfect queen.

But her uncle had cruelly dashed her hopes. Instead, Hortense was married off at the age of fifteen to the clinically mad Armand de la Porte, Marquis de Meilleraye, whom the cardinal made duc Mazarin so that his own name would live on.

A religious fanatic and maniacal prude, Armand psychologically abused Hortense and locked her away from the world so that she would be free of its many temptations. He fired her servants if she expressed any kindness toward them, and willfully took a paintbrush and chisel to her late uncle's priceless collection of Old Masters in which any nudity was displayed. Any mention of something even remotely sexual drove him further off the deep end. It was the most dreadful match imaginable for the hedonistic Hortense, who realized that she had no alternative but to flee, which in 1666 she did—disguised as a man.

The cross-dressing, pistol- and saber-wielding Hortense became an exotic adventuress, traveling to Savoy in Italy, where she ended up as the mistress to Charles Emmanuel II, the married duke who had once asked Cardinal Mazarin for her hand. She penned her memoirs—an exceptionally rare thing for a woman to do at the time—which justified her flight from her wacko spouse and expiated herself for her infidelities. When the Duke of Savoy died, his widow told Hortense in no uncertain terms that she was no longer a welcome houseguest. So Hortense hit the road once more, eventually arriving in London in 1675 at the age of thirty, with a train of twenty liveried nobles, a parrot, and a little Moorish pageboy named Mustapha. The French ambassador de Courtin had once described England as a haven for all women who had quarreled with their husbands, and Hortense was no exception.

Charles's younger brother James and his new Duchess of York—Hortense's relation, Mary of Modena—welcomed the colorful traveler into their social circle. Hortense briefly stayed at one of the Yorks' houses in St. James's, and was soon a fixture at court.

According to the French ambassador, who was quite impressed with Hortense's beauty and vivacity, he had never seen "anyone who so well defies the power of time and vice to disfigure." In other words, Hortense's debaucheries had not aged her nor dimmed her luster.

Charles's old passion for her soon burned anew. "Mme. Mazarin is well satisfied with the conversation she had with the king of England," reported the French envoy. One result of this "conversation" was a town house in Chelsea, where the sovereign set her up in style. Gossips soon spread the word that Charles would spend hours beneath Hortense's window, gazing up like a lovestruck spaniel in the hope of glimpsing the brunette beauty.

Though they referred to Hortense as "the Roman whore" because she was related to Mary of Modena, the monarch's subjects blackened her reputation with the Gallic-tinted brush as well. They were disgusted that "the king should send of another

French whore when one already [Louise de Kéroualle] had made him poor."

But Hortense was never a serious candidate for *maîtresse en titre*. For one thing, her nature was too peripatetic to enjoy a gilded cage at Whitehall. For another, she reveled in her bohemian lifestyle. For a third, she was emphatically bisexual.

"Each sex provides its lovers for Hortense," an English courtier observed. Her affairs included the visiting Prince of Monaco and the Countess of Sussex, Anne Palmer—Charles's then-pregnant teenage daughter by the former royal mistress Barbara Castlemaine. Anne occupied her mother's old apartments directly above the king's bedchamber, and it was said that each morning Charles would ascend the secret back stairs connecting the two apartments in the hopes of catching his daughter in bed with Hortense. Neither of Anne's parents were terribly amused by her passion for Hortense; Barbara briefly shoved the rebellious teen into a Parisian convent, where Anne spent much of her time smothering Hortense's portrait with kisses and the rest of it bribing the abbess to release her whenever she felt the urge to depart.

When one of Hortense's lovers was killed in a duel, she briefly considered retiring to a convent—given Hortense's predilections, not so dire a penance as one might assume. Charles was greatly amused by the notion.

Considering her incapability for fidelity, perhaps it was for old time's sake that Hortense was permitted to remain in the sovereign's seraglio. Flouting royal protocol, she never addressed him as "Your Majesty." But the king seems not to have minded. Hortense and Charles provided variety for each other. The Duchesse Mazarin was not nearly as demanding as his other mistresses, content to maintain her Chelsea salon peopled with artists and intellectuals while collecting her £4,000 (roughly $1 million) pension from the king.

It was Louise de Kéroualle who felt most threatened by

Hortense's existence. Hortense boasted birthright, breeding, and beauty. Her slender figure, thanks to horseback riding, swimming, and swordplay, looked great in anything she chose to wear, including the menswear ensembles that so excited king and court and scandalized the envious ladies. She was accomplished in many disciplines and well versed in languages and literature. In short, except for her rampant promiscuity, as far as Louise was concerned, Hortense had the whole package.

But Hortense didn't consider herself a rival. She simply didn't want the top-dog honors as much as Nell Gwyn or Louise craved them. Supremely self-aware, Hortense was too wild and craved variety too much to be domesticated as the perfect royal paramour. She couldn't have cared less about affairs of state. Hortense was a sensualist, not a politician.

After Charles's death in 1685, Hortense remained in England, residing on Paradise Row. She still collected a portion of her pension from his successors, James II and William III. Although she was in her forties, one of her admirers during the beginning of William's reign was Arnold Joost van Keppel, William's rakish young page, who would eventually be made 1st Earl of Albemarle. At the time, Keppel, twenty-three years younger than Hortense, was merely a colonel in the Horse Guards.

But when Hortense discovered that Albemarle had fallen in love with her visiting daughter, Marie-Charlotte, and had begun to see her on the sly, the duchess, understandably, fell to pieces.

Faced with the ugly fact that her own daughter was her rival, the great beauty deteriorated rapidly. Alcoholism destroyed her looks and her health, and her penchant for high-stakes gambling bankrupted her. She retired to a country home, and passed away there in 1699 at the age of fifty-three. The wealthiest heiress in Europe during her youth, she died so hopelessly in debt that the bailiffs wanted to enumerate her lifeless body among her goods and chattels.

It was Hortense's insane estranged husband Armand who redeemed her, so to speak. She had successfully avoided him for thirty-three years, but now that she had expired, the duc Mazarin had come to claim her. Armand purchased her body from her creditors, carting it all over France so that he could keep an eye on her. He finally buried her in the family crypt.

JAMES II OF ENGLAND/ JAMES VII OF SCOTLAND

1633–1701

RULED 1685–1688 (DEPOSED)

*J*AMES WAS THE SECOND SURVIVING SON OF CHARLES I and Queen Henrietta Maria. He was created Duke of York in 1644 when he was eleven years old. Two years later, during the English Civil War, he was captured and imprisoned at St. James's Palace in London. In April 1648, James escaped, disguised as a girl, with his elder brother, Charles. The boys went to Holland, where their sister Mary and her husband, Prince William II of Orange, reigned.

During the early years of Charles II's reign, James distinguished himself as commander of the Royal Navy and Lord High Admiral. But when Charles passed the first Test Act, making it a precondition for any public officeholder to take communion in the Church of England, the secretly Catholic James resigned his commission.

At the age of fifty-one, he became king upon Charles's death on February 6, 1685. Soon thereafter, the Duke of Monmouth,

Charles's illegitimate son by Lucy Walter, asserted his claim to the throne as Charles's heir, raised an army against James, and was subsequently executed for treason.

James undid many of the exclusionary acts passed against Catholics during Charles's reign. After he suspended the penal laws in the autumn of 1685, the House of Commons protested, so James suspended all parliamentary activity, dissolving the Parliament entirely in 1687. He also purged the judges of the high court.

On April 4, 1687, James issued a Declaration of Indulgence aimed at religious toleration of Catholics. The following year, a second Declaration of Indulgence prohibited Anglican ministers from preaching against the Catholic religion.

This was too much for the Bishop of London. He and six laymen—known as the Immortal Seven—extended an invitation to Prince William (III) of Orange, James's nephew as well as his son-in-law, since William was wed to James's oldest daughter, Mary, to come to England for the purposes of protecting liberty and property, and to assert Mary's claim (as the daughter of James) to the throne.

William of Orange landed in England on November 5, 1688, with a large army behind him. By that time, public opinion had so turned against James that his military refused to fight for him. Hyperaware of his father's fate on the scaffold—though he still believed himself king—he surrendered the throne in the blink of an eye. James made a cosmetic attempt at negotiation with William. Then, after sending his second wife, Mary of Modena, and their infant son to the Continent, James sneaked out of London. He arrived in France on Christmas Day 1688, placing himself under the protection of Louis XIV.

His three-year reign was one of the least successful in British history, though it would lead to massive government reform under the reign of his successors, William and Mary. James never forgave his daughter for "usurping" his throne.

After an unsuccessful attempt at fomenting rebellion in Ireland—where William's army knocked the stuffing out of him at the Battle of the Boyne on July 1, 1690—James retired to France. There he was content to enjoy his favorite sports—hunting and womanizing—until he was felled by a brain hemorrhage on September 16, 1701. James's coffin was placed in the Chapel of St. Edmund in the Church of the English Benedictines in Paris. The tomb was desecrated during the French Revolution and his remains disappeared.

Mary of Modena, who married James in 1685, survived him by seventeen years, dying of breast cancer on May 7, 1718, the same disease that had claimed James's most successful mistress and first wife, Anne Hyde, on March 31, 1671.

James II of England/James VII of Scotland
and Anne Hyde 1637–1671

The prodigiously buxom and flirtatious Anne Hyde was the daughter of Edward Hyde, a Wiltshire lawyer who turned to politics, becoming Charles II's chancellor. Her contemporaries noted her intelligence, though they admitted she was not very pretty; in fact, Anne was most often described as a cow. A hearty eater during an era when slenderness was the vogue at court, the girl's booty came in for some serious ribbing in a popular rhyme:

> With chanc'lor's belly, and so large a rump,
> There, not behind the coach, her pages jump.

For several years before the Restoration, Anne had been a maid of honor to Mary, the Princess Royal, sister of Charles and James. But it was in Paris at the exiled court of the Queen Mother Henrietta Maria where Anne first met Mary's brother James, the Duke of York.

The stuttering duke was stiff and reserved, with a downer of a personality, but by all accounts, James, tall, blue-eyed, and fair, was even more of a rake than his less classically handsome brother, Charles. It certainly wasn't charm or affability that was the chick magnet—in fact, James was considered rather slow and plodding, particularly compared to the exceptionally bright and witty Charles. But then again, James didn't attract the beauties of the age, as did his elder brother. On James's embracing of Catholicism as well as loose women, Charles observed, "My brother will lose his throne for his principles and his soul for a bunch of ugly trollops." He jested that James's mistresses were so universally hideous that his priests must have given them to the duke as penance.

With Anne Hyde, however, "dismal Jimmy" (as Charles's famously clever mistress Nell Gwyn called him) must have scintillated. Apparently their affair grew passionate after the exiled court had moved to The Hague. After the Restoration, Anne's father sent for her, and she returned to London, fat and glowing—but as Anne was always fat and glowing, her father didn't notice that she was also pregnant.

Hyde should have congratulated himself on the fact that his daughter had inherited his canny political skills, because in August 1659, Anne had successfully convinced the duke to sign a marriage contract. After that, they cohabited intermittently and clandestinely as man and wife.

On Anne's return to England, realizing they'd be caught sooner or later, James sneaked into Worcester House, her father's home, with an Anglican chaplain in tow. The chaplain married Anne and James in a private ceremony on September 3, 1660. Only after they were legally wed did Anne's new husband throw himself upon the king's mercy, begging him to allow them to publicly marry.

King Charles summoned Chancellor Hyde, a portly Polonius who had known nothing of his daughter's affairs until the news was broken to him by two of his friends, the Marquis of Ormonde and the Earl of Southampton. Hyde assured the monarch that as soon as he got home to Worcester House, he would toss Anne out into the street as a strumpet. At the suggestion that Anne might actually be married, the politician then changed his tack, ranting that he would sooner see his daughter be the king's whore than the duke's wife—and if Anne were really married to James, she should be thrown into a dungeon in the Tower of London and an Act of Parliament passed to behead her.

"And I shall be the first man to propose that to Parliament!" Hyde shouted.

Charles endeavored to smooth things over, but poor Anne ended up locked in her room. However, Anne's sympathetic mother managed to sneak the duke into her daughter's chamber for conjugal visits.

But Anne, a mere commoner, had unintentionally created an international incident.

The Queen Mum, Henrietta Maria, came over from Paris "to prevent so great a stain and dishonor to the Crown." Then a group of courtiers was enlisted to convince James of his wife's rampant promiscuity—and therefore, her unsuitability to be his duchess. Anne was traduced by men who had never even met her, all claiming to have bedded her. It seemed that every man in England had crawled out of the woodwork to testify to Anne's lasciviousness, each sworn statement more outlandish than the last.

Charles didn't believe a word of it, and assured his increasingly livid chancellor that his daughter was being unjustly slandered. As Anne lay abed, the birth of her baby imminent, the king sent his most trusted ladies to attend her.

But that wasn't the end of it. Anne, shrieking with labor pains, was forced to endure another torment. The oh-so-sensitive Bishop of Winchester visited her bedside and demanded, "Whose child is it of which you are in labor? Have you known any man other than the Duke of York?" Anne responded in the negative, and probably spat out a lot of other negative things to the bishop besides.

Enter Henrietta Maria, in high dudgeon at Dover, ready to defend her son's good name and tar Chancellor Hyde with the brush of treachery for daring to marry an undeserving creature of his own lowly brood into the royal house—little realizing that she and the chancellor were on the same side.

Charles stepped in and averted a crisis by making Hyde a baron, with a gift of £20,000 (well over $4.3 million today) to sustain the honor. By the time the groom's mother reached London, she was greeted by the bride's father, now Baron Hyde of Hindon, a peer of the realm. The following year Charles made Hyde Earl of Clarendon.

The dowager queen's argument about the worthiness of Anne Hyde's family had thus been gracefully nipped in the bud, and eventually, Henrietta Maria grew to accept her new daughter-in-law.

Anne was clearly the dominant partner in the marriage, yet she could not prevent James from returning to his rakish ways soon after their union was legalized in the eyes of family and state. "The duke is in all things but his codpiece led by the nose," Samuel Pepys observed.

Anne coped with her husband's frequent infidelities by overeating. She was also perpetually pregnant, giving birth to eight children in nearly as many years, but only two daughters, Mary and Anne, survived to adulthood. The rest died in infancy.

After suffering from cancer for three years, Anne finally succumbed to the disease in 1671, a few weeks after giving birth to her eighth child. In her final days, she also became a secret convert to Catholicism.

One evening after enjoying a hearty dinner at Burlington House, Anne retired to pray, and then collapsed in the chapel. A frantic James sent for the Bishop of Oxford, but by the time he arrived, Anne was incoherent.

She died at St. James's Palace in her husband's arms, with the words "Duke, Duke, death is terrible. Death is very terrible." She was buried in Westminster Abbey.

The Duke of York subsequently married a fifteen-year-old Italian princess, the willowy Mary of Modena, who became his queen in 1685 on the death of Charles II. Mary was twenty-five years younger than her husband and bore him two children.

Anne Hyde is one of the few royal mistresses to end up marrying her lover, and one of only six profiled in this volume, the others being Katherine Swynford; Anne Boleyn, Jane Seymour, and Kathryn Howard—the three mistress-wives of Henry VIII; and Camilla Parker Bowles.

Anne's two daughters each went on to become Queen of England, and both would make their mark in British history. Mary, born on April 30, 1662, would marry William of Orange and become a key player in the Glorious Revolution that would overthrow her own father and place herself and her husband on the English throne. Her younger sister, Anne, born on the sixth of February in 1665, would inherit her mother's corpulence as well as her father's crown. Under Queen Anne, England and Scotland were combined into a single nation in the Act of Union signed on May 1, 1707, thereby making Anne Hyde's younger daughter—the issue of the woman who was such a "stain and dishonor to the Crown"—the first monarch of Great Britain.

WILLIAM AND MARY

WILLIAM III

1650–1702

AND MARY II

1662–1694

RULED (JOINTLY WITH MARY) 1689–1694

WILLIAM RULED ALONE 1694–1702

THOUGH RAISED A PROTESTANT, MARY STUART WAS THE oldest daughter of the Catholic James, Duke of York (the future James II). When Mary was just fifteen years old, her father informed her that she was to be married to her lovestruck twenty-five-year-old first cousin, William, Prince of Orange—a taciturn asthmatic with a slight hunchback. Those were only three of the reasons that the bride spent the entire wedding ceremony weeping copiously.

The ceremony took place at St. James's Palace in London on November 4, 1677. They must have looked like a seventeenth-century version of the *Mutt and Jeff* cartoons—skinny, sallow, lanky-haired William, a whole five inches shorter than his rosy-cheeked, big-boned teenage bride with her alabaster skin and luxuriant dark curls.

The bridegroom was the last of the House of Orange-Nassau, which had ruled the Independent Dutch Republic since William's great-grandfather, "William the Silent," founded it in the mid-sixteenth century. His mother was Mary Henrietta Stuart, the sister of Charles II and James, making William James's nephew as well as his son-in-law.

As the Dutch Republic's Stadtholder, William was an able ruler and an accomplished military commander, despite his spindly stature. For six years he bravely resisted French aggression in the Netherlands. In 1678, when a peace was concluded without any concessions on the Dutch side, William was hailed as a Protestant hero across Europe.

The thirty-eight-year-old William and twenty-seven-year-old Mary acceded to the English throne in "the Glorious Revolution" of 1688, becoming the first joint rulers of England. However, their coronation did not take place until February 1689, after Parliament convened a special session, in which Mary and William were formally invited to become queen and king on the proviso that the executive authority be placed in William's hands. The new monarchs also had to agree to a Declaration of Rights (entered in the statute books as the Bill of Rights) that condemned the way James II had used his prerogative in the matter of dispensing the laws.

An affable people-pleaser and a good-natured soul, throughout her reign Mary was very aware that many subjects considered her a "usurper" of her father's throne, but over time the English did embrace her as a beloved queen.

The pensive William was at the official helm, but he spent nearly every spring and summer overseas on military campaigns. In his absence, the governance of the realm was placed squarely in Mary's hands, and she proved a highly competent and effective administrator.

Several major changes took place during the reign of William and Mary, planting the seeds of a constitutional monarchy. The Triennial Act required that a new Parliament convene every three years. A Mutiny Act prevented a king from keeping a standing army in peacetime without the consent of the House of Commons. William strengthened the expansion of trade at home and abroad in 1694 by founding the Bank of England, which provided for secure long-term government borrowing, financing trade ventures and foreign-policy interests.

Mary died of smallpox on December 28, 1694, at the age of thirty-two, and was buried at Westminster Abbey. In exile in France, James refused to allow his daughter to be officially mourned, so bitter was he at her role in his enforced abdication.

One of the cornerstones of William's reign after Mary's death was the 1701 Act of Settlement that required all future monarchs to be members of the Church of England, and forbade the sovereign to leave the country without parliamentary permission.

William continued to advance policies of tolerance. Freedom of the press was granted in 1695, and religious restrictions were loosened (for all but Roman Catholics). Jews were no longer compelled by law to observe the Christian Sabbath and Quakers were not penalized for refusing to swear under oath.

William survived Mary by more than seven years. He never remarried. On March 8, 1702, at the age of fifty-one, William died of pneumonia after a fall from a horse broke his collarbone. It was rumored that his horse stumbled into a molehill, prompting James's supporters, the Jacobites, to anthropomorphize the little burrower by toasting "the little gentleman in the black velvet waistcoat." He died clutching the hand of his closest adviser, Hans Willem Bentinck, Earl of Portland. When the corpse was undressed it was discovered that William had worn Mary's ruby and diamond ring along with a lock of her hair tied around his left arm with a black ribbon. He had loved her more than he had ever revealed.

William was buried in Westminster Abbey alongside his queen. Because William's marriage to Mary was childless, the crown passed to James II's younger daughter, Anne, with whom the vibrant Stuart dynasty would end.

MARY II
and Frances Apsley 1668–1727

WILLIAM III
and Elizabeth Villiers 1655–1733
and Arnold Joost van Keppel 1669/70–1718

Mary was only nine years old when she and her younger sister, Anne, were sent to live at Richmond Palace with the bustling family of Sir Edward Villiers, whose wife, Frances Howard, was their governess.

At the age of twelve, Mary developed a raging crush on the twenty-one-year-old Frances Apsley, the beautiful daughter of Sir Allen Apsley, the king's hawks keeper, and later Governor of the Tower of London. The adolescent Mary was enamored of lurid romances and cross-dressing theatrical performances; in her love letters to Frances she pilfered their pen names, Clorine and Aurelia, from a theatrical masque by John Crowne titled *Calisto, or the Chaste Nymph*, which Mary and Anne had performed at court. "There is nothing in this heart, breast, guts, or bowels but you shall know it," Mary wrote to her sweet "husband."

Clearly influenced by the pastoral poetry that was so popular at the time, Mary rhapsodized,

> *I would be content with a cottage in the country, a cow, a stuff petticoat and waistcoat in summer and cloth in winter, a little garden to live upon the fruit and herbs it yields, or if I could not have you so to myself I would go a begging, be poor but content—what greater happiness is there in the world than to have the company of them one loves to make your happiness complete.*

Mary assured Frances that she was her

> *. . . humble servant to kiss the ground where you go, to be your dog on a string, your fish in a net, your bird in a cage, your humble trout. . . . I may, if I can tell you how much I love you, but I hope that is not doubted. I have given you proofs enough. If not, I will die to satisfy you, dear, dear husband. If all my hairs were lives, I would lose them all twenty times over to serve or satisfy you.*

No ambiguity there. Mary sent her letters to Frances furtively, fully aware that her governess would not have approved of the tenor of her correspondence.

But the feeling between Mary and Frances was not entirely mutual. Even if Frances were inclined to favor women, her pursuer was, after all, not much more than a child, a motherless, romantic adolescent who very much needed to love and be loved. And Frances probably saw no harm in humoring Mary by maintaining the fiction of a passionate connection. She was, perhaps, the only one in Mary's rarefied little sphere who showed her some genuine affection.

As soon as she heard the news that she was to wed her wheezing first cousin, Prince William III of Orange, Stadtholder of the Netherlands, the fifteen-year-old bride-to-be wrote tearfully to Frances:

> *If you do not come to me some time today, dear husband, that I may have my bellyful of discourse with you, I shall take it very ill . . . for I have a great deal to say to you concerning I do not know how to tell in the letter. If you do come, you will mightily oblige your faithful wife, Mary Clorine.*

Frances Apsley's name was significantly missing from the list of ladies-in-waiting asked to accompany Mary to Holland. As William seemed to play a role in deciding who would go, perhaps he had been delicately warned of Mary's passionate attachment to the young woman. Mary did not even get to bid good-bye to Frances. Sir Allen had fallen gravely ill and Frances was attending him.

Meanwhile, rumors that William was gay surfaced from time to time over the years as well, although given the chance to cat around, he had numerous heterosexual liaisons, most of which were kept well under wraps. It's possible that when William was fourteen years old he developed a crush on Hans Willem Bentinck, who that year entered his household as a pageboy. Ten years later, when William was felled by smallpox, he was certain that Bentinck had saved his life by sharing his bed, as it was commonly believed that a healthy person sleeping beside a smallpox patient would draw some of the illness into themselves. Bentinck would go on to become William's closest and most trusted adviser. In 1689, after the Glorious Revolution, William naturalized Bentinck a British subject and created him Earl of Portland and made him a Knight of the Garter in 1697.

In any event, if rumors of William's homoerotic bent were true, he was supremely lucky to have been mated with a wife whose inclinations, at least during her youth, were distinctly Sapphic.

Their wedding night was an embarrassment. It was the custom of the times for the bridal couple to be escorted to the marital chamber and officially put to bed, to begin the performance for which they were united. Evidently, William was less than enthusiastic about his conjugal duties, because King Charles II, the couple's lusty uncle, had to exhort the groom, "Now, nephew, to your work! Hey! St. George for England!"

After their wedding celebration, Mary and William returned to Holland. Left behind in London, Frances Apsley was unsure how things stood between her and her epistolary lover now that Mary had married.

In a surviving draft of a letter she penned to Mary, Frances lamented,

> *Since it was my hard fate to lose the greatest blessing I ever had in this world, which was the dear presence of my most beloved wife, I have some comfort that she is taken from me by so worthy and so great a prince . . . Your Highness has put a hard task upon me to treat you with the same familiarity as becomes a fond husband to a beloved wife he dotes upon . . . I think what the scripture says that man and wife are but only one body and then your heart is mine, and I am sure mine is yours . . . I must ask your pardon for my presumption, yet since my life depends upon it, for I can live no longer than your favor shines upon me, it will be a great charity in your Highness to continue your love and bounty to a husband that admires you and dotes upon you and an obedient servant that will always serve and adore you.*

Reading between the lines, it sounds like Frances is asking Mary for a job. Although a position was not forthcoming, Mary had not forgotten Frances, nor her passion for her. When she became pregnant, Mary wrote to her adored "husband," assuring her that

I have played the whore a little; because the sea parts us, you may believe that it is a bastard.

Mary miscarried that fetus, but she and William remained diligent in their duty to beget an heir. However, it doesn't sound like they had a whole lot of fun going about it. Mary told a friend, "He comes to my chamber about supper time upon this condition—that I will not tire him with multiplicity of question, but rather strive to recreate him."

When she was just a girl, Mary had once remarked to Frances Apsley with regard to her own father's infidelity to her young stepmother, "In two or three years men are always weary of their wives and look for a Mrs [mistress] as soon as they can get them."

Unfortunately, this proved to be the case with her own marriage. William was satisfying his more amorous urges in the arms of his clandestine mistress, Elizabeth Villiers, a woman whose pedigree connects many of the dots of the Stuart dynasty's romantic history.

Elizabeth's mother was Frances Howard, governess to both Mary and Anne. As a daughter of Sir Edward Villiers, Elizabeth had been a playmate of Mary's back at Richmond. Both Elizabeth and her sister, Anne Villiers—who fell in love with and married William's confidant, Hans Bentinck—came to Holland with Mary after she married William. Elizabeth's cousin, Lady Castlemaine, was one of Charles II's most notorious mistresses. Her great-uncle, the 1st Duke of Buckingham, George Villiers, had been the lover of King James I.

Elizabeth had inherited none of Lady Castlemaine's extraordinary beauty, but the spindly William, with a nose like an eagle's beak, was no Dutch Adonis. Elizabeth had a cast in her eyes that made her myopic; according to the great satirist and statesman Jonathan Swift—a dear friend of hers, no less—"the good lady squints like a dragon." Another contemporary wrote, "One can't imagine her arousing desire."

The twenty-year-old Elizabeth caught the prince's interest in 1677, soon after the royal wedding, when she was traveling with Mary's entourage to Holland. To throw gossips off the scent, she flirted mercilessly with a Scottish mercenary, Captain Wauchop, but no one was fooled. By 1679, everyone was whispering about her affair with William, and by 1680, she was his acknowledged mistress.

William wasn't as interested in "Squinting Betty's" looks as in her intelligence. What made Elizabeth so alluring, particularly to a man who didn't place a premium on carnality, was her quicksilver wit. And unlike William's young wife, his mistress was a stimulating conversationalist. Although Mary was kind and eminently affable, her education had been sorely lacking. Gone were the days of the Renaissance when princesses received a thorough schooling in the arts, sciences, and humanities. Women of Mary's era were expected to be vacuous and ornamental.

Historically, no one expected a king to be in love with—and therefore, sexually faithful to—a wife that had been selected for him. William was no exception, but at least—unlike his uncle, Charles II—he attempted to be discreet about it. William would tell Mary that he was up working late on dispatches, and she swallowed his excuses, although she probably would have been glad of her husband's attention on a more frequent basis. Her only solace was her ongoing correspondence with Frances Apsley. It might also have comforted her to know that Hans Bentinck, an extremely straight arrow, regardless of whatever sort of affection William had once harbored for him, was disgusted by his sister-in-law's behavior with the prince.

With spies well placed in Mary's household, her father, James II, eventually caught wind of William's affair with Elizabeth. James was afraid that Mary would seek a divorce, or else that William would look to get rid of her in order to marry Elizabeth. Henry VIII had set a literally dangerous precedent.

Faced with a confirmation of the liaison she'd long sought to ignore, Mary was openly humiliated. One night, she staked out Elizabeth Villiers's apartments, and caught her husband tiptoeing out the door at two a.m.

Mary exploded then and there, accusing William of infidelity. When they had both calmed down a few days later, his response was, "What has given you so much pain is merely an amusement; there is no crime in it." William accused Mary's servants of plotting against him and several of her closest attendants were summarily dismissed.

The queen decided to handle the matter on her own. As Elizabeth was still one of her ladies-in-waiting, Mary dispatched her to England with a letter for King James, requesting her father to detain Elizabeth. But the clever mistress opened the letter herself and delivered it instead to her own father. Sir Edward Villiers advised Elizabeth to head directly back to Holland and beg the royals to reinstate her.

Mary refused to see Elizabeth on her return. But William compelled her to welcome his mistress into her household again. Elizabeth ended up residing with her sister Katharine, where William continued to visit her.

Over time, however, Mary begrudgingly came to accept the situation. Elizabeth was in the retinue that accompanied William and Mary to England in 1688 when they became king and queen. For services rendered to her, Mary granted her childhood companion and lady-in-waiting ninety thousand acres of property in Ireland that had belonged to her father, James, when he was Duke of York. Some historians have stated that the land grant was William's idea and that Mary wept to see her father's property bestowed upon her husband's mistress. In any event, unfortunately for Elizabeth, that grant was revoked by Parliament in 1699.

Mary's friendship with Frances Apsley fizzled out. In 1682, Frances had married the much-older Benjamin Bathurst, a director of the East India Company. She had not even told her correspondent about her marriage, and Mary was quite hurt to learn of it through the grapevine.

When Mary's sister, Anne, became Princess of Denmark, she found places in her London household for both Frances and Benjamin. Because of the Stuart sisters' sibling rivalry, Frances's new position as Anne's retainer made her a potentially untrustworthy confidante, as anything Mary dared share with her might be repeated to Anne. In any case, Mary, now a queen and in love with her actual husband, seemed to have outgrown her epistolary one.

When William was off fighting in Ireland, supporters of the former king, James II, spread the rumors that William's lover was pregnant and that William and Mary's marriage was on the rocks, neither of which was true. To halt the malicious gossip William sent a letter to his bishops ordering them to preach against adultery and the pervasive practice of openly kept mistresses. Meanwhile, the king continued his romance with Elizabeth, though he at least endeavored to be more discreet about it.

In December 1694, when Mary fell ill with smallpox, she began to put her affairs in order, burning much of her personal correspondence, including her youthful letters. The absence of these documents may account for the scant information we have regarding her relationship with Frances Apsley. Mary had also burned her diaries in 1677 before she left for Holland.

On her deathbed, Mary begged her husband to dismiss his mistress. Early in their marriage, she had come to adore William, ever after fearing she would lose half of herself every time he went off to war. His long affair with Elizabeth Villiers, even if it had grown platonic over time, had broken her heart. William, who slept by his dying wife on a camp cot, could not refuse this final request.

He pensioned off the forty-year-old Elizabeth with a gift of lands worth £30,000 a year (over $7.2 million today) and arranged a marriage to her cousin, Lord George Hamilton, the fifth son of the 3rd Duke of Hamilton. Elizabeth wed Hamilton on November 25, 1695, and the following year he was made Duke of Orkney.

Elizabeth's marriage proved to be a happy one. She bore three healthy children, and as the Countess of Orkney became a noted hostess during the era of the Hanoverian kings. She entertained both George I and George II at Cliveden, her estate in Buckinghamshire.

The seventy-year-old former royal mistress was present in all her glory at the coronation of George II in 1727. An eyewitness noted that "she exposed a mixture of fat and wrinkles, and before a considerable pair of bubbies a good deal withered, a great belly that preceded her; add to this the inimitable roll of her great eyes and her gray hair which by good fortune stood directly upright, and 'tis impossible to imagine a more delightful spectacle."

She died on April 19, 1733, at the age of seventy-six.

After William pensioned off his mistress in 1694, he focused on grieving for his late wife. William had never been made so distraught as he was by Mary's death. According to Bishop Burnet, the king had uncharacteristically sobbed that "during the whole course of his marriage he had never known one single fault in her: there was a worth in her that nobody knew besides himself." The king remarked that "from being the happiest," he was "now going to be the miserablest creature on earth." His wife might not have been his favorite lover, but she had been a true partner.

He never remarried, nor did he rekindle his romance with Elizabeth Villiers. His new fascination was one of his page-boys, a rakish fop named Arnold Joost van Keppel. Keppel had captured the king's attention when he suffered a riding acci-dent in 1691, an eerie echo of the James I–Robert Carr affair. But it was not until after Mary's death—when she, and by her directive, Elizabeth Villiers, were both out of the picture—that William fixated on Keppel.

Keppel was a ladies' man as well. Toward the beginning of William's reign, when Keppel was a mere colonel in the Horse Guards, he commenced a torrid affair with a sultry older woman, Hortense Mancini, who had been one of Charles II's mistresses. Then he dumped Hortense for her daughter, Marie-Charlotte, but that relationship did not last long.

William was displeased at Keppel's catting about, but he cared for him too much to keep him out of favor for too long.

Hans Bentinck warned William that his affection for Keppel was giving rise to rumors that they were lovers. William an-grily replied, "It is a most extraordinary thing that one could have no esteem of friendship for a young man without its being criminal." True, but the king's response is pretty much word for word the same one he'd given Mary when she caught him sneaking out of Elizabeth Villiers's boudoir.

Bentinck couldn't remain at court and watch his sovereign self-destruct. After serving as ambassador to France, he re-turned to England in 1699, preferring to retire after thirty-five years of faithful service rather than watch the king make a fool of himself over Keppel.

William bestowed numerous grants of money and property on his new favorite, and ennobled him to the peerage, creating him 1st Earl of Albemarle on February 10, 1697, and making him a Knight of the Garter in 1700. Keppel proved himself an able military commander and settled down as he matured, marrying a Dutch woman in 1701, with whom he had two children.

Despite the rumors about his relationship with William, if the king had been homosexual, the world would have heard about it long before they decided to gossip about Keppel. Servants could be bought for a song, and foreign ambassadors were always eager to send damaging information back to their homelands. Certainly Bentinck, the straight arrow in every way who knew William better than anyone, would have raised the issue of the king's proclivities years before the Keppel kerfuffle.

Although the scandal reached international proportions as the gossip spread from drawing rooms to military camps to foreign courts, what is most likely is that the middle-aged William saw the young, flamboyant Keppel as the son he never had. Or not. In any event, the king's outsized indulgence toward his protégé sparked jealousy from others—particularly his oldest and dearest friend, the man who had risked his own life to save his sovereign's.

But toward the end of William's life, Bentinck renewed their friendship, visiting William every day. And William died clutching Bentinck's hand to his heart. Bentinck was sixty years old when he succumbed to the lung disease pleurisy seven years later, on November 23, 1709.

Keppel-made-Albemarle was also at the dying king's bedside. William is said to have pressed the keys to his private cabinet and drawers into the earl's hand and whispered, "You know what to do with them." Although it was probably a straightforward request, anyone looking for a gay slant between the two men can spend years analyzing William's final directive to his favorite.

Albemarle died on May 30, 1718, at the age of forty-eight. His direct descendants include Prince Charles *and* Camilla, Duchess of Cornwall.

ANNE

1665–1714
RULED 1702–1714

The last of the Stuart monarchs, Anne was the younger daughter of King James II and his first wife, Anne Hyde. She spent her early childhood in France in the hope of a cure for her rheumy eyes. Unfortunately, no remedy was found, and Anne would always squint, giving the shy girl a permanently petulant expression. In 1670, she returned to England, and just a year later her mother died. The six-year-old Anne and her older sister, Mary, were sent to live at Richmond with the family of Sir Edward Villiers and his wife, Frances Howard, the girls' governess. They were raised there alongside the six Villiers daughters and a number of other girls thought to be suitable companions for the young royals, including Frances Apsley and Sarah Jennings.

On July 28, 1683, King Charles II married his eighteen-year-old niece Anne to Prince George of Denmark. Evidently, George had a strong sense of marital obligation, because Anne gave birth seventeen times in as many years and endured several miscarriages as well. The great tragedy of her life is considered by many to be that none of her children survived to adulthood. In any case, from constantly being pregnant her weight continued to balloon, so that by the end of her life, purpose-built hoists had to haul her about in a most unregal fashion, plopping her into extra-sturdy chairs. She always suffered from ill health, including morbid obesity, gout, and porphyria, the metabolic disorder that contributed to the demise of her relative King George III.

Because she was a younger sister, Anne had never been groomed for the throne. On March 8, 1702, when she became queen at the age of thirty-seven on the death of King William III, she lacked any serious background in statecraft. Her indolent husband (whom she grew to love very much) preferred to take a backseat, so Anne was forced to step up to the plate and work hard. She proved a diligent sovereign.

For most of her reign, England was involved in the war of the Grand Alliance against France. The Duke of Marlborough, John Churchill—husband of Anne's favorite, Sarah—planned successful campaigns and achieved three notable victories.

Anne's reign is also notable for the May 1, 1707, Act of Union, uniting England and Scotland as one realm, henceforth to be known as Great Britain. During her rule, territorial gains and economic privileges led to the foundation of the British Empire.

Anne faced significant criticism that her political decisions were too often influenced by her favorites, Sarah Churchill and Abigail Masham. One detractor complained that the country was governed from Anne's bedroom by a bunch of dictators in petticoats.

Despite her evident preference for women, Anne was despondent when her husband died in 1708. She did not remarry. Her only child to survive infancy was her eldest son, William, Duke of Gloucester, who died at the age of eleven on July 29,

1700. As William and Mary had no heirs either, Anne became the last of the Stuart dynasty.

According to the terms of the 1701 Act of Settlement enacted during William's reign, the English crown had to pass to Anne's nearest Protestant relation, paving the way for the Hanoverian dynasty and the Georgian era.

Suffering from suppressed gout and severe dropsy that led to erysipelas (a high fever accompanied by a bacterial infection below the skin), Anne died on August 1, 1714, at the age of forty-nine. She was buried in Westminster Abbey in a coffin so enormous that it was practically square. Anne was succeeded by her second cousin, George Ludwig, the eldest son of Sophia, the late Electress of Hanover, who ascended the English throne as George I.

ANNE

and Sarah Churchill, Duchess of Marlborough 1660–1744

and Abigail Masham, Baroness Masham c. 1670–1734

Sarah's father, an MP named Richard Jennings (sometimes spelled Jenyns), died when she was just eight years old. But because he had made a favorable impression on the Duke of York, Jennings's daughters, Frances and Sarah, were given positions as maids of honor to the Duchess of York, Mary of Modena. Sarah was thirteen years old in 1673 when she joined the duchess's household.

Her friendship with James's younger daughter, Anne, began to blossom in 1675, when Anne was only ten. For the next twenty-five years, Sarah would remain Anne's bosom companion and confidante.

When Anne became queen, she installed Sarah as a Lady of the Bedchamber. They corresponded frequently when they were apart, but their pet names for each other were hardly the lofty pseudonyms Mary and Frances Apsley employed. Anne and Sarah were the far more prosaic Mrs. Morley and Mrs. Freeman.

Describing Anne's feelings for her in the third person, Sarah wrote:

> *Every moment of absence she [Anne] counted a sort of tedious lifeless state. To see her [Sarah] was a constant joy, and to part with her for ever so short a time a constant uneasiness . . . She used to say she desired to possess her wholly and could hardly bear that she should ever escape this confinement into any other company.*

However, the two women wanted decidedly different things from their relationship. On Anne's side, it was the yearning for the consummation of a physical passion for the sensuous, honey-haired Sarah. Sarah felt no more for the corpulent Anne than the affection one heterosexual female feels for a very dear friend. But she knew very well which side of the bread had the butter. Referring to herself, Sarah wrote:

> *She had too great a sense of her favor not to submit to all such inconveniences to oblige one she saw loved her to excess . . . yet their tempers were not more different than their principles and notions on many occasions appeared to be.*

Unlike Anne, Sarah was blazingly straight. She was seventeen years old in the winter of 1677 when she secretly wed John Churchill, a dashing soldier who used to return from his military campaigns and make love to her with his boots on. No wedding date was recorded and only the Duchess of York was informed of it, so that Sarah could retain her position as a maid of honor, a sinecure reserved for virgins.

Churchill had a rakish past. A man who had to make his own way in the world, at one point he'd been the lover of Barbara Villiers, Countess of Castlemaine.

Both John and Sarah proved to be good friends to Anne and her husband, Prince George of Denmark. In 1688, when King James threatened to arrest Anne and George if they joined William of Orange against him, Sarah spirited Anne out of London, conveying her to safety in Nottingham, where William had many supporters, while John delivered George, without incident, to William's army camp.

Sarah's prominence in Anne's household was a bone of contention between the two sisters. Perhaps Mary, who had to leave Frances Apsley behind, was jealous that Anne was able to enjoy *her* favorite's daily companionship. When Mary became queen, she was determined to prevent Anne from bringing Sarah to court. A despondent Anne dramatically threatened to "shut myself up and never see the world more, but live where I may be forgotten by human kind."

Anne told Sarah, "If I had any inclination to part with dear Mrs. Freeman, it would make me keep her in spite of their teeth." And then—in a classic display of sibling rivalry—Anne took Mary's precious Frances Apsley, now Lady Bathurst, into her own household.

But where Sarah was concerned, there was more at stake than sisterly disaffection. John Churchill's military successes had earned him an elevation to the peerage. For his valiant leadership in the Glorious Revolution of 1688, King William made him Earl of Marlborough, but only a few years later, Marlborough fell from grace. He was known to have corresponded with the exiled James II and was suspected of turning Jacobite. As such, both John and Sarah Churchill posed a threat to William and Mary's throne. And for Anne to retain Sarah in her household, particularly as her most intimate confidante, was potentially treasonous.

Mary also believed that Anne was sharing some of the allowance she received from Parliament with Sarah. And it infuriated her that Sarah, in consort with a few of Anne's other well-placed friends, including the Duke of Somerset, had brought the matter of Anne's allowance (a parliamentary annuity of £50,000—nearly $13.5 million today) straight to the House of Commons, instead of taking it up with the monarchs.

In 1692, things came to a head. Marlborough was dismissed from court when his signature was discovered on an incriminating document supporting James II. The earl was stripped of his offices and was briefly imprisoned in the Tower of London.

Mary confronted her much larger little sister and demanded that she now release the traitor's wife from her service. Anne refused, defiantly appearing at court with Sarah beside her. Mary retained her dignity in the moment, but fired off a letter to Anne excoriating her for daring to bring her tainted favorite to court as "the strangest thing that ever was done." Anne replied that her sister's rebuke would have zero effect on her conduct.

The two Stuart sisters never reconciled, and Sarah was the wedge that had created the irrevocable rift. Even after Anne had experienced her umpteenth stillbirth and Mary came to visit her, the queen used the occasion to discuss the Sarah Problem. Anne, weak and exhausted from her maternal ordeal, never forgave Mary for making her feel worse, and they never saw each other again.

After Mary's death, William restored Anne, as well as Marlborough, to his favor, having learned that the treasonous document bearing the earl's signature was a forgery intended to discredit him. Another European war loomed on the horizon and the king had need of the duke's martial skills.

When Anne became queen, Sarah was the acknowledged

power behind the throne, while Marlborough's military prowess on the Continent made him a national hero. Anne offered Churchill a dukedom, but Sarah refused at first, citing the tremendous financial burden of maintaining such an honor. So the queen ameliorated matters by granting her favorite a lifetime annuity of £5,000 ($1.4 million today)—payable by Parliament—and an additional £200 (roughly $56,000) from the Royal Privy Purse, as well as a number of royal offices and titles, including Keeper of the Privy Purse. The Churchills accepted the dukedom. And Anne bestowed on John the honor of the Garter and made him Captain-General of the army.

As much as the new duchess begrudgingly acknowledged that Anne, being the sovereign, was her better, Sarah, as bossy, outspoken, and competitive as she was witty, lively, and charming, was clearly the dominant partner in their relationship.

The ambitious Sarah assumed the role of Anne's manager and agent, officially controlling the queen's finances and acting as gatekeeper to all who sought her audience. She was quick to give her frank opinion of any matter, even if it differed from Anne's. Few royal mistresses ever had such influence on government policy and affairs, or got away with openly contradicting the sovereign, often with thinly veiled contempt for the royal point of view.

The Duchess of Marlborough did have something that the queen never would. Sarah had given birth to two sons and four daughters, which made her feel vastly superior to Anne, and she parlayed her influence with the queen to secure positions for each of her girls.

Sarah also scored an appointment as a Lady of the Bedchamber for one of her poor relations, Abigail Hill, a young lady described by a contemporary as being inclined to "give . . . a loose to her passions."

In short order, the horse-faced Abigail replaced Sarah in Anne's affections. In 1707, when Abigail married Samuel

Masham, a gentleman of the queen's household, Sarah learned about it through backstairs gossip, while Anne had not only been an honored guest at the wedding but had given Abigail a magnanimous dowry of £2,000 (well over $500,000 today) from the Privy Purse.

Sarah, who lamented that Abigail "could make a queen stand on her head if she chose," wrote in her memoirs:

> *My cousin was an absolute favorite. Mrs. Masham came often to the Queen when the Prince was asleep, and was generally two hours in private with her.*

It's possible that Abigail supplanted Sarah because she was willing to give the queen what Sarah would not—sexual gratification. Or, the intimacy could have been purely political. Sarah was a staunch Whig while Abigail was a firm Tory, the party that was consistently promonarchy. And by 1704, when Abigail was established in the queen's household, Sarah was absenting herself frequently from court to give pro-Whig political lectures across the realm. Sarah was an astute politician with a keen intellect in an era when a woman with such "masculine" skills was an anomaly.

Additionally, Anne craved kindness and affection from her favorites in return for their preferment, and Sarah was most unwilling to play the game. She didn't fawn or flatter and her frankness with Anne often reached the point of insensitivity.

If the shrewd and gorgeous Sarah was the queen's Anne Boleyn, Abigail was her Jane Seymour. She was quietly compassionate, a homely nurturer who was content to give every impression that her ego took a backseat to her loving lady's. At the same time, she was busily promoting the interests of her Tory cousin, the MP Robert Harley.

Both Abigail and Sarah pressed their advantage with Anne to appoint ministers of their party preference, thereby exercising a tremendous influence on government policy from behind the scenes. But there was one appointment that Abigail could not convince the queen to make. Anne refused to elevate her new favorite to the peerage, because she was loath to lose Abigail as a Lady of the Bedchamber, a position that required the retainer to sleep in the same room with the sovereign. So Anne told Mrs. Masham that "it would give great offence to have a peeress lie on the floor."

In 1708, rumors of a royal affair abounded and dirty little ditties circulated about Anne and Abigail. The final verse of one such tune says it all:

> Her secretary she was not
> Because she could not write
> But had the conduct and the care
> Of some dark deeds at night.

Almost gleefully, Sarah strode into Anne's bedchamber brandishing the broadsheet. She cautioned the queen that the gossip had reached Europe and was being spread across the Continent. Her memoirs recounted the conversation.

> . . . I remember you said at the same time of all things in this world you valued most your reputation, which I confess surprised me very much, that your Majesty should so soon mention that word after having discovered so great a passion for such a woman, for sure there can be no great reputation in a thing so strange and unaccountable . . . nor can I think that having no inclination for any but of one's own sex is enough to maintain such a character as what I wish may be yours.

But Anne stubbornly refused to end the affair with Abigail. And Sarah was trying her royal patience. When Anne's husband,

Prince George, died in 1708 and Anne was overcome with grief, Sarah—the only one at court who refused to don mourning clothes because she thought the queen shed crocodile tears—unadvisedly referred to the late king in Anne's presence as "that dreary corpse."

That same year, under the influence of the Marlboroughs, there were cries from the House of Commons that Abigail was an undue influence on the queen, with calls for her dismissal. Anne herself met with individual MPs and "with tears in her eyes" begged them to oppose the formal motion to cashier her concubine. Instead, Anne dismissed the duchess from her service.

After Sarah left the court, some discrepancies were discovered in her accounts as Keeper of the Privy Purse. This information was used to blackmail Sarah when she threatened to publish a book about life at Anne's court, which would include excerpts from the queen's private correspondence. Sarah's embezzlement was swept under the rug, and in exchange she agreed to withhold publication of her sensational memoirs. (The volumes were finally published in 1742, twenty-eight years after Anne's death.)

Anne appointed Abigail Keeper of the Privy Purse in 1711 and her husband was created Baron Masham in 1713. After Anne's death in 1714, the baroness retired into private life, dying on December 6, 1734, at the age of sixty-four.

Sarah, Duchess of Marlborough, became one of the richest women in Europe, returning to favor with the Hanoverians after Anne's death. She left an architectural legacy, Blenheim Palace (which she never liked, calling it "that great heap of stones"), and lived to the ripe old age of eighty-four, dying on October 18, 1744. Her distinguished descendants include Winston Churchill and Diana, the late Princess of Wales.

THE
HANOVERS
1714–1901

George I

❧❧❧

1660–1727

Ruled 1714–1727

"German George," the great-great-grandson of James I and founder of the Hanoverian dynasty, was the first English monarch to reign pursuant to the Act of Settlement, which required the crown to pass to the nearest Protestant relation of the deceased sovereign. Before being called to do so, he was Elector of Hanover, a tiny German duchy known for its mercenary soldiers and an annual carnival internationally renowned for its licentiousness.

The fifty-four-year-old George arrived in his new country on September 29, 1714. He knew only a few words and fractured phrases of English on his arrival. His refusal to learn much more of the language during his reign reinforced the British prejudice against him as a stranger in their midst, remote and uninterested in their concerns. State business was conducted in French instead, the international language of diplomacy.

Homesick for Hanover, George spent as little time in England as possible. But his sojourns home were more than idyllic holidays; as he was still Elector of Hanover, he could not effectively govern the duchy long-distance. And it was clear to everyone which realm he preferred. George mightily disliked and distrusted his British subjects. The feeling was mutual; the English mocked him mercilessly for his coarseness, as well as for his exceptionally odd taste in mistresses.

There was no queen of England during George I's reign. In 1682, back in Hanover, George had been forced into an exceedingly loveless marriage with his high-strung, gorgeous, sixteen-year-old first cousin, Princess Sophia Dorothea of Celle. George divorced his wife in 1694, after her long-standing love affair with a studly Swedish mercenary became a public embarrassment.

George's political legacy includes the Septennial Act of 1718, which called for parliamentary elections every seven years, creating stability in the House of Commons for the first time, and leading to the MPs' increased influence in government affairs. But his reign was most characterized by financial scandals and an acrimonious feud with his son, the Prince of Wales, the future George II, because the father had chosen his mistresses over his son's mother, made her life hell, and then banished her to honorable captivity till the end of her days. In other words, the usual stuff.

The king consistently refused to give his heir a role of his own in government affairs, so the sociable prince formed his own parties in both houses of Parliament, and he and his wife hosted a rival court in their home, Leicester House. George I then deprived his son of every royal perquisite, including the participation in any matters of state. He took his children from him, and at one point plotted to have the Prince of Wales killed, or at the very least deported.

In 1720, the economy nearly collapsed when a speculative get-rich-quick scheme, known as the South Sea Bubble—the Enron scandal of its day—caused a run on the Bank of England. George's gangly mistress, by then the Duchess of Kendal, was one of the principals who successfully bribed and swindled her way to a fortune, attaching her royal lover's name to the South Sea proposal as well.

On the morning of June 10, 1727, a day after eating a surfeit of fruit, George suffered an apoplectic fit and was dead within twenty-four hours. His son succeeded him, becoming George II.

GEORGE I

and Sophia Charlotte von Kielmansegg, Countess of Darlington and Countess of Leinster 1678–1725 and (simultaneously) Ehrengard Melusine von der Schulenburg, Duchess of Kendal and Duchess of Munster 1667–1743

The words of Horace Walpole (the eighteenth-century diarist and son of the king's First Minister, Sir Robert Walpole) paint a colorful description of George I's two hideous mistresses. His depiction of the zaftig Sophia Charlotte von Kielmansegg, Countess of Darlington, is particularly grotesque:

> *Lady Darlington . . . whom I remember by being terrified at her enormous figure, was as corpulent and ample as the duchess was long and emaciated. Two fierce black eyes, large and rolling beneath two lofty arched eyebrows, two acres of cheeks spread with crimson, an ocean of neck that overflowed and was not distinguished from the lower parts of her body, and no part restrained by stays—no wonder that a child dreaded such an ogress,*

and that the mob of London were highly diverted at the
importation of such a seraglio ... and indeed nothing
could be grosser than the ribaldry that was vomited out
in lampoons, libels, and every channel of abuse, against
the sovereign and the new court and chanted even in
their hearing about in the public streets.

Surely the Disney animators had this pair in mind when they
drew the ugly stepsisters in *Cinderella*.

Of course, their royal lover was no Adonis either. George's
family were the Guelphs of Hanover, and all Guelphs shared a
number of rather unfortunate physical traits. They tended to
be chinless wonders with bulging blue eyes, and a complexion
that turned beet red at the slightest discontent—a frequent occurrence, since the Guelphs also tended to be hot-tempered.

George was indoctrinated into the delights of debauchery, probably as a teenager, by the Countess Platen, a painted doxy who
also happened to be his father's *maîtresse en titre*. The countess
procured a nice girl for George, as fat and blowsy and greedy as
herself: Sophia Charlotte von Kielmansegg, the wife of the Hanoverian court's *Oberstallmeister*, or Master of the Horse.

Her name was both a hint and an inside joke, because
George's sister was also named Sophia Charlotte. Although the
countess had numerous lovers, it was widely assumed that the
woman whom Platen had placed in the prince's bed was her
own daughter by the boy's father, Duke Ernest Augustus, Elector of Hanover, making the happy young couple half siblings.
The Countess Platen was a piece of work of historical proportions. Although George was recreationally sleeping with her
daughter, the countess was also instrumental in brokering the
prince's marriage to his first cousin, Sophia Dorothea.

The luscious, chestnut-haired, doe-eyed Sophia Dorothea
mistakenly assumed that George would ditch his mistress once
they were married; George, however, continued to prefer his

flabby, grasping trollop. Sophia Dorothea couldn't stand her husband anyway, but no one likes to be publicly humiliated. Still, in October 1683, the newlyweds managed to beget a son and heir, George Augustus.

But instead of giving up his mistress for his beautiful wife, George made things worse. In 1685, while Sophia Dorothea was on an Italian holiday with her father-in-law, Duke Ernest Augustus, George found an additional lover among his mother's maids of honor.

This new object of his desire, Ehrengard Melusine von der Schulenburg, was freakishly tall and anorexically thin. The formidable and elegant Electress Sophia couldn't fathom how her son could love a woman who looked like a scarecrow. "Look at that malkin and think of her being my son's passion!" she exclaimed to a friend. Actually, many people found Melusine patient and pleasant, with a kind disposition, so if one were to look beneath the surface, the prince's infatuation with her was not entirely surprising.

When George's wife, the princess, returned from her vacation to find that her husband had taken up with a *second* hideous mistress, she was livid. But Sophia Dorothea must have kissed and made up with George for just long enough to become pregnant again. Their daughter—also named Sophia Dorothea—was born in 1687. But after a particularly acrimonious celebration of the girl's birth, where George nearly strangled his wife in public, the battling Hanovers wanted nothing more to do with each other.

As heedless and selfish as she was lovely, in 1688 the princess commenced a torrid affair with a tall, handsome, and rakish Swedish mercenary in her husband's army. By the time he fell shako over spurs for Sophia Dorothea, Count Philip von Königsmarck had left his boots on the floor of many a European lady's boudoir. But his liaison with the Hanoverian princess was True Love.

They exchanged lurid love letters and spent as much time in each other's arms as possible. Finally, they planned to elope. But Königsmarck was waylaid, and the stories about his subsequent murder are as colorful as they are varied. What is certain is that he was ambushed—either on the open road or in the Leine Palace—and that he fought back valiantly, wounding one of his assailants. His body disappeared entirely.

George had ignored his wife's infidelity for eight years because Philip was such a crack soldier and one of the best swordsmen in Europe. But enough was enough. A kangaroo court found Sophia Dorothea guilty of "malicious desertion," and on December 28, 1694, her marriage to George was legally dissolved—a relief to the princess as well, who was now officially rid of a husband she found revolting. Sophia Dorothea was "banished" to a lovely moated country home in Ahlden, where she lived out the rest of her days in what most of us would consider luxury. Although her children were taken away and raised by their paternal grandmother, Sophia Dorothea would not have been the recipient of any mother-of-the-year trophies, so this sacrifice was probably for the best.

Meanwhile, of course, George continued to enjoy the charms of his two lovers. By then, Melusine—acknowledged since 1691 as George's *maîtresse en titre*—had given him two daughters, who were immediately reborn as her "nieces." She would give him a third daughter in 1701. Although he never acknowledged paternity of any of the girls, George did make sure they were very well provided for as they were growing up and they were included in his intimate family circle.

In 1714, the news arrived that Queen Anne had died and the mistresses learned that George would become King of England.

In England it was a common practice for places at court, army commissions, and even votes to exchange hands for money. The cost of living in London was extremely high and a courtier was expected to maintain a certain style of living. Anti-

Hanoverian propaganda penned by British contemporaries who feared the influx of foreigners and resented the enthusiastic German co-opting of the unbridled traffic in patronage has been handed down through the centuries as fact. A twenty-first-century examination of the behavior of George I's entourage has revealed that much of the eighteenth- and nineteenth-century reports, while they contain elements of truth, have also been exaggerated. Nevertheless, the accounts of the Germans' rampant corruption, retailing of government offices and contracts, and zealous greed for British money were popularly believed at the time and are not entirely false. Although it should now be taken with a grain of salt, the anti-Hanoverian version of events is too delicious to omit.

So . . .

The two mistresses caught up with their lover before he reached the English Channel and were quick to voice their concerns about his sailing off to rule a bunch of unruly regicides. But George allayed their fears, assuring his darlings that "the king-killers are my friends."

Back in Hanover, the Germans had been accustomed to having their fingers in the government till. Once they reached the shores of England, George exhorted his entourage to continue this behavior with gusto! He encouraged them to take whatever they could get, stealing it hand over fist like everyone else.

The thirty-nine-year-old zaftig Sophia Charlotte (dubbed "the Elephant" by the British) and the übersvelte forty-seven-year-old Melusine (whom they nicknamed "the Maypole") enthusiastically obeyed their lover's advice. They plundered the Treasury and the royal commissaries like pirates on the high seas. The story of George I and his monstrous mistresses is less about sex than it is about rape—the rape of English money, titles, and property, even of Queen Anne's jewels and personal effects—by the pair of fraüleins.

All but hanging out a shingle reading "Influence Peddlars,"

the two Teutonic marauders made tens of thousands of pounds accepting bribe after bribe of money and jewelry, selling government offices in England, positions on the Continent, even colonial governorships in America. The king had settled an income on each of his women, but it wasn't nearly enough. It was never enough. Melusine was receiving an allowance from George of £7,500 a year (almost $2 million today), but she coveted the household allowance, too. And when the post of Master of the Horse became vacant, she didn't care whether her lover appointed a replacement—she demanded the salary.

King George naturalized his mistresses as British subjects and ennobled them each to life peerages, first in Ireland and then in England. The Elephant was made Countess of Leinster and Countess of Darlington. As proof of the suppositions that she was George's half sister, her letters of patent bore the words *"consanguineum nostrum"* (of our blood), and her Brunswick coat of arms included the bar sinister, the heraldic emblem for a royal bastard.

George granted the Maypole a number of Irish estates, but everyone knew that collecting the rents on them was dodgy, and therefore the income was uncertain. So the king gave her four English titles, the loftiest being Duchess of Kendal, by which she is known today.

Evidently, Kendal was a pro at taking everything but criticism. After she brought him to court, the journalist Nathaniel Mist was fined and imprisoned for publishing an anonymous letter in his *Journal* that read:

> *We are ruined by trulls, nay, what is more vexatious, by ugly trulls, such as could not find entertainment in the most hospitable hundreds of old Drury.*

Although the Elephant was better liked among the English for her gregariousness, her good taste, and her sparkling conversation, of the two women, it was Melusine, Lady Kendal, who behaved like the morganatic wife of the king. She had apartments in St. James's Palace and acted as George's hostess at official events. Sir Robert Walpole remarked that she was "as much a queen of England as ever any was, though she would sell the king's honor for a shilling."

And did. Lady Kendal was the Ken Lay of her day, becoming spectacularly rich off of speculative investments, bribes from wannabe government officials, salaries, rents, and annuities. She was also, perhaps, the first known political lobbyist, on the payroll of a collective of investors known as the South Sea Company, which concocted a historic stock swindle that included a proposal to take over the massive national debt at a five percent annual rate of interest.

Bribery of public officials reached a peak when the Duchess of Kendal put the king on the South Sea Company's payroll. Allegedly, George received what amounted to a hefty licensing fee for lending his name to the scheme.

The premise had been concocted by the Earl of Oxford and a cadre of cronies, who in 1711 took seed money from duties collected on various imported goods and funneled it into a company that had a charter to trade in the South Seas. The company told the public that King Philip V of Spain was enthusiastically cooperating with the venture, providing ships and free passage along Spanish-controlled trade routes to the Pacific, where gold and silver abounded. The more shares in the venture you purchased, the greater your percentage of the treasure to be plundered from this mythical Pacific paradise. No one bothered to ask if Philip was really involved.

Preying on the national passion for wagering, shares in the speculative (and fictional) venture were sold hand over fist and the price soared, while the South Sea Company's principals pocketed the cash. The company's promoters made a windfall for themselves and their friends. The scheme, known as the

South Sea Bubble, bilked the greedy, the hopeful, and the naïve out of millions. By August 1720, the shares reached a 1,000 percent dividend buoyed by a hysterical belief in the high return the investments would receive when the financed ships returned with treasures from the West. The Exchange Alley at Cornhill was mobbed by Londoners from all walks of life. Tories and Whigs found themselves in the same camp, united by avarice. King George himself amassed an enormous profit.

And then suddenly, panic began to set in after it was rumored that the initial investors were starting to sell off their shares. Each of George's lovers raked in huge profits by selling high, and his reign was seriously tainted by the scandal. When the list of people who had used undue influence to pressure investors to buy the bogus stock was read aloud in Parliament, right up at the top were his two mistresses, as well as most of his chief ministers and the secretaries of the Treasury.

By the mid-1720s, the Maypole, now pushing sixty, evidently lost interest in collecting bribes and suddenly got religion. She began attending Lutheran services several times every Sunday in the vain hope, perhaps, of making up for lost time. But the ministers refused to give her the Eucharist because she was living in a state of adultery.

Countess Darlington, the Elephant, died at her home in St. James's Palace on April 20, 1725, and was buried four days later in Westminster Abbey.

In June 1727, the sixty-seven-year-old monarch embarked on his fifth excursion to Hanover since the beginning of his thirteen-year reign as King of England. On June 9, his little entourage stopped en route in Delden, Holland, at the home of a friend, Count de Twillet. There George enjoyed an enormous supper, overindulging in a dessert of oranges and strawberries. Inexplicably, many historical accounts refer to "several water melons" as the lethal fruit. Whatever roughage he consumed, despite a dreadful bellyache the following day, the king was eager to get back on the road. When he reached Ibbenburen, he suffered an attack of apoplexy.

A contemporary described the incident: "He was quite lethargic, his hand fell down as if lifeless, and his tongue hung out of his mouth. He gave, however, signs of life by continually crying out as well as he could articulate, 'Osnabrück! Osnabrück!' [the name of his birthplace]." This account does not appear to make it into other twenty-first-century discussions of the king's final hours.

A modern version of events has George reaching Osnabrück, lapsing in and out of consciousness along the way, and briefly raising his hat to acknowledge that he recognized his surroundings once he'd arrived at his birthplace. According to the Historical Register, his last words were in French—*"c'est fait de moi"* (I am done for!). He died in the early hours of the morning on June 11, 1727. George I was buried near his mother's monument at the Leineschloss Church in Hanover.

The Duchess of Kendal was not with the king when he died, having lagged behind at Delden for some unrecorded reason. When she received the news of her beloved's demise, she became hysterical, tearing her hair and beating her breast like the heroine of a Greek tragedy. The duchess went into seclusion in Germany for three months. At that point the new king, George II, welcomed her back to England, where she lived out the remainder of her days on her various estates. She died in bed on May 10, 1743, at the age of seventy-six.

GEORGE II

❧❧❧

1683–1760
RULED 1727–1760

*I*N 1705, WHILE HIS FATHER WAS STILL ELECTOR OF HAN-over, the twenty-two-year-old George married Princess Caroline of Anspach in a match arranged by his grandmother, the dowager Electress. Caroline was not a classic beauty. Her features were somewhat coarse, but she was blond and blue-eyed and had fabulous boobs. Competent and pragmatic, Caroline soothed her husband's childish temper tantrums and insisted that he learn the language when the family went off to England in 1714. And after George II became king, it was Caroline who acted as regent when he left the country.

A talented soldier, George had distinguished himself at the Battle of Oudenarde in 1707, and his father was so jealous of his accomplishment that he pulled the plug on Junior's military career. It was not until thirty-six years later, when he defeated the French at Dettingen in 1743, that he got to flex his martial muscles once more. George II was the last British monarch to lead his troops into battle.

George is perhaps best remembered for his role in the Jacobite rebellion of 1745. "The Young Pretender," the grandson of James II (through James's son by Mary of Modena), better known as Bonnie Prince Charlie, took up arms against George II's forces and made a bid for the English throne. Born in 1720, Bonnie Prince Charlie was raised in Rome, where his family enjoyed the protection of the Pope. Many of the Highland clans supported the Jacobites (James's followers) and rallied to the cause, backing the restoration to the throne of the Catholic Stuarts. Bonnie Prince Charlie's grandfather, James II of England, had of course also been James VII of Scotland.

On April 16, 1746, the Young Pretender's forces were decimated by the British army, led by the morbidly obese Duke of Cumberland, George II's younger son. In retreat, Bonnie Prince Charlie fled to the Highlands. After fifty-eight years of uprisings and skirmishes, the Jacobite threat was finally extinguished.

Having sat on the throne for thirty-three years, a constipated George II died at the age of seventy-two on October 25, 1760, while straining to use the toilet at Kensington Palace. The official cause of death was "an aortic dissection." He was buried beside his wife in Westminster Abbey, having given specific instructions that the side of his coffin be removed so that their remains could be together. Frederick, the heir apparent, had suffered a burst abscess after receiving a blow from a cricket ball, dying on March 20, 1751, at the age of forty-four. So George II's grandson, George III, succeeded him as King of England.

♔

GEORGE II
and Henrietta Howard 1688–1767

Although George II and his father never seemed to agree on anything, they shared one particular quirk: a passion for pulchritude. According to one of George II's contemporaries, "not a woman came amiss to him if she were very willing and very fat." The English derived as much entertainment from mocking the son's choice of concubine as they had enjoyed scorning the father's.

And yet Lord Hervey, Vice Chamberlain of the Royal House-hold, observed of George II, "Though he is incapable of being at-tached to any woman but his wife, he seemed to look upon his mistresses as a necessary appurtenance to his grandeur as a Prince rather than an addition to his pleasure." When Queen Caroline died in 1737, her grieving husband avowed that he "never saw a woman worthy to buckle her shoe." It didn't mean he didn't sleep with them, though, while she was very much alive.

The plump and homely Henrietta Howard was the daughter of Sir Henry Hobart, who was killed in a duel when she was a little girl. By the time Henrietta was thirteen years old, she was orphaned. She became a ward of the Earl of Suffolk, and at the age of eighteen married the earl's youngest son, Charles, an of-ficer in the dragoons.

They moved to London and Henrietta secured a position as a Lady of the Bedchamber to the Princess of Wales. But Henri-etta and her husband were so poor that they had been forced to chop off her hair and sell it to a wig maker so they could afford to come to court. Although her marriage had been a love match, Charles Howard was straight out of a Central Casting call for profligate, boorish drunks. So it's not surprising that when the Prince of Wales winked in Henrietta's direction in 1723, she was grateful for his paltry offer of £2,000 a year (about $538,000 nowadays) to become his mistress.

Henrietta was universally liked at court, amiable, and hon-est. And soon she was the acknowledged mistress of the Prince of Wales. According to Horace Walpole, "his time of going down to Lady Suffolk was seven in the evening: he would fre-quently walk up and down the Gallery looking at his watch for a quarter of an hour before seven, but would not go till the clock struck." A courtier once suggested that perhaps the two were just talking, to which Walpole replied that this scenario was highly unlikely, as Henrietta was so deaf, and George's "passions so indelicate."

But George Junior's adulterous father just couldn't tolerate his son's extramarital happiness. In 1727, George I paid Henrietta's inebriated no-account husband to stand under the prince's window at Leicester House and shout for his wife. The gathering bystanders realized that the king had put Howard up to it, and enjoyed a laugh at both men's expense.

For Henrietta, however, the matter was deadly serious. Backed by George I, Howard was seeking a reconciliation that would have meant her dismissal from Caroline's household and her enforced retirement to the country. Howard assumed custody of their young son, and Henrietta became a political pawn in the tug-of-war between the royal Georges. The king viewed her as an unpleasant influence on the prince's politics and wanted her neutralized. For several tense weeks she feared being kidnapped.

When George I died that year, Henrietta's position became less precarious. Her lover was now the king. Howard was bought off with a £1,200 annuity (over $263,000 today); he and Henrietta were legally separated on February 29, 1728.

Ordinarily, George II's affairs had little effect on his wife. Caroline of Anspach was smarter than her husband and prettier than his mistresses. By all accounts, George and Caroline loved each other very much, and were the rare royals to share a bedroom. But often the king came to bed very late, or left the room rather early. The Archbishop of York archly remarked that he "was glad to find her Majesty so sensible a woman as to like [that] her husband should divert himself."

However, where Henrietta was concerned, the queen could not bring herself to be indifferent. Caroline enjoyed humiliating her waiting women, and took especial care to single out Henrietta. And Henrietta's royal lover, instead of leaping chivalrously to her defense, joined in the fray. One day while Henrietta was securing a scarf about Caroline's creamy throat, George yanked it off, cruelly telling his mistress, "Because you have an ugly neck yourself, you love to hide the queen's!" Henrietta somehow endured the torment.

Although Henrietta and Charles were separated when he became Earl of Suffolk in 1731, she was entitled to remain his countess. Henrietta's new position made her too exalted to remain a Lady of the Bedchamber, so Queen Caroline made her Mistress of the Robes. She was also, of course, still mistress to the king.

Henrietta had staying power, remaining George's mistress for twenty years. And when the king decided it was time to trade her in for a newer model, there was an outcry at court. Lord Hervey remarked that "one would have imagined that the King, instead of dropping a mistress to give himself up entirely to his wife, had repudiated some virtuous, obedient, and dutiful wife in order to abandon himself to the dissolute commerce and dangerous sway of some new favorite."

And after two decades of civilly accepting Henrietta's horizontal position with her husband, the queen voiced her opinion on the matter: George should keep Henrietta. After all, Caroline feared the influence of a new favorite as well. The king was incensed at her meddling. "What the devil do you mean by trying to make an old, dull, deaf, peevish beast stay and plague me?" he demanded of his wife.

Suffolk died in 1733, and the following year Henrietta lost her position at court. By 1734, George had tired of her, and the queen dismissed her from her service. Henrietta married the Honorable George Berkeley, the son of the Earl of Berkeley, in 1735 and enjoyed the better part of her remaining years at her Palladian estate, Marble Hill, in Twickenham. There, she presided over a glittering literary salon, hosting such notable minds and wits as Jonathan Swift and Alexander Pope—who wrote a quatrain about Henrietta that encapsulated her effect on the people who loved her:

> *I knew a thing that's most uncommon*
> *(Envy be silent and attend!)*
> *I knew a reasonable woman,*
> *Handsome and witty, yet a friend.*

Henrietta's second husband died in October 1746; she spent the rest of her life making improvements to Marble Hill and concealing the extent of her debts from her friends. She died there on July 26, 1767, at the age of seventy-eight or -nine.

GEORGE II

and Amalie Sophie Marianne von Wallmoden 1705–1765

After Henrietta, George pleasured himself with a bevy of dubious beauties. And Queen Caroline shared her husband's taste for titillation. Understanding that kings have needs, she occasionally acted as George's procuress—provided that his lovers were uglier than she was. And when he visited Hanover, he delighted in sharing the graphic details of his amorous exploits in juicy letters home.

During a visit in 1735, the king waxed particularly rhapsodic about Amalie Sophie von Wallmoden, a voluptuous dusky beauty twenty-one years his junior. The daughter of a Hanoverian general, in 1727 Amalie had married the *Oberhauptmann* of Calenberg, Gottlieb Adam von Wallmoden, whom she bore two children.

It took George thirty pages to tell his wife about his new inamorata's charms, crowing to Caroline, "I know you will love Madame Walmoden [sic] because she loves me!"

However, the queen's remarkable tolerance for his affairs evanesced after George hung a full-length portrait of his new mistress directly opposite their marital bed. And in 1736, when he insisted on returning to Germany to visit Madame von Wallmoden, a scamp sent a broken-down nag trundling through the London streets with a placard affixed to its rump advising, "Let nobody stop me. I am the King's Hanover equipage going to fetch His Majesty and his whore to England."

George wanted to bring his amorous souvenir home with him; but Caroline was adamantly against it, as were George's ministers, including Sir Robert Walpole, who feared that a German influence so intimately connected with the king might have a devastating effect on the British government. So George's lover remained in Germany, and in 1737, he and Caroline patched up their marital differences.

But by November of that year, Caroline was very ill. She'd suffered from gout for years, and that summer had succumbed to an attack of colic. But it was complications that had followed the birth of her last child, Princess Louisa, in 1724, that eventually felled the queen. She lay in agony for a week, and on her deathbed, tearfully asked her husband if he planned to take another wife.

"*Non, non, j'aurai des maîtresses,*" the sobbing king assured his beloved spouse ("No, no, I shall have mistresses").

Caroline died on November 20, 1737, at the age of fifty-four. The following June, Madame von Wallmoden arrived in England and was promptly installed as George's *maîtresse en titre*. Her husband had accompanied her. But with Amalie playing official hostess and royal concubine, there was clearly no role for him, so he returned to Hanover and divorced her in 1740.

On February 8, 1740, George naturalized Amalie a British subject and elevated her to the peerage, creating her Countess of Yarmouth. She wasted no time setting up shop for the purposes of bribes and influence peddling. After demanding £30,000 (over $6.6 million today) from her royal lover, rather than open the Privy Purse, George gave her permission to choose two candidates for the peerage and pocket a £15,000 bribe from each of them!

On George II's death in 1760, he left his lover a strongbox containing "about ten thousand pounds" (a little over $2.7 million today), according to Horace Walpole. The king's dour successor, his grandson, George III, sent her packing back to the Continent, so the Countess of Yarmouth decamped to Hanover, where she died of breast cancer in 1765.

GEORGE IV

1762–1830

REGENT 1811–1820

KING 1820–1830

WHEN GEORGE WAS FIFTEEN YEARS OLD, HIS TUTOR, DR. Richard Hurd, presciently observed, "He will either be the most polished gentleman or the most accomplished blackguard in Europe, possibly an admixture of both."

After several romances that earned the Prince of Wales an especially notorious reputation as well as a secret marriage on December 15, 1785, to the Roman Catholic Maria Fitzherbert, on April 8, 1795, George married his first cousin, the slatternly and odiferous Caroline of Brunswick. It was a match made *only* because the king had agreed to pay his son's debts, which at the time amounted to over £600,000 (nearly $88 million today).

His father, George III, had struggled with bouts of "madness," which are now believed to have been manifestations of porphyria, a rare metabolic disorder that was most likely passed into the Hanover line through the Stuarts. In fact, George I's cousin Anne, the last Stuart monarch, is also believed to have suffered from porphyria, though with a less drastic effect on her overall health.

Symptoms of porphyria include discolored urine (often bluish black); abdominal pain; a weakness in the limbs; and mental issues leading to paranoia, derangement, and hysteria (which is why George III's contemporaries, who knew nothing of porphyria, were certain he'd gone mad).

After it was determined that King George was no longer mentally sound enough to continue to rule, on February 5, 1811, the forty-eight-year-old Prince of Wales was made Regent. George III died on January 29, 1820, and the regent, then fifty-seven, was crowned George IV.

He was one of the most erudite and cultivated of all English monarchs, and a great patron of the arts. The Regency, and later George IV's reign, were characterized by lavish balls and crowded assemblies, and the introduction of that daring new dance from the Continent—the waltz. Often viewed through rosy lenses, the Regency is one of the most popular settings for romance novels, depicted as a kinder, gentler era where manners mattered—the age of Jane Austen's novels. In fact, Austen was George's favorite author, so she had no choice but to dedicate *Emma* to him, although she despised the prince's shabby treatment of his wife, Princess Caroline of Brunswick.

As Prince of Wales, George was perversely and obstinately in favor of anything his father was against. George III was a staunch Tory; so "Prinny" supported the Whigs. But once he became king, George IV switched allegiances and became a Tory himself, shutting out the very men who had helped his cause when he was floundering in financial and romantic straits. And although the prince had secretly married the Catholic Maria Fitzherbert, he stubbornly refused to grant Catholic emancipation. Politically, there is little in the "credits" column of

George IV's reign, other than his decision as regent to continue to ally with Spain in the Peninsular War against Napoleon.

Unfortunately, George IV had so much promise, but did precious little with it, squandering the public's goodwill with his lechery and lavish spending, while during his regency and reign soldiers and sailors went unpaid. "Luddite" laborers were threatened with redundancy by machines that sped up, but cheapened, their craft. And in Ireland there were threats of civil war.

Possessing the Hanoverian corpulence, George's weight matched the size of his ego, swelling to well over three hundred and fifty pounds in his final years. The man who had once been so vain that he had asked Beau Brummel to mentor him in all things sartorial refused to go out in public, so ashamed was he of his elephantine appearance.

George IV died at the age of sixty-seven on June 26, 1830, as the result of a burst blood vessel in his abdomen. He was succeeded by his younger brother William, Duke of Clarence, who ruled as William IV.

GEORGE IV
and Mary Robinson 1757–1800

On December 3, 1779, readers of the London daily papers would have seen an advertisement announcing:

Drury Lane
By Command of their Majesties
The sixth time these ten years

At the Theatre Royal in Drury Lane
This Day will be Presented
The Winter's Tale
(altered by Garrick from Shakespeare)

Mary Robinson, one of the theatre company's leading luminaries, was assigned the central role of Perdita, the shepherd girl who falls in love with a handsome prince and does not learn until the denouement that she herself is really a princess.

In her day, Mary was a glamorous superstar renowned for her fashion sense; she was an enormous trendsetter, and her influence extended to her choice of theatrical costumes as well as her offstage ensembles, which included scandalous appearances at the London pleasure gardens wearing breeches. On the night of the command performance for the royal family, rather than attire herself in frothy flounces, which was the standard costume for such heroines, Mary chose something more rustic, which would show her figure and her abundant auburn hair to advantage: a tight-fitting red jacket and matching ribbons in her hair.

One of her costars, a Mr. Smith, remarked, "By Jove, Mrs. Robinson, you will make a conquest of the prince; for tonight you look handsomer than ever."

The compliment didn't help dispel Mary's preperformance jitters. And when the seventeen-year-old heir to the English throne fixed his attention on her, the twenty-two-year-old married actress was so discombobulated that she raced through her lines with the speed of a runaway horse. But George Augustus Frederick, Prince of Wales, wasn't paying much attention to the script. He was utterly entranced by Mary's appearance and vivacity, and could see little else.

By the final scene, Mary realized just what an impact she

had scored. Recalling the momentous event in her memoirs, she wrote, "with a look that I shall never forget, he gently inclined his head a second time; I felt the compliment and blushed my gratitude." At the end of the performance, the actors lined up across the stage and waited respectfully while the royal party exited in front of them. The Prince of Wales again inclined his head to Mary, a gesture that was not missed by anyone remaining in the house, and certainly not by Mary's fellow performers. The heir's attention was the talk of the company.

Mary endeavored to modestly downplay George's subtle flirtations, but inside she was all aflutter. The middle-class girl from Bristol who had become a "household name" in her own right now secretly gave her imagination free rein.

The day after the command performance, the prince's confidant, Viscount Malden, paid Mary a call. He was bearing a gushing letter addressed to "Perdita" from an admirer calling himself "Florizel." According to her memoirs, Mary said to Malden, "Well, my lord, and what does this mean?"

"Can you not guess the writer?" replied the viscount.

" 'Perhaps yourself, my lord,' cried I gravely."

Malden assured her that he would never presume to offer such florid compliments on so short an acquaintance. The Prince of Wales, however, was unconcerned with that sort of etiquette. Mary remained skeptical about the identity of her epistolary admirer until Malden visited the following day with another letter, purportedly from the prince, in which His Highness assured her that he would give her a demonstrable sign of his attraction for her that evening at the oratorio, a religious concert where the young prince and his family were to be in attendance.

Through Malden, who now became the couple's official courier, Mary reminded the prince that she was a married woman, and that if she were to attend the concert, it would be in the company of her husband. By that time, Mr. and Mrs. Robinson, who had wed in April 1773, when Mary was all of fifteen years old, had unofficially parted ways, divorce being a near impossibility for the English middle class. Mr. Robinson was an unemployed, hard-drinking, hard-gambling womanizer who kept two mistresses, and Mary was well rid of him. But for an actress, a profession notorious for its lack of respectability, being married, however unhappily, lent a woman a measure of propriety.

At the oratorio, the prince, sitting in his box, engaged in an elaborate pantomime, where he seductively touched his glass to his lips, and pretended to write something on the edge of the box. Soon, the daily papers were buzzing with tidbits of gossip about the pair; and from salons to coffeehouses, the buzz centered on the prince's fancy. "Florizel" wrote to his "Perdita" almost daily. Mrs. Robinson would become the first in a long line of George's mistresses.

But not yet.

Mary was a sensible young woman. She understood that her giddy epistolary romance might as well have been written in the sand they used to set the ink. George continually pressed her for a private meeting, but Mary was not yet willing to surrender her charms. For one thing, the prince—though he seemed to have no qualms about taking a married woman as his mistress—emphatically believed that the theatre was a disgraced profession. If Mary were to become his lover, she would have to relinquish her stage career, an uncomfortable trade-off. Not only was she a bona fide stage star who loved her job, but Mary was one of the few women of her day who had managed to secure an independent living, supporting herself, her wayward spouse, and their young daughter solely on the income she made as an actress. And it was quite an impressive income, even if Mary did have a penchant for spending every penny of it on clothes and new carriages.

But George was an eager pup and unwilling to be forestalled.

He begged Mary to visit him disguised as a man, but the actress, renowned for showing off her legs in "breeches parts," dissuaded him. He sent her his portrait in miniature, ringed with diamonds. Even when their liaison ended, Mary cherished the portrait; in early 1782, Sir Thomas Gainsborough painted Mary holding it, and when her other possessions were auctioned off to pay her debts, she clung to this tiny treasure. Describing the miniature in her memoirs, Mary wrote, "Within the case was a small heart cut in paper, which I also have; on the one side was written '*Je ne change qu'en mourant.*' On the other, 'Unalterable to my Perdita through life,'" more or less the English translation of the French phrase written on the flip side of the heart.

Although Mary delighted in their passionate correspondence, she still kept the prince's person at arm's length. "I recommended him to be patient till he should become his own master; to wait until he knew more of my mind and manners before he engaged in a public attachment to me and, above all, to do nothing that might incur the displeasure of the royal family."

To prove his earnestness and his devotion, the prince sent Mary a promissory note or bond for £20,000 (nearly $4 million today), payable upon his coming of age, although His Highness would not turn twenty-one until August 12, 1783. When Mary opened the envelope, she burst into a flood of astonished tears, convinced by the magnanimity of the gesture that the prince was taking her concerns seriously. Were she now to cast off her lucrative career to become a royal mistress, her financial sacrifice would not be overlooked.

Finally, Mary consented to a meeting with His Royal Highness. Lord Malden brokered the nocturnal liaison, which took place just beyond the iron gates of Kew Palace. Literally cloaked, the would-be lovers exchanged furtive words and sighs, but their interview was abruptly halted when they heard noises coming from the palace. The prince scurried indoors while Mary (and Malden) beat a hasty retreat for the little boat that had transported them downriver. But that intimate meeting had done much to sway Mary's inclinations from esteem to ardor. During just a few minutes together she had become utterly smitten. "How my soul would have idolized such a husband," she wrote in her memoirs.

Within weeks, Mary gave her notice to the manager of Drury Lane, the playwright (and MP) Richard Brinsley Sheridan. The savvy manager capitalized on Mary's increased notoriety, adding more appearances in order to pack the house as frequently as possible through her final, emotional, farewell performance on May 31, 1780.

Mary finally surrendered her body to her royal lover at the unprepossessing Three Swans inn on Brentford, an islet in the Thames. The lovers would have further assignations at a small brick house not far from Kew.

One week after her final stage appearance, Mary's behavior created another scandal when, as the prince's invited guest (and everyone knew why), she sat in the Lord Chamberlain's box during the King's Birthday celebration at St. James's Palace. Bad enough that an actress should be in their exalted midst, but the haute ton was doubly mortified when Mary immodestly trumpeted her position. During the first dance with the Lady Augusta Campbell, who bestowed a posy of roses upon him, His Royal Highness asked a courtier to bring the buds to Mary, who made a great show of placing them in her décolletage.

She set up house in Cork Street, Mayfair, as befitted a *maîtresse en titre*, but footed the bill for her own establishment, although it was frequented by the Prince of Wales and his circle of friends, providing a welcome respite from his parents, the repressive monarchs.

Already a celebrity as an actress, once she became a royal

mistress, Mary's allure multiplied. "Whenever I appeared in public, I was overwhelmed by the gazing of the multitude," she wrote in her memoirs. "Even in the streets of the metropolis, I had scarcely ventured to enter a shop without experiencing the greatest inconvenience. Many hours have I waited till the crowd dispersed, which surrounded my carriage."

She began flashing her status around town, gadding about in a coach that bore the emblem of her initials entwined with George's, surrounded by a border that tapered at its apex into something resembling a coronet. She took a side box at the theatre, a location customarily the privilege of the titled and otherwise well-heeled. Despite the fact that Mary had once been queen of that very stage, her detractors thought she should have been relegated to the upper balcony, where the trolling prostitutes plied their trade.

The caricaturists, ever vicious, turned Mary and her royal lover into a popular subject for ridicule. It was then, as the prince's mistress, and for the role in which she had first caught his eye, that Mary Robinson earned the sobriquet that would follow her for the rest of her life, no matter what her profession or who she was sleeping with. Everyone now called her "the Perdita," which literally means *the lost girl*, a term more apt than people knew for this young woman whose father had abandoned their family when she was a little girl, and who as an adult would go from man to man seeking not merely material comforts but a fulfilling and enduring love.

And then, one day in mid-December 1780, when Mary believed herself at the zenith of her popularity and the prince's affection, she received a brief message from George: "*We must meet no more,*" it read. Mary was startled, shocked, and devastated. She summoned one of her carriages and drove posthaste for Windsor. It was night when she approached the castle, her carriage passing another coach heading back to London carrying Elizabeth Armistead, a burgeoning courtesan. Evidently, her royal lover had taken a new mistress.

Days later in London, Mary begged George to take her back, and they had a passionate reconciliation at Lord Malden's town house; but her relief was short-lived. The following day, Mary's carriage passed the prince's in Hyde Park and he gave her the cut direct, refusing eye contact and rattling right by her coach as if he never knew her.

Mary was well and truly lost now, and a laughingstock to boot. Her friends cautioned her against renewing her stage career, for no one wanted to see her triumph. Out of a job, and bereft of a protector, Mary made the difficult decision to publish their love letters. Naturally, she realized that the correspondence would become a bestseller and would provide the income necessary to support herself and her little girl.

When the prince's father got wind of Mary's intentions, he knew it was time to get involved. No way was this upstart actress going to bring down the House of Hanover by publicizing the heir's immature indiscretions. Wanting to make the whole bloody embarrassing issue disappear, the king dispatched Colonel George Hotham, the prince's treasurer, to negotiate a settlement with Mary. Mary chose a "second" as well: Lord Malden. The talks dragged on for more than half a year. By July 1781, Mary was still reminding the king that she had been compelled to relinquish her profession and her respectability as a married woman because she truly believed the prince loved her and would always provide for her, as he had so often promised to do.

The king's final offer, through Hotham, was £5,000 (a whisper under $900,000 today) for the letters—all or nothing. Mary was left with no choice, but wanted it stipulated that the money was for the return of the letters, not as payment for services rendered to the prince. In other words, she considered herself the prince's girlfriend, not his whore. "I never would or could have made him ampler restitution, as I have valued those letters as dearly as my existence & nothing but my distressed situation ever should have tempted me to give them up at all," she wrote in her memoirs.

Although Mary despised gamblers, she decided to throw the dice once more. Five thousand pounds would scarcely cover her debts, leaving her with little to live on, and she had no immediate prospects of an independent income. She still had the £20,000 bond the prince had given her. Hotham argued that the document was invalid because the prince, being underage, had no authority to make such a promise.

Nevertheless, it did bear the official seal and His Royal Highness's true signature, insisted Mary. However, she was willing to forfeit the bond in exchange for an annuity, and cited considerable precedent for English kings and princes providing annuities for their cast-off mistresses. Hotham did his best to stand his ground on behalf of the crown, but Mary had a point. Besides, she wasn't about to relinquish the promissory note without compensation, because in two years' time, when Prince George turned twenty-one, the document might very well be viewed as perfectly legitimate.

They settled on a £500 annuity (nearly $90,000 today), with half-payment of the sum to be given to Mary's daughter, Maria Elizabeth, upon Mary's demise. This petty squabbling over financial matters, which didn't reach a full accord until late August 1781, was an ugly denouement to what had begun so romantically.

As the years wore on, Mary and her prince became cordial acquaintances and often moved in the same social and political circles. At the very least, the glimmer that remained from that initial glow of young love was enough not to turn the pair against each other irrevocably.

When Mary died in 1800 at the age of forty-three, her request that two locks of her hair be cut off and sent to two former paramours was fulfilled. One of the recipients was her lover of fifteen years, Colonel Banastre Tarleton. The other man who received an auburn curl was the Prince of Wales, and it is said that he was buried with it.

♔

GEORGE IV
and Maria Fitzherbert 1756–1837

Maria Anne Smythe came from a Catholic Royalist family. Between the ages of twelve and sixteen, she was educated at an English convent school in Paris. At eighteen, she wed Edward Weld, a wealthy landowner twenty-six years her senior, who died after a fall from his horse just three months into their marriage. Three years later, in 1777, Maria married Thomas Fitzherbert, who came from an illustrious and highly respected Catholic family. She bore Fitzherbert a son, but both husband and child died in the South of France in 1781.

By 1784, Maria was twenty-seven years old, with a £1,000 annuity (nearly $187,000 today) from Thomas Fitzherbert, a respectable annual income for a childless young widow. Following Fitzherbert's death, she traveled extensively through the Continent's most picturesque towns and Alpine villages, endeavoring to assuage her grief.

Her uncle, Henry Errington, finally coaxed her back to England, and one evening that March he convinced her to attend the opera with him. That night her fate was to change dramatically. According to a contemporary's account, "She left the opera leaning on Henry Errington's arm, and when at the door, with her veil down waiting for the carriage, the Prince came up to him and said, 'Who the devil is that pretty girl you have on your arm, Henry?' On being introduced, the Prince is said to have been transfixed, unable to tear his eyes away from the lovely face half hidden by the veil. Then her carriage drew up and she was able to make her escape."

Six years Maria's junior, George found her entirely irresistible, although she was not a classic beauty. Women, in particular, were inclined to think her somewhat "fat." Her chin was considered too "determined" and there was rather a vast amount of cheek along the sides of her oval face, described by contemporaries as "a very mild benignant countenance without much animation." She even mocked her own aquiline "Roman Catholic" nose. But she made up for it with her hazel eyes, silky blond hair, and flawless complexion. More important, everyone who knew Maria Fitzherbert thought the world of her sweet temper and demure, yet utterly uncloying, nature. Respected and respectable, she was kind and compassionate—the utter antithesis of the typical grasping, opportunistic royal mistress.

By March 10, 1784, just days after George demanded an introduction to the mysteriously veiled beauty, rumors abounded that the Prince of Wales was making "fierce love to the widow Fitzherbert," and it was expected that he would succeed in his quest. What the gossips hadn't counted on was Maria's impeccable dignity. Although he peppered her with invitations to Carlton House, Maria, accepting some of them, while declining others, made it quite clear to the heir apparent that she had no interest in becoming his mistress.

So he proposed marriage.

Maria countered with every pragmatic reply. She was a devout Catholic with no intentions of renouncing her faith. Should she marry him, it would be in defiance of both the Royal Marriages Act (which prohibited a royal under the age of twenty-five from marrying without the king's permission) *and* the Act of Settlement (which barred any Catholics, or anyone married to a Catholic, from inheriting the crown). Were

Maria to marry George, it would cost him his throne. Even a secret marriage would violate both laws.

But the prince was uninterested in anything approaching a rational argument. He practically stalked Maria, showing up at her doorstep at all hours and threatening to do himself some bodily injury if she did not surrender.

The prince could be seductively disarming, but he was also spectacularly manipulative, selfish, and insensitive—all the ugliest qualities of royal entitlement. If Maria would not consent to be his, he would die. And he meant it. He had frequently dissolved into hysterical protestations of love, but had failed to move her.

On July 8, 1784, the prince stabbed himself just badly enough to make it look like a credible suicide attempt. Late that evening four men from his household showed up at Maria's doorstep insisting that she return to Carlton House with them immediately. The distracted faces of the prince's men convinced Maria that they weren't kidding, but to preserve her honor from malicious gossip, she insisted that their mutual friend Georgiana, Duchess of Devonshire, accompany her as a chaperone and witness.

At Carlton House, they found the prince tearing at his bandages. He threatened to rip them off and bleed to death in front of Maria if she refused to marry him. As George continued to toy with his bandages, bleeding through his shirt, Maria relented. She signed a paper consenting to marry him, and the duchess pulled a ring from her own finger, as the prince had none of his own to bestow upon his bullied bride.

Immediately after the women departed, Georgiana wrote up a deposition stating that Maria was aware that a written promise extracted under such threats was invalid, thus protecting themselves against the illegality of the bedside agreement. The following day Maria went abroad in the hope that the whole messy business with the prince would blow over.

Throwing temper tantrums like a spoiled brat, the twenty-two-year-old heir apparent wept uncontrollably, tore at his hair, and banged his head against hard objects. He desperately wished to follow Maria, but could not leave the country without his father's permission. From Brighton, the prince wrote to Maria so frequently that French authorities were concerned that some espionage was afoot and arrested three of his couriers. When the packets turned out to contain sheaves of billets-doux, the French ministers had to laugh and shrug, *"Ahhh, l'amour."*

The letters routinely pledged George's eternal fidelity to Maria. In an eighteen-page love note, George told Maria that he now "looked upon himself as married. You know I never presumed to make you any offer with a view of purchasing your virtue. I know you too well," he insisted. Imploring her to return to him, the prince signed this letter, "Not only the most affectionate of lovers but the tenderest of husbands."

The constant heart beat extremely irregularly, however. If only Maria could have known that the Prince of Wales was temporarily consoling his sorrows in the arms of other women, she might have remained in France forever.

Instead, in October 1785, after receiving more suicide threats from the ever-manipulative George, Maria wrote to tell him that she *might* consent to marry him. The prince accepted her "maybe" as a "yes" and was over the moon.

Just in case Maria *might* change her mind, the bombardment of desperate love notes continued. Written on November 3, a forty-two-page letter closed with the words "Come then, oh come, dearest of Wives, best and most sacred of women, come and for ever crown with bliss him who will through Life endeavor to convince you by his love and attention of his wishes to be the best of husbands and who will ever remain under the latest moments of existence." He signed the letter "Unalterably thine."

By late November, having spent more than fifteen months in France, Maria resolved to return to England and commit herself to the prince. "I know I injure him and perhaps destroy forever my own tranquility," Maria wrote to Lady Anne Barnard, her former traveling companion on the Continent. By this time, she had fallen in love with the twenty-three-year-old George.

It was not easy to find a clergyman willing to risk the wrath of heaven and earth to perform a blatantly illegal wedding ceremony, secretly uniting a Roman Catholic to the underage (according to the 1772 Royal Marriages Act) heir. Finally, a young curate, the Reverend John Burt, was located—in the Fleet, where he was incarcerated for debts. Burt struck a hard bargain: he would marry the prince to Mrs. Fitzherbert for £500 (almost $98,000 today), payment of all his debts, the appointment as one of the prince's chaplains, and a future bishopric.

The ceremony was performed on the frosty afternoon of December 15, 1785, behind the curtained windows and locked doors of Maria's Park Street parlor. The twenty-eight-year-old bride wore a simple suit of traveling clothes. Maria's uncle, Henry Errington, and one of her brothers, John Smythe, stood as witnesses, endangering themselves if their complicit participation was ever discovered. The prince's friend, Orlando Bridgeman, stood guard outside the door. After the groom and the two witnesses signed the marriage certificate, George gave it to Maria to keep.

Although the marriage was illegal in the eyes of the state, it was valid in Church law. Any issue of the marriage would therefore be considered illegitimate according to English civil law, but legitimate by canon law.

The happy couple honeymooned at Ormley Lodge on Ham Common. After that came the systematic public denials of their marriage, particularly in Parliament, where George's friend, Richard Brinsley Sheridan (who knew the truth) vehemently denounced the prince's marriage to Mrs. Fitzherbert as a fiction. The prince's mentor, the fiery Whig orator Charles James Fox, accepted George's denial that "there not only is not, but never was, any grounds for those reports . . . so maliciously circulated," and vociferously insisted in the House of Commons that any "reports" of such a union were baseless rumors.

Maria was mortified by the deceit. From then on, Fox would remain her bitter enemy. Thanks to him, her precious reputation was in tatters and her position impossible. Fox "had rolled [her] in the kennel like a street-walker . . . he knew every word was a lie." She and George had agreed to *just say nothing at all* when they were confronted with the question. He had broken a vow already. True, if it were known for certain that she was George's legal wife, he would never inherit the throne and—perhaps worse—their union could spark a civil war. Anti-Catholic sentiment still ran high. But with their secret marriage *openly and publicly denied*, she seemed no better than the prince's whore. She had never wanted to be a royal mistress.

At least the king's brothers, the dukes of Cumberland and Gloucester, were very cordial to her and treated her as one of the family. Gloucester wrote to his nephew, "I have seen so much of her that I think I can with truth say she has few like her. I am convinced she loves you far beyond herself—I only allow myself to rejoice that the two people I have every reason to love the most, seem to be so happy in each other, and must last because there is so much good temper and good judgment." Unfortunately, those fine qualities turned out to be possessed by only one of the newlyweds.

Although the few people who knew the truth were sworn to secrecy, caricatures of the prince and Mrs. Fitzherbert appeared in every shop window. A clandestine royal marriage, true or not, was the talk of the town.

Mary Frampton's diary for 1786 refers to Mrs. Fitzherbert calling on her mother in London. "If ever the prince loved any woman, it was she: and half London, had he thrown his hand-kerchief, would have flown to pick it up . . . Mrs. Fitzherbert's very uncomfortable life since her connection with the Prince affords as strong a lesson as was ever given in favor of virtue, for she never desired any benefit."

The Earl of Denbigh wrote to Major Bulkeley on March 4, 1786, "Surely there cannot be any truth in the Report of the Prince being married to a Catholic widow? Is it believed or not? If true, the consequences may be dreadful to our posterity." Denbigh also asked the same question of the Reading Clerk of the House of Lords, Matthew Arnot. Arnot replied on March 14, "The marriage you allude to, I fear, is but too well founded in fact."

Charles James Fox was aghast to discover that he had been duped. Crossing paths with the Whig firebrand at Brooks's, Henry Errington (another version of the event names Orlando Bridgeman instead) told Fox, "I hear you have denied in the House the Prince's marriage to Mrs. Fitzherbert. You have been misinformed. I was present at the marriage."

As furious as she was with Fox, Maria realized that he would not have publicly shredded her reputation in Parliament without a cue from the prince. Her only recourse was to cut off all contact with her husband.

His reaction was to fall "exceeding ill" with "an inward complaint and a high fever." Once again, George threatened suicide if Maria didn't return to him. She had no choice but to relent, fearful that if she refused, he might actually go through with it.

George's carriage was seen every morning at Maria's door. She had precedence at every function. He let it be known that Mrs. Fitzherbert was to receive the courtesy of any social invitations extended to him, and if precedence could not be waived in her favor by other hosts, His Royal Highness would refuse to attend their affairs. He was as solicitous and attentive to her in public as if she was his legal wife, but Maria had insisted on maintaining separate residences.

That July, those who glimpsed Mrs. Fitzherbert with the prince in Brighton were certain she was visibly pregnant. Most people believe that Maria had at least one child, and possibly two, by the prince; and she never denied having any. On the death of George IV in 1830, Lord Stourton, one of her executors and her eventual biographer, asked her to sign a declaration written on the back of her marriage certificate that read, "I, Mary Fitzherbert, testify that my Union with George P. of Wales was without issue."

"She smilingly objected on the score of delicacy," said Stourton. Surely she would have signed the endorsement without hesitation if she had never given George any children. Considering their relationship lasted several years, it is more likely than not that she became pregnant by him and carried to term.

Her first child may have been born in the early autumn of 1786. There was a baby boy given the name of his foster father, James Ord, who was taken first to Bilbao, Spain, and then to Norfolk, Virginia, raised by prominent Catholic families and afforded the best education available. James Ord's paternity was never clearly established, but if it became known that the heir apparent had fathered a Catholic son, it would have irrevocably destroyed George's chances of ever becoming king. For all her maternal instincts, assuming James Ord *was* their son, Maria would never have ruined her beloved husband's destiny.

The Regency Crisis of 1789 came and went. George III recovered from his bouts of madness and the issue of whether the Prince of Wales was suited to be his father's regent became moot. But his choice of rakish friends remained an issue. Ironically, Maria Fitzherbert, who still loved him in spite of his numerous character flaws, was the only sobering influence on him. But even she was powerless to keep him from the wildly drunken debaucheries he enjoyed amid "the most depraved" company of his cronies, including Fox and Sheridan.

By the winter of 1793, Maria's marriage to the prince was floundering. Their diverging tastes had become an increasing problem. Maria preferred intimate, quiet evenings at home and her husband's excesses were wearing very thin. They often quarreled about it, and it was said that they were drifting apart.

The following summer, his debts had swelled to upwards of £50,000 (nearly $8.5 million today), and Maria was lending *him* money out of her £3,000 (roughly $560,000) royal annuity!

But the greatest source of tension was caused by the prince's philandering. Throughout their relationship he had dallied with other women and there was nothing for Maria to do but suffer in quiet dignity, because the legality of their union was to appear a mere rumor. While they were married, the prince had an affair with Anna Maria Crouch, a mercenary singer-actress who demanded several thousand pounds from him before she would bestow her charms. After haggling a bit over her price, the prince eventually extricated himself from the entanglement with a heavier purse than he had anticipated, but he had not learned a lesson from it.

Instead, he commenced a relationship with the forty-one-year-old former Frances Twysden, who had become the beautiful but diamond-hard Lady Jersey, cleverly introduced to him by the queen in the hopes of detaching her son from his Catholic inamorata. Married to the 4th Earl of Jersey, who was thirty-five years her senior, her ladyship was one of the Devonshire set, the fast crowd of Whigs who orbited around the glamorous Duchess of Devonshire, Georgiana.

No mere fling, the prince's affair with the witty and accomplished Lady Jersey was to change all of their lives. The contemporary diarist Nathanial Wraxall referred to the tall brunette's "irresistible seduction and fascination." This architect of the destruction of George's relationship with Maria was also an arch manipulator. Robert Huish, a contemporary biographer of the Prince of Wales, likened Lady Jersey to "a type of serpent—beautiful, bright, and glossy in its exterior—poisonous and pestiferous."

The prince was not the ambitious Lady Jersey's first extramarital conquest, but he was her most illustrious one. As soon as she had insinuated herself into his heart she began to systematically evict its other residents, starting with Mrs. Fitzherbert. Lady Jersey convinced George that the reason he was so unpopular was because Maria was a Roman Catholic—but he might redeem himself if he married a Protestant princess. To save his ratings George had to end his relationship with Mrs. Fitzherbert.

On June 23, Maria received a note from the prince just as she was about to depart for Bushy Park, the residence shared by the Duke of Clarence and his mistress Dorothy Jordan. The note expressed George's regrets at being unable to join her, as he had just been called to Windsor.

That evening, Captain Jack Willet-Payne, the head of the prince's household, arrived at Bushy Park with a subsequent letter from his employer, tersely telling Maria that their relationship was over and "he would never enter my house again."

Maria paled and immediately begged to excuse herself, saying that she would prefer to drive home alone. On reaching her residence, the devastated Mrs. Fitzherbert endorsed the bottom of the first note with the words "This letter I received the morning of the day the Prince sent me word he would never enter my house." Then she wrote the two-word explanation for George's cruelty to her: "Lady Jersey."

Marriage was also the only way out of the hole, according to the king. Because George's marriage to Maria had been so officially denied, and even (or particularly) because the Catholic

Maria would not confirm it herself at peril to the prince's ability to inherit the throne, most people accepted him as a bachelor. And because the prince had been under the age of twenty-five and had not gained the sovereign's consent to wed, Parliament and the Anglican Church would have deemed the marriage to Mrs. Fitzherbert invalid.

To encourage George to do his duty, the king promised that his heir's debts would be paid the day he wed. So on April 8, 1795, the Prince of Wales married his first cousin, Princess Caroline of Brunswick. At that time, his debts had surpassed the sum of £600,000—nearly $88 million in today's economy. He was being dunned in the street. Despite his rank, tradesmen had begun to refuse his custom.

Maria bore the prince's marriage stoically. She pointedly ignored George when, two days before the royal wedding, he rode back and forth in front of her house, desperate to get her attention, so he could show how much he missed her. But later in the year, the prince began to resent his enforced separation from Maria. He confessed to Lord Moira, "It's no use. I shall never love any woman but Fitzherbert," repeating the same sentiment to the Duke of Clarence. He urged his friends to show her the same attention as they had done before the split.

On January 12, 1796, having been married less than half a year to the now-pregnant Caroline, the Prince of Wales wrote his last will and testament, bequeathing all his "worldly property . . . to *my Maria Fitzherbert, my wife, the wife of my heart and soul.* Although by the laws of this country she *could not avail herself publicly of that name, still such she is in the eyes of Heaven, was, is, and ever will be such in mine . . .*" The will indicates the desire to be buried with "the *picture of my beloved wife, my Maria Fitzherbert . . .* suspended round my neck by a ribbon as I used to wear it when I lived *and placed right upon my heart.*" If she predeceased him, he wanted her to be disinterred and buried beside him, with the adjoining sides of their coffins cut away so they could lie together, while "to her who is called the Princess of Wales, I leave one shilling."

The prince sought a reconciliation with Maria during the summer of 1798. By then he had separated from Caroline for good and was bored with his mistress, Lady Jersey. Mrs. Fitzherbert felt sorry for Caroline, believing her to be poorly used by the prince; and according to George's factor, Colonel John McMahon, she "entertained an ill opinion of him," and still considered the prince "among the friends of Lady Jersey." Her answer, therefore, was *no*.

The prince tried again to woo her back in February 1799, this time employing the Duchess of Rutland as a go-between. Her Grace was deputized to tell Mrs. Fitzherbert that "there *never was an instant*" when he did not care for her, adding that "everything is finally at an end in another quarter," an assurance that his affair with Lady Jersey was over.

A week later, he read a newspaper report of Maria's death in Bath. The prince was utterly bereft. "To describe my feelings, to talk even of the subject is totally impossible, for I could neither feel, think, speak; in short, there was almost an end to my existence."

The account turned out to be false, but it exponentially increased the prince's desire to rekindle their romance. Once again, he assumed his desperate stance. In a letter sent to Maria in June 1799—which took him two days to compose—he melodramatically begged her, "Save me, save me on my knees I conjure you from myself. IF YOU WILL NOT ADHERE TO YOUR PROMISE I WILL *claim you as such, prove my marriage*, relinquish everything for you, rank, situation, birth, and if that is not sufficient, my life shall go also."

Whenever he became emotionally distraught, he would suffer physically as well. The prince was by now liberally dosing himself with laudanum (it was soon his most frequent "mixer" with his postprandial brandy) and insisting on being bled with alarming frequency.

With her son's health in such jeopardy, the queen got involved. While Her Majesty never would have countenanced Mrs. Fitzherbert as a *legitimate* daughter-in-law, the entire royal family was genuinely fond of her. Queen Charlotte, in her own handwriting, begged Maria to be reconciled with the prince.

Mrs. Fitzherbert's resolve began to weaken. She advised the prince that a rapprochement would be possible only if they could maintain separate residences, and he would have to consider her his sister, rather than his wife or mistress. But more important, she refused to return to the prince unless the Pope passed judgment on whether their marriage was valid.

The prince was on tenterhooks while they awaited a decision from Rome. Finally, the Pope ruled that Maria Fitzherbert was the true wife of the Prince of Wales in the eyes of the Catholic Church, as long as His Royal Highness was penitent for his sins. If so, then Maria was free to return to him.

Maria considered the next eight years of her life her happiest. Their reconciliation became official. And on July 4, 1799, the *Times* reported that "a gentleman of high rank and MRS. FITZHERBERT are once more *Inseperables*. Where one is invited, a card to the other is a matter of course." By the early spring of 1800, the couple was frequently seen out together in public. Unaware of the Pope's sanction of their union, people were shocked to see the usually modest Mrs. Fitzherbert make such a display of herself.

Despite the prince's imprimatur of social approval, Maria now found herself snubbed by the very members of the haute ton who had previously welcomed her most warmly. Lady Holland deplored such hypocrisy, writing, "Every prude, dowager and maiden visited Mrs. Fitzherbert before, and all the decline of her favor scarcely reduced her visitors; but now they all cry out shame for doing that which she did notoriously five years ago. There is a sort of morality I can never comprehend."

Between 1801–4, the Prince of Wales used his influence to secure Maria's adoption of Minney Seymour, the youngest child of their friends Lord Hugh and Lady Horatia Seymour, who had died within a couple of months of each other. In 1799, Minney's parents had asked Mrs. Fitzherbert to look after the little girl, who at the time was not much older than an infant. Seymour was an admiral posted to Jamaica, and the ailing Horatia sought a cure in Madeira. They had never intended for Maria to become Minney's permanent guardian, but she had grown so attached to the little girl that she could not bear to relinquish her into the custody of her aunt and uncle, as stipulated in the terms of the Seymours' wills. When the case finally reached the Court of Chancery in 1804, the ruling went against Maria and the prince, who the Seymours had considered an entirely unsuitable parental influence on their little daughter regardless of his rank and title.

Abusing that rank and title, the prince brought the case to the House of Lords, the highest appeals court in the land, where Maria was granted permanent custody of little Minney. Despite the initial misgivings of the Seymours' surviving family, Mrs. Fitzherbert was a wonderful and doting mother, and "Prinny" a generous, loving, and playful father—far kinder to Minney than he was to his real daughter, the ungovernable Princess Charlotte, who reminded him far too much of her slatternly mother.

Maria and the prince may have had another child in addition to "James Ord"—if Ord indeed was their son. A little girl named Maryanne Smythe (a version of Maria's birth name) was born around 1800, but she did not enter Mrs. Fitzherbert's household until 1817. Maryanne was passed off as Maria's niece, the daughter of her younger brother John—although official records reflect that John and his wife had no children. Some proof that Maryanne was really Maria's daughter lies in an 1828 letter from Mrs. Fitzherbert in which she sends her regards to Maryanne's husband, closing with the words "Say a thousand kind things from me to my *son in law* and believe me ever most affectionately . . ."

Maria had twice risked all to be the prince's consort, but the only thing in which he was constant to her was his inconstancy. In 1806, he began to chase Minney Seymour's aunt, Isabella, Marchioness of Hertford. The marchioness, who had met the prince during Minney's adoption proceedings, was ambitious, married, and two years his senior. According to Princess Lieven, Lady Hertford was "a luxurious abundance of flesh," and Mrs. Calvert described her as "without exception the most forbidding, haughty, unpleasant-looking woman I ever saw." By July 1807, the corpulent forty-seven-year-old rival had the Prince of Wales firmly within her clutches. Ironically, in gaining Minney, Mrs. Fitzherbert lost the prince.

Maria's influence with George waned in direct proportion to the ascendance of Lady Hertford. The scheming marchioness convinced the prince to drop his commitment to Catholic emancipation. She broke Maria's heart by encouraging George to continue to see her even as their romance had all but faded. Lady Hertford's intention was to slowly ooze her way into *maîtresse en titre* status, so that no one would notice a clean break of George's affections toward Maria, thereby reducing the effect of damaging gossip. When Lady Hertford was there, Maria hated to visit the hothouse atmosphere of the Marine Pavilion, the prince's opulent Brighton residence; nothing could have been more humiliating. But when the prince requested her attendance, she had no choice but to comply.

Yet by December 1809, Maria, now fifty-three years old, had endured enough of Prinny's flagrant fickleness. She wrote him a letter on the eighteenth of the month, explaining why she could not accept his most recent invitation:

> *The very great incivilities I have received these past two years just because I obeyed your orders in going there was*

*too visible to everyone present and too poignantly felt by
me to admit of my putting myself in a situation of again
being treated with such indignity . . . I feel I owe it to myself not to be insulted under your roof with impunity.*

Saddened by Maria's note, the prince assured her that nothing would ever make him "deviate from or forget those affectionate feelings" he had "ever entertained for her."

On February 5, 1811, the prince was sworn in as Regent. He
hosted a fete for himself at Carlton House on June 19, where
two thousand guests (except for Princess Caroline and their
daughter Charlotte, who weren't invited) celebrated the inau-
guration of the Regency. Although George had sent Maria a
gown, she refused to attend because she was not to be seated at
his table, where the two hundred most honored guests would
be placed. His insult was keenly felt; for decades Maria had
received the honors of his consort and wife at his own table, as
well as that of every other host and hostess who had invited the
prince to attend their events. On a copy of her letter to the regent declining his invitation and advising him that she would
never again cross his doorstep, whether at Carlton House or
the Pavilion in Brighton, she wrote the words "copy of a letter
written to the Prince, June 7, 1811, when persuaded by Lady
Hertford not to admit me to his table."

That contretemps spelled the end of their romance. If Maria
was truly the love of his life, then Prinny had a warped idea of
that sacred and noble sentiment. He playacted at it, a master
of creating and sustaining melodrama, but he had no clue how
to reciprocate the genuine article when offered, and was incapable of constancy, wounding the hearts and reputations of
those—especially Mrs. Fitzherbert—who had succumbed, however reluctantly, to his charm. He twice abandoned Maria, his
protestations of undying fidelity and sacrifice worth less than
the paper they were scrawled on.

The regent became king at the age of fifty-seven upon the death of his father on January 29, 1820. Now George IV, he and Maria rarely crossed paths, but evidently she was never terribly far from his thoughts.

In June 1830, when the king was dying, he refused to have her visit his bedside, because he was ashamed of his appearance. But he eagerly seized her "get well soon" letter, and after reading it placed it under his pillow. On June 26 at three fifteen a.m., Maria Fitzherbert was made a widow for the third time.

The new king, George IV's younger brother, William IV, the former Duke of Clarence, returned eight of the nine portraits of her that had been in George IV's possession, but Mrs. Fitzherbert wondered what had happened to the missing image—a miniature painted by Maria Cosway that had been set with brilliants in a locket.

Minney had remained George's pride and joy, even after Maria had broken with him for good. She knew that the king had wished to be buried with Maria's portrait about his neck, and for some time she felt too shy to admit its whereabouts to her adoptive mother. When Minney finally told her the king had gone to his grave with it, she said that "Mrs. Fitzherbert made no observation but soon large tears fell from her eyes."

William IV unhesitatingly continued to dispense Maria's annual pension (now £10,000 [over $1.4 million today], although George had changed his 1796 will that had initially left her everything). She signed a release against any claim to George IV's property. When the new king called on her in Brighton, Maria showed him her marriage certificate to his elder brother, and William's eyes filled with tears.

Maria now spoke openly of her marriage to George, and William's court happily accepted her as a respected in-law.

The remainder of Maria's life was gracious and genteel. She was a devoted mother and grandmother to Minney and Maryanne and their children, hostessing parties, traveling throughout

England and abroad, and when in Brighton, attending the Church of St. John the Baptist every week for confession. Only a young charwoman was permitted to remain in the building on these occasions, and she was told by the priest to curtsy deeply to the mysteriously veiled old lady, "for maybe it was the queen of England and maybe not."

One day in March 1837, Maria collapsed. She died at her Brighton home on Easter Monday, March 27, at the age of eighty, and was buried on April 6 in St. John the Baptist Church. The ring finger of her stone effigy is carved with three wedding bands.

Caroline of Brunswick, Princess of Wales

1768–1821

Queen of England (Uncrowned) 1820–1821

The "Delicate Investigation" and
The Bill of Pains and Penalties

I never did commit adultery but once, and I have repented of it
ever since. It was with the husband of Mrs. Fitzherbert.

—CAROLINE OF BRUNSWICK

Once upon a time there was a Princess of Wales who
was wed to the prince in an arranged marriage. She knew she
was on uneven footing from the start because the prince only had
eyes for his nearly-middle-aged mistress—the very woman who
thought the match would be a good idea in the first place, knowing that the new princess would prove no rival. Although the
prince repeatedly assured his bride that the mistress was "just a
good friend," the new princess didn't for a moment believe it.

To get back at her husband for his flagrant infidelities, the
lonely and sexually rapacious Princess of Wales unwisely re-
sorted to numerous affairs—some were mere flirtations, perhaps, and others were full-blown flings—until the house of cards
came down around her head and she was accused of immoral

conduct and adultery. Although her husband was as guilty of the same offense, she was better at manipulating public opinion. Getting her story into the press before he did resulted in her martyrdom as the victim of a hypocritical, tin-eared monarchy.

Most of this sounds eerily familiar, doesn't it? But two hundred or so years before Princess Diana, there was Caroline of Brunswick.

First cousin to the Prince of Wales, Caroline was the second daughter of the unhappy marriage between Karl II, the Duke of Brunswick-Wolfenbüttel, and George III's favorite sister, Augusta.

The prince had not planned to take a wife—beyond Maria Fitzherbert. It was only the sheer magnitude of his debts, and his father's promise to pay them on his wedding day, that spurred his decision to find a suitable bride. The pickings were slim; only Protestants were legally eligible because of the 1701 Act of Settlement, and most of those princesses were to be found in the postage-stamp-sized Prussian duchies.

The persnickety George spent less time choosing a bride than he did a pair of boots, dismissively quipping, "One damned German frau is as good as another." He told his father "very abruptly" in August 1794 that he was ready to begin "a more creditable line of life" by marrying. His choice of words is telling.

According to the Duke of Wellington, "Lady Jersey made the marriage simply because she wished to put Mrs. Fitzherbert on the same footing with herself, and deprive her of the claim to the title of lawful wife." Lady Jersey chose a wife for her royal lover with "indelicate manners, indifferent character, and not very inviting appearance, from the hope that disgust for the wife would secure constancy for the mistress."

In the autumn of 1794, James Harris, Earl of Malmesbury, was dispatched to Brunswick, charged with bringing the princess back to England for a royal marriage. After meeting an embarrassed Caroline on November 28, his diary entry describes her "pretty face—not expressive of softness—her figure not graceful—fine eyes—tolerable teeth, but going—fair hair and light eyebrows, good bust—short, with what the French call '*épaules impertinentes*' [broad shoulders]. Vastly happy with her future expectations . . ."

She also had an overly large head that looked far too big for her squat, no-necked body. Although her pale, clear complexion was much praised, she was also too fond of her rouge pot.

The twenty-six-year-old Caroline was not in any way presentable. Malmesbury remained in Brunswick for several weeks, endeavoring to instill even the most rudimentary elements of decorum, discretion, and personal hygiene. Malmesbury also discovered that Caroline's undergarments—her "coarse petticoats and shifts and thread stockings"—were filthy and smelled rank, "never well washed or changed often enough." She evinced no hurry to remedy the situation until Malmesbury insisted on it, making a point of telling her that the prince was "very delicate" and expected "a long and very careful *toilette de propreté*."

The Duke of Brunswick candidly told Malmesbury on December 5 that his daughter was "no fool, but she lacks judgment. She was strictly brought up, and necessarily so." Caroline's high spirits required a firm hand, which the duke hoped the Prince of Wales would exert. Little did Karl know that, temperamentally, George was all too similar to Caroline.

Malmesbury began to lay the groundwork for the necessary taming of the shrew. He instructed Caroline "never to talk politics or allow them to be talked to her." He cautioned her never to "be familiar or too easy" with her ladies, reminding her that she could "be affable without forgetting she was Princess of Wales."

When Caroline asked the earl, point-blank, about Lady Jersey, whom she reckoned was "an intriguante," Malmesbury advised her never to display any jealousy of her husband. If she suspected him of an infidelity, she was to feign ignorance, pretending not to notice it.

With every admonishment, Caroline promised Lord Malmesbury that she was very anxious to please her prince. "She entreats me also to guide and direct her," Malmesbury wrote. "I recommend perfect silence on all subjects for six months after her arrival." By December 16, Malmesbury had formed the impression that Caroline "had no *fond* [depth], no fixed character, a light and flighty mind, but means well and well disposed; and my eternal theme to her is *to think before she speaks, to recollect herself.*"

Caroline's departure from Brunswick was scheduled for December 21. On the day before, her mother, Augusta, received an anonymous letter, warning her that Lady Jersey was not to be trusted, that she would be a bad influence on Caroline and put into her head the notion to take lovers. The duchess unwisely showed Caroline the letter.

But Augusta's bad judgment gave Malmesbury the cue he needed to instruct Caroline on the issue of adultery and how it applied to the future Queen of England. The earl warned Caroline that "anybody who presumed to *love* her was guilty of *high treason* and punished with *death*, if she was weak enough to listen to him; so also was she. This startled her."

But the loose-moraled Caroline's astonishment was born of incredulity. She laughed uproariously, dismissing Malmesbury's dire warning as though she had no intention of taking him seriously.

On Easter Sunday—April 5, 1795—at St. James's Palace, the prince and princess met for the first time. Observing the protocol she had struggled to absorb, Caroline curtsied deeply to George. According to Malmesbury, "He raised her (gracefully enough) and embraced her, said barely one word, turned round [and] returned to a distant part of the apartment."

"Harris, I am not well, get me a glass of brandy," the prince said curtly to Malmesbury.

The earl, embarrassed for both Caroline and the prince, diplomatically endeavored to smooth things over. "Sir, had you not better have a glass of water?"

"No," the prince replied, adding an oath presumably too crude for Malmesbury to record in his diary. "I will go directly to the queen." George then turned on his heels and strode out of the room without another word.

An astonished Caroline inquired of Malmesbury (in French), "My God! Is the prince always like that? I find him very fat and nothing as handsome as his picture."

The match, made first in haste and then in Hanover, might just as well have begun in hell.

Was it Caroline's looks or her body odor that had repulsed the Prince of Wales? More than once, Malmesbury had cautioned the princess to wash herself thoroughly *all over.*

That night, Caroline's first in London, was an unmitigated disaster. Insulted that Lady Jersey was present at their dinner table—seated right between her and George—the princess could not keep silent after all, implying that she knew perfectly well that her ladyship was the prince's mistress.

Years later, Caroline told Lady Charlotte Campbell, "The first moment I saw my *futur* and Lady Jersey together, I knew how it all was, and I said to myself, 'Oh, very well!' I could be the slave of a man I love; but one whom I love not, and who did not love me, impossible—*c'est autre chose.*"

Over the next few days, as the wedding approached, the monarchs subtly offered their heir an "out." Her Majesty drew the prince aside and told him, "You know, George, it is for you to say whether you can marry the Princess or not." The king grew uneasy as well, admitting to his wife, in what may have been his most lucid moment of the decade, that he would accept the responsibility for breaking off what might be a disastrous match.

At the London gentlemen's clubs, the betting books were full of wagers as to whether the royal wedding would actually take place.

But His Royal Highness was dreaming of a clean credit report; as distasteful as things were, he was not about to back out. Caroline didn't care for the prince any more than he did for her, but she was ever the pugnacious Brunswicker, duty- and honor-bound to hold her head high and see it through. She knew the prize was not George—it was to be Queen of England.

Caroline and George were married in the Chapel Royal on the evening of April 8, 1795. Clad in silver tissue lace festooned with ribbons and bows, the bride glittered with diamonds and grinned from ear to ear, almost bursting with happiness. In contrast, the piss-drunk groom, who had made it down the aisle literally supported by two unmarried dukes, wept through the ceremony when he wasn't ogling Lady Jersey. At one point, the prince rose to his feet in the middle of the service, looking as though he was about to bolt. He received dirty looks from his father and the Archbishop of Canterbury, and the king admonished his heir to assume the position again.

But the most potentially embarrassing hitch came when the archbishop set down the book after asking whether "any person" knew "of a lawful impediment." The air was thick with tension. Would someone mention Mrs. Fitzherbert, the Catholic woman George had secretly married a decade earlier? It was certainly the cue to do so. The archbishop looked long and hard from the prince to the king and back again. The chapel remained silent and the ceremony continued.

Guests didn't know what to make of it all. "What an odd wedding," observed Lady Maria Stuart.

On his wedding night, through a haze of brandy, the prince must have gritted his teeth and thought of £600,000, fantasizing about paying off his debts and beginning to spend afresh, starting with all the improvements he wished to make to Carlton House.

Caroline was mortified, humiliated, and disgusted by his behavior. She confided to Lady Charlotte Campbell, "Judge what it was to have a drunken husband on one's wedding day, and one who passed the greatest part of his bridal night under the grate, where he fell, and where I left him."

But it got worse. George told Lord Minto, "Finding that I had suspicions of her not being *new*, she the next night mixed up some tooth powder and water, colored her shift with it and . . . in showing these she showed at the same time such marks of filth both in the fore and *hind* part of her . . . that she turned my stomach and from that moment I made a vow *never to touch her again*. I had known her three times—twice the first and once the second night—it required no small [effort] to conquer my aversion and overcome the disgust of her person."

Miraculously, during one of George's three drunken and disappointing performances in the bedroom, he had gotten Caroline pregnant. On January 7, 1796, she gave birth to "an *immense* girl," Princess Charlotte. Times had changed; the monarchy was constitutional, and the Renaissance-era reasons for preferring a male heir were moot. Upon Charlotte's birth, because a daughter could also inherit the throne (as long as she was, according to the 1701 Act of Settlement, a legitimate descendent of Sophia, Electress of Hanover—the mother of George I), the succession was now secured.

The kingdom rejoiced. So did the Prince of Wales. His duty done, he assured Malmesbury that "the child just born . . . certainly will be the last as I declare I can never approach her again, for she never washes or wipes any part of her body."

By mid-April, Caroline, lonely and humiliated, complained to her husband that she would no longer spend her days being shut in with no other company but his spiteful mistress, who had been assigned to act more or less as Caroline's full-time companion and minder. George immediately became shocked, appalled, insulted! He castigated Caroline for assuming such an indelicate thing about Lady Jersey and wounding her noble character. They were just good friends, George insisted.

In the spring of 1796, the Waleses decided to live apart, and by December the formal separation agreement was finalized. But the double standard by which Caroline was expected to abide is anathema to modern women. The prince felt perfectly at liberty to cat around as much as he liked, while he expected Caroline to socialize only with the people named on a list he'd drawn up, and to remain chaste, or at least discreet.

After the split, Caroline indiscreetly shared her opinions of her estranged husband's failings in certain areas, causing the Earl of Minto to remark, "I fancy the *mutual* disgust broke out at that time, and if I can spell her *hums* and *haws*, I take it that the ground of his antipathy was his own *incapacity*, and the distaste which a man feels for a woman who *knows* his defects and humiliations."

There may be some truth to Minto's observation. One reason the prince had so avidly desired to rid himself of Caroline was because she was not as advertised. George told Malmesbury, "Not only on the first night there was no appearance of blood, but her manners were not those of a novice. In taking the liberties natural on these occasions, she said, *'Ah mon dieu, qu'il est gros!'* (Oh, my god, it's big!), and how should she know this without a previous means of comparison."

By 1799, she was in her new residence, Montague House. There she entertained several of the most prominent cabinet ministers—including the PM himself, William Pitt. Caroline was giving full rein to her flirtatious personality.

One of Caroline's favorites was George Canning, the twenty-nine-year-old member of the Control Board (and a future PM). Evidently, Caroline threw herself at Canning during the summer of 1799 and he didn't turn down what was offered, despite having just lost his heart to Miss Joan Scott, the woman he would eventually marry.

Another rumored lover was the artist Thomas Lawrence, who briefly resided at Montague House over the winter of 1800 while he was working on a portrait of Caroline and Charlotte. And from 1801 to 1802, the princess appeared to be more than just good friends with the naval hero and diplomat Sir Sidney Smith, who was observed coming and going at all hours. "I have a bedfellow as often as I like," she boasted. "Nothing is more wholesome."

Around 1801, Caroline struck up a friendship with her neighbors, Sir John and Lady Douglas. She insinuated herself into their lives, and the ambitious and scheming Lady Douglas was treated to the full measure of the princess's madcap (or just plain mad) behavior. When Lady Douglas was pregnant, Caroline confided that she, too, was enceinte, leading her ladyship to eventually conclude that Willy Austin, an indigent infant adopted by the princess in 1802, was in fact Caroline's own son.

Caroline loved children, but after Charlotte had been taken from her and given a separate establishment, the prince sought to exclude her from seeing their daughter with any degree of regularity, and from having any input in the girl's education. To fill the void, Caroline "adopted" a number of children— orphans or the offspring of destitute parents who could not afford to feed so many mouths. She placed the children with nearby foster mothers, and they were always welcome to come and play at Montague House.

Willy Austin had been born on July 11, 1802, to the wife of a cashiered Deptford shipwright. Babe in arms, Sophia Austin had sought Caroline's assistance in reinstating her husband's employment. The princess offered to care for the little boy herself, and ten days later, Sophia returned with little Willikins, as Caroline would call him. Assured that her son would be given the best of everything, Sophia released him to Caroline.

No sooner had Caroline set up Willy's nursery than a new man, the handsome naval captain Thomas Manby, arrived in Greenwich and entered her life.

Lady Douglas, swiftly revealing herself to be no true friend to Caroline, told the prince about a Montague House dinner party at which the princess played footsie with Manby under the table, while above board she flirted quite outrageously and evenhandedly with both Manby and Sidney Smith. When the meal ended, Caroline rose from the table and headed for the door, turning back to glance significantly at Manby. When Smith spied Caroline and Manby kissing behind the door, he left the table, never to return to Montague House.

At another dinner party, Caroline disappeared with Manby for nearly an hour, leaving her embarrassed guests to fend for themselves.

Caroline's behavior was becoming increasingly shocking. According to Lady Hester Stanhope, "How the sea-captains used to color up when she danced about, exposing herself like an opera girl . . . she was so low, so vulgar! . . . I plainly told her it was a hanging matter that she should mind what she was about."

Unwisely, Caroline never seriously credited anyone's warnings that her sexual escapades were treasonous offenses.

Caroline had either discovered the products of Yardley and Floris or else her lovers were not as hygienically fastidious as her estranged husband. Then again, she was the Princess of Wales. She was rich enough, she was a terrific hostess, and she clearly loved to have a good time. Not only that, she was the mother of the young heir presumptive. With the king ailing and mentally deranged, and the Prince of Wales unhealthily obese, Caroline might at any moment become the most powerful woman in England.

And if that's not enough inducement for a man to catch her when she threw herself at him, Caroline no doubt became better and better looking with each glass of claret.

Toward the end of 1804, the air was thick with rumors about Caroline's indiscreet conduct. Captain Manby received two anonymous letters bribing him to reveal the extent of his "intimacy" with the Princess of Wales. Although the prince assured everyone that he was looking forward to letting justice take its course, behind the scenes, he had been assiduously endeavoring to dig up as much dirt as possible.

On May 29, 1806, after the PM, Lord Grenville, had presented the evidence of Caroline's indiscretions, King George appointed a secret commission of cabinet ministers to examine the witnesses who had provided it. At issue was whether Caroline and Charlotte's visits should still be subject to "restriction and regulation," pursuant to a thorough investigation of her conduct. In the meantime, Caroline was "deprived by a positive order" from seeing her daughter at all. Until she married in 1816, the hoydenish Charlotte remained an unfortunate pawn in the ugly squabbles between the battling Hanovers; neither of her parents wanted anything to do with her unless it would cause pain to the other one.

The proceeding, called "the Delicate Investigation," commenced on June 1, 1806, with Lady Douglas's sworn statement, written in December 1805, that the child brought to Caroline's house in the summer of 1802 was the princess's biological son. Lady Douglas was certain that Sir Sidney Smith was Willy Austin's father, knowing of Caroline's partiality for the naval man. She told the commission that "Sir Sidney Smith had lain with her [Caroline]; that she believed all men liked a bedfellow, but Sir Sidney better than any body else."

But Sophia Austin swore under oath that the child was indeed hers and that she visited him regularly at Montague House.

Lord Moira testified that a box belonging to Captain Manby (who Princess Charlotte believed to be Willy's father) had been opened by a friend, who found inside it a portrait of Caroline "with many souvenirs hanging to it," including a leather bag containing "hair of a particular description and such as his friend said he had been married too long not to know that it came from no woman's head."

Lord Ellenborough, the Lord Chief Justice, jocularly suggested that the hair found in the bag would have to be compared with its supposed source in order for it to become admissible evidence.

However, despite the statement made in the witness box by her former footman Samuel Roberts that "the Princess is very fond of fucking," the investigators were unable to obtain any incontrovertible proof of Caroline's infidelity.

Accusations, denials, hearsay, rumor, and innuendo characterized "the Delicate Investigation." Tales of soiled sheets and skulking about in the night titillated the commissioners. Some testimony was contradictory, other statements seemed coerced, and some allegations were clearly manufactured by those who nurtured grudges against the Princess of Wales, or those who feared losing their situation and therefore sought to protect her.

Finally, some genius thought to check for any documentation on Willy Austin's birth, leading to the Brownlow Street Hospital records, where, plain as day, Sophia Austin's testimony was revealed to be absolutely factual.

On July 4, 1806, the Lord Commissioners rendered their verdict: "There is no foundation for believing that the child now with the Princess is the child of her Royal Highness, or that she was delivered of any child in the year 1802; nor has anything appeared to us which would warrant the belief that she was pregnant in that year, or at any other period within the compass of our inquisition."

Although Caroline had been found innocent of giving birth to a bastard, the commission found enough merit in the allegations of sexual misconduct, particularly with regard to Captain Manby, for her behavior to warrant further scrutiny.

The king was fond of his niece, and he adored his grand-daughter Charlotte, now ten years old. But after the spotlight of inquiry had revealed Caroline's moral character (or lack thereof) to be unwholesome, if not illegal, he had no alternative but to terminate all social intercourse between Caroline and the royal family, including—or perhaps especially—the impressionable Charlotte, who would one day become queen.

On February 5, 1811, the Prince of Wales was sworn in as Regent. Now that he, and Caroline, were one step closer to the throne, it was vital to George to prevent her from ever sitting on it beside him.

But in endeavoring to exclude Caroline from society, they compelled her to choose her lovers from outside it, creating a bigger nest of hornets that would end up stinging everyone.

Craving a less repressive atmosphere, during the first week in August 1814, at the age of forty-six, she embarked for the Continent, attended by an assortment of English companions. As her ship put out to sea, she was observed to be weeping.

In Italy, she met thirty-two-year-old Bartolomeo Pergami, a stud of a man over six feet tall, with curly black hair and thick dark mustachios. He had come to her lodgings for a job interview, and finding no one to meet him, wandered through the rooms, eventually discovering a short, stout lady endeavoring to dislodge her skirts from a piece of furniture. Pergami gallantly assisted her in releasing her gown, and Caroline hired him immediately, assigning him to ride ahead to her next destination and secure lodgings and fresh horses for her entourage.

Pergami came from a well-heeled Crema family and had been a quartermaster in the Austrian Viceregal army, serving in the Russian campaign of 1812 as a courier for General Pino. He was now unemployed, allegedly for killing a higher-ranking officer in a duel, and was also conveniently separated from his wife. Caroline acquired Pergami's relatives along with the dashing Bartolomeo, loading them with favors and financial gifts.

She decided to "go native," but her unfortunate attempt to look Italian was comical. Caroline covered her fine blond hair with a curly black wig and darkened her eyebrows with kohl until she looked like an ancestor of Groucho Marx. In an effort to darken her pale Germanic complexion, she reddened her cheeks until she resembled a circus clown. Overindulging in the local cuisine, she packed on more weight. At balls, she danced with abandon until her high-waisted gowns slipped off her shoulders and her considerable bosom bounced out of the few inches of fabric that strained to contain it.

With a mandate to provide irrefutable proof of Caroline's adultery, the Regent's spies filed regular reports to the crown on Caroline's outrageous conduct. What must George have thought when he read about the time his estranged wife plopped a pumpkin shell on her head, explaining that the unusual chapeau kept her cool? Or the news that she had appeared more than once at a formal ball attired (to her mind) like a Roman goddess, which meant remaining entirely nude from the waist up? Or that she had traveled through the streets of Genoa in a coach shaped like a conch shell with a pageboy dressed as Cupid in flesh-colored tights leading her matched pair of tiny ponies? Presumably costumed as Venus, Caroline had been clad in her black fright wig and a diaphanous tunic that barely grazed her knees. Beside her sat her thirteen-year-old adopted protégé, Willy Austin, whom she referred to as "the little Prince," although it had already been satisfactorily proven that he was not her biological son.

At Catania, Pergami received the Order of Malta when Caroline explained to the Grand Master that the other men in her entourage could not be knighted because they were Protestant. Discovering that she could not appoint Pergami to the rank of chamberlain because English court protocol stipulated that only a nobleman could hold that position, she bought her lover an estate and a barony, creating him Barone Pergami della Francina, Order of Malta.

Caroline and her entourage cruised the Mediterranean on a polacca. She rode into Jerusalem on an ass, a deliberate allusion to Jesus. There, she founded the Order of St. Caroline, naming Pergami as its Grand Master, adopting the motto of England's Order of the Garter, *"Honi soit qui mal y pense"* (Evil be to him who evil thinks).

News that the Princess of Wales was consorting with a mob of undistinguished foreigners shocked the English aristocracy. When the Duke of Devonshire heard that Caroline had "a Mameluke outside her carriage," he replied that "it was not so bad as having a courier inside."

On May 2, 1816, Princess Charlotte married Prince Leopold, the third son of the Duke of Saxe-Coburg-Saalfeld. Not only had Charlotte finally escaped her repressive, infantilizing upbringing, it was a love match. Her mother, traveling abroad, was not present at the wedding. Nor was Caroline at her daughter's bedside when, after fifty hours of agonizing labor, on November 5, 1817, the princess was delivered of a stillborn boy.

Five hours later, in the early morning hours of November 6, the twenty-one-year-old princess was dead, most probably from a postpartum hemorrhage or an infection that was misdiagnosed and then mistreated. Her grieving husband, Leopold, robbed of his chance to become England's king consort, returned to the Continent and remarried. He eventually became King of the Belgians, and was the uncle of Queen Victoria.

Caroline was living in Pesaro, on the east coast of Italy, when she received the sorrowful report, quite by accident, that Charlotte and her infant had died. The princess's household, always on the lookout for news of Charlotte's *accouchement*, intercepted the English monarch's courier, who was en route to Rome. Evidently, the crown had thought it was more important to inform the Pope of the princess's death than to tell her mother about it.

When she heard the dreadful news, the Princess of Wales fainted. Contrary to the propaganda disseminated by her husband, Caroline was *very* affected by Charlotte's death (as well as her chance to be a grandmother and eventually queen mum). She began to suffer severe headaches and bouts of extreme melancholy.

With their daughter dead, George no longer felt any need to be remotely kind to Caroline. In 1818, casting himself as the most abused and tormented man ever to walk the face of the earth, the Regent wrote to his Lord Chancellor illuminating the need for "unshackling myself from a woman who has for the last three and twenty years . . . been the bane and curse of my existence," and who "now stands prominent in the eyes of the world characterized by a flagrancy of abandonment unparalleled in the history of women, and stamped with disgrace and dishonor."

That summer, although the cabinet had been reluctant to sanction a second proceeding at taxpayer expense that would only result in another royal scandal, the Regent dispatched a three-man commission to Milan "for the purposes of making enquiries into the conduct of Her Royal Highness the Princess of Wales since she quitted England in the month of August 1814."

The Milan Commission interviewed more than eighty-five witnesses, most of whom were Italian servants who gave their statements through interpreters—and afterward laughingly shared all the sordid details with their friends at the local tavern, mocking the somber-suited Englishmen who were paying them so much for their stories that they didn't need to work again.

The prince's British investigators amassed "a great body of evidence," but upon their return to England with their brimming portfolios the Regent was advised that he could not obtain a divorce "except upon proof of adultery, to be substantiated by evidence before some tribunal in this country."

Not only that, Caroline could always raise the issue of *her husband's* numerous extramarital liaisons, including his marriage to Maria Fitzherbert and a potential charge of bigamy. Although some historians have maintained that Caroline was even more upset by the existence of Mrs. Fitzherbert than she was by Lady Jersey, the princess was quite sympathetic toward Maria, avowing, "That is the prince's true wife; she is an excellent woman; it is a great pity for him that he ever broke with her."

On July 13, 1819, the Milan Commission presented its report to the cabinet. After reviewing it, they decided on July 24 that the report did not contain enough evidence to assure that the Princess of Wales would be found guilty of adultery with Bartolomeo Pergami in an English court of law.

Caroline was in Italy at Leghorn (Livorno) in 1820 when she received a letter from Henry Brougham advising her of the death of George III on January 29 and urging her to return to England immediately; she was now Queen of Great Britain. But another letter informed her that the new king would take no action against her *unless* she set foot again on English soil. She would remain queen, but uncrowned.

One of George IV's first acts as king was to insist that Caroline's name be struck from the church liturgy, so that the country would not be exhorted to pray for her by name every Sunday. When Caroline heard about her husband's intention, she grew livid. Adding insult to injury, she then learned that she was not to be called the queen after all, but simply Caroline of Brunswick. This was intolerable; she was going home.

Her lawyer, the Whig MP Henry Brougham, now secretly working on the king's behalf, tried to talk her out of returning, advising her to remain abroad in exchange for a £50,000 annuity (over $6.2 million today), retention of her title, and all rights as Queen of England. But Caroline wasn't going to be bribed. Having left her foreign entourage behind, on June 5, she landed at Dover, prepared to greet her subjects.

It was noted by the *Times* that after a five-and-a-half-year absence, "Her blue eyes [were] shining with peculiar luster, but her cheeks had the appearance of a long intimacy with care and anxiety." She was now fifty-two years old.

Now that she was queen, she dressed herself with all the decorum of a criminal defendant on arraignment day. Her bodices fully covered her ample poitrine right up to her nonexistent neck. Her gowns were somber-hued, her bonnets modest and fashionable.

At Dover, the people unhorsed her carriage and pulled it themselves through the streets. It was just the sort of enthusiastic welcome the king and his government had dreaded. Caroline was cheered all the way to London with shouts of "God Save the Queen" and "No Queen, No King." She had become the people's symbolic victim of an abusive, repressive, and hypocritical monarchy. The press called her "the injured queen."

After receiving such a warm welcome from her subjects, Caroline was prepared to live abroad forever in exchange for the allowance, but now the king felt it was not punishment enough. He stubbornly clung to the liturgy issue. Not only that, he wanted a legal divorce.

Luckily for the queen, her purported affair took place outside of England and her presumable lover was a foreigner. *Pergami* could not have committed treason against a king and crown not his own; therefore, if *he* was not treasonous, neither was Caroline. Consequently, when George brought the Milan Commission documents to both houses of Parliament, he urged the government to consider a Bill of Pains and Penalties, the only remedy available to him that would punish Caroline for her alleged adultery with Bartolomeo Pergami.

The Secret Committee comprised of fifteen lords convened on June 20, to review the contents of the notorious "green bags" that contained the intelligence amassed over the years by the Milan Commission.

On July 5, the Bill of Pains and Penalties was introduced

into the House of Lords. The bill sought "to deprive Her Majesty Caroline Amelia Elizabeth of the title, prerogatives, rights, privileges, and exemptions of Queen Consort of this Realm, and to dissolve the marriage between His Majesty and the said [Queen] Caroline."

Caroline was accused of committing her first adulterous act with Pergami on November 14, 1814, in Naples. A witness had seen imprints of two bodies on her bed in the morning.

But from the start, there were problems. For one thing, the Bill of Pains and Penalties permitted the king to achieve what none of his equally adulterous subjects could obtain: a divorce "without clean hands." The Whig lords were solidly against the bill. Several Tories, including some of the king's closest friends, didn't think it prudent to proceed, fearing that the defense would drag His Majesty's numerous skeletons from his closet. And many of the clerical lords would only vote for the bill if the divorce clause was removed.

On August 17, 1820, the first day of her trial, Caroline rode in triumph to the House of Lords, dressed in a modest black sarcenet gown. Two of her former lovers were among the 258 peers charged with judging her conduct.

The streets became seas of white handkerchiefs, brandished by women enthusiastically showing their support of Her Majesty.

Acrimonious grandstanding characterized the first humid days. It was so uncomfortably hot that Caroline, her dress ungainly bunched up all around her and spilling over the sides of her chair, fell asleep in her unintentional cocoon, prompting Lord Henry Holland's couplet:

> *Her conduct at present no censure affords.*
> *She sins not with courtiers, but sleeps with the Lords.*

A salaciously entertaining parade of witnesses for the prosecution provided a circus that lasted two weeks. Several of them had braved beatings from "Queenite" mobs when they reached Dover.

Testimony from former servants, reiterating what they had told the Milan Commission, blew the wax out of the peers' ears. Pergami was seen in the middle of the night tiptoeing through the corridors, candle aloft; Caroline was observed sitting on Pergami's lap as they kissed, or sitting next to him on a bed. Hotel maids swore they had removed two chamber pots from the queen's boudoir and stained sheets from her bed. They had also observed Pergami's slippers peeking out from beneath it. Pergami had also been spotted with his hand on Caroline's thigh or caressing her bare breast.

Teodoro Majocchi recalled the queen and her purported lover sharing a tent pitched on the deck of the polacca during the Mediterranean voyage. And the captain of that vessel testified that he saw Caroline go below to take her bath (a bath!), accompanied only by Pergami (whom other witnesses said routinely helped her dress). The captain had also seen Caroline messing up Pergami's bed (presumably to make it look slept in).

Pergami soon became the pet of the satirists' pens. Punning wittily on titles of royal preferment, one wag wrote:

> *The Grand Master of St. Caroline*
> *Has found promotion's path.*
> *He is made both Night Companion*
> *And Commander of the Bath.*

Louise Demont, a Swiss *femme de chambre* formerly in Caroline's employ, testified that on some occasions, having just left Caroline undressed, she saw Pergami making his way to the queen's bedroom. "I have also seen Pergami in the Princess's room when she was at her toilette when she had no skirts on. Pergami turned round and said, 'Oh! How pretty you are. I like you much better so.'"

A former courier and equerry, Giuseppe Sacchi, really woke up the lords. He testified that in the course of his duties to ride beside Caroline's coach, late one evening his horse passed the carriage (at what pace, one wonders), and he glimpsed Caroline and Pergami, slumbering side by side. "Her Royal Highness had her hand upon the private part of Mr. Pergami and Pergami held his own upon that of Her Royal Highness. . . . Once Pergami had his breeches loosened and the Princess's hand was upon that part."

At the end of the sixteenth day of testimony, the prosecution rested its case.

But now it was the defense's turn. Caroline's ambitious lawyer, Henry Brougham, had abandoned the king and returned to her camp after recognizing that anyone who represented the queen would make a national name for himself. Once he accepted the case, he was anything but halfhearted in his vigorous defense. So slender that he was almost swallowed by his black robe and horsehair wig, he systematically demolished the testimony of the prosecution's witnesses—establishing that Demont and Sacchi had been dismissed for stealing gold coins from Caroline's strongbox, and that many of the witnesses had been paid by the government for their testimony and appearance at the trial.

"Was it not a curious thing that these people, all of them poor, should be brought over to England to live in luxury and idleness and should be in receipt of great rewards?"

Brougham also keenly illuminated the inconsistencies contained in the witnesses' testimony, characterizing the prosecution's case as the "tittle-tattle of coffee-houses and alehouses, the gossip of bargemen on canals and . . . cast-off servants," denouncing the Milan Commission as "that great receipt of perjury—that storehouse of false swearing and all iniquity."

The trial sold a lot of newspapers; everyone eagerly awaited the latest sordid revelation—even though they were sometimes a little *too* sordid. Ladies began keeping the papers out of reach of their maids, but soon their overly protective husbands were hiding the daily news from *them*. People and the press talked of little but the queen's trial. It was as if nothing else was happening in England, let alone in the rest of the world.

Aware of this phenomenon, Caroline, who had learned how to manipulate public opinion, copied the press on a letter she sent to her husband. Probably ghostwritten by Brougham because Caroline's use of English had never become sophisticated, the queen wrote, "From the very threshold of your Majesty's mansion the mother of your child was pursued by spies, conspirators, and traitors . . . You have pursued me with hatred and scorn, and with all the means of destruction. You wrested me from my child . . . you sent me sorrowing through the world, and even in my sorrows pursued me with unrelenting persecution."

Cue the violins. From eyewitness reports given by people who *liked* Caroline, she had never done less than *gaily gallivanted* through the world. But even if no one credited her fiction, they believed her husband to be just as ill behaved and licentious, if not worse.

Lord Ellenborough spoke for his fellow peers when he conceded that "the queen was the last woman any one would wish his own wife to resemble," yet he voted against the bill. The opinion of many of the lords reflected that of John Bull. In the words of Henry Brougham, "all men, both in and out of Parliament . . . admit everything to be true which is alleged against the Queen, yet, after the treatment she had received since she first came to England, her husband had no right to the relief prayed by him or the punishment sought against her."

As the case approached its conclusion there were daily displays of support for Caroline. Calling themselves the Queen's Guards, thousands of citizens, armored and marching in lockstep, proclaimed, "The Queen's Guard are Men of Metal!"

Thomas Creevey, a contemporary, recorded the events, estimating crowds of ten thousand people assembled in Piccadilly. "I should like any one to tell me what is to come next if this organized army loses its temper," he observed.

The prosecution presumably had the same reaction. After closing arguments were made, the bill received three readings, where the charges were restated and the matter then put to a vote. Following the first reading on November 6, 1820, a protracted debate resulted in 123 members who voted "Content" (Aye) and 95 who voted "Not Content" (Nay).

Caroline's conviction was no longer the slam dunk the king had been assured of. The government withdrew the Bill of Pains and Penalties four days later after the third reading when, at 108 to 99, only nine votes separated the ayes from the nays. George's brothers, the equally adulterous dukes of York and Clarence, were most vociferously (and hypocritically) "Content," shouting out their approval of the bill. But the crown uncomfortably conceded that if the outcome was this close in the Lords, the bill would never pass in the Commons, where the king's numerous extramarital infidelities, as well as the Mrs. Fitzherbert issue, would surely sink his case. Fear of mob violence was another reason the government withdrew the bill.

The Lords had decided to punish the king for his hypocrisy rather than condemn the queen for her adultery.

Toward the end of her young life, Princess Charlotte had observed, "My mother was bad, but she would not have become as bad as she was if my father had not been infinitely worse."

George was so shocked by the withdrawal of the bill that he

considered abdicating and leaving permanently for Hanover, which he would continue to rule as the duchy's Elector.

Caroline was too exhausted to rejoice. Lady Charlotte Campbell observed that the queen "appeared worn-out in mind and body. The desolateness of her private existence seemed to make her very sorrowful: she appeared to feel the loss of her daughter more than at any previous moment, and she wept incessantly."

The outcome of Caroline's trial was the obverse of poor Anne Boleyn's: the innocent Anne had been convicted by a cadre of powerful enemies, while the undoubtedly guilty Caroline was acquitted by a consortium of powerful friends.

So the matter was laid to rest. And a popular satirical verse made the rounds of coffeehouses:

> *Most gracious Queen we thee implore*
> *To go away and sin no more,*
> *Or, if that effort be too great,*
> *To go away at any rate.*

For the next three days, the major cities in Britain were illuminated in celebration. After that, everyone was ready to move on—when a thirteenth-hour witness crawled out of the woodwork. Iacinto Greco, Caroline's former Sicilian cook, came forward a few days after the trial, claiming that, on opening a door after dinner one evening, he discovered "the Princess on the sofa at the further end of the saloon—Pergami was standing between her legs which were in his arms—his breeches were down, and his back towards the door—at which I was. I saw the Princess's thighs quite naked—Pergami was moving backwards and forwards and in the very act with the Princess." Pergami turned his head, noticed Greco, and the cook was fired the next day.

Asked why the devil he hadn't stepped forward during the

trial, Greco explained that his wife had told him the English would cut off his head. In any event, his information came too late. The books were closed.

George then took every precaution to prevent Caroline from being rightfully crowned alongside him. He hired beefy prize-fighters, captained by the champion pugilist Gentleman Jackson, to guard the doors to Westminster Abbey, the palace, and the hall on Coronation Day, July 19, 1821. The queen arrived, dressed to the nines, and demanded entry, but was humiliatingly turned away.

That evening, the uncrowned queen hosted a dinner party and tried to mask her distress with a forced gaiety. When her uproarious laughter suddenly turned to copious weeping, the guests realized how bitterly wounded she was. One described "tears of anguish so acute that she seemed to dread the usual approach of rest."

Within days of the coronation, Caroline suffered an obstruction and inflammation of the bowels. And at ten twenty-five p.m. on August 8, 1821, she died. This Queen of England who never reigned, and was the only monarch in British history to have been subjected to a Bill of Pains and Penalties, was just fifty-three years old. At her request, she was buried in Brunswick.

George IV was aboard the royal yacht when he received the news, retiring to his cabin for the remainder of the day. The court was ordered to go into mourning for all of three weeks. The nation was not required to officially mourn their queen at all.

Bartolomeo Pergami, who never saw Caroline again after she returned to England in 1820, died in 1842 after a fall from his horse.

George IV survived his wife by nine years, dying in 1830. As eccentric and often disliked as Caroline had been, his popularity was even lower. For all his aesthetic sensibilities, throughout his life George IV was a hypochondriac, a moral hypocrite, an emotional bully, a glutton, a drunkard, and a womanizer.

After he died on June 26, 1830, as the result of a burst blood vessel in his abdomen, the *Times* of London editorialized (on July 16) that "There was never an individual less regretted by his fellow creatures than this deceased king."

FREDERICK, DUKE OF YORK

1763–1827

and Mary Anne Clarke 1776–1852

$\mathcal{M}$ARY ANNE CLARKE WAS A REAL-LIFE FOLK HEROINE, a child of the London gutters whose beauty captivated a prince and whose business acumen landed them both in court.

She was born in the colorful location of Ball and Pin Alley, White's Alley, near Chancery Lane, and was raised by a compositor named Farquhar who was either her father or her step-father.

Mary Anne eloped at the age of fifteen with Joseph Clarke, the son of a builder. She bore him two daughters, although their marriage was not legalized until 1794. She had greater aspirations, however.

George III's sons were notorious for their womanizing, and it never much mattered to any of them whether the petticoats they raised were made of woolen stuff or of silk. Mary Anne quite evidently fit into the former category when she captivated the king's second son, the randy Prince of Wales's younger brother, Frederick, Duke of York and Albany, sometime around 1803.

Thirteen years Mary Anne's senior, the rakish duke promised her an annual income of £12,000 (nearly $1.7 million in today's economy) to be dispensed in monthly installments. Unfortunately, the king and queen kept the purse strings tight when it came to dispensing their sons' allowances, which meant that Frederick's payments to Mary Anne amounted to only a fraction of what he had promised her.

This was bad news for Mary Anne, who had already set herself up handsomely in a fine town house in Gloucester Place staffed by a raft of servants, including three male cooks. She dressed like a duchess, kept a stable of ten horses, and entertained lavishly, dining on plate once owned by the duc de Berri. Many of her purchases were acquired on credit, thanks to the generosity of ambitious merchants who were eager to gain the custom of a duke's mistress.

Frederick, who had married a daughter of the King of Prussia in 1791 and separated from her soon afterward, was Commander in Chief of the armed forces. The duke was also a bishop, which enabled him to confer preferments in the Church.

Having grown rather accustomed to her ostentatious lifestyle, the enterprising Mary Anne decided she would rather parlay her benefactor's position into an income than get tossed out onto the street (or into prison) for debt. She spread the word underground that, for a consideration, she would use her influence with her royal lover to gain a man a military commission or promotion. Mary Anne would pin the list of her clients' names to the bed curtains at Gloucester Place as a little reminder to her paramour, or add it to the duke's own lists, relying on his usual practice of never reading what he was signing.

In 1806, when their affair ended, Mary Anne sought a financial settlement from the duke. When Frederick would not meet her terms, she threatened to publish an account of their love affair, including the details of her little business on the side.

Surprisingly, things dragged on for another three years without the public getting wind of either the sexual liaison or the promotions scandal. It was only when her former lover took up with another woman, Mrs. Carr, that Mary Anne sought revenge. She became involved with two men, Major Dillion and Colonel Gwyllym Lloyd Wardle, MP for Okehampton.

Wardle was making a career for himself rooting out corruption in army contracts involving Frederick, Duke of York. Naturally, Mary Anne's name surfaced, and in 1809, Wardle brought the scheme to the attention of Parliament.

On February 1, Parliament opened an inquest into any wrongdoing committed by the duke and his former mistress. Eight charges were brought against Frederick for improper use of his military patronage, but it was Mary Anne Clarke who charmed the parliamentarians and captured the public's giddy attention.

The luscious brunette appeared for the hearings dressed in a revealing gown with a plunging décolleté and flirted shamelessly with the ministers. "I cannot tell you because it was indelicate," she replied to several questions regarding her private life. During her testimony, her answers were so saucy that one of her *inquisitors* offered her a bribe of three hundred guineas to join him for "supper."

On March 18, 1809, Frederick resigned his office as Commander in Chief in order to avoid further damage to his reputation.

Following his resignation, Frederick was mutilated in effigy by angry mobs in Suffolk and York, protesting his immoral lifestyle; and for a time, the familiar "heads or tails" call in a coin toss was replaced with "dukes or darlings."

Astonishingly, although Mary Anne was blatantly guilty, on December 10, 1809, she was acquitted. All charges were dismissed against the duke as well. His dealings with Mrs. Clarke had been accounted careless, but it could not be proved that Frederick had actually known of any wrongdoing—even though he had clearly profited by the sale of commissions.

As is often the case in tales of corruption, the scourge is as tainted as the target. The following year, Wardle's star sank into the sea when Francis Wright, an upholsterer, sued him for nonpayment of a bill for furnishings purchased for Mary Anne's establishment. During the trial it was revealed that Wardle and Mary Anne had enjoyed a relationship prior to the 1809 parliamentary investigation, and it did not sit well with the jury that the two of them had negotiated over the duke's involvement in the commissions scandal. In open court Mary Anne claimed that Wardle had bought her testimony in the 1809 inquest by promising to furnish her home.

Mary Anne published *The Rival Princes*, her account of the entire sordid affair. In the book, she accused Wardle of being in league with one of Frederick's younger brothers, the Duke of Kent, who had offered her £10,000 (a shade over $1 million today) to ruin her royal lover's reputation. The volume included several of her love letters to and from Frederick.

Also that year, in exchange for the suppression of her tell-all memoirs, Mary Anne Clarke's representative, Sir Edward Taylor, negotiated a settlement with the Duke of York for £7,000 (almost $738,000 today) and a pension of £400 a year (slightly more than $42,000). All but one copy of her confessional was destroyed. The remaining edition was placed in a lockbox in Drummond's Bank.

Parliament voted to reinstate the duke as Commander in Chief in 1811, and Frederick proved himself a capable administrator. Chastened, perhaps, by his embarrassingly public shaming, he helped introduce a system where men were promoted on merit rather than by nepotism, and founded military academies to provide better training for the armed forces.

Frederick suffered an attack of dropsy in 1826, and never got to be king, dying on January 5, 1827, at the age of sixty-three, three years before his elder brother, George IV, expired. His estranged wife, who preferred animals to people, had died in 1820 on her estate, Oatlands House, in Surrey, surrounded by her exotic menagerie.

Wardle was not returned to Parliament in the 1812 elections. According to Mary Anne Clarke, he was reduced "to selling milk about Tunbridge." In 1815, deeply in debt, he decamped to the Continent, dying in Florence at the age of seventy-one on November 30, 1833.

But Mary Anne just couldn't leave well enough alone. In 1813, she was convicted of libel for publishing "A Letter to the Right Hon. William Fitzgerald" and served nine months in prison. After her release, she left England, spending the rest of her life abroad, mostly in Brussels and Paris, entertaining numerous lovers, including the Marquess of Londonderry, and making good marriages for her daughters.

On June 21, 1852, Mary Anne Clarke died in Boulogne, at the age of seventy-six.

Her descendant, the twentieth-century author Daphne Du Maurier, fictionalized Mary Anne Clarke's already colorful life in her 1954 novel, *Mary Anne.*

WILLIAM IV

1765–1837

RULED 1830–1837

and Dorothy Jordan 1761–1816

Her face, her tears, her manners were irresistible. Her smile had the effect of sunshine, and her laugh did one good to hear it. Her voice was eloquence itself; it seemed as if her heart was always at her mouth. She was all gaiety, openness, and good nature. She rioted in her fine animal spirits, and gave more pleasure than any other actress, because she had the greatest spirit of enjoyment in herself.

—WILLIAM HAZLITT, 1815

Warning: do not read this entry before bedtime. It is a horror story.

Dorothy Jordan was one of nine children born to Grace Phillips, a vicar's daughter-turned-actress, and Francis Bland, a judge's son and the heir to Derriquin Castle in County Derry. Francis had eloped with Grace when they were both underage, and therefore their "marriage" was illegal. His father refused to recognize the union and disowned him. When Dora was just thirteen, Francis left his large family in the lurch and legally married an English heiress.

By the time she met William, Duke of Clarence, the third son of King George III and Queen Charlotte, Dora already had three daughters and was at the top of her profession, known far and wide as the finest comedic actress in England. Her oldest child, Fanny, was born after Dora was raped or at the very least seduced by Richard Daly, the very married manager of the Dublin theatre where she made her stage debut. With her mother, a pair of siblings, and her baby in tow, in 1782 Dora fled to England, auditioning in Leeds for Tate Wilkinson's company.

Wilkinson "christened" Dora "Mrs. Jordan." In an era where actresses were generally considered no better than prostitutes, the "Mrs." conveyed an element of respectability, giving the impression that there was, or had at one time been, a husband.

"Why, said I, my dear, you have crossed the water, so I'll call you 'Jordan,'" said Wilkinson.

Dora liked the inside joke, so it stuck. There never was a Mr. Jordan.

In 1784, at the age of twenty-three, she made her London debut at Drury Lane, scoring an immediate artistic and commercial success. Dora's wholesome appearance stood her in good stead in the comedic roles that were her greatest triumphs. She was short and small-waisted with a perfectly proportioned figure, terrific legs that were shown to great advantage in the trouser roles, and a mop of brown curls. Although she was not a classic beauty by Georgian standards, her nose and chin being too prominent, her face was charming and very expressive. Dora was also so nearsighted that she took to wearing her spectacles on a slender gold chain about her neck.

For five years Dora lived with the son of one of Drury Lane's investors, Richard Ford, a lawyer and future MP. They called each other Mr. and Mrs. Ford. Dora bore Richard a son, who didn't live long enough to be named, and two daughters, Dorothea Maria ("Dodee") and Lucy. But as time dragged on, it was becoming clearer that the marriage proposal Ford had promised Dora before they set up housekeeping would never be forthcoming.

This left Dora in an ideal position toward the end of 1791 to give some credence to a new admirer. The young Duke of Clarence, four years her junior, had been making his amorous intentions known to her since February. Fully aware that the Hanover princes had a habit of wooing and jilting in a most callous fashion, she hesitated. Perhaps Ford was the safer bet after all.

Being of the blood royal, William was accustomed to getting his own way. When he was thirteen, his father had sent him off to the navy. As a fourteen-year-old midshipman, he saw action when the British fleet captured a Spanish flagship, which was promptly renamed the *Prince William*. He returned to London a hero, but his naval career was all downhill from there. William lost his princely polish and picked up all the sailors' bad habits: drinking, swearing, and whoring. Even Horatio Nelson couldn't talk sense into him. And when the prince was given his own ship, he turned into a bully—a captain too fond of the lash who did not respect the orders of his superior officers. The Admiralty couldn't get him out of the water fast enough.

In 1783, William's disappointed parents sent him to Hanover for two years to learn some manners from his German cousins. It didn't work. But he did learn to fornicate standing up. The teenage prince wrote home to his elder brother George, complaining of the dearth of agreeable (or compliant) women, indignantly adding that he was compelled to perform

> . . . *with a lady of the town against a wall or in the middle of a parade. . . . Oh, for England! And the pretty girls of*

*Westminster; at least to such as would not clap or pox me
every time I fucked.*

But this was not the side he showed to Mrs. Jordan. For all
their faults, George III's sons were renowned for their irresistible charm. Most of them weren't much to look at, though. The
fair-haired William was of middling height with all the traits
of the Hanover physiognomy—the bulging blue eyes, long nose,
florid complexion, and nonexistent chin. But he had a genuine
warmth about him, and the twenty-six-year-old duke was desperate for love and affection; not only that, royalty conferred
some of its magic on those who traveled within its exalted
sphere. The thirty-year-old Dora might have seen it all in her
theatrical career, but she was not immune to the aura. Add to
this William's jolly and kind behavior toward her children, and
as a mother she was won.

On October 13, 1791, the duke wrote a triumphant letter to
the Prince of Wales, having ascertained for certain that Dora
and Richard Ford had never been legally married, and therefore, she would be his.

> *I have all proofs requisite and even legal ones. . . . Suspend
> then judgment till we meet. . . . I am sure I am too well
> acquainted with your friendship to doubt for a moment
> you will, my dear brother, behave kindly to a woman who
> possesses so deservedly my heart and confidence, and who
> has given me so many unequivocal and steady proofs of
> the most uncommon steady attachment.*

Aware of the way the princes of the blood had behaved toward the actresses they professed to admire, Dora had secured
an arrangement from William, who was now Duke of Clarence, having been gazetted in 1788. For the consideration of
£3,000 prior to consummation (nearly half a million dollars

today) and an £840 annual allowance (a little more than $152,000), to be paid quarterly, Dora would agree to be his mistress. It sounds mercenary, but such agreements were the way of the world.

Offstage, Dora was more the anxious mother than the flamboyant bon vivant. She could be quite retiring, rarely joining in a conversation, as though she needed a good script in order to be clever or witty. "What a task you give me to tell you how much I love you," she wrote to the duke in one of her early letters. Although she assured William of her feelings, she did not want to conduct their courtship in public, anxious about what the servants might say. And she begged the duke to delay their moving in together because she was "of a very shy disposition." Dora offered to meet him somewhere in the country instead—"*any where* out of town."

As soon as rumors began to circulate about the new glamour couple, the press gleefully pounced. The caricaturists and satirists had a field day and soon every shop window was hung with scurrilous cartoons.

In the eyes of the press and the public, because she was an actress, Dora was therefore a gold digger. Jests abounded that she collected her weekly salary from the Royal Treasurer. Worse, *Bon Ton* magazine reported that since she had taken up with the duke, Dora had become a neglectful mother.

Nothing was further from the truth, and Dora enlisted Richard Ford to write a letter upholding her maternal integrity.

> . . . *her conduct has been as laudable, generous, and as like a fond mother as in her present situation it was possible to be. She has indeed given up for their use every sixpence she has been able to save from her theatrical profits. She has also engaged to allow them £550 per an. [nearly $100,000 in today's economy] . . .'tis but bare justice for me to assert this as the father of those children . . .*

This was not propaganda. It was as true in 1791 as it would be in 1811. Nearly every penny Dora earned went to the support of her children—including saving for dowries, educations, and paying off gambling debts.

By 1795, Ford was married, with a legitimate son. He cut Dodee and Lucy out of his 1798 will, dying in 1806.

As a couple, Dora and William were generally good for each other. Although he was not clever or smart, William was warm and outgoing, energetic, and passionately in love with her. Dora supplied consistency, stability, and devotion, as tenderly maternal as she was amorous. She even managed to curb her royal lover's drinking, although she couldn't prevent him from doing "hard duty" on his visits to the Prince of Wales.

One satirist mused:

> *She's in truth the best feather you have in your cap.*
> *How you got her, to me, I must own, is a wonder!*
> *When I think of your natural aptness to blunder.*

But it took Dora a while to find her footing in the relationship. William could be very overbearing at times (which angered her sister, Hester, who was caring for the girls while Dora was at the theatre). Other times, he could be very needy. And because he was on a fixed income of £12,000 (a little more than $2.1 million today), he was not a good provider. A terrible money manager, he was almost permanently in debt, and his allowance payments to Dora were spotty at best.

A verse by Peter Pindar, the popular poet and satirist, swiftly made the rounds of every coffeehouse in London.

> *As Jordan's high and mighty squire*
> *Her playhouse profits deign to skim*
> *Some folks audaciously inquire*
> *If he keeps her or she keeps him.*

Two things the couple excelled at were motility and fertility. Dora bore William ten children (five of each) in twenty years, and there were a few miscarriages along the way as well. She was forty-five years old when she gave birth to her last child. All ten of their offspring were healthy and reached adulthood, a rarity in those days.

Each time Dora gave birth, she returned to the stage as soon as possible, not simply because she adored her career but because she had to maintain her family. Small wonder that as soon as she slowed down long enough to catch her breath and take stock, she was assailed by a bout of melancholy.

She breast-fed her own babies in an age when they were usually farmed out to a wet nurse. She did all the things a stay-at-home mother would have done for them, while managing a career that demanded very long hours, extensive travel, and full-bore energy at every moment. When she was on the road, touring the provinces, Dora's letters to William—the house-husband—were full of sweet domestic concerns about the children's colds, as well as griping about insensitive theatre managers and grueling schedules.

In the winter of 1796, after Dora and William had presented a model of domestic bliss for four years, King George grudgingly came round to accepting the situation. Although it did not result in any official recognition of their children, it led to a terrific home and an occupation for William. In January 1797, Dora and the duke inspected Bushy, the king's gift to his third son. Bushy House was a red-brick mansion dating from the reign of Charles II, surrounded by thousands of acres of parkland, of which William was to be the Ranger. Feeling professionally emasculated by his father as well as by Dora, the duke would have preferred a naval commission, as his veins were blue with seawater, but the Admiralty collectively shuddered at the idea.

Bushy became their idyll, a relaxed pastoral landscape that

was an optimal location for raising a family. The children, finally given a surname—FitzClarence—romped and played with their menagerie of dogs, ponies, and birds. Their parents told them bedtime stories. During their years there Dora enjoyed a vast measure of comfort and security, and delighted in William's genial help with their brood. For any era, and particularly for the eighteenth century, the duke was an extremely "hands-on" father.

William Boaden, a friend of Dora's who had been a guest at Bushy House, expressed his admiration for the way Dora "devoted herself to [William's] interests and his habits, his taste and domestic pleasures." He observed, "Whoever has had the happiness of seeing them together at Bushy saw them surrounded by a family rarely equaled for personal and mental grace; they saw their happy mother an honored wife, in every thing but the legal title, and uniformly spoke of the establishment at Bushy as one of the most enviable that had ever presented itself to their scrutiny."

Despite the fact that this was exactly the sort of family picture George III desperately desired for his children (barring the absence of legality, of course), there remained no formal acceptance from Windsor. However, the king and queen must have said something to William, because during the early years at Bushy Dora wrote to her lover, who was visiting his parents, to say, "A thousand thanks, dear love, for your kind letter. . . . I am proud of their Majesties' notice of the dear children. . . ."

William missed Dora dreadfully during her frequent absences while she toured the provinces. At the end of 1805, he asked her to give up her stage career and devote herself entirely to their family. It represented a huge sacrifice for Dora, emotionally, professionally, and financially, but she acquiesced, and remained off the boards for the next year and a half.

In 1809, when William went to Windsor to press his father for a naval appointment, he wrote the forty-seven-year-old

Dora an extremely touching letter. It bears a mention because only two years later, he would adopt a very different attitude.

> *Thro' your excellence and kindness in private life I am the happiest man possible and look forward only to a temporary separation to make that happiness more compleat from having provided for our dear children. My love and best and tenderest wishes attend you all at Bushy . . . Adieu till we meet and ever believe me, dearest Dora, Yours most affectionately . . .*

After Drury Lane burned to the ground on February 24, Dora had immediately pitched in, playing benefits to help the displaced stagehands. William then, inexplicably, stopped attending her performances and exercised his royal prerogative to "prohibit" Dora from appearing on a London stage. No reasons were discussed or given. Suddenly, William's dignity took precedence over her career and her renown. On the heels of these new restrictions, however, came the urgent need for funds. There were always debts and William had no employment. So Dora was free to continue to tour the provinces, jouncing about on rutted dirt roads from town to town.

As she always was when she was on the road, Dora was distressed to be separated from her beloved family. Her insightful letter perfectly encapsulates the mixed emotions and the demands of professionalism that remain the actor's burden today.

> *I drive you all from my mind as much as I can during the time I am employed, but then you all return with a double force and my dreams are confused and disturbed to a degree.*

She was now pushing fifty, no longer slim-waisted, but by no means stout. And yet early in 1811, performing at Bath, Dora felt at the top of her game.

I really think, and it is the opinion of several critics here that have known me from my first appearance in London, that I am a better actress at this moment than I ever was.

Her audiences were as appreciative as ever. But back home at Bushy, a sea change was taking place. William's attitude had cooled significantly; he made it clear that he was indifferent as to whether Dora went or stayed.

Things were changing. Her children by William were growing older and were now invited to attend royal events with their father, from which Dora was barred. Her other children's roles evolved as well. Lucy, her younger daughter by Richard Ford (and her traveling companion on the road) moved on, marrying Colonel Hawker, a man old enough to be her father. As a settled matron, Lucy could no longer accompany her mother on her provincial engagements. So Dora's oldest daughter, the miserably married Fanny Alsop, assumed Lucy's duties, but seemed overly fond of dosing her mother's wine with white poppy syrup—laudanum—much to Dora's distress.

When the Prince of Wales became Regent, William, now in his mid-forties, grew one step closer to the throne. He had to marry. And the Royal Marriages Act of 1772 prevented him from wedding the illegitimate commoner with whom he had resided for twenty years, because the king would never consent to it.

He began to pay not very subtle court to Catherine Tylney-Long, a twenty-two-year-old heiress. Dora began to realize what was happening, and in some way resigned herself to the inevitable, writing to William:

I frequently feel myself a restraint on your pleasures, and this idea makes me unhappy, even in the midst of my family . . . You see, I already consider you as an old friend, and tell you everything I think.

How she must have swallowed her pride to write those words! And yet she rather hoped that the duke would be able to sustain her as his mistress. After all, she was the devoted mother of their children, and couldn't imagine breaking up the home.

On October 2, 1811, Dora received a letter from William, asking her to meet her in Maidenhead three days later. Although there is no record of what transpired, William must have told Dora that—after twenty years—it was all over between them. From then on, he endeavored to avoid her, and the negotiations for her extrication from the relationship were conducted by factors. Dora did not even have her own advocate against the vast royal machine.

The gossip mill churned up the rumors of a royal split, as well as William's almost immediate, and bumbleheaded, proposal of marriage to Miss Tylney-Long—who summarily rejected him. Everyone wondered what would become of poor Mrs. Jordan. Even the regent's daughter, Princess Charlotte, expressed her sympathy, endorsing Dora as a "true friend to [the duke] and a most affcte. mother."

Dora's children by William were shocked and wondered about their future. Now fourteen, their second son, Henry, who had been sent to join the navy at the age of eleven, immediately took up the cudgels on his mother's behalf, writing to his elder brother, George:

> . . . were he not my father I could and would say more . . .
> My God!! To think that our father should have done such
> a thing [proposed to Miss Tylney-Long] . . . if this be true
> I will never more go home except once to see my Dear
> Mother whom I consider as a Most Injured Woman . . . I
> could not believe my eyes when I saw the paper which
> contained Distressing truth I scarcely know how I write I
> am nearly mad I think I shall run away home . . .

No one dared to openly criticize the duke for his callous conduct toward the devoted and faithful woman who loved him dearly, who had never once given him cause for complaint, and who had cared for him and their children with every ounce of her energy and every penny she earned.

The trusting Dora was misled by the royal machine, which assured her that she would be well provided for after the split, and so she "went quietly," assuming that their representations were genuine. In fact, she was kicked out of Bushy with no arrangements made for her residence elsewhere. She lost custody of her children once they reached the age of thirteen. For decades Dora Jordan had been living proof that an actress need not be licentious or loose. In fact, William had scarcely objected to her performing career while she was raising their children. However, under the new arrangement, Dora would not be permitted to see them if she continued to pursue a profession that was of dubious moral value. This distasteful restriction would effectively deprive her of her income and her life's work if she ever wanted to spend time with her beloved children.

The deed of settlement was formalized on December 23, 1811. Her three daughters by other men were again guaranteed £200 a year as they had been in the 1791 agreement that cemented Dora's arrangement with the duke. Of William's £12,000 annual allowance, Dora was to receive £4,400 (a bit more than $451,000), to sustain a home, horse and carriage, and provide for her younger daughters. She would lose half that income if she participated in any activity (including both public and private performances) that the duke might consider "unfavorable to the morals, manners, or habits of the said children."

It was a travesty.

But it got worse. A rumor began to circulate that Dora was planning to publish her private correspondence with William.

Dora was so distressed by it that she packed up the hundreds of letters she had sentimentally saved and delivered them to one of William's factors, saving only four letters "because they do him credit for candor and justice."

She moved to Cadogan Place and tried to begin anew. When the duke brought their children for their prearranged visits, he went around to the back-door servants' entrance to avoid running into their mother.

Money, or the lack of it, remained a problem. When Dora told William's adviser, John Barton, that she needed to resume her profession in order to pay the bills, Barton coolly belittled the longtime royal mistress by informing her that far from the duke's objection to her theatrical career, it was a matter of perfect indifference to His Grace.

So, taking Barton at his word, Dora returned to the stage. And she pragmatically covered her derrière in case there might be any backlash from William, by telling the newspapers (before William had a chance to react) that the duke had been the embodiment of kindness in allowing her to pursue her profession and thereby provide for herself. Although Dora had been treated abominably by the royal family, she was more regal and dignified than any of them and never spoke a single unkind word against William.

But the separation had taken its toll on her emotionally. She wrote to her son George, "I begin to feel that acting keeps me alive. In fact, it keeps me from thinking." Still, close friends like William Boaden noticed a difference in her performances; glimmers of her private despair occasionally intruded on her professionalism. But after a career that spanned nearly four decades, exhausted and disappointed by the dwindling houses, she retired from the stage without fanfare in 1815, giving her final performances in July and August at the seaside resort of Margate.

At the end of August, Dora discovered that her son-in-law, Frederick March—Dodee's husband—had bled dry her Coutt's bank account. All the wind went out of her sails. Dora hadn't an ounce of fight left. Terrified of being arrested for debt—the same fate that befell her friends Mary Robinson and Emma Hamilton—she decided to flee to the Continent, where her creditors could not legally reach her. She landed at Boulogne, took a little coastal cottage in nearby Marquetra, and sought anonymity by calling herself Mrs. James. Although Dora had relied upon John Barton to handle the arrangements of disposing of her property, Barton never informed the duke of her plight. Nor did anyone take the thieving Mr. March to court on her behalf.

In the wee hours of the morning on July 5, 1816, at the age of fifty-four, Dora Jordan died in a rooming house in St. Cloud, alone and impoverished in a country not her own. It was only through the energetic intervention of "an English gentleman of some weight" that she was buried in the local cemetery. Being an actress and a Protestant counted as two strikes against Dora in Catholic France. Her headstone was paid for by the Woodgates, an English couple from Essex, who were said to have visited Dora shortly before her death. Dora's epitaph, engraved by the theatre historian John Genest, was a lengthy Latin encomium ending with the words *"Mementote Lugete"* (Read it and Weep).

Two of her children, Frederick FitzClarence and the devoted Lucy, could have reached her in time, had they known she was ill.

At the time Dora left England, William himself was so deeply in debt he'd considered giving up Bushy and moving with their half-royal children to St. James's Palace. We do not know how he felt when he heard of Dora's death. He was utterly silent, not even referring to it in his letters to their children. Yet years later, surrounded by portraits of her, with tears in his eyes, the duke remarked to others what a good woman she was.

After trying his luck with a few more marriageable heiresses, in 1818 the duke finally wed Princess Adelaide of Saxe-Coburg and Meiningen, who was "very ugly, with a horrid complexion." Adelaide gave William five children, none of whom survived infancy. But she was a terrific stepmother to the FitzClarence girls, who admired her very much, in part, perhaps, because she insisted that all the portraits of Dora Jordan remain on the walls at Bushy.

After Dora's death, one of her daughters revealed that the duke had never repaid some £30,000 (more than $3.2 million today) that he had borrowed from Dora.

At six a.m. on June 26, 1830, the sixty-four-year-old duke was awakened with the news that his elder brother, George IV, had died and that he was now King of England.

The royal bum had hardly warmed the throne when the press took him to task for his callous treatment of his former mistress. Finally, someone dared to mention the immorality in a man's refusing to do his duty by the mother of his children, rather than the scandal of not being married to her. One paper wrote:

> The people . . . have witnessed a man who has inundated his country with bastards, and deserted the deserving but helpless mother of his offspring, and finally left her to perish like a dog in the streets, and to be buried as a pauper at the public charge when she ceased to maintain him by her exertions.

On the other hand, the *Morning Post* continued to complain about the indecency of the new king riding about in his carriage accompanied by his illegitimate children.

Was it Dora's fault that their children were bastards? No—it was George III's. His Royal Marriages Act of 1772, which was intended to prevent his wayward sons from engaging in *mésalliances*, instead had the effect of sending them into the arms of mistresses whom they couldn't wed. William and Dorothy's healthy brood of ten children, raised in a loving and stable home, were exactly the ideal family George III had envisioned for his heirs. And yet Dora herself, a loving, hardworking pragmatic soul and devoted mother—was persona non grata because of her lack of birthright.

Although Dorothy had been dead for fifteen years, one of William's first acts as king was that of a lover's repentance toward the woman he had reduced to penury and disgrace. He commissioned a statue of Dora with two of their children from Francis Chantrey, the leading sculptor of the day. The marble tableau—an odd cross between a Madonna and a Greek Muse—features Dora breast-feeding their infant. It was not completed during the king's lifetime, and languished in the artist's studio (where an eighteen-year-old Queen Victoria admired it). At the time, because the subject was a notorious fallen woman, the sculpture was deemed too immoral to be displayed in a public place. Since 1980, it has been on view in the Portrait Gallery at Buckingham Palace, where the living Dora would have been denied entry.

William was considered a relatively decent king, if not a very bright one. His reign was marked by a struggle for parliamentary reform and the attempt to rid the country of the "rotten boroughs"—the sparsely populated districts that had the same voting power as more densely inhabited ones.

The seventy-one-year-old king was felled by a serious illness in the spring of 1837. He died at Windsor Castle on June 20, and was buried on July 8 in the vault at St. George's Chapel. William was succeeded on the throne by his niece, Victoria, the daughter of his late younger brother Edward, Duke of Kent.

In 1884, a two-volume biography titled *The Life and Times*

of William IV was published. It was a perfect example of high Victorian literature and mores, in that there was no mention whatsoever of Dora Jordan and her two-decade love affair with the future king, except in the unsatisfying sentence:

> *The king had formed a connection with a well-known actress . . . there is no need to do more than to chronicle the fact, as the subject is a distasteful one.*

VICTORIA

1819–1901

RULED 1837–1901 (GREAT BRITAIN AND IRELAND)

EMPRESS OF INDIA 1877–1901

VICTORIA'S FATHER, THE DUKE OF KENT, DIED WHEN SHE was just a few months old. Her mother, the German-born princess Victoire of Saxe-Coburg-Saalfeld, deliberately shielded her from her "wicked uncles" so that she could never be tainted with even the slightest whiff of the immorality that was the hallmark of the Hanoverian monarchy. Victoria was to represent a fresh start, the future of England, rather than an extension of its dissolute past.

When she was just eighteen years old, Victoria acceded to the throne on the death of her uncle, William IV. By all accounts the diminutive sovereign possessed remarkable poise for one so young and with such enormous responsibility on her slim shoulders. Her modest yet regal demeanor immediately won her the praise of her ministers as well as her subjects.

On February 10, 1840, three years after becoming queen, Victoria married her first cousin, Albert of Saxe-Coburg-Gotha.

It was most definitely a love match; the twenty-year-old queen had giddily fallen head over heels for the tall, mustachioed German, and with thumping heart, *she* had proposed marriage to *him*. It was one of the last times she took the reins in their relationship. Victoria and Albert had nine children and worked diligently to promote the royal family as the archetype of English domestic bliss, a model for the middle classes to emulate.

When, after twenty-one years of marriage, Albert died of typhoid fever on December 14, 1861, part of Victoria died with him. Widowed at forty-two, she continued to rule the country through the prism of Albert's eyes, emphasizing his most keenly held virtues of discretion, decorum, and duty, as well as strict moral rectitude (even to the point of prudery), leading her subjects by example. She went into permanent mourning for Albert, retiring from public life for a number of years, which left her open to severe criticism from her subjects, her ministers, and the press. During these reclusive years, her intimate friendship with a Scottish gillie, John Brown, created a national scandal.

Victoria was the longest-reigning monarch in British history, lending her name to an era that spanned two-thirds of the nineteenth century. During her sixty-three years, seven months, and two days as queen, the British Empire reached its zenith, covering a quarter of the world. But imperial expansion exacted its price, notably the 1857 Sepoy Massacre in India and the two South African Boer Wars.

Trade was so extensive, and the available goods so exotic, that the English became an acquisitive population, packing as much bric-a-brac into their gaslit homes as humanly possible. The Industrial Revolution, the steam engine, and the invention of the telegraph changed the way people lived, worked, communicated, and traveled, transforming the English economy.

Victoria survived six assassination attempts during her reign, but on January 22, 1901, she died of a cerebral hemorrhage at the age of eighty-one, marking the end of the House of Hanover. She was interred beside her beloved Albert at Frogmore mausoleum in Windsor Great Park. She was succeeded by her eldest son, who was crowned Edward VII at the age of fifty-nine. One of his first acts as king was to destroy the myriad monuments his mother had erected in memory of her beloved John Brown.

👑

"MRS. BROWN",
QUEEN VICTORIA
and John Brown 1826–1883

From their very first visit to Scotland in 1842, Victoria and Albert had been enchanted by its wild beauty and by the simplicity and genuineness of its people. "All seemed to breathe freedom and peace," Victoria observed, and the royal family was eager to establish a presence there. Victoria bought the lease to Balmoral, "a pretty little castle in the old Scotch style," after its owner, Sir Robert Gordon, dropped dead over his morning kippers on October 8, 1847.

At Balmoral, the rugged John Brown, seven years the royal couple's junior, was one of their gillies, an attendant on the family's hunting and fishing excursions. He was one of nine children, born in Craithie, Aberdeenshire, to a tenant farmer, or crofter. Brown had no formal education, but Victoria found him "discreet, careful, intelligent [and] attentive."

This stalwart and handsome Highlander, with his russet hair and beard and his thick muttonchop whiskers, soon became an indispensable retainer. The queen's physicians had prescribed riding as a remedy against her increasing stoutness. Victoria would have no one else lead out her pony, so Brown was promoted to chief gillie. In 1858, Albert handpicked him to be his wife's personal servant in Scotland.

After Albert died on December 14, 1861, Victoria was stricken to the point of collapse. She slept with her consort's coat on top of her, clutching his nightshirt like a lover. Other clothes of Albert's were strewn about the bed so that his presence and his scent were omnipresent. The Blue Room at Windsor where he spent so much time became a shrine to Albert, his personal effects maintained the way he had left them. In fact, Victoria turned the entire kingdom into a memorial to her late husband. "*His* wishes—*his* plans about *every* thing, *his* views about *every* thing are to be *my law*! And no *human power* will make me swerve from *what he* decided and wished."

As the 1860s plodded on, the queen became reclusive, refusing to appear in public or attend to the duties of state, such as opening Parliament. People thought she was literally going mad, so excessive was her mourning. All she desired to do was sit and weep. According to Lord Clarendon, "She believes that his eye is now constantly upon her, that he watches over every action of hers and that in fact, she never ceases to be in communication with his spirit."

Feelings were running high against the queen's selfishness in abandoning her public duties in order to wallow in her misery. Her subjects had sympathized with her at first, but as the years dragged on, they wanted her to snap out of it already! In March of 1864, a large placard was affixed to the gates at Buckingham Palace: "These commanding premises to be let or sold, in consequence of the late occupant's declining business."

Enter John Brown.

Fears for Victoria's health brought Brown and Her Majesty's pony Lochnagar from Balmoral to Osborne, her estate on the Isle of Wight. But John Brown was far more than a personal trainer. He was a connection to Albert, someone who had known her husband well in happier times.

The Queen of England was in a very difficult position. She was friendless. Victoria had no former playmates or schoolfellows to surround herself with, because she had been raised apart from other children. It was inappropriate to confide in her ladies-in-waiting or her younger children; besides, she never had much use for her offspring, preferring Prince Albert over any of them, individually and collectively. Her older children were starting families of their own, often in far-flung countries on the Continent. And Victoria could be surprisingly shy in the presence of the upper classes, often at a loss for conversation. She was far more comfortable among the middle classes, who shared her tastes and values, and most at ease among the hardworking, honest Scots laborers.

It was Victoria who was the constitutional monarch. Because Albert was just her spouse, her prince consort—not even king consort—he had no official role in the government. Victoria lamented that their marriage reversed the natural order of things: man was supposed to master woman. Victoria's ministers always acknowledged that there were two sides to her that needed constant massaging: the queen, and the woman. And all through her life, the woman needed to be cherished. Not only that, she seemed to crave a strong man to put her in her place.

Brown was that and more. He was legendarily blunt and outspoken (to the point of rudeness, according to the royal family), and soon became the queen's gatekeeper. No one was admitted to see Victoria unless he approved. The devoted Brown, who never took a single day off in eighteen and a half years of service, saw to her every need. The two of them developed a daily routine that Victoria found very comforting.

A letter from the queen to her eldest daughter, Vicky, sums

up her personal as well as psychological reasons for her devotion to John Brown:

> He comes to my room—after breakfast & luncheon to get his orders, & everything is always right—he has such an excellent head and memory . . . is besides so devoted, & attached & clever . . . It is an excellent arrangement & I feel I have here always in the house, a good, devoted soul . . . whose only object and interest is my service, & God knows how much I want to be taken care of . . . And in this house where there are so many people, & often so much indiscretion & no Male head now—such a person is invaluable.

When Victoria became morose, Brown, in his charmingly brusque way, would provide a reality check. Once, when he was trying to fasten her riding bonnet for her, the stalwart Scot demanded of the glum little monarch, "Hoots, Wumman! Can ye no hold yerr head up!" On another occasion, when she appeared for her morning ride in mourning, he exclaimed, "What are ye daeing with that auld black dress on again? It's green-moulded." Victoria rustled off to put on a different gown.

Not too many other people wanted Brown to be so ubiquitous. Her family, in particular the Prince of Wales, felt that the upstart servant took far too many liberties; his informality was an affront. Who else would dare to address the Queen of England as "Wumman"? Only Brown was permitted to smoke where Her Majesty might be exposed to the noxious tobacco fumes she detested. Not only that, he was frequently drunk. Victoria was well aware of this fault, but even when his inebriation prohibited him from attending to his duties, when he was found passed out on his bed at the hour appointed for her morning ride, she never dignified the reason with a reaction.

She often rode out with Brown to a little secluded cottage beyond Balmoral, bringing only a picnic hamper, as a few ladies-in-waiting trotted dutifully several paces behind her. A maid of honor was shocked to learn that the repast was neither terribly regal nor terribly ladylike. "She don't much like tea. We take oot biscuits and spirits," Brown told her. In fact, the distiller John Begg had created a special blend of Scotch whisky for Her Majesty, her beverage of choice when the occasion called for a little nip.

Her ministers and advisers feared Brown's undue influence on an already vulnerable woman. Only Henry Ponsonby, one of Victoria's personal secretaries, had a different perspective. According to Ponsonby, Brown "was the only person who could fight and make the Queen do what she did not wish," which was viewed as a good thing by those who desperately sought to put her back into the public eye. And things could be worse, Ponsonby reminded the critics. At least Brown had no political agenda to press.

Ponsonby, like Brown, was in daily contact with Victoria, and better than most people, he understood the nature of their friendship. The secretary assured Brown's detractors that "while certainly a favorite," he was "only a servant and nothing more. One only had to know the Queen to realize how innocent" this odd-seeming relationship was. Although she despised the English class system as an artificial construct, when it came to her relationship with staff and retainers, Victoria had extremely rigid ideas about the natural order of things.

Nevertheless, the press disregarded anything approaching a kernel of truth. By 1866, word had gotten out that Victoria and her personal Highland servant had a special relationship, leading to a crop of salacious and unchecked rumors about Victoria's inappropriate affection for John Brown. It was variously written and reported that Brown was "the queen's stallion," that she was "in an interesting condition" as a result of their love affair. It was also reported that he was the medium through which the queen contacted Albert's spirit and that Victoria fervently believed that this spirit now inhabited John Brown's body, making it perfectly acceptable to sleep with him. The most frequent comment was that Victoria and Brown were secretly married, thus inspiring the queen's nickname, "Mrs. Brown."

In 1868, Victoria published *Leaves from a Journal of Our Life in the Highlands*. Dedicated to Albert, it was intended to be an instructive little volume on the royal family's exemplar of domestic felicity and "kind and proper feeling towards the poor and the servants." Footnotes discussing the particulars of the servants' careers and characters shone a bright light on Brown and fueled speculation of an improper relationship between the gillie and the queen.

She had more or less made him one of the family. It galled her children that Brown even rode on the queen's coach. But on one frightening day in 1872, if it hadn't been for Victoria's "big man in livery," Her Majesty might have been assassinated.

As the queen's carriage was about to pass through the Golden Gate to Buckingham Palace, the eagle-eyed Scotsman caught sight of the pistol-waving Arthur O'Connor, a seventeen-year-old Fenian—one of the revolutionaries committed to independent rule in Ireland—and hopped off the coach.

"It is to good Brown and his wonderful presence of mind that I so greatly owe my safety, for he alone saw the boy rush round and followed him," a relieved Victoria acknowledged. She awarded Brown a special gold medal for devoted service—which was never bestowed on anyone else during her sixty-three years as queen—and an annuity of £25 (a measly $3,069.54 today). Albert Edward, the Prince of Wales, who was always jealous of his mother's attentions to Brown, grumpily complained that his younger brother, Prince Arthur, had behaved just as bravely and their mother had only given *him* a gold pin.

In the middle of March 1883, Brown caught a severe cold after the queen sent him out in an icy wind, traveling by dog cart on the hunt for a pair of assailants who had threatened one of the queen's ladies in Windsor Great Park. Although he insisted on returning to his duties, by March 25, Brown had developed a high fever. Fluid-filled swellings had broken out on his face and head, a relapse of the bacterial disease erysipelas from which he had suffered in the past.

The fifty-seven-year-old favorite remained gravely ill in the Clarence Tower at Windsor. Delirium tremens set in, probably owing as much to Brown's inability to sneak a drink of whisky as to his fever.

Rheumatic complaints prevented Victoria, now sixty-three, from climbing the tower stairs to visit her beloved Brown. So as not to aggravate her, the queen was not told how ill he was until the end was inevitable.

On March 27, John Brown died. Victoria was distraught. It was like losing Albert all over again. Her youngest daughter, Princess Beatrice, helped her up the winding steps to Brown's room, where the funeral service was performed. Placed atop the coffin were a wreath of white flowers and myrtle, and a card reading "from his best and most faithful friend, Victoria R.I." He was buried at Craithie, his birthplace.

Brown's room in Clarence Tower was to remain exactly the way he had left it, just as Victoria had insisted on enshrining Albert's Blue Room at Windsor. A fresh flower was to be placed on his pillow every day. The eulogy in the *Court Circular* was fives times the length of the one written for Victoria's favorite prime minister, Benjamin Disraeli. She commissioned monuments to Brown at each of her royal residences, and his was the only memorial at Frogmore not commemorating a member of her family. The celebrated sculptor Joseph Edgar Boehm created a life-sized statue of the Scot; its plinth bore an inscription written by England's poet laureate Alfred Lord Tennyson:

> *Friend more than servant, Loyal, Truthful, Brave!*
> *Self less than Duty, even to the Grave.*

The agonized queen wrote to her daughter Vicky:

I feel so stunned and bewildered. He protected me so—that I felt safe! And now all, all is gone in this world and all seems unhinged again in thousands of ways . . . the shock—the blow, the blank, the constant missing at every turn of the one strong powerful arm and head . . . This anguish that comes over me like a wave . . . is terrible. . . . God's will be done, but I shall never be the same again.

In 1884, Victoria published a sequel to her *Leaves from a Journal* covering the years from 1862 to 1882 and dedicated to her "Loyal Highlanders, and especially to the memory of my devoted personal attendant and faithful friend, JOHN BROWN. He is daily, nay hourly, missed by me, whose lifelong gratitude he won by his constant care, attention, and devotion."

The public devoured the book, but the royal family was not amused. The queen and "Bertie," the Prince of Wales, had tussled over its publication. Bertie had advised her to stick to private circulation because her memoir cast unpleasant speculation on the nature of her relationship with Brown, a comment that his mother found distinctly hypocritical, given her son's notoriously rakish behavior.

When Victoria died on January 22, 1901, she was wearing (among other rings) Brown's mother's wedding band, which he had given her in 1883. As soon as the royal family had paid their last respects, her physician, James Reid, placed Brown's photograph and a lock of his hair in the queen's left hand, discreetly concealed by a small bouquet. Nestled amid numerous totems belonging to members of the royal family, she was buried clutching these mementos.

Long after their deaths, the titillating gossip about Brown and the queen persisted, and it can't be entirely dismissed. Catherine Walter, a popular prostitute colorfully known as

"Skittles" (who numbered the Prince of Wales among her customers), shared information with another one of her clients, a politician and poet named Wilfred Scawen Blunt, regarding conversations she had with the sculptor Edgar Boehm at the time Boehm was creating (on Victoria's commission) a bust of John Brown. Having witnessed firsthand the interactions between his patron and his subject, Boehm told Skittles that he didn't doubt for a moment that there was a very special spark between them.

The alleged conversations between courtesan and artisan seem to suggest that Her Majesty was intimate with John Brown. Blunt's "Secret Diary," sealed according to the terms of his will until 1972, revealed Boehm's belief (as told by Skittles) that the queen had allowed Brown "every conjugal privilege" during their jaunts to the little house in the hills.

More than two decades after Brown's death, Dr. James Reid was asked by King Edward VII to retrieve a box containing more than three hundred letters referencing John Brown that had been written by his late mother to her factor at Balmoral, Dr. Alexander Profeit. Profeit's son was threatening to blackmail the king with the contents of the correspondence. Reid read the letters after collecting them, and in his diary noted that "many of them" were "most compromising." After Edward read the letters, they disappeared; presumably he burned them.

A thorough reading of Victoria's character would probably lead to the conclusion that the passionate letters were heartfelt and sincere expressions of her own devotion to the one person who had been her closest confidant and had known her best in the years after her beloved Albert's death. Believing that her late husband omnisciently watched her every moment from his lofty cloud beside St. Peter, it is highly doubtful that Victoria knew John Brown carnally, or even that she hinted at—much less graphically alluded to—that level of intimacy in her correspondence with a third party. And surely, from the *Leaves* to the monuments, Victoria would never have publicly trumpeted her admiration if their friendship had been improper. This was not a case of hiding an indiscretion in plain sight.

Edward VII himself had enough infidelities to fill several volumes of memoirs, and though his aged mother's epistolary effusiveness over a man not his father may have given him the creeps, the king's reaction to the letters might not have had very much to do with middle-class morality. Bertie, who never liked Brown, probably could not countenance the idea that his widowed mother, who had never been fond of him, had instead, in the wake of his father's demise, embarrassingly lavished every shred of her devotion on a servant.

SAXE-COBURG-GOTHA

1901—1910

EDWARD VII

1841–1910
RULED 1901–1910
KING OF THE UNITED KINGDOM OF
GREAT BRITAIN AND IRELAND AND
THE BRITISH DOMINIONS BEYOND THE SEAS
EMPEROR OF INDIA

*I*T WAS QUEEN VICTORIA'S WORST NIGHTMARE THAT HER eldest son and heir would end up emulating George IV's excesses. Not only did Albert Edward—known as Bertie—live up to her fears, he exceeded them. His behavior was so decadent that for the first time in British history, there was serious, and open, talk of a republic.

On March 5, 1863, at the age of twenty-one, the five-feet-seven-inch Bertie wed one of his fourth cousins, a daughter of Prince Christian of Denmark, the slightly taller eighteen-year-old Princess Alexandra Caroline Marie Charlotte Louise Julie of Schleswig-Holstein-Sonderburg-Glucksberg—mercifully known as Alix. Like her husband, the slender and lovely Alix was not an intellectual. But her sweet temperament and ubiquitous grace made her an instant favorite among her new subjects. Unfortunately, she had inherited a form of deafness (otosclerosis), and by the time she'd given birth to her last child, Alix had lost almost all her hearing. As a result, it was difficult for her to keep pace with their witty and vivacious social set or to converse in any meaningful way with her husband.

Considering him an indolent wastrel and not very bright, for decades Victoria shut Bertie out of all state affairs. Not until the 1890s, in the last years of her life, did she allow him access to official papers. Several of Victoria's prime ministers suggested a role for him in Ireland, but the queen always scotched the idea.

The Prince of Wales finally ascended the throne at the age of fifty-nine on January 22, 1901. He ruled as Edward VII, declaring that his father was the only Albert who should be enshrined in his subjects' memories. Edward VII was the first English king to be ruler of "the British Dominions beyond the seas," a reference to the colonies of the vast British Empire, which he continued to build and struggled to maintain.

Edward's cosmopolitan sensibilities, affinity for people of other colors and religions, and his genial bonhomie made him an ideal roving ambassador. It was a good fit for the portly prince for whom restlessness had always led to boredom. As king, he was instrumental in achieving what no English monarch before him could do: the 1904 Entente Cordiale marked the end of centuries of Anglo-French rivalry and cemented a lasting peace between the two countries. And he achieved it in large measure due to a compliment he'd paid the previous year to a pretty French actress!

And yet it's not as a skilled diplomat, but as "Edward the Caresser"—the nickname bestowed by the expat novelist Henry James—that Bertie entered the pages of history.

His flirtations were legion—from Cockney chorus girls to the *grandes cocottes* of Parisian brothels, and from the Brooklyn-born mother of Winston Churchill (the former Jennie Jerome) to Sarah Bernhardt. A passing naval officer on the royal yacht once overheard Bertie through the walls of his cabin exhorting his latest conquest to "Stop calling me 'Sir' and put another cushion under your back!" Although there were three women who qualified as a *maîtresse en titre*—Lillie Langtry, Daisy Brooke, and Alice Keppel—there were countless others, simultaneously and in between.

Bertie never lost his slight German accent, but he frequently lost his temper. He loved yachting and blood sports, fat cigars, fast motorcars, and fast women. He specialized in killing time while waiting for the crown by patronizing racetracks and theatres, country house parties, casinos, and brothels.

After suffering a series of colds in April 1910, Bertie died at Buckingham Palace on the night of May 6. His last sentient expression was that of gladness that his racehorse Witch of Air had won the 4:15 at Kempton Park. Edward's second son succeeded him, as George V.

His nine-year reign, known as the Edwardian era, epitomized a world of glamour and gaiety, country tweeds, shooting parties, and roast beef with Yorkshire pudding on Sundays. A welcome escape from the dark, restrictive decades of Victorianism and a return to the pageantry of the monarchy, it was England's last Age of Innocence. Just four years after Edward's death, the winds of war would reek of mustard gas, thanks to his nephew, Kaiser Wilhelm of Germany.

EDWARD VII
and Lillie Langtry 1853–1929

Emilie Charlotte Le Breton was born on the Channel Island of Jersey to the Dean of Jersey, a handsome serial philanderer, and the beautiful but impoverished Londoner for whom she was named. A tomboyish hoyden who regularly roughhoused with her six brothers, she hated her French-sounding moniker, much preferring her nickname, Lillie, earned because her skin was so unusually fair.

In 1874 at the age of twenty-one, the tall, long-legged beauty with waist-length russet hair and deep blue eyes married the twenty-six-year-old Irish landowner Edward Langtry, the owner of a rather spiffy vessel. She had known him for only six weeks. "To become mistress of the yacht I married the owner," Lillie admitted. She had a lifelong fascination with sailing and racing, but her big dream was to take London's social world by storm.

A chance meeting at the Westminster Aquarium with a former neighbor from Jersey resulted in an invitation to a house party. Lillie's looks, wit, and unaffected mien utterly charmed the guests and soon she and Ned were mingling with London's smart set. Lillie bloomed, but Ned, an outdoorsman, hated every minute of it.

Lillie's beauty, her vivacious spirit, and her perfect hourglass figure, daringly unsupported by stays in an age when women corseted themselves practically to asphyxia, captivated London society, from socialites to artists. Oscar Wilde idolized her to the point of walking around the streets of London with a lily in his hand, and worshipfully sleeping on her doorstep until her husband tripped over him. Edward Millais's portrait of her in a simple black dress, titled *A Jersey Lily* (which became her nickname), was so popular when it was exhibited to the public that the Royal Academy had to rope it off.

Photography, the new media rage, turned Lillie into one of the "P.B.'s"—professional beauties—whose photos were for sale in postcard form on nearly every London street corner. Now, everybody knew her name, including the most famous man in the kingdom, a renowned connoisseur of feminine beauty.

Lillie met the bearded, slightly portly Albert Edward, Prince of Wales, in May 1877, at an intimate supper (ten guests only) hosted by their mutual friend, the dashing amateur arctic explorer Sir Allen Young. Bertie arrived late, flush from another engagement. An important one, Lillie assumed, "for some glittering orders and the blue ribbon of the Garter added to his regal appearance."

Lillie was standing by the fireplace, her long, Titian-red hair coiffed in her usual style, an unadorned coil at the nape of her neck. She was wearing the only gown she owned, a simple black dress with cream lace cuffs that had been sewn for her by a Jersey modiste. The black dress served double duty; she was in mourning for her favorite brother, Reggie, who had died in the winter of 1876 after a tragic riding accident.

According to Lillie's memoir, *The Days I Knew*, she hadn't known the reason for the dinner party, unaware of the identity of the guest of honor.

Suddenly there was a stir, followed by an expectant hush, a hurried exit of Sir Allen, then a slight commotion out-side, and presently I heard a deep and cheery voice say: "I am afraid I am a little late." Sir Allen murmured something courtier-like in reply, and the Prince of Wales, whose face had been previously unfamiliar to me except through photographs, appeared in the doorway of Strat-ford Place drawing-room.

The twenty-three-year-old Lillie was so overwhelmed that although she was seated next to the prince, she could barely muster the guts to make conversation. But they'd made a con-quest of each other. Soon Bertie was calling at the Langtrys' Eaton Place flat. In Hyde Park, he rode with Lillie (who turned heads in her form-fitting habit) in full view of the public.

Such outings made Mrs. Langtry even more of a public fig-ure, and turned Mr. Langtry into a figure of fun. Society's rigid (though wildly hypocritical) rules dictated that for propriety's sake a husband had to accompany his wife when in mixed company.

But it was soon common knowledge that the woman who had immediately impressed Bertie as "a beautiful hound set upon its feet" was the prince's first official *maîtresse en titre*.

Alexandra, the beautiful Danish-born Princess of Wales, seemed to like Lillie personally, and was always warm and gracious to her. Alix displayed a surprising generosity of spirit, even sending for the royal doctor to attend Mrs. Langtry at her home after she was taken ill during a ball at Marlborough House. Beautiful, slightly simple, and extremely deaf, Alix was adept at feigning ignorance. Or perhaps she had made peace with the fact that there was nothing she could do to stop Bertie's philandering.

Ned Langtry, however, had an Irish temper, and though he was a gentleman and not brought up to work (making him socially acceptable in the circle in which he now moved), he was also not raised to turn a blind eye to adultery. Mr. Langtry bitterly resented his wife's unusual status—though the prince and Lillie were never seen alone together—as well as the toll it took on his ego, increasingly finding solace in the bottle. Ned was not above making scenes, once disrupting a house party at Lord Malmesbury's estate when he snatched Lillie's blotting paper from the escritoire and held it to a mirror, revealing the text of her rather indiscreet thank-you note to the Prince of Wales. The Langtrys' row became the stuff of legend, with Lillie livid that his lordship's servants had ignored their employer's instructions and not burned the guests' blotting paper every day.

As a balm to Ned's vanity, the prince gave him a pair of monogrammed cufflinks and arranged for him to be presented to the queen, which mollified him for a while.

Lillie was presented at court some months later, resplendent in a low-cut ivory brocade gown with a nine-foot train that began at her shoulders. Her hair was dressed with three tall ostrich plumes that daringly mimicked the Prince of Wales's crest. Unfortunately, she was presented third to last on an exceptionally hot afternoon, and both Lillie and Queen Victoria were debilitated by the time her turn came. Ordinarily, the queen didn't remain for the entire three p.m. Drawing Room, leaving the late-afternoon presentations to her daughter-in-law, Princess Alexandra. Lillie, who was somewhat panicked about meeting her lover's mum, had been counting on this changing of the guard, as Alexandra was already fond of her. But Victoria was anxious to see who her son was sleeping with, and endured the entire Drawing Room. When Lillie was finally presented to Her Majesty, "there was not even the flicker of a smile on her face, and she looked grave and tired."

Still, it was a huge deal to have been presented at court, though Lillie would later write that there was an awful lot of fuss and preparation for an interview that went by in an eye blink. But now Lillie was eligible to attend balls at Buckingham Palace, which naturally were the most glittering and glamorous events of the season. It's hard to imagine today's monarchy being so tolerant of such overt adulterers waltzing about their rooms and drinking their champagne. In fact, Queen Elizabeth refused to acknowledge Camilla Parker Bowles during Camilla's lengthy extramarital affair with Prince Charles. But during the Edwardian era, adultery—which had become the norm among generations of men who had married for money—was far less of a scandal than divorce.

Lillie's sense of fun enchanted the thirty-six-year-old prince. He fell in love with her spirit as well as her remarkable outer beauty, and wanted the world to know it. He showered Lillie with jewelry, and when a society hostess finally persuaded her to ditch her black dress, claiming her husband had a horror of the color, Lillie's wardrobe went from drab to resplendent—subsidized, as was the custom, by her royal paramour. The prince legendarily hated to see the same dress twice. Lillie admitted in her memoirs that their only quarrel came when she wore the same gown to two successive balls, not expecting Bertie to be at both of them.

At one point during their three-year affair, Bertie bitterly complained, "I've spent enough on you to build a battleship," to which Lillie wittily riposted, "and you've spent enough in me to float one."

In 1877, the first year of their relationship, Bertie set her up in a little red-brick house in Bournemouth, where they resided like a couple of married bourgeoisie. From 1878 to 1880, Mrs. Langtry was the prince's official mistress, and for the first two of those years they were surprisingly faithful to each other. In fact, Lillie wasn't even sleeping with her husband.

During their third year together, the prince whisked Lillie off to the Continent. There they enjoyed the delights of Vienna and Paris—where he openly kissed her on the dance floor at Maxim's.

But their commitment to mutual exclusivity was waning. The prince began to stray, dallying with the celebrated French actress Sarah Bernhardt and other women. Meanwhile, Lillie was enjoying an affair with the man who was said to be the great love of her life, her childhood friend Arthur Jones.

The prince introduced her to his German cousin, Prince Louis of Battenberg, who had become a British national in order to realize his dream of serving in the Royal Navy. As Wales had privately predicted, throwing Lillie together with young Battenberg, dark and dashing, and closer to her age, had the expected conclusion. But soon the pair was wildly in love (which wasn't in the script) and Lillie was pregnant (which *really* wasn't in the script). As Lillie had been concurrently sleeping with Wales, Battenberg, and Arthur Jones, the hot potato of paternity was up for grabs. As it was, no one claimed responsibility beyond Bertie's sending Lillie from Jersey to

France during the final months of her pregnancy, where (unlike England) there was no law requiring that all births be recorded.

On March 8, 1881, Lillie gave birth to a daughter she named Jeanne-Marie. At first, she pretended to be the girl's aunt. When she finally revealed herself to be Jeanne-Marie's mother, Lillie kept the identity of her papa a secret—in her view, protecting the girl from the taint of illegitimacy by allowing Jeanne-Marie to assume that her father was Ned Langtry. Lillie believed Jeanne-Marie's father to be Prince Louis—who during her pregnancy had conveniently received a new naval posting, sending him halfway across the world and out of Lillie's life.

Fully three years after her royal affair with the Prince of Wales began, the story went to press. *Town Talk* published reports of Lillie's infidelities, which led not to a divorce proceeding but to a libel suit, resulting in the editor's incarceration for eighteen months! Smart alecks quipped earnestly, "There was nothing between the Prince of Wales and Lillie Langtry; not even a sheet."

But the combination of an ugly trial and tabloid exposure was the final button on their love affair.

As the prince's mistress, Lillie had said that "my only purpose in life was to look nice and make myself agreeable." But when her royal affair ended, she had to make a living. She took acting lessons and began to perform onstage, starting cautiously by appearing in charity events where her celebrity cachet, rather than her talent, was in the spotlight. Yet Lillie soon proved herself worthy of critical review. Step by step, getting her theatrical feet wet by performing in the provinces, she finally landed a contract with the Haymarket Theatre in London, where she made a brilliant success of it. Soon, her calendar was filled with international engagements. She toured America in a seventy-five-foot-long private railway car and invested her earnings in real estate and racehorses.

It's hard to miss the irony that as a royal mistress and obvious adulteress, Lillie was permitted to hobnob with high society and dance at Buckingham Palace, but as an actress, the same hostesses closed their doors to her. In fact, the palace had a rule prohibiting actors and tradesmen from darkening their gilded doorstep. But Lillie and Bertie, who encouraged his circle to receive her despite the stigma attached to theatricals, remained friends. When she performed in London, he never missed an opening night, frequently arriving with Princess Alexandra, and enjoying the after-theatre supper parties that Lillie hosted.

She became an American citizen, and bought property in California, thereby establishing residency. In a California court she divorced Ned Langtry. Langtry remained so obsessed with her fame and beauty that he would ask rail porters to describe her appearance to him in detail. He received a quarterly allowance from Lillie until he died, a dazed and confused alcoholic, in a lunatic asylum. Lillie did not attend the funeral, but sent a wreath. The card read simply "In Remembrance—Lillie Langtry."

In 1899, the forty-six-year-old actress married Lord Hugo de Bathe, a twenty-nine-year-old playboy who spent Lillie's money as fast as she could earn it. Lillie and her daughter remained estranged, a rift that widened when in 1902 one of Jeanne-Marie's wedding guests told the bride that her father was really Prince Louis of Battenberg. By the way, this makes Jeanne-Marie the great-aunt of Prince Charles.

On the death of his mother in 1901, Bertie became King Edward VII. During his decade-long reign he continued to enjoy extramarital affairs with impunity. At his coronation, three of his former official mistresses, including Lillie and Sarah Bernhardt, were seated in a special area, referred to by wags as "the King's Loose Box." And on May 20, 1910, Lillie was present at his funeral, at which Edward's beloved wirehaired fox terrier trotted alongside the cortege, bearing a golden collar inscribed "My name is Caesar; I belong to the King." In accordance with her late husband's wishes, Alexandra gave the dog to Lillie.

Lillie died at her home in Monaco in 1929, after a brief illness. She was seventy-five years old.

👑

EDWARD VII

and Frances Evelyn "Daisy" Greville, Countess of Warwick 1861–1938

Blond, blue-eyed, slim Daisy Greville was one of the "modern women" who were the rage of the age in the last quarter of the nineteenth century. Both her father, Colonel Charles Maynard, and his father, the 3rd Viscount Maynard, died in 1865, so at the tender age of four, Daisy inherited their enormous wealth and property. Her position in society placed her on Queen Victoria's short list for a royal bride for her youngest son, but it wasn't Prince Leopold's bed she wound up in. Daisy eventually ended up with Victoria's eldest son.

But first, she married—and for love. At the age of twenty, Daisy wed twenty-eight-year-old Lord Brooke, heir to the Earl of Warwick and Leopold's aide-de-camp, at Westminster Abbey. Her future royal lover, the Prince of Wales, and his wife were honored guests at the lavish ceremony.

"Brookie" adored her, but after Daisy did her duty by giving birth to a son and heir in 1882, she plunged headfirst into the whirlwind social life of the well heeled and well bred. She was a pleasure-loving thrill seeker, who once drove her motorcar three hundred miles nonstop from Easton Lodge to Land's End just to admire the view from the craggy seacoast. She loved hunting and wild house parties, and drove a four-in-hand with masterful skill. In her form-fitting riding habit, her fashionably fringed hair peeking out from her stylish bowler, she was often seen cantering along Rotten Row in Hyde Park. And she raised her skirts and spread her legs to climb atop that newfangled contraption called the bicycle, inspiring the rollicking music hall song "Daisy, Daisy."

"Brookie" was usually complaisant when his sexually insatiable wife strayed from their bed. But in 1889, her three-year love affair with a dashing naval commander, Lord Charles Beresford, became a public scandal.

Casting herself as "Beauty in Distress," the distraught Daisy poured out her troubles to the graying, portly prince, twenty years her senior. "He was charmingly courteous to me and at length he told me that he hoped his friendship would make up in part, at least, for my sailor-lover's loss. He was more than kind." And then, as Daisy glanced up from her tear-stained lashes, "I saw him looking at me in a way all women understand."

Ultimately, Daisy emerged from the Beresford contretemps relatively unscathed, mostly because she had acquired a new trophy from the emotional debris: Prince Albert Edward. "He was a very perfect, gentle lover," Daisy recalled. "He had manners and was very considerate, and from a woman's point of view, that's a great deal. Then he was remarkably constant and adored me exceedingly. I grew to like him very much. I think anybody would have been won by him."

Daisy was twenty-nine years old, extremely beautiful, and blazingly intelligent when she ensnared the heart of the Prince of Wales. Bertie fell head over heels in love with her. Her aristocratic background enabled her to fit in perfectly with his vibrant social circle, known as the Marlborough set. And yet, she could not seem to steer clear of scandal.

In 1890, Daisy got the prince in hot water after leaking

the details of an illegal baccarat game during a house party at which Bertie was present when Sir William Gordon-Cummings was caught cheating. After Bertie confided in Daisy, she blabbed about the whole affair to everyone she knew, earning her the nickname "the Babbling Brooke." In what became one of the most celebrated trials of the late nineteenth century, Gordon-Cummings filed a libel suit against those who had accused him, one of whom was the Prince of Wales. England could talk of nothing else for weeks, focusing on Bertie's pleasure-loving lifestyle and his unsuitability to become king.

In 1891, the Lord Charles Beresford affair got a second wind after Lady Charles's sister published a semifictional account of it, merely changing the name of Brooke to Rivers. Daisy's reputation suffered tremendously, and Brookie briefly contemplated divorcing her, but the prince stood by his lover. The royal affair *and* the marriage weathered the storm.

At Daisy's estate, Easton Lodge, where Bertie was by now a regular visitor, the lovers would tryst in the pretty little summer house tucked away on the grounds. Daisy had a rail station built closer to her house so that the prince could more easily reach her on his private train. They cooed lovingly to each other in German and exchanged rings. Bertie, who had been married for twenty-eight years, referred to his new love as "my own adored Daisy wife," closing his letters with "For ever yours, Your only love."

"He wrote me a letter twice or three times a week, telling me everything that had happened to him. He expected me to write frequently, and if I didn't he used to say I had hurt him," Daisy admitted. And he never forgot special occasions, such as Christmas, birthdays, and anniversaries, always sending cards and charming presents. One wonders what Queen Victoria might have thought when Bertie gave his mistress a ring that had been inscribed "To Bertie from his affectionate parents A. and V.R., July 9, 1860."

The affair was more than slightly lopsided. Daisy "like[d] Bertie very much" but had never loved him the way he adored her. After all, he was fiftyish, balding and portly, and reeked of cigars. She indiscreetly confided to a friend that the prince was rather "boresome as he sat on a sofa holding my hand and goggling at me." What she loved was the élan her royal affair afforded her, the cachet of being *maîtresse en titre*.

In 1893, Daisy became Countess of Warwick on the death of her father-in-law, inheriting Warwick Castle and an enormous fortune. Now, she entertained on an even grander scale; her house parties were renowned for the variety of pleasures on offer to her guests, both indoors and out. Her opulent wardrobe was the stuff of society columns.

As time passed, Bertie grew less cautious about appearing with Daisy in public, squiring her to the finest restaurants, and even to church. Alix, who'd taken her husband's affair with Lillie in stride, did not care at all for his new inamorata. Where Lillie had been so happy, even awed, to be included amid the upper crust at Marlborough House and Sandringham, and was always gracious and genuinely deferential to her hostess, Daisy was *from* that crowd and behaved with all the heedless entitlement of the aristocracy. And when Daisy became Bertie's acknowledged *maîtresse en titre*, Alix refused to entertain her at either of their official residences. The Princess of Wales was hurt by her husband's lack of discretion with Daisy, openly humiliated by Bertie's insensitivity and by his mistress's boldness. Lillie had behaved like a good friend in the royal presence, but Daisy—vain, outspoken, and eighteen years younger than Alix—left no one to wonder about the nature of her relationship with the prince.

Even as Daisy's lifestyle typified the excesses of the age, in 1892 she fell under the influence of the bushy-bearded Socialist W. T. Stead, a fiery-gazed newspaper editor. Embracing Stead's ideals with the same fervor she employed in planning dinner parties, Daisy promised to lecture the prince on his moral responsibilities to his subjects. Bertie listened good-naturedly for a time, but Daisy ultimately recognized that "there was a perpetual struggle between his sense of duty and a desire to conceal from himself that all was not well with the best of all possible worlds. . . . Those who revealed unpleasant things were not liked the better for it."

In January 1898, pregnant with her second legitimate son, Daisy finally ended her nine-year royal affair, writing two letters: one to Bertie and the other to Alix. According to Bertie's reply (Alix didn't write back), his wife was genuinely moved by both the gesture and the sentiment behind it. "Certainly the Princess has been an angel of goodness throughout all this, but then she is a Lady and never could do anything mean or small." He closed his letter to Daisy by writing, "Though our interests, as you have often said, lie apart, still we have that sentimental feeling of affinity which cannot be eradicated by time . . ."

In truth, Alix was far less forgiving of the affair than her husband had led Daisy to believe. Her younger son, Prince George, wrote to his wife, Princess May of Teck, "In case you should hear from Lady Warwick asking you to become a President of a Charity of hers, refuse it. Motherdear has done so and wishes you to do the same."

After Bertie became king in 1901, Lord Esher was dispatched by the palace to tactfully give Daisy a warning (in her words) "that he thought it would be well for all concerned if my close association with great affairs were to cease, as it was giving rise to hostile comment, which distressed Queen Alexandra." Shortly before Esher's visit, the queen had written Daisy a rather cordial note, to the same effect.

By 1907, at the age of forty-five, Daisy was going broke. She was offered a substantial sum to pen her memoirs, but refused. If she told all, she'd be ostracized by the very people she needed, and if she remained "tame," no publisher would front the extravagant advance she required to remain afloat.

However, as her debts mounted, she tried a slightly different tack. After Edward VII's death in 1910, between her high living and her Socialist causes, Daisy ran up debts of £100,000—over $14 million in today's economy. In 1914, with the aid of Frank Harris, a notoriously sleazy journalist, she let it be known that she was about to publish her amorous correspondence with the late king. Her real intention was to "ransom" the letters, figuring that Buckingham Palace would buy her off. Instead, Edward's successor, his son George V, immediately took Daisy to court, claiming the palace owned the copyright to the love letters. The matter was hushed up for the next fifty years and finally came to light in 1960 amid a discovery of the papers belonging to a man named Arthur du Cros, who had acted as a go-between for Daisy and the palace.

Daisy devoted the rest of her life to Socialist causes and stood for Parliament in 1923, coming in third. By the 1930s, her fortune was entirely gone, as were her looks. She was too fat to get out of a chair without assistance, but she remained flamboyant to the last. At Easton Lodge, where she maintained a vast menagerie, she was often seen toddling about at feeding time, a feather boa trailing in her substantial wake. She hoped that upon her death her home would be used as a wildlife preserve. "I am a very happy woman," Daisy said at the time. And she meant it.

Daisy died on July 26, 1938, at Easton and was buried in the family crypt at Warwick.

♔

EDWARD VII
and Alice Keppel 1868–1947

Ring out the old; ring in the new was the watchword as the infant year of 1898 breached its way through the New Year's celebrations. The "Babbling Brooke" was swiftly becoming water under the bridge and a new love—Alice Keppel—entered Bertie's life. Alice would remain his *maîtresse en titre* until he literally drew his last breath.

She famously told an interviewer that her "job" was "to curtsy first and then hop into bed."

The daughter of a Scottish baronet, Admiral Sir William Edmonstone, Alice possessed "superabundant vitality." She was twenty-nine years old when she met the fifty-six-year-old Bertie early in 1898. "An understanding arose almost overnight," according to a royal biographer. Glowing with good health, witty, vivacious, and fashionable, the petite yet voluptuous brunette was married to George Keppel, a very tall (six feet four), mustachioed army officer. Alice had already made her mark among the smart set as a bright and delightful conversationalist who, supposedly, never had an unkind word for anyone. Honest, energetic, and practical, her character was absent all malice or prejudice. Consequently, she was tremendously popular. Her elder daughter, Violet, said "she resembled a Christmas tree, laden with presents for everyone." And a contemporary of Alice's maintained that "she not only had a gift of happiness, but she excelled in making others happy."

And yet, the woman knew how to work it. Sir Osbert Sitwell described how the soignée Alice "would remove from her mouth for a moment the cigarette which she would be smoking through a long holder and turn upon the person to whom she was speaking her large, humorous, kindly, and peculiarly discerning eyes." And she had a way of seductively lifting the veil of her hat so slowly that every male waited with bated breath to catch a single tantalizing glimpse from her blue-green eyes.

Certainly, the initial spark between Alice and her prince was based on sexual attraction—at least from Bertie's point of view. But he soon discovered that underneath Alice's masses of raven hair, beyond the curves, was a woman who was as kind as she was compassionate, as amusing as she was discreet, in short, the perfect "royal friend." Even Alix had to begrudgingly appreciate the way Alice kept Bertie's hairtrigger temper in check. Alice truly loved him, and was the ideal mistress for an aging royal: undemanding and uncritical, a skilled lover who was just as accomplished a bridge player and raconteur.

Many people spoke of her *discretion*—the anti-Daisy in that regard. But there were witnesses who remember her horning into every photograph of Bertie taken during country house parties. Her presence, while delightful to just about everyone but Alix, was most certainly a visible one. Mrs. Keppel milked her royal affair shamelessly, but it wasn't entirely her "fault." Her unique position, so to speak, made her the most sought-after woman in diplomatic, social, and political circles, consulted by men and women at all levels who wished to gain the ear of the man who would be king.

As soon as it was apparent to high society that Alice had superseded Daisy as Bertie's *maîtresse en titre*, they fell over themselves to extend invitations. A few upper-crust snobs snubbed her, to be sure, and from time to time Bertie would grow mischievous, such as at the dinner party where he seated his mistress next to the Archbishop of Canterbury. But Alice was so good at comporting herself prudently in public that His Grace was certain that her relationship with the king could not possibly be anything but platonic. One wonders what the Archbishop might have thought of the "hanging harness complete with footholds" that Bertie had constructed in his private chamber, which enabled the 224-pound prince to—*ahem*—get it up.

However, Alice's constant presence—for the last twelve years of Bertie's life—was one of the factors that caused Alix to retreat into the private world inside her head and to devote herself even more assiduously to her children and their pets. Hostesses tied themselves in knots wondering how to handle the protocol of inviting both princess and mistress—or having to choose between the two women. Bertie hated to appear where his mistress was unwanted, and when he did, he was guaranteed to be grumpy about it. On the other hand, he endeavored to be sensitive to Alix, much as he often ended up humiliating her. Yet Alix and Alice were both so impeccably well mannered that no one would have thought there was the slightest hint of animosity between them.

After Bertie became king in 1901, Alice Keppel's much-vaunted discretion made her an ideal conduit between the monarch and his ministers. Unlike Daisy Warwick, Alice never used her position to influence him politically, nor had she any interest in doing so. But she had a way of presenting a topic to him so that he was willing to listen and give it credence, even if his personal opinion differed. The Viceroy of India remarked that "there were one or two occasions when the King was in disagreement with the Foreign Office, and I was able, through her, to advise the King with a view to the foreign policy of the government being accepted."

The chic and articulate Mrs. Keppel, dubbed "La Favorita," was at the center of it all, a highly visible—and equally respected—member of his court. As all good mistresses do, she made it her business to learn which subjects interested her lover and to become well informed about them. According to the Duchess of Marlborough, Alice "invariably knew the choicest scandals, the price of stocks, the latest political move; no one could better amuse [the king] during the tedium of the long dinners etiquette decreed."

Gone were the days of wide-open privy purses. Instead, Bertie gave Alice a number of shares in a rubber company, which in time earned her £50,000 (almost $7.5 million today), and he also engaged his own bankers and financial advisers to handle her investments.

Keeping up appearances as a *maîtresse en titre* was difficult and very expensive. Although the king subsidized her wardrobe, she always had to be dressed in the latest fashions—and Edwardian ladies changed clothes four times a day. Hosting king-sized parties also took a tremendous toll on a courtier's—or courtesan's—purse.

And Alice was evidently an exceptional entertainer. According to Sir Harold Acton—a writer, aesthete, and bon vivant of the next generation, who was a child during the Edwardian era—"None could compete with her glamour as a hostess. She could have impersonated *Britannia* in a *tableau vivant* and done that lady credit." One wonders if he realized that he was alluding to another royal inamorata, Charles II's love Frances Teresa Stuart, the model for Britannia.

Life for a royal mistress, even one such as Alice Keppel, was precarious. As much as Bertie adored and valued Alice, he was not faithful to her. The official mistress, like the wife, learned to tolerate his infidelities, smilingly making the most of his presence when he deigned to bestow it. Although he was involved with several married ladies, he was never separated from Alice for very long. They weekended together, and Bertie's green brougham (his least flashy carriage) was a frequent fixture in front of the Keppels' Portman Square town house.

This fastidiously dressed royal fashion plate must have been very much in love with Alice to have cheerfully indulged her two young daughters, Violet and Sonia, in a betting game the girls invented to see whose slice of buttered toast would be the first to make it from "Kingy's" knee to the floor as it slid down the stripes of his perfectly creased trousers. Alice's daughters recalled Bertie's good nature in letting them use his pants as a ski slope for their breakfast, and the impression he left with the children lingered in the air. "He had a rich German accent and smelled deliciously of cigars and *eau de Portugal*," the girls recalled.

Alice and Bertie spent every Easter together in Biarritz,

where they shopped, strolled, dined, gambled, and played cards. Although she was an accomplished bridge player, Bertie once chided Alice for making a foolish call. Without missing a beat, the witty mistress apologized to her royal lover, quipping that she could never "tell a king from a knave."

For propriety's sake, Alice was always a guest at the villa rented by the financier Sir Ernest Cassel. However, neither spouse accompanied Alice and Bertie on these annual trips, which would extend from early March to early April. In Biarritz, Alice Keppel reigned supreme. In fact, Alix would use "Biarritz" as a byword to mean "Alice," as in "that horrid Biarritz."

As time passed, George Keppel, the ultimate *mari complaisant*, developed a genuine affection for "Kingy." A ladies' man himself, the dashing officer truly considered it his patriotic duty to sacrifice his wife to the greater good of the monarch(y). When their finances dwindled drastically from trying to afford the extravagant lifestyle expected of a royal mistress, the gentlemanly Keppel gamely accepted a Buyers Association position with one of Bertie's yachting companions, the tea magnate Sir Thomas Lipton. Their friends were shocked; it was embarrassing enough that he was a public cuckold—but to be forced to go into *trade* to support his wife's position was about as vulgar and low as things could possibly get. Conveniently, George's territory included North America. And George himself never uttered a single word of complaint or reproach. He once said of Alice, "I do not mind what she does as long as she comes back to me in the end."

It makes a nice little historical link to mention that George Keppel was a descendant of Arnold Joost van Keppel, 1st Earl of Albemarle, the foppish former pageboy who had been King William III's favorite in his waning years. Regardless of the actual nature of William's fascination with his Keppel, the Edwardians were fairly certain they knew what it was all about. When George Keppel noticed a friend reading a book by Oscar Wilde, he professed his abhorrence of the author because of Wilde's notorious homosexual predilections. "A frightful bounder," Keppel said. "It makes one puke just to look at him." To this, the friend's son, Harold Acton, wondered aloud, "Did Alice Keppel ever remind him that he was descended from William III's minion, who was created Earl of Albemarle for his *beaux yeux*?"

Whenever possible, Alix tried to see the humor in her husband's relationship with Mrs. Keppel. Alice lost her figure over the years, and it was a matter of some pride (and glee) to Alix that she had managed to remain as svelte as she was on her wedding day. One afternoon, Alix happened to be glancing out of a window and saw Bertie and his aging mistress riding together in an open carriage that was just pulling into the drive. The sight of the two very plump figures bouncing off each other was so amusing that Alix summoned one of her ladies-in-waiting to come and look, so they could enjoy the laugh together.

Yet there were most certainly times when the queen's patience with her wayward husband and his too-obvious friendship with Mrs. Keppel almost entirely frayed. In 1910, Alix quarreled about it with Bertie before his annual pilgrimage to Biarritz. He had been ailing since February—couldn't he forgo the trip this year? And when Bertie caught another chill there, Her Majesty was quick to blame the mistress for the king's illness. If he had not been at "that horrid Biarritz. . . ."

On May 6, 1910, when Alice Keppel heard that Bertie was dying, she located among her papers a letter he had written to her several years earlier, in which he declared that, if he were ever ill again, Alice should be admitted to his bedside. The note had been written after Alix had debarred the royal mistress from her husband's sickroom. But now, Alix could not countermand the king's written order. As Alice sat beside her dying lover, stroking his hand, the queen turned her back, discreetly pretending to ignore them.

Bertie hoarsely whispered to his wife, "You must kiss her. You must kiss Alice."

Swallowing her pride, Alix stiffly complied. The two courtiers in the room at the time, Lord Esher and Sir Francis Laking, recalled Alix shaking the mistress's hand and coolly saying something to her along the lines of "I'm sure you always had a good influence over him," before turning her back on Alice and walking over to the window.

When the king lapsed into a coma, Alix muttered to Laking to "get that woman away." But Alice refused to budge and became hysterical. As she was bodily dragged from the room, she sobbed, "I never did any harm. There was nothing wrong between us. What is to become of me?" She was taken into another room, where she remained for some hours, until she was composed enough to leave the palace.

Esher—never very fond of Mrs. Keppel—wrote in his diary that day, "Altogether, it was a painful and rather theatrical exhibition and ought never to have happened."

After the royal mistress departed, the queen finally poured out her heart to Laking. Years of pent-up humiliation and frustration bubbled out uncontrollably. "I would not have kissed her, if he had not bade me," Alix wept. "But I would have done anything he asked of me. Twelve years ago, when I was so angry about Lady Warwick, and the King expostulated with me and said that I should get him into the divorce court, I told him once for all that he might have all the women he wished, and I would not say a word; and I have done everything since that he desired me to do about them. He was the whole of my life and now he is dead, nothing matters."

Lord Esher couldn't figure out why the queen was smiling at her husband's corpse until he guessed that for the first time in forty-seven years of marriage, Alix had Edward all to herself.

As she gazed at Bertie's lifeless form she murmured to Esher, "After all, he loved me best."

Alice was shocked to find herself prevented from signing the official condolence book at Marlborough House. In accordance with Alix's wishes, the new monarch, George V, and his consort, Queen Mary, had given orders to forbid the late king's mistress from insinuating herself in any way.

They had to reach a compromise, however, when Bertie's corpse lay in state at Westminster Hall. The courtiers feared that if Alice were prohibited from a final farewell, there might be another scene even more hysterical—and certainly more public—than the one at Buckingham Palace. So on the night of May 17, 1910, after the doors of Westminster Hall were closed to the public at ten p.m., Mrs. Keppel was escorted to the purple-draped catafalque containing her former lover's coffin. Alice had her final moment to say good-bye, and after one last curtsy, was escorted outside and helped into her closed carriage.

After Edward's death, the Keppel household was plunged into deep mourning. Little Sonia Keppel asked her father, "Why does it matter so much Kingy dying?" Through genuine tears, the cuckolded husband replied, "Because Kingy was a very, very wonderful person."

Slipping through a side door of the chapel, Alice wore full mourning to her lover's funeral, swathed in floor-length black veils, with ebony-colored ostrich plumes adorning her hat, a carbon copy of the grieving queen. But after the official mourning period, the Keppels fled the glare of the publicity spotlight, embarking on a two-year tour of Asia.

On their return to England in 1912, George and Alice resumed their opulent lifestyle, entertaining lavishly, as warmly devoted to each other as ever. They also purchased l'Ombrellino, a villa in Tuscany, where they would visit for several months during the year, becoming part of the Anglo-Italian expat culture. It was in Italy that they both died, within two months of each other, in 1947. Alice was seventy-eight years old and George was eighty-one.

But during the 1930s and into World War II, the Keppels had remained in London, residing at the Ritz on Piccadilly. Alice was in the hotel dining room on December 11, 1936, when King Edward VIII announced his abdication in order to marry his twice-divorced American sweetheart, Wallis Warfield Simpson.

Everyone in the room heard Alice's reaction. In her famously thrilling, husky voice, the former royal mistress very audibly sniffed, "Things were done much better in *my* day."

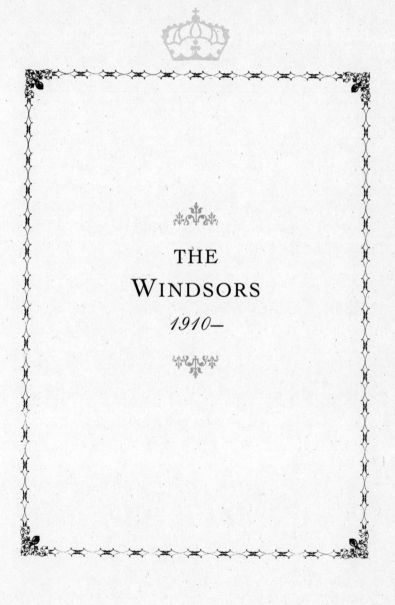

THE
WINDSORS
1910–

EDWARD VIII

❧❧❧

1894–1972
RULED JANUARY 20 TO DECEMBER 11, 1936
(ABDICATED)

*K*NOWN AS THE KING WHO ABDICATED FOR LOVE, Edward VIII was the grandson of the larger-than-life Bertie, Edward VII. The younger Edward, whom the family called "David" (the last in a string of his seven first names), was the eldest son of the bearded and brusque former Royal Navy officer King George V. His mother was the quiet and remote English-born Princess May of Teck, who had inherited her German father's courtesy title and was known as Queen Mary. Edward ascended the throne on January 20, 1936, on the death of his father.

As Prince of Wales, Edward and his brothers were raised in a far more middlebrow environment than some of their predecessors. Perhaps this egalitarian atmosphere instilled in them more of a connection with their subjects once they became kings. Edward attended Oxford, but he left the university in 1914 at the start of World War I. Although his role was a noncombative one, his life was often in danger during his service, and former soldiers would always regard him as one of their own.

As a child the handsome, blond Edward was somewhat fragile, bullied by both his overbearing nanny and his gruff father, whose legendary temper was often unleashed on his oldest son. He grew up to be a dapper, charming, somewhat fey-looking bon vivant, a man who came of age during difficult times for England. After the war years, he spent a lifetime working hard to convince people that there was more to him than the merry playboy whose day consisted of golf, naps, and cocktails, followed by long evenings cavorting at nightclubs with the "bright young things" of café society. Not raised to appreciate culture, including his own country's contributions to it, he was an anti-intellectual who, while the rest of the world was suffering the effects of the Great Depression, decided it was a good idea to charter a friend's yacht, remove the library to make room for more alcohol, and host a floating house party headed for Fascist Italy—until someone talked him out of the destination.

Yet for all the frivolity, as king he displayed the common touch that John Bull had missed for decades. Edward VIII was the hero of the middle and working classes, of former servicemen, and of the impoverished miners from the South Wales Black Area. Visiting the economically devastated region early in his reign, a shocked and appalled Edward famously remarked, *"Something must be done."* That sentence became a catchphrase for the politicians who wanted him out of the way once he announced his intention to marry Mrs. Wallis Simpson, a twice-divorced American.

Edward's parents, unlike previous sovereigns, had hoped that their children would marry for love, and therefore didn't rush them into passionless dynastic arrangements. Little did they suspect that, where Edward was concerned, what seemed on the surface to be a blessing was, for the British Establishment, far more of a curse.

Practically tricked into abdicating by a prime minister who withheld crucial information from the king regarding the extent of his popularity, on December 11, 1936, after reigning for less than a year, Edward VIII gave up his crown. Because Edward had no children, his shy younger brother acceded to the throne in his place, ruling as George VI. Edward would henceforth be known as His Royal Highness The Duke of Windsor. He spent the rest of his life with his beloved Wallis, the mid-twentieth-century equivalents of jet-setters, discreetly exiled from England for their pro-Nazi sympathies at a time when Hitler's rise to power was becoming more ominous by the day and an increasing threat to Britain.

The brief reign of Edward VIII is so entirely tied to his relationship with the woman for whom he gave up his throne that to separate it from their love story does both a disservice. And it truly *was* a love story. Edward VIII had insisted on marrying only the woman he adored, was willing to sacrifice everything to do so, and made good on his promise. For all his unpalatable political sensibilities, he was a true romantic.

Edward, Duke of Windsor, died on May 28, 1972. His brother, George VI, continued to rule England until his death in 1952 at the age of fifty-six, when the crown passed to the current queen, his oldest daughter, who acceded to the throne as Elizabeth II.

Edward VIII
and Wallis Warfield Simpson 1895 or '96–1986

Bessie Wallis Warfield came from modest Baltimore beginnings. At one point her mother ran a boardinghouse to make ends meet. But even as a child, the future Duchess of Windsor possessed an overdeveloped sense of entitlement, and somehow managed to receive just about everything she demanded. "So many cows are called Bessie," she declared as a girl, ditching her detested first name in favor of her middle one. Though it wasn't exactly Wallis's fault that she arrived only seven months after her parents' marriage, she entered the world something of a scandal, and her behavior would continue to shock the Western world for the next eight decades.

Wallis was no real-life Daisy Buchanan, though. For one thing, her looks were anything but conventionally attractive. Her nose was lumpy, with a bulbous tip; her jaw resembled carved granite; there was a large mole on her chin below her lower lip; her hands, which an English aristocrat once referred to as "peasant paws," were large and ugly, with stubby fingernails.

Meeting her in London in the 1930s, Cecil Beaton, a distant relative by marriage of Wallis's second husband, Ernest Simpson, took the measure of her immediately. Beaton is probably best known to Americans as the designer of the fabulous black-and-white costumes for the Ascot scene in *My Fair Lady*. His impression of Wallis sounds like the low-class flower girl Henry Higgins bets he can pass off as a duchess. "She looked coarse. Her back was coarse and her arms were heavy. Her voice had a high nasal twang. She was loud and brash, terribly so—and rowdy and raucous. Her squawks of laughter were like a parrot's." Of course, when Wallis *did* become a duchess, Beaton revised his opinion and found many charming things to say about her features.

Wallis walked out on her first husband, the bisexual navy pilot Earl Winfield "Win" Spencer, when he proved to be a depressive and moody alcoholic and a sexual sadist who would tie her to the bedposts and beat her.

Yet Wallis was still married to Spencer when she commenced a passionate affair with the man who would become her second husband, the gentle, understanding, and very patient

Anglo-American businessman Ernest Aldrich Simpson. After she divorced Win, she wed Simpson in 1928, and it was he who provided her entrée into the royal enclave.

Wallis Simpson met Edward, the Prince of Wales, then England's—if not the world's—most eligible bachelor at a house party in Leicestershire given on January 10, 1931, by the prince's then mistress, Lady Thelma Furness. It wasn't long before she would leave her indelible stamp on the British high society of the 1930s, introducing them to hot hors d'oeuvres, and giving the world the credo "You can never be too rich or too thin."

The ambitious Wallis—who was very much like the prince in every way—saw in him what she wanted to see. The homely girl from Baltimore was bowled over by the power he wielded. "His slightest wish seemed always to be translated into the most impressive kind of reality. Trains were held; yachts materialized; the best suites in the finest hotels were flung open; airplanes stood waiting." What woman's head wouldn't be turned?

Soon Edward was a regular visitor to the Simpsons' home. The thirty-five-year-old Mrs. Simpson, rail-slim and seductive, set her cap for the heir to the throne, taking advantage of Lady Furness's holiday in New York to make her move. Juggling her husband and her new paramour was not always easy, yet Wallis was confident of her own abilities, boldly telling her aunt Bessie, "It requires great tact to manage both men. I shall try to keep them both."

To Wallis, Edward was the ultimate fairy-tale prince. But people wondered what *he* saw in *her*. One answer is that Wallis—who by now had perfected the "metallic elegance" for which she would become famous—never fawned on him, and he was a man who was used to women doing just that.

The Prince of Wales fell in love with Wallis in 1934, later writing in his memoirs that one day she "began to mean more to me in a way that she did not perhaps comprehend.

My impression is that for a long time she remained unaffected by my interest."

In Edward's own words, "I admired her forthrightness. If she disagreed with some point under discussion, she never failed to advance her own views with vigor and spirit. That side of her enchanted me . . . From the first, I looked upon her as the most independent woman I had ever met."

Eventually, their passion became mutual. Wallis fell in love with the prince during a Mediterranean cruise aboard Lord Moyne's yacht, the *Rosaura*. She, too, experienced the sudden realization that something had shifted in their relationship, that her emotions were now engaged, passing "the undefinable boundary between friendship and love." The prince gave her a diamond and emerald charm, which she didn't disclose to Ernest, who was conveniently in America on business. Soon the lovers developed a private language, referring to themselves as WE (for Wallis and Edward) in their love notes.

Edward's good friend Walter Monckton, who had known him since they were at Oxford together, observed: It was "a great mistake to assume that he was merely in love with her in the ordinary physical sense of the term. There was an intellectual companionship and there is no doubt that his lonely nature found in her a spiritual comradeship. . . . No one will ever really understand the story of the King's life, who does not appreciate . . . the intensity and depth of his devotion to Mrs. Simpson."

Wallis was presented to Edward's parents only once and the reception was distinctly chilly. In the autumn of 1934, she attended a lavish Buckingham Palace ball. Wallis mingled among the glittering and distinguished guests, at one point lingering by a window overlooking Queen Mary's famous flower beds, the pride of the nation. A palace servant overheard Wallis remarking, "Of course, when I live here, this will all be tennis courts." Her comment spread like wildfire from the royal back stairs to every London pub. Wallis had made her first set of enemies in the servants at Buckingham Palace.

Edward and Wallis soon became nearly inseparable, while Ernest disappeared on business trips to New York. But unlike George Keppel, another husband whose wife had become the official royal mistress, Mr. Simpson wasn't willing to swallow his humiliation and discreetly keep up appearances. Understandably, their marriage disintegrated.

To chivalrously spare Wallis's reputation, they set up a classic scenario that would automatically lead to a charge of adultery. A woman was hired to share a hotel room with Ernest, and—Shock! Horror!—the two were discovered in flagrante. In order to keep the news out of the papers, Wallis subsequently sued Ernest for divorce in the quiet town of Ipswich. However, there was much speculation at the time that Wallis was in fact divorcing Ernest in order to marry Edward—which would have put the king in collusion—a situation that was unethical, if not strictly illegal. Wallis was eventually granted a divorce on October 27, 1936, although her decree would not become absolute until the following spring.

So, she was still married to Ernest Simpson when Edward's father, King George V, died on January 10, 1936. Yet, Edward, now king, refused to keep their affair under wraps, breaking royal protocol by watching the proclamation of his accession from St. James's Palace with his mistress at his side.

Edward VIII then found himself faced with a constitutional crisis—the possibility of a rift with his own government over the choices he wished to make in his personal life. Prime Minister Stanley Baldwin stated that if Edward insisted on wedding Wallis anyway, Baldwin would have no alternative but to resign, leading to a mass mutiny of cabinet ministers and the collapse of the government. If Edward were compelled to re-form the government he would be hard-pressed to find support—or so he was told.

Though the royals were popular with the people, it would be disastrous to the health of the realm to have a serious division between the sovereign and his government. In the twentieth century, although the British monarchy still played a vital role, its duties had become more ceremonial than political. Parliament and the government ministers really ran the country. Nevertheless, the monarch had a very public duty, and was fully expected to perform it faithfully, upholding centuries of tradition.

There were no laws forbidding an English monarch from marrying a commoner, *or* a divorcée, *or* a foreigner. After all, nearly every queen of England was born in a country on the Continent. What made Wallis Simpson off-limits as queen consort material was that her two ex-husbands were still thrashing about. Dead ex-husbands might have been all right, but living ones presented a thorny legal issue for a Church that didn't condone divorce. Therefore, Wallis could never be married in the Church of England—and the King of England was also the Supreme Governor of the Church.

And if Edward insisted on marrying a woman whose two former spouses were alive and well, he would not only incite a mass exodus among his cabinet, but he could not expect to uphold his title of Defender of the Faith while remaining King of England. Edward had two choices: ditch Wallis or abdicate the throne. No one, not even Wallis, expected him to do the latter.

However, Edward's subjects were unaware of the official minutiae that would prevent him from marrying his girlfriend while remaining king. A large number of Britons just wanted him to be happy, delighted that he had found True Love, no matter who his lady was or what her background had been.

Boxes of supportive letters and telegrams marked "top secret" were locked away in Windsor Castle until 2003. Many of these were compassionate notes from the working and middle classes, calling Edward "the People's King" and endorsing his relationship to Wallis. It has only been in the past few years that historians have been able to see the side of the story that was suppressed—the massive public opinion in the king's favor. The correspondence firmly supported the "modern" view that Edward could marry whomever he bloody well liked! Some even felt that Wallis was simply the government's excuse to get rid of a king who was determined to behave like an individual.

However, although many of the letters were addressed directly to his attention, the king may never have seen them, or he might not have been so hasty to abdicate. After all, kings didn't open their own mail. And Edward's Private Secretary, Major Alexander Hardinge, was very much aligned with Prime Minister Stanley Baldwin's government.

At the time, Baldwin carefully spun the information to suit his own purpose and that of his government, casting Wallis as the ultimate outsider who was costing the popular Edward his subjects' love and support. He kept the king unaware of the truth—that the people were largely behind him—and instead informed Edward that they would never accept the twice-divorced American (a double stigma) as their queen.

To give Baldwin some credit, this was partly true. There were certainly rumblings to that effect from more distant corners of the empire. Prime ministers of several of the British Dominions, including Canada and Australia, were emphatically against Wallis's having any role or status whatsoever in their empire. But there was also doubt in some of the Dominions that abdication was the right thing to do if the king insisted on marrying Mrs. Simpson.

Eamon de Valera, the prime minister of the Irish Free State, reminded Baldwin that Edward was a very popular king, even in Ireland, and that "every avenue ought to be explored before he was excluded from the throne." He added that "many—especially young people—throughout the Empire would, in these democratic days, be attracted by the idea of a young king ready to give up all for love."

It is doubtful that the Irish PM's concerns were forwarded to the king.

Therefore, operating on the information Baldwin had supplied to him, Edward proposed the idea of a morganatic marriage, where Wallis's status as a commoner would remain unchanged and she would have no title and none of the rights of a queen consort, such as the succession to the throne of any children she might bear Edward. But Baldwin rejected the king's suggested compromise, informing His Majesty of the Dominions' position and citing a lack of parliamentary precedent for the existence of a king's wife who was not the queen, nor had any other official role or title. Regardless of *public opinion*, in order for a morganatic marriage to be viable, new legislation would have to be enacted in England, as well as in each of the Empire's Dominions, requiring constitutional changes in each venue. It would have been a lengthy process, and Parliament was unwilling to undertake it. Therefore, the king's proposal was not a feasible solution.

Yet, abdication *had* to seem like the king's idea. If the people were to get wind of the fact that the government had doctored the information to make it appear that the chips were stacked against the king, public opinion would be extremely divided.

For all his Fascist sympathies, Edward was very concerned with upholding the sanctity of the democracy. Keen to avoid "the scars of civil war," he buckled under the pressure of his government—exactly the opposite of Henry VIII, who steamrolled over his *ministers* when they sought to deprive him of his chosen bride. If Edward had flagrantly disregarded Parliament and made a stand, it would have divided his country.

Wallis and Edward shared a tearful farewell before she departed for the Continent on a well-advised holiday. In the arched doorway of Edward's home, Fort Belvedere, the king told Wallis,

"You must wait for me no matter how long it takes. I shall never give you up."

Wallis had finally achieved what she wanted—or had she?

Back in February 1936, Wallis had written to Edward, "I am sad because I miss you and being near and yet so far seems most unfair . . . Perhaps both of us will cease to want what is the hardest to have and be content with the simple way" (which presumably was for her to remain his mistress, rather than become his wife). And in a document made public in the year 2000 that was signed by Mrs. Simpson shortly before Edward's December 11, 1936, abdication, Wallis had written (partially under duress from the prime minister's office) that she "has abandoned any interest in marrying His Majesty."

Decades later, she insisted, "I told him I didn't want to be queen . . . All that formality and responsibility . . . I told him that if he stayed on as king, it wouldn't be the end of us. I could still come and see him and he could still come and see me. We had terrible arguments about it. But he was a mule. He said he didn't want to be king without me, that if I left him he would follow me wherever I went."

Made nearly four hundred years later, this argument is the very antithesis of Anne Boleyn's insistence to Henry VIII that he must push for their marriage because she refused to be a royal mistress. *Wallis* was *genuinely content* to remain the king's *maîtresse en titre*, if it meant that he would keep his crown—provided he remained a bachelor and wed no one else in a marriage of convenience.

Although journalists in the United States and on the European continent had kept their readers informed of Windsor and "Wally's" affair, the English press did not publish the story of the king's impending abdication until a week before the event. The reason is surprising. It had nothing to do with protecting the privacy of the couple, but was intended to prevent an informed public that might be sympathetic to the Windsors from swaying the powerful Establishment or aristocracy from its plan to replace Edward with his younger brother George, the more pliant Duke of York.

In such an extremely class-oriented society, the conservative Establishment could not yield to the great unwashed masses. By telling Edward that public opinion was heavily against a marriage to Wallis, Baldwin had in fact "fixed up" the situation to yield the desired result before the people of England had in fact heard a word of what was going on.

The formal Instrument of Abdication was executed at ten a.m. on December 10, 1936. And on December 11, 1936, at one fifty-two Greenwich Mean Time, he renounced his throne, the first English monarch to voluntarily relinquish the crown. In a radio broadcast that day, Edward told his former subjects, "I have found it impossible to carry the heavy burden of responsibility, and to discharge my duties as King as I would wish to do, without the help and support of the woman I love." Parts of the speech were ghostwritten by Winston Churchill, who was advising Edward, and who strongly opposed the PM's efforts to force the king's hand. Other lines of Edward's speech bore the distinct imprint of Wallis Simpson, though she would claim that she knew nothing about his abdication until it was practically a fait accompli.

The Church's opinion of Edward's exercising his desire over his duty was crystal clear, when in a 1936 radio broadcast, Archbishop Cosmo Gordon Lang intoned, "From God he had received a high and sacred trust. Yet by his own will he has abdicated—he has surrendered the trust. With characteristic frankness he has told us his motive. It was a craving for private happiness. Strange and sad it must be that for such a motive, however strongly it pressed upon his heart, he should have disappointed hopes so high and abandoned a trust so great."

But, unlike centuries of his predecessors, Edward didn't

want some sleazy hole-in-the-wall intrigue. He wanted a wife. And he wanted that wife to be Wallis.

On December 12, 1936, the day after his abdication, Edward sailed for France. Complying with an alleged "agreement" with the new king—his younger brother George VI—Windsor and Wally would never again permanently reside in England. Edward wrote in his memoirs, "HMS *Fury* slid silently and unescorted out of Portsmouth Harbor. Watching the shore of England recede, I was swept by many emotions. If it had been hard to give up the throne, it had been even harder to give up my country. . . . The drawbridges were going up behind me."

On March 8, 1937, the former King Edward VIII was granted the title Duke of Windsor. It never sat well with the other royals that Wallis would now be a duchess.

Wallis obtained her decree absolute finalizing her divorce on May 3, 1937, and she married Edward on June 3, in a tiny French town at the home of a confirmed Fascist who was developing a workforce production system for Adolf Hitler. The bride wore a suit of blue silk crepe and a wedding ring fashioned of Welsh gold by a loyal former subject. No member of the royal family or the court was present, on instructions of Edward's younger brother, the new king, George VI.

They honeymooned in a private railway car (affixed to regular trains) that had been loaned to them by Benito Mussolini. Among other stops, they visited Munich, where Hitler warmly received them, chatting with the newlyweds for two hours. When Hitler learned of Edward's abdication, he had glumly moaned, "I have lost a friend to my cause!"

The Windsors lived the life of expatriates in France. By all accounts, it was Wallis who supplied the backbone in their relationship. She whipped him every way but literally (one assumes) and he seemed to enjoy it. When she commanded him, in front of a group of their friends, to "take off my dirty shoes and bring me another pair," Edward fell to his knees and removed her footwear, relishing every moment of his humility. No wonder that their social set referred to him as Wallis's "lapdog."

Edward's friend "Fruity" Metcalfe had no problem sharing his opinion of Wallis with their mutual friends. "God, that woman's a bitch! She'll play hell with him before long."

One evening during a dinner party the Duke of Windsor asked the butler to deliver a message to the chauffeur regarding his plans for the following day. Wallis raised her hands and slammed them on the table. You can probably still hear the silver and stemware rattling. "Never—never again will you give orders in my house!" the duchess shouted at her adoring husband. Then in a belated effort to smooth things over, Wallis explained to the mortified guests, "You see, the duke is in charge of everything that happens outside the house, and I on the inside."

Utterly cowed by his wife's outburst, Edward mumbled his apologies—but to the hostess, or to their guests?

"No one will ever know how hard I work to try to make the little man feel busy," Wallis once confided to a friend during their postabdication peregrinations.

To Edward, it had been worth exchanging his kingdom for this former Baltimore colt, despite the oft-repeated joke that the king who had once been Admiral of the Fleet had become "the third mate on an American tramp."

During World War II, the duke was initially assigned to the British Military Mission in France, but he wasn't doing his own country any favors. In fact, there was no doubt as to the specifics of Edward's politics after Rudolph Hess reported to Hitler, "There is no need to lose a single German life in invading Britain. The Duke and his clever wife will deliver the goods." As a thank-you gift, in the event of a German victory over the Allies, the führer intended to restore Edward VIII to the English throne. Wallis, of course, would be his queen consort.

However, as Hitler's agenda became more apparent, the duke and duchess of Windsor were essentially exiled to a place where their pro-Nazi sentiments could do little to harm British policy.

George VI put an ocean between the crown and his older brother, distancing the current monarchy from its former, politically incorrect sovereign by sending Edward to Nassau to be Governor and Commander in Chief of the Bahamas. Bored out of their minds, the Windsors managed to spend as little time there as possible, taking off for shopping sprees in Manhattan or Palm Springs. They were living large while their country endured the dangers and deprivations of wartime. Wallis's annual clothing budget at the time was somewhere in the neighborhood of $25,000—nearly $351,000 today.

She was ever fashion-conscious for her husband as well. Wallis had been telling him for years that white dinner jackets at black-tie parties were passé, but the duke insisted on remaining unfashionable—high treason to his wife. One night, at a Palm Beach soiree, Wallis grabbed a tray of hors d'oeuvres from a passing waiter, shoved it into Edward's hands, and exclaimed, "Here! If you're going to dress like a waiter, you might as well act like one!"

In 1941, the FBI launched an investigation into the Windsors' Nazi connections. It was revealed that during Germany's 1940 invasion of France, Wallis had been passing information to Joachim von Ribbentrop, Hitler's foreign minister. Some sources are certain that they had trysted in 1936 when von Ribbentrop was ambassador to Britain. Allegedly, the ambassador had seventeen carnations delivered to Wallis every day for a while, representing the number of times the pair had slept together. And an American journalist, Helen Worden, wrote that the duchess kept a framed photo of von Ribbentrop in her

Bahamian bedroom, an allegation that the duke vociferously denied.

In all likelihood, Wallis was not entirely faithful to her "lap-dog," though their contemporaries never believed that *sex* was the glue that kept the couple together. Nor did sex appear to be one of the most vital aspects of any of Wallis's relationships. In 1950, thirteen years after Wallis wed Edward, she embarked on an affair of sorts with Jimmy Donohue, a flamboyantly gay American playboy twenty years her junior.

Donohue often traveled with the Windsors as a threesome, and the duke didn't seem to mind when Wallis and Jimmy, their heads conspiratorially inclined toward each other, giggled like a pair of schoolgirls. Edward also didn't object to his wife's traveling alone with Donohue, despite Jimmy's provocative endorsement of Wally's talents. "She's marvelous! She's the best cock sucker I've ever known!"

Their affair lasted into the mid-1950s.

From the time of her husband's abdication until she and Edward grew too frail and infirm to travel, they enjoyed the peripatetic lifestyle of the bon vivant. The duke and duchess of Windsor did little but attend parties and galas, shop, and play golf. They stayed with friends and acquaintances—often for months at a time. When they departed, they left behind reams of unpaid phone bills and legions of untipped servants. Wallis took every opportunity to remind her husband of his fallen state whenever his demands were not met in a timely fashion or in full. "Don't forget, darling, you're not King anymore," she would scold.

After battling several illnesses, including throat cancer, probably caused by a lifetime of cigarette smoking, on May 28, 1972, Edward died, one month shy of his seventy-eighth birthday. He lay in state in Windsor, but not in Westminster Hall, where late British monarchs are traditionally honored before burial. It was at Windsor that Wallis paid her respects to his bier on June 3, their thirty-fifth wedding anniversary. The former Edward VIII was interred in the royal burying ground at Frogmore, where he often played as a boy.

By the time she reached her mid-seventies, Wallis's health was deteriorating as well. In 1973, at the age of seventy-eight, she fell and broke her hip. A few months later, she suffered a number of fractured ribs in a second fall. Doctors had difficulty inserting the anesthesia tube down her throat because it was so tight from her numerous cosmetic surgeries.

The duchess's chief solace during her declining years seemed to be the iced vodkas she would frequently nurse, served to her in silver cups. But the consumption of all those spirits, plus her increasing dementia, did not diminish the lady's much-vaunted rudeness. In 1974, unhappy with either the room service or the menu at New York's Waldorf-Astoria, she phoned down to the chef and screeched, "This is the Duchess of Windsor! Are you the son of a bitch who sent this fucking trout up here?"

Wallis spent the last five years of her life in complete seclusion. She died in Paris at her home in the Bois de Boulogne on April 24, 1986. Several members of the royal family, including her surviving sister-in-law Queen Elizabeth the Queen Mother, and Queen Elizabeth II, attended the funeral service and the burial, as they witnessed Wallis, Duchess of Windsor, interred beside her beloved Edward. Maybe they just wanted to be sure she was really out of their lives.

Charles, Prince
of Wales

༺ ༒ ༻

B. 1948

*T*HE MAN KNOWN AS CHARLES PHILIP ARTHUR GEORGE,
His Royal Highness The Prince of Wales, Earl of Chester,
Duke of Cornwall, Duke of Rothesay, Earl of Carrick, Baron
Renfrew, Lord of the Isles, and Prince and Great Steward of
Scotland, was born on the night of November 14, 1948, to the
Princess Elizabeth, who stood next in line to the English
throne. His father is Elizabeth's fourth cousin, the Greek-born
Prince Philip, Duke of Edinburgh.

When Charles was just three years old, his mother acceded
to the throne on the death of his fifty-six-year-old grandfather,
George VI, in February 1952. This left the new queen, just
twenty-five years old, with little time to devote to her young
family.

His parents raised him at arm's length and he often shivered
from the chill. Prince Philip was a stern figure and rebuked
Charles for what he perceived to be a lack of rigor and robust-
ness. In 1962, he enrolled his thirteen-year-old firstborn in his

own alma mater, Gordonstoun, a rigid academy on Scotland's northeast coast.

Eventually, Charles completed four terms at Trinity College, Cambridge, where he asserted himself by pursuing his own choice of subjects—not his father's—reading anthropology, archaeology, and history.

On July 1, 1969, the twenty-year-old heir was invested as Prince of Wales at the medieval Welsh castle Caernavon. After completing his tour of his new kingdom he returned to Cambridge, and the following year Charles met the woman who would become his great love—Camilla Shand. But Charles was about to embark on five years of military service, so Camilla got on with her life, marrying Andrew Parker Bowles.

In 1976, the twenty-eight-year-old Prince of Wales returned from his tour of duty and began serially, though not particularly seriously, dating. Soon, his family, the country, and the press started pressuring him to do his royal duty by settling down.

In 1980, he began to court Lady Diana Spencer, the youngest of the 8th Earl Spencer's three daughters, and the royal romance sold so many newspapers that half the kingdom might as well have been deforested. But when Charles seemed to dither about proposing, his father put his foot down, advising him to pop the question ASAP, before the popular rumors about lovers' trysts aboard the royal train effectively ruined Diana's reputation—which would also have rendered her a less eligible choice to become Britain's future queen.

So, on February 24, 1981, Buckingham Palace announced the engagement of Prince Charles and Lady Diana Spencer. The royal wedding took place in St. Paul's Cathedral on July 29, amid copious pomp and circumstance. Charles was thirty-two years old, and Diana only nineteen.

On June 21, 1982, the Waleses welcomed their first child, Prince William, into the world. Two years later, in September

1984, Prince Harry, their second son, was born. But there had been trouble in Paradise almost from the moment Charles and Diana had wed. The stresses of Diana's official responsibilities, coupled with her awareness that her husband had never entirely forsaken Camilla, drove the princess to bulimia. Only on occasion would there be glimpses of warmth within the royal marriage, of what might have been able to blossom, had each of them given the other a fighting chance. Instead, Charles and Diana continued to drift apart, the prince rekindling his romance with Camilla while Diana consoled herself in the arms of a number of different men.

The couple formally separated in 1992.

In November 1995, Diana was interviewed by Martin Bashir on a current affairs television program called *Panorama* (taped on the incendiary Guy Fawkes Day and broadcast nine days later on Prince Charles's forty-seventh birthday). On national television, she aired the royal couple's dirty linen and accused the Windsors (and most pointedly Her Majesty) of being out of touch with the times.

The palace had had enough. After consulting the prime minister and the Archbishop of Canterbury regarding its feasibility, with their concurrence the queen decided to order her son and Diana to divorce. Their marriage was dissolved on August 28, 1996. Diana was killed a year later, during a high-speed automobile chase in Paris on August 30, 1997.

Charles discreetly continued his affair with the now-divorced Camilla until public opinion against her had noticeably relaxed. On April 9, 2005, Charles wed Camilla in a civil ceremony at the Guildhall in Windsor. Camilla's title is Her Royal Highness The Duchess of Cornwall. She and Charles reside at Clarence House in London, formerly the home of Charles's grandmother, the late Queen Mother.

As Prince of Wales, Charles has involved himself over the decades with a number of nonprofit charitable trusts, and has spoken extensively on his two passions, architectural preservation and organic farming.

If Elizabeth II is still on the throne at the end of 2008, then Charles (who will celebrate his sixtieth birthday that November 14) will have beaten Edward VII's record for remaining Prince of Wales for the longest amount of time.

DIANA, PRINCESS OF WALES
1961–1997
and James Hewitt b. 1958

Lady Diana Frances Spencer, the third daughter of the 8th Earl Spencer, could trace her aristocratic lineage to the reign of James I, who created the 1st Baron Spencer. The title was upgraded to an earldom by George III in 1765. Diana was all of nineteen years old, rosy-cheeked and packing on a bit of puppy fat, modestly working as a kindergarten teacher and nanny when her destiny changed forever.

As a child Diana, whose step-grandmother was the prolific romance novelist Barbara Cartland, had dreamed of a fairy-tale happily-ever-after. Immersing herself in Cartland's rose-colored canon, Diana longed for a real-life handsome prince who would sweep away the unpleasant memories of a broken home. Her adulterous mother deserted the family for the arms of a wallpaper magnate, and had been regarded as a pariah ever since. Her father was often absent. When he remarried, he conveniently forgot to inform his four children of the fact and presented it to his offspring as a fait accompli.

So, the ruggedly masculine prince whose muscles rippled like Fabio's and whose eyes smoldered like onyx would of course give Diana the perfect life she craved and all the love she believed she'd been denied. In fact, as a sixteen-year-old one of her favorite Cartland novels was titled *Bride to a King*, and from the first moment she met Prince Charles, she romantically decided to save herself for him—despite the fact that he'd barely given the chubby teen a second glance at the time, and even if he wasn't ruggedly handsome and his eyes didn't exactly smolder. Her imagination could fill in that part.

Diana's family home was Park House in Sandringham, the guesthouse right on the grounds of the royal estate there. One day when Diana was a little girl, her father informed his children that they were going to drive over to visit the royal family, who had invited them to a party. Diana, stubborn to a fault, according to those who knew her well, threw a temper tantrum at what other girls might consider a wildly glamorous prospect. After Diana's energetic protests that she hated the "strange atmosphere" there, her humiliated father was faced with ringing the queen to send the Spencer family's regrets.

Yet a dozen years later, Diana was on the verge of becoming one of them, although from the outset she hadn't exactly received the support of the people who should have offered it the most. Her mother, now Frances Shand Kydd, accompanied Diana to her first wedding gown fitting, but then kept her distance as the grand plans for the Big Day unfolded. The bride's maternal grandmother, Lady Fermoy, a lady-in-waiting to the Queen Mother, warned Diana that she would not fit in. "Their sense of humour and lifestyle are very different. I don't think it would suit you," cautioned Diana's wise granny.

Biographers dispute whether Diana was a sacrificial lamb that fateful July 1981 morning in St. Paul's Cathedral, *or* if her wedding day was the delirious culmination of all her Barbara Cartland–fueled romantic fantasies, *or* if Diana was the finest actress in the world at masking her ruthless ambition to become the future Queen of England—knowing all the while by that point that she would share the fate of many a predecessor and never secure her royal husband's love.

The heir had briefly dated Diana's older sister Sarah, so Diana must have known that Charles was, as romantic novels might word it, an indifferent lover—more Prince Chilly than Prince Charming.

But there was an easy explanation for Charles's coolness toward his potential marriage prospects: he'd rather be somewhere else. The love of his life was always in the picture, even if there were times when her image was closer to the frame. Knowing how desperately in love Charles seemed to be with Camilla, even during their awkward courtship, it's doubtful that Diana was so naïve as to think that things would change with matrimony. Did she stubbornly (or optimistically) believe that *her* relationship with him would be utterly different?

Sources interviewed for Tina Brown's recent biography of Diana refer to her extreme youth and inexperience, an unworldliness that left her ill prepared for the monumental responsibilities that she would face as Princess of Wales and future queen. They also point to Diana's prenuptial ecstasy over the fact that, as she put it, "He's the one man on the planet who is not allowed to divorce me." After they became engaged, she seemed to believe that once he was hers, she, younger and far more beautiful than her rival, could persuade him to forget all about Camilla.

Like Charles II's queen, Catherine of Braganza, Diana ended up in the unfortunate position of actually falling intensely in love with her Charles, a man who married out of duty and who never really loved her to begin with.

Consider this awkward little episode: During their February 24, 1981, BBC interview, when the journalist asked the newly engaged couple if they were in love, Diana immediately replied,

"Of course." In contrast, Charles's response could have frozen beer. "Whatever 'in love' means," he answered feebly. According to Tina Brown's biography of Diana, the print media chose to excise the prince's gut-plummeting words from their coverage of the interview.

After they married, Charles's infidelity mortified and humiliated Diana. But she figured out how to play the role of the wronged woman to the hilt, considered by many to be the first Windsor who truly understood the art of public relations, the power of the media, and the influence of the tabloid press— "the most artful practitioner of the media game," according to Tina Brown. As a pre-Charles teen, Diana had avidly devoured the tabloids and was familiar with the names of their staffers and the interests of their readership. Diana *was* their readership.

But Charles's adultery was only a part of Diana's rage for adulation, a craving that manifested itself, according to Ms. Brown, in her need for constant attention, affection, and confirmation that she was worthy and lovable, whether such reassurance came from a journalist or from the many lovers she took in an effort to heal her psychic and romantic wounds. Diana herself admitted, in reference to her relationship with her bodyguard, Barry Mannakee (but the remark could just as easily have pertained to the other men from whom she sought comfort and adulation), "I was . . . desperate for praise, desperate."

Mannakee, though initially starstruck by Diana's beauty and charisma, realized just how needy the princess was when his role shifted from protector to paramour. He found her quite a handful and realized he was in over his head.

Diana made frequent daily calls to some of her paramours, in which she demanded continual affirmation of their adoration, and went into a snit if they dared to admit that they had other obligations as well. "I just don't get him," Diana told a friend, upset that her great heartthrob, the thirty-six-year-old cardiologist Hasnat Khan, spent so much time at the hospital instead of with her. "He's always so busy and his work is so important to him."

Sometimes her behavior bordered on stalking. According to Diana's chauffeur Barry Hodge, when she was involved with the Islamic art dealer Oliver Hoare in 1992, the princess phoned her married lover up to twenty times a day. She left so many hang-ups that Mrs. Hoare feared the family were targets of terrorists and insisted that her (reluctant) husband inform the police. Scotland Yard traced the calls to a number of different phone lines, one of which was Diana's mobile; three were located in Diana's residence, Kensington Palace, in rooms "rented by the office of HRH the Prince of Wales." And Tina Brown's biography of Diana asserts that during her affair with Dr. Khan in 1995, Diana paged him at the hospital just as frequently.

James Hewitt, the Londonderry-born Captain of the Life Guards, the unit responsible for protecting the royal family, either took his responsibilities to the extreme or failed miserably at them, depending on one's point of view. From the start, Hewitt sensed that he had been set up all along by The Firm (as the royal family referred to themselves), which was looking for a way to halt Diana's affair with Barry Mannakee. The latter died in a motorcycle accident on May 22, 1987, which Diana always deemed suspicious.

Diana's first encounter with James Hewitt took place in Buckingham Palace in the fall of 1986. The twenty-six-year-old princess was standing alone at the foot of a staircase, backlit and barefoot, in a sheer summer dress, shoes in hand. Hewitt, two years her senior, had just exited a meeting regarding the impending marriage of Prince Andrew and Sarah Ferguson. Diana looked up and saw Hewitt in his uniform with its dashing red jacket. She gave him the seductive sidelong glance immortalized in countless photographs and purred, "Like the outfit."

She then arranged for Hewitt to be invited to a courtiers' cocktail party hosted by her friend Hazel West, where she enthused about her love for horses and all but roped the cavalry officer into offering her riding instructions. As a cover for what would soon become a clandestine affair, Diana engaged Major Hewitt to teach Princes Harry and William as well.

Hewitt quickly became something of a boy toy, or at least a kept man. Diana showered him with gifts of jewelry, clothing, and accessories, the way Albert Edward, Prince of Wales, did with Lillie Langtry a hundred years earlier.

In her love affairs, the princess was anything but "shy Di." Both Hewitt's memoirs and Tina Brown's biography of Diana assert that it was the princess who made the first move with Hewitt, taking advantage of a rare private moment in the Officers' Mess to lean in and kiss him. "I need you. You give me strength. I can't stand it when I'm away from you. I want to be with you. I've come to love you," Diana told her swain, her eyes brimming with tears. She orchestrated their relationship with military precision, arranging for close friends to accompany them as "beards." She even informed her personal protection officer Ken Wharfe of their illicit activities. Wharfe referred to Hewitt as a "protest fuck." After all, Charles was rubbing Diana's nose in his adulterous affair with Camilla Parker Bowles.

And, according to Hewitt, "there was a tacit understanding between Diana and Charles that I was part of her life in the same way that Mrs. Parker Bowles was a part of Prince Charles's life."

But Diana was so careful about keeping her affair with Hewitt a secret that she would rumple her lover's bedsheets to make it appear as though he had spent the night in his own room.

Tina Brown contends that with Hewitt, Diana evidently received the earth-shattering orgasms she'd craved. And he brought out the sportswoman in her, though Diana would eventually confess to Hewitt, "I hated every minute I spent sitting on a horse. I only did it for you." Her previously bulimic figure grew tanned and fit and she ate properly and healthfully. "Only one thing went wrong," Hewitt would later admit. "We fell in love."

From Diana's perspective, viewed with twenty-twenty hindsight, *much* went wrong. "His head was inside his trousers," she bitterly griped. Eventually, she would claim that Hewitt was "about as interesting as a knitting pattern."

But Diana had plenty of her own issues. She was needy and possessive, and routinely fumed when a paramour had other concerns, even outside of his control. The princess went ballistic when Hewitt was compelled to take another posting. She cut off all communication with him for three months after he told her he was being sent to Germany to command a Sabre Squadron. In 1990, he was posted to the Gulf and she was obliged to rewrite her fantasy script of a happily-ever-after romance, recasting herself as the solider boy's girl back home. The princess sent Hewitt contraband bottles of whiskey and a gold cross that matched the one she wore, bearing the engraved inscription "I will love you forever," in addition to a continual stream of letters and care packages, some of which contained girlie magazines.

Privately, however, Diana confessed to Ken Wharfe that Hewitt had gotten "too serious." And her tin soldier made an unforgivable misstep when he posed for a press photo-op atop his armored tank, waving one of her blue airmail letters. The photographer Ken Lennox overheard him shouting, "Look what I have got in my hand—you would pay a fortune for it."

Hewitt had crossed the bounds of discretion. The rest of the world did not need to learn what The Firm already knew. Hubristically, he had flown too close to the sun, and now it was going to scorch him.

Naturally, the newspapers ran with it. Nigel Dempster, writing for the *Daily Mail* on March 15, 1991, delivered the headline "Di's Dashing Pal to Tell of Desert Deeds."

Nine days later, Emma Stewardson, Hewitt's ex-girlfriend, sold her confessional, "I Lost My Lover to Di," to the *News of the World.*

In *Love and War*, Hewitt's memoir detailing his affair with Diana, he claims that the Stewardson story was a clever tweaking of the facts, since he and Emma had split up long before he became involved with Diana.

But at the time, the public didn't know that, and wouldn't, until Hewitt's book was published nine years later.

The damage had been done.

In the wake of the fallout from Hewitt's Desert Storm debacle, Diana instructed the Kensington Palace switchboard to patch him through only on her instructions. He had lost the privilege of having her current mobile number. When she deigned to take his phone calls, Diana reminded her paramour of the importance of secrecy and discretion.

According to myriad biographies of Diana, Hewitt was only one of several men, married and single, wellborn and working class, whom the Princess of Wales took to bed. But he was the only one who kissed and told for a hefty publishing advance. Ever since their romance was made public in 1991, Hewitt had fended off lucrative offers to sell his story. Once jilted, however, he began to self-destruct. He was twice fined by the army for disobeying orders, and failed his promotion exams—by one point, allegedly—a scenario that Hewitt was certain was rigged. "My card had been marked for some time," he admits in *Love and War*. After the handsome and muscular former cavalry officer's tell-all hit the bookshelves in 1999, two years after Diana's death, he was quickly branded the "Love Rat" and "the vilest man in Britain."

In 1994, Hewitt had been booted out of the service with

only a £40,000 severance check and a paltry £6,600 annual pension. Well, a boy's got to eat, doesn't he?

His tongue was loosened by a £300,000 check from the *Daily Express.* In a series of interviews, Hewitt coyly divulged enough to the journalist Anna Pasternak to keep her readers guessing, and cooperated with Pasternak for her lurid exposé of their correspondence in the book *Princess in Love.* Diana was devastated that he had sold her down the Thames for a book deal. She would not live to see their love letters stolen from a safe in Hewitt's home by his deceitful Italian fiancée, Anna Ferretti, who tried to sell them to the *Mirror* for £150,000. A fiasco ensued, in which no one came off looking good.

To illustrate how much times had changed since the Tudors, the disclosure of their adulterous affair in 1994 amounted to a confession of treason. According to a fourteenth-century law that was still on the books, Hewitt would have been beheaded for his crime, while Diana could have suffered the same fate, or been publicly burned at the stake, the option Henry VIII chose not to exercise for Anne Boleyn.

Although Hewitt had told Anna Pasternak that his affair with Diana began in 1986, it had been such a well-kept secret until Pasternak's 1994 exposé that many believed the royal liaison had begun even sooner. There had been intermittent speculation in the press as to whether Hewitt, and not Charles, had fathered Prince Harry, Diana's second son. Supposedly, when Charles first saw the redheaded infant prince, he grew quite upset, because he thought he didn't resemble the child— and had a pretty good notion who did. Actually, Harry resembles a raft of redheaded Spencers, and Charles's initial disappointment was put down to the fact he had hoped for a girl instead.

Speaking to London's *Sunday Mirror* in September 2002, Hewitt insisted that although he had been Diana's secret lover for five years, he was not Harry's father, reiterating that they had not met until two years after the prince's birth. "Admittedly the red hair is similar to mine and people say we look alike." However, he added, "I have never encouraged these comparisons, and although I was with Diana for a long time I must state once and for all that I'm not Harry's father." In referring to official photos taken that year to mark the prince's eighteenth birthday, Hewitt said, "Looking at the pictures I have to say he's a much more handsome chap than I ever was."

In 2005, Hewitt underwent the ultimate publicity stunt—a past-life regression—conducted by a man named Tony Rae, who specializes in such astral journeys. On Channel Five's program *Under Hypnosis*, the trance-induced Hewitt admitted that his affair with Diana began much earlier than 1986, and he had lied to protect her.

By then, Hewitt's dignity had already been taking a nosedive for a couple of years. In February 2003, the BBC reported that Hewitt was trying to sell Diana's love letters (the original documents). A year later he was arrested in Chelsea on suspected cocaine possession. In 2006, he sunk even lower, appearing on a reality TV show, *The X Factor: Battle of the Stars*.

Diana remains endeared to us forever as a tragic (and tragically flawed) heroine. We knew as much about her frailties—her eating disorders, alleged suicide attempts, unloving and chilly marriage, and hideously impossible in-laws—as we did of her myriad charitable works and her seemingly endless compassion for anyone who suffered even the slightest pain. All of it contributed to her image as "the People's Princess."

Diana reached her zenith in an age when the world demanded a right to know everything about someone. Ironically, that which made Diana so famous and so iconic—her talented collusion with the press—is what ultimately killed her. She perished in a speeding sedan alongside Dodi Fayed, her flashy forty-two-year-old beau of only six weeks' acquaintance, during an attempt to evade a hellish cavalcade (two motor scooters, three motorcycles, and five automobiles) of aggressive paparazzi.

"The camera was Diana's fatal attraction," Tina Brown observed in her biography of the princess. "It had created the image that had given her so much power and she was addicted to its magic, even when it hurt."

In a sad postscript, Prince Charles finally "got it" when—after learning of Diana's Paris accident, but not yet informed of its dreadful outcome—he admitted to Mark Bolland, his assistant private secretary, "I always thought that Diana would come back to me, needing to be cared for."

CHARLES, PRINCE OF WALES
and Camilla Parker Bowles b. 1947

She might not have been a stunner to look at, but she had an opening line that couldn't be beat. The popularly repeated story goes that on a rainy day in 1970 at a polo match at Windsor, feisty Camilla Shand marched up to Charles Philip Arthur George, Prince of Wales—you can just imagine her tweed skirt, quilted Barbour jacket, and muddy boots—and told him, "My great-grandmother was the mistress of your great-great-grandfather."

Supposedly following this setup line with the brazen question "How about it?" it was the come-hither equivalent of presenting her credentials for the position, boldly suggesting that she and Charles might like to continue what Edward VII and Alice Keppel began.

Tina Brown, Princess Diana's most recent biographer, relates a different story in *The Diana Chronicles*. According to Brown, Camilla appraised Prince Charles's horse with a gimlet eye and in an opening gambit huskily said, "That's a fine animal you have there, sir."

Whichever line is genuine, the effect was the same, whether or not Charles had already heard the rumors that the candid Camilla was terrific in bed. The heir to the English throne was intrigued. Camilla and Charles began a relationship, and by all accounts they were quite suited to one another in every way but one. Though Charles was likely keen on making her his wife, Buckingham Palace wouldn't hear of it. Camilla, from a proper family, and with all the right education—at the Queens Gate School in South Kensington, and at finishing schools in France and Switzerland—was quite obviously not a virgin, and old royal traditions die hard.

The two were more or less compelled to officially move on. And absence had made the heart falter rather than grow fonder after only about a year, when in 1971 Charles entered the Royal Navy. In 1973, while the prince was still performing his military duty, the twenty-five-year-old Camilla married another old flame, the cavalry officer Andrew Parker Bowles. They had two children together: Tom, born in 1975, and Laura, born in 1979.

But in August 1979, the literally explosive murder of Charles's favorite relative and chief confidant, his "Uncle Dickie," Lord Mountbatten, sent the grief-stricken thirty-year-old Charles back to Camilla's consoling arms. Mountbatten, the victim of a political assassination, was killed, along with two others, by agents of the Irish Republican Army when a bomb concealed aboard his fishing boat was blown up by remote control.

The Prince of Wales began to spend considerable time in the company of Camilla and her husband. In 1980, Charles and the Parker Bowleses attended a soiree during which the prince and Camilla spent considerable time on the dance floor, French-kissing in full view of the appalled guests—and Camilla's husband.

A bounder himself, according to several sources (including his wife), Parker Bowles observed, according to Tina Brown, "HRH is very fond of my wife . . . and she appears to be very fond of him." Seven years later, Parker Bowles would be promoted to Commanding Officer of the Household Cavalry.

Meanwhile, back in 1980, the quest for a proper virgin bride for Charles continued, even as his relationship with Camilla was rekindled—while her marriage to Parker Bowles understandably began to collapse. Ironically, it was Camilla who nudged her lover into the arms of the nineteen-year-old, diffident yet radiant English rose, Lady Diana Spencer.

Viewed as young and unworldly enough to be pliably molded into the perfect complacent consort, Diana, a noblewoman from a prominent and prestigious line, filled all the proper criteria for the future Queen of England. And although she had previous boyfriends, including having very briefly dated the notoriously randy Prince Andrew (who had been a girlhood crush), Diana was allegedly *intacta*. She famously told an interviewer, "I had to keep myself tidy for what lay ahead," meaning her fantasy marriage to Prince Charming. If Barbara Cartland novels had taught her nothing else, it was that fast girls don't get the future king.

There was only one major obstacle: Charles was madly in love with Camilla, even confessing to his valet, Stephen Barry, that Mrs. Parker Bowles "was the only woman he had ever loved."

But the prince did his duty, no doubt gritting his teeth and thinking of England when he married Diana on July 29, 1981, in a royal wedding watched around the world. Goggle-eyed romantics from New York to New Delhi stayed up late or woke up early to stake out a seat in front of the television, as a Cinderella-style coach transported the beautiful blond bride. She was wearing a voluminous silken confection of a gown that would be copied for years.

Rumors soon surfaced of marital trouble, trouble that had in fact persisted throughout the prince's lukewarm courtship of Diana. As the wedding gifts had poured into the palace in advance of the big day, Diana discovered among them a gift box for Camilla that contained a stunning bracelet engraved with the entwined initials F and G—according to one source, for Fred and Gladys, Charles and Camilla's pet names for each other. (According to Tina Brown, the letters stand for "Girl Friday," Charles's nickname for Camilla.) And Charles's valet, Stephen Barry, admitted that Charles had likely spent the night of the prewedding ball in Camilla's arms.

During his honeymoon with Diana aboard the royal yacht *Britannia*, Charles phoned Camilla every day. According to Barry, the prince was a man unmoored without her.

Camilla was a frequent visitor to Highgrove, Charles's beloved Gloucestershire retreat, and knew the manor's layout better than Diana did. The Parker Bowleses resided only sixteen miles away at Bolehyde Manor, which made Highgrove particularly convenient for a royal tryst. Charles and Camilla's tight-lipped Gloucestershire clique treated them as a couple.

According to Diana's personal protection officer Ken Wharfe, on one occasion the princess had her suspicions confirmed that the minute her back was turned Charles took advantage of the occasion to rendezvous with Camilla. Not too many months after Charles had surprised Diana with a romantic seventh-anniversary celebration at Highgrove, one Sunday afternoon, as Diana headed back to London from weekending there with her husband, about a half hour from Highgrove, she urged Ken Wharfe to turn the car around and head back there. Sure enough, Camilla's car was in the driveway. The prince's lover did in fact play châtelaine at Highgrove quite often in Diana's absence. Prince Charles's official biographer, Jonathan Dimbleby, records that the affair with Camilla resumed in 1986, though Tina Brown seems to believe that date simply became the standard party line. Some royal biographers believe it; some beg to differ. Brown is among the writers who are convinced that Camilla and Charles resumed their affair in or by 1983, the year before Charles and Diana's second son, Prince Harry, was born. In fact, Diana had admitted that it was a miracle Harry got conceived at all, so infrequently were the Waleses having sex together by then.

Where hundreds of years ago a royal scandal was whispered about among the envious and ambitious bluebloods at court, nowadays, thanks to freedom of the press, pernicious paparazzi, and, more recently, the Internet, royal adulterers are tried in the court of public opinion. Camilla and Charles—though he came out the worse for it—were thoroughly excoriated (amid titters and giggles) when the press released the "Camillagate tapes," transcripts of the December 18, 1989, mobile phone conversation that Charles had with his lover, in which he passionately murmured his desire to be reincarnated as Camilla's tampon.

The transcript was first published in 1992 by the Australian weekly periodical *New Idea* and was soon afterward picked up by fifty-three news outlets internationally. In London, it was the *Daily Mirror* that published it. These days, the transcript can easily be Googled and located on a number of Web sites, where it is available in its entirety.

Then again, according to an ex-girlfriend, the Prince of Wales prefers to be called "Arthur" during the throes of ecstasy, which can't help but make one wonder about Excalibur. So much for Charles being remembered for his keen interests in such comparatively mundane subjects as architectural preservation and organic farming!

Toward the end of 1992, in a bit of classic British understatement, Buckingham Palace reluctantly conceded that Charles and Diana had been having some marital problems. In December, the Waleses would officially separate. Eventually, they brought their case to the press, each of them seeking to sway the tide of public opinion in their favor.

In an interview on June 29, 1994, with the BBC's Jonathan Dimbleby, Charles confessed that he had in fact been unfaithful to Diana during their marriage. But he immediately issued a disclaimer of sorts, telling Dimbleby, "Until it became irretrievably broken down, both of us having tried."

The reaction of the *Daily Mirror* was, "He is not the first royal to be unfaithful, but he is the first to appear before 25 million of his subjects to confess."

The following year, when Diana appeared on *Panorama*, she invoked the specter of Camilla, bitterly telling the television journalist Martin Bashir, "There were three of us in this marriage, so it was a bit crowded." It must have been a dreadful situation for Diana to have fallen in love with her husband, only to be forced at every turn to acknowledge his long-standing infidelity—but this time in an age when people were supposed to marry for love, and when the official royal mistress was an archaism that should have been relegated to the proverbial dustbin of history.

All three of them—Camilla, Charles, and Diana—were caught between the ridiculously conflicting exigencies of duty and desire, and the palace's stubborn refusal to admit that times had changed. If Charles had been permitted to wed Camilla in the first place, an infinite amount of pain, and eventually tragedy, might have been avoided.

In 1995, Camilla and Andrew Parker Bowles divorced. A year later, Charles divorced Diana. Interestingly, it has been said of Camilla that the love of her life was Parker Bowles, not Charles, though she has always remained the *prince's* grand passion. Perhaps the canniest royal mistresses (and Camilla's got the genes to prove it) comprehend that it is always preferable, if not profitable, for your lover to care more about you than you do for him.

Lest anyone assume that annuities and financial gifts to royal mistresses are a thing of the past, in 1995, Camilla's grocery shopping for her new Wiltshire estate was performed by Charles's Highgrove butler. The bills were sent to the Prince of Wales's account. And after Charles divorced Diana and Camilla was acknowledged as Charles's lover, his *maîtresse en titre*, he awarded her a wardrobe allowance. Charles eventually covered her £130,000 debt at Coutts bank and gave Camilla an annual stipend of £120,000, which over time increased to £180,000 per annum.

Diana's tragic death in August 1997 once more put the spotlight on Charles's infidelity. Many people expressed the wish that if only he had been kinder to Diana, had loved her the way she loved him, hadn't cheated on her and then rubbed her nose in it, had dumped Camilla for good and really tried to make the royal marriage work, then Diana would never have been in that sedan with Dodi Fayed.

The thought had even occurred to Charles himself. The prince told his private secretary, Stephen Lamport, "They're all going to blame me."

People also found a way to blame Camilla as the temptress and interloper who didn't do the noble thing and allow her former lover to be a faithful husband. To the mortification of the House of Windsor, Diana's death effectively deified her. Though Camilla and Charles were now fully free to proclaim their coupledom, the months following Diana's death would have been the worst possible moment to do so from a public relations standpoint.

So Camilla receded from the spotlight. Not until 1999 did she and Charles appear together publicly as a couple. It took another year for the queen to remove the royal blinders and acknowledge Camilla's relationship with her son by attending a luncheon at which the prince's lover was also present. Three years later, in 2003, Camilla moved into the prince's residence, Clarence House.

In 2002, the Church of England was finally dragged kicking and screaming into the modern age when it ended the centuries-old practice of prohibiting divorced persons with living ex-spouses from being married in the Church. This had been the sticking point when it came to the subject of whether Charles could wed Camilla, because as the King of England he would also become the titular head of the Anglican Church. The old law is also what had tripped up Edward VIII and Wallis War-field Simpson and prevented their marrying—not that Wally was American, a commoner, or even that she was a double di-vorcée. Nowhere in the British Constitution are any of these three issues a valid barrier to a royal marriage. The issue had been that the mistresses' former spouses still lived.

Now Camilla would be able to marry her prince—so long as Charles received permission from his mum the sovereign, in accordance with the Royal Marriages Act of 1772. It was also important that in the intervening years since Diana's tragic death, the tide of public opinion had begun to flow in Camilla's favor. No one changed his mind and suddenly found her a raving beauty, but she did pick up some hair, makeup, and wardrobe tips. The clothing allowance probably helped. Her appearance morphed from what-to-wear-while-mucking-out-the-stables to one of appropriately matronly elegance (ridiculous hats aside). What seems to have happened was a combination of time's ability to heal all wounds and the public's realization that the real Cinderella story was Charles and Camilla's. He had loved her passionately for thirty-five years. Yes, poor Di-ana was savaged by it, but now her memory could remain en-shrined as immortal and beloved while Camilla and Charles became the poster children for Love Conquering All, giving hope to dowdy middle-aged singletons in every corner of the earth.

On April 9, 2005, the romance that Diana viewed as a nightmare and Charles saw as a fairy tale had a happy ending for him when he wed Camilla in a civil service at the Guildhall in Windsor. The Archbishop of Canterbury had gone so far as to bless their marriage, averring that their union in no way prohibited Charles from becoming King of England, or the titular head of the Anglican Church. (After all, known adulterers have done so for centuries; why should twenty-first-century hypocrisy be any different?)

Charles's mother, Queen Elizabeth II, did not attend the Guildhall ceremony. It sounds like grist for the gossip mill, but the queen averred that to attend a civil wedding was not in keeping with *her* position as Supreme Governor of the Church of England. The civil ceremony was followed later that day by the blessing of their union in St. George's Chapel, at which Her Majesty did put in an appearance.

At the time, public sentiment—however it may have changed in Camilla's favor since the death of Princess Diana—would likely not have withstood the title of Princess of Wales bestowed on the woman who shattered Diana's hopes for wedded bliss. On her marriage to Charles, Camilla was made Duchess of Cornwall. But if Charles becomes king, because she is his wife, Camilla will in fact be Queen of England unless a public outcry compels the British cabinet to raise an objection and insist that the marriage be considered morganatic. A morganatic marriage would mean that Camilla's status or rank as a commoner would remain unchanged, even if Charles were to accede to the throne, and she would not become his queen consort in any formal or officially recognized way. In other words, Camilla would still be Charles's legal wife of course, but she would not be his queen.

However, according to a statement from Clarence House, it has been agreed upon that should Charles ascend the throne, Camilla's official title will not be queen, but HRH The Princess Consort.

Still, the effects of Camilla's long-term adulterous liaison with Prince Charles extend beyond the prurient interests of the curious reader of *Hello* magazine. For one thing, many still regard her as the interloper who made life hell for the martyred Princess Diana. As of June 2007, 73 percent of Britons did not want to see Camilla as their queen. Indeed, two-thirds of them would like their next king to be Prince William, the elder son of Charles and Diana, who stands next in line to his father.

Whether Charles chooses to ascend the throne after Elizabeth II is his decision, but one that may have lasting implications on the state of the British monarchy, its relevance, and its official stewardship of the Church of England. While British royal history is rife with adultery, if Charles were to become king, he would be the first divorced English-born monarch ever. Henry VIII, after all, technically, had his marriages annulled.

Then again, despite vociferous public outcry at the time, England's monarchy successfully survived the sexual excesses of such serial adulterers as Henry VIII, Charles II, George IV, and Edward VII. And from Eleanor of Aquitaine to Catherine of Braganza to Princess Alix of Denmark to Diana, Princess of Wales, royal consorts have fruitlessly begged their husbands to relinquish their mistresses and give *them* a cuddle instead.

But it is a truth universally acknowledged that the more things change, the more they stay the same.

Acknowledgments

Thanks are due to my editor, Claire Zion, for giving me the opportunity to dive head-first into the field of historical nonfiction. To my agent, Irene Goodman, I owe perpetual thanks; and I suppose it wouldn't hurt to thank my fifth-grade teacher, Barbara Thatcher (wherever she is), for turning me into a history geek. Thanks are also due to the members of the Beau Monde, the Romance Writers of America's subset of Georgian- and Regency-era writers, whose individual and collective encyclopedic knowledge of the periods is just as valuable to a historian as to a novelist. Merci to Mme. Cecile Droz at my alma mater, the Fieldston School, who translated George I's last words. Finally, I must acknowledge the New York City Public Library system, which made a daunting amount of research more manageable. I've never been happier to see my tax dollars at work.

Selected Bibliography

Andrews, Allen. *The Royal Whore: Barbara Villiers, Countess of Castlemaine*. Philadelphia: Chilton Book Company, 1970.

Appleby, John T. *Henry II the Vanquished King*. New York: The Macmillan Company, 1962.

Aronson, Theo. *The King in Love: Edward VII's Mistresses*. New York: Harper and Row, 1998.

Ashley, Maurice. *The Stuarts*. Antonia Fraser, ed. Berkeley and Los Angeles: University of California Press, 2000.

Beauclerk, Charles. *Nell Gwyn: Mistress to a King*. New York: Atlantic Monthly Press, 2005.

Brown, Tina. *The Diana Chronicles*. New York: Doubleday, 2007.

Byrne, Paula. *Perdita*. New York: Random House, 2004.

Cantor, Norman F. *The Last Knight: The Twilight of the Middle Ages and the Birth of the Modern Era*. New York: HarperCollins, 2004.

Cawthorne, Nigel. *Sex Lives of the Kings and Queens of England*. London: Prion, 1994.

Clive, Mary. *This Sun of York: A Biography of Edward IV*. New York: Alfred A. Knopf, 1974.

Coote, Stephen. *Samuel Pepys*. New York: Palgrave, 2001.

Crosland, Margaret. *The Mysterious Mistress: The Life and Legend of Jane Shore*. Phoenix Mill, Thrupp, Stroud, Gloucestershire: Sutton Publishing, Limited, 2006.

Davenport, Hester. *The Prince's Mistress: A Life of Mary Robinson*. Gloucestershire: Sutton Publishing, Limited, 2004.

David, Saul. *Prince of Pleasure: The Prince of Wales and the Making of the Regency*. New York: Atlantic Monthly Press, 1998.

Doherty, Paul. *Isabella and the Strange Death of Edward II*. New York: Carroll & Graf, 2003.

Farquhar, Michael. *A Treasury of Royal Scandals*. New York: Penguin Books, 2001.

Fraser, Antonia. *Mary Queen of Scots*. New York: Bantam Dell, 1969.

———. *The Wives of Henry VIII*. New York: Alfred A. Knopf, 1993.

Fraser, Antonia, ed. *The Lives of the Kings & Queens of England*. Berkeley, Los Angeles, London: University of California Press, 1999.

Fraser, Flora. *The Unruly Queen: The Life of Queen Caroline*. New York: Alfred A. Knopf, 1996.

Gillingham, John. *Richard I*. New Haven, London: Yale University Press, 1999.

Gristwood, Sarah. *Perdita*. London, Toronto, Sydney, Auckland, Johannesburg: Bantam Press, 2005.

Hamilton, Elizabeth. *William's Mary*. New York: Taplinger Publishing Co., Inc., 1972.

Hatton, Ragnild. *George I*. New Haven: Yale University Press, 2001.

Herman, Eleanor. *Sex With Kings*. New York: William Morrow, 2004.

———. *Sex With the Queen*. New York: HarperCollins, 2006.

Hewitt, James. *Love and War*. London: Blake Publishing, Ltd., 1999.

Hibbert, Christopher. *Edward VII: The Last Victorian King*. New York: Palgrave Macmillan, 2007.

———. *George IV: The Rebel Who Would Be King*. New York: Palgrave Macmillan, 2007.

———. *Queen Victoria: A Personal History*. New York: Basic Books, 2000.

Hicks, Michael. *Edward IV*. London: Hodder Headline Group, 2004.

Lamont-Brown, Raymond. *Alice Keppel & Agnes Keyser: Edward VII's Last Loves*. Great Britain: Sutton Publishing, 2005.

Langtry, Lillie. *The Days I Knew*, 2nd ed. London: Hutchinson & Co., 1925.

Leslie, Anita. *Mrs. Fitzherbert*. New York: Charles Scribner's Sons, 1960.

Lucraft, Jeannette. *Katherine Swynford: The History of a Medieval Mistress*. Thrupp, Stroud, Gloucestershire: Sutton Publishing, Ltd., 2006.

Mackie, R. L. *King James IV of Scotland*. Edinburgh, London: Oliver & Boyd, 1958.

Mangan, J. J. *The King's Favour: Three Eighteenth-Century Monarchs and the Favourites Who Ruled Them*. Gloucestershire: Sutton Publishing, Ltd., 1991.

Mortimer, Ian. *The Greatest Traitor*. New York: St. Martin's Press, 2003.

Pepys, Samuel. *The Diary of Samuel Pepys*. New York: Modern Library Edition/Random House, 2001.

Plowden, Alison. *Caroline and Charlotte: Regency Scandals*. Thrupp, Stroud, Gloucestershire: Sutton Publishing, Ltd., 2005.

Princess Michael of Kent. *Cupid and the King: Five Royal Paramours*. New York: Touchstone, 1991, 2005.

Robb, Nesca A. *William of Orange: A Personal Portrait, Volume Two: 1674–1702*. New York: St. Martin's Press, 1966.

Robinson, Mary. *Memoirs of the Late Mrs. Robinson, written by herself, with some posthumous pieces*. M. E. Robinson, R. Phillips, eds., 1801.

Rosvall, Toivo David. *The Mazarine Legacy: The Life of Hortense Mancini, Duchess Mazarin*. New York: Viking Press, 1969.

Rowse, A. L. *Homosexuals in History*. New York: Carroll & Graf, 1977.

Shaw, Karl. *Royal Babylon*. New York: Broadway Books, 1999.

Starkey, David. *Six Wives: The Queens of Henry VIII*. New York: HarperCollins, 2003.

Strachey, Lytton. *Elizabeth and Essex: A Tragic History*. New York: Harcourt Brace Jovanovich, 1928.

Tomalin, Claire. *Mrs. Jordan's Profession: The Actress and the Prince*. New York: Alfred A. Knopf, 1995.

Waller, Maureen. *Ungrateful Daughters: The Stuart Princesses Who Stole Their Father's Crown*. New York: St. Martin's Press, 2002.

Warren, W. L. *Henry II*. Berkeley: University of California Press, 1973.

Weintraub, Stanley. *Edward the Caresser: The Playboy Prince Who Became Edward VII*. New York: Simon & Schuster, 2001.

Weir, Alison. *Henry VIII: The King and His Court*. New York: Ballantine, 2001.

————. *Katherine Swynford: The Story of John of Gaunt and His Scandalous Duchess*. London: Jonathan Cape, 2007.

————. *Queen Isabella*. New York: Ballantine Books, 2005.

————. *The Life of Elizabeth I*. New York: Ballantine, 1998.

————. *The Six Wives of Henry VIII*. New York: Grove Press, 1991.

Williams, Neville. *The Tudors*. Antonia Fraser, ed. Berkeley: University of California Press, 2000.

Williams, Susan. *The People's King: The True Story of the Abdication*. New York: Palgrave Macmillan, 2004.

Wilson, A. N. *The Rise & Fall of the House of Windsor*. New York and London: W. W. Norton and Company, Inc., 1993.

Young, Michael B. *King James and the History of Homosexuality*. New York: New York University Press, 2000.

WEB SITES

www.britannia.com

www.1911encyclopedia.org

www.middle-ages.org.uk

www.englishhistory.net

www.nellgavin.com

www.tudorhistory.org

www.publications.bham.ac.uk

www.marie-stuart.co.uk

www.oup.co.uk

www.englishmonarchs.co.uk

www.oxforddnb.com

www.britainexpress.com/royals/charles.htm (article reprinted from *The Royal Report*)

www.scotshistoryonline.co.uk/charlieb.html

www.princeofwales.gov.uk

ARTICLES

Aronson, Theo. "Keppel, Alice Frederica (1868–1947)." In *Oxford Dictionary of National Biography*, edited by H. C. G. Matthew and Brian Harrison. Oxford: OUP, 2004. www.oxforddnb.com/view/article/37632 (accessed August 27, 2007).

Brock, Michael. "William IV (1765–1837)." In *Oxford Dictionary of National Biography*, edited by H. C. G. Matthew and Brian Harrison. Oxford: OUP, 2004. www.oxforddnb.com/view/article/29451 (accessed August 27, 2007).

Courtney, W. P. "Wardle, Gwyllym Lloyd (1761/2–1833)." In *Oxford Dictionary of National Biography*, edited by H. C. G. Matthew and Brian Harrison. Oxford: OUP, 2004. Online ed., edited by Lawrence Goldman, January 2007. www.oxforddnb.com/view/article/28725 (accessed August 28, 2007).

Hibbert, Christopher. "George IV (1762–1830)." In *Oxford Dictionary of National Biography*, edited by H. C. G. Matthew and Brian Harrison. Oxford: OUP, 2004. Online ed., edited by Lawrence Goldman, October 2005. www.oxforddnb.com/view/article/10541 (accessed August 27, 2007).

Horrox, Rosemary. "Shore, Elizabeth [Jane] (*d.* 1526/7?)." In *Oxford Dictionary of National Biography*, edited by H. C. G. Matthew and Brian Harrison. Oxford: OUP, 2004. www.oxforddnb.com/view/article/25451 (accessed October 4, 2007).

Kilburn, Matthew. "Howard, Henrietta, countess of Suffolk (*c.*1688–1767)." In *Oxford Dictionary of National Biography*, edited by H. C. G. Matthew and Brian Harrison. Oxford: OUP, 2004. www.oxforddnb.com/view/article/13904 (accessed August 26, 2007).

Kilburn, Matthew. "Wallmoden, Amalie Sophie Marianne von, suo jure countess of Yarmouth (1704–1765)." In *Oxford Dictionary of National Biography*, edited by H. C. G. Matthew and Brian Harrison. Oxford: OUP, 2004. Online ed., edited by Lawrence Goldman, October 2006. www.oxforddnb.com/view/article/28579 (accessed August 26, 2007).

Matthew, H. C. G. "Edward VII (1841–1910)." In *Oxford Dictionary of National Biography*, edited by H. C. G. Matthew and Brian Harrison. Oxford: OUP, 2004. Online ed., edited by Lawrence Goldman, May 2007. www.oxforddnb.com/view/article/32975 (accessed August 27, 2007).

Matthew, H. C. G. "Edward VIII [*later* Prince Edward, duke of Windsor] (1894–1972)." In *Oxford Dictionary of National Biography*, edited by H. C. G. Matthew and Brian Harrison. Oxford: OUP, 2004. www.oxforddnb.com/view/article/31061 (accessed November 24, 2007).

Matthew, H. C. G. and K. D. Reynolds. "Victoria (1819–1901)." In *Oxford Dictionary of National Biography*, edited by H. C. G. Matthew and Brian Harrison. Oxford: OUP, 2004. Online ed., edited by Lawrence Goldman, May 2007. www.oxforddnb.com/view/article/36652 (accessed August 27, 2007).

Ranger, Paul. "Jordan, Dorothy (1761–1816)." In *Oxford Dictionary of National Biography*, edited by H. C. G. Matthew and Brian Harrison. Oxford: OUP, 2004. Online ed., edited by Lawrence Goldman, January 2006. www.oxforddnb.com/view/article/15119 (accessed August 27, 2007).

Reynolds, K. D. "Brown, John (1826–1883)." In *Oxford Dictionary of National Biography*, edited by H. C. G. Matthew and Brian Harrison. Oxford: OUP, 2004. www.oxforddnb.com/view/article/37231 (accessed August 27, 2007).

Reynolds, K. D. "Clarke, Mary Anne (1776?–1852)." In *Oxford Dictionary of National Biography*, edited by H. C. G. Matthew and Brian Harrison. Oxford: OUP, 2004. Online ed., edited by Lawrence Goldman, January 2007. www.oxforddnb.com/view/article/5520 (accessed August 26, 2007).

Reynolds, K. D. "Conyngham, Elizabeth, Marchioness Conyngham (1769–1861)." In *Oxford Dictionary of National Biography*, edited by H. C. G. Matthew and Brian Harrison. Oxford: OUP, 2004. www.oxforddnb.com/view/article/45483 (accessed September 16, 2007).

Reynolds, K. D. "Diana, princess of Wales (1961–1997)." In *Oxford Dictionary of National Biography*, edited by H. C. G. Matthew and Brian Harrison. Oxford: OUP, 2004. Online ed., edited by Lawrence Goldman, October 2006. www.oxforddnb.com/view/article/68348 (accessed November 21, 2007).

Smith, E. A. "Caroline (1768–1821)." In *Oxford Dictionary of National Biography*, edited by H. C. G. Matthew and Brian Harrison. Oxford: OUP, 2004. www.oxforddnb.com/view/article/4722 (accessed August 27, 2007).

Stephens, H. M. "Frederick, Prince, duke of York and Albany

(1763–1827)." Rev. John Van der Kiste. In *Oxford Dictionary of National Biography*, edited by H. C. G. Matthew and Brian Harrison. Oxford: OUP, 2004. Online ed., edited by Lawrence Goldman, January 2007. www.oxforddnb.com/view/article/10139 (accessed August 26, 2007).

Taylor, Stephen. "Caroline (1683–1737)." In *Oxford Dictionary of National Biography*, edited by H. C. G. Matthew and Brian Harrison. Oxford: OUP, 2004. www.oxforddnb.com/view/article/4720 (accessed August 26, 2007).

Walker, Simon. "John, duke of Aquitaine and duke of Lancaster, styled king of Castile and León (1340–1399)." In *Oxford Dictionary of National Biography*, edited by H. C. G. Matthew and Brian Harrison. Oxford: OUP, 2004. Online ed., edited by Lawrence Goldman, May 2006. www.oxforddnb.com/view/article/14843 (accessed September 28, 2007).

Walker, Simon. "Katherine, duchess of Lancaster (1350?—1403)." In *Oxford Dictionary of National Biography*, edited by H. C. G. Matthew and Brian Harrison. Oxford: OUP, 2004. www.oxforddnb.com/view/article/26858 (accessed September 28, 2007).

Weil, Rachel. "Villiers [Hamilton], Elizabeth, countess of Orkney (*c.* 1657–1733)." In *Oxford Dictionary of National Biography*, edited by H. C. G. Matthew and Brian Harrison. Oxford: OUP, 2004. www.oxforddnb.com/view/article/28290 (accessed August 26, 2007).

NB: Financial calculations from British pounds in a given year to American dollars as of 2006 (which is as far as the Web site goes as of this writing) were obtained from: www.measuringworth.com/calculators. Since one British pound was roughly equivalent to $2 in 2006 and remains more or less $2 as of this writing in 2007, I doubled the pound amount calculated from the year in question to its current (2006) worth, and the figures I provided "in today's economy" and similar wording are rounded numbers, not intended to be an exact calculation but to give readers a general sense of the value of the monetary bequest then and now.

Photo by Ron Rinaldi

LESLIE CARROLL is the author of several works of contemporary women's fiction, and, under the pen name Amanda Elyot, a number of works of historical fiction. She and her husband, Scott, currently reside in New York City. *Royal Affairs* marks her debut in the field of historical nonfiction. Meet the author at www.tlt.com/authors/lesliecarroll.htm.

Let's dish the dirt on royal affairs!
Please visit www.royalaffairs.blogspot.com to chat with me about the scintillating lives and sizzling affairs in the book, and juicy tidbits about other affairs that didn't make the final cut. Book club leaders are invited to set up a "tryst," choosing a day all to yourselves, where I'll discuss the book interactively with your members.

941.0099 Carroll, Leslie.
CAR
          Royal affairs.

$14.00 WITHDRAWN

DATE			